Fodor's

BOSTON

Welcome to Boston

Bursting with Yankee pride, Boston attracts visitors for its rich past and vibrant present. From Boston Common to Faneuil Hall to Fenway Park, the city is a hub of American history and culture. Buzzing neighborhoods such as the North End, Beacon Hill, and the Back Bay mix venerable landmarks and lively street life. On the other side of the Charles River is bustling Cambridge, home of Harvard University and MIT. As you plan your upcoming travels to Boston, please confirm that places are still open and let us know when we need to make updates by writing to us at this address: editors@fodors.com.

TOP REASONS TO GO

★ **Historic Icons:** The Freedom Trail links sites from the American Revolution's start.

★ **The Charles:** The river's bridges and esplanade reward exploration by foot or boat.

★ **Great Museums:** The Museum of Fine Arts and New England Aquarium satisfy curious minds.

★ **Stylish Shopping:** Newbury and Boylston Streets give shopaholics a boutique buzz.

★ **Cuisine:** Seafood restaurants and chef-led hot spots fuel a booming restaurant scene.

★ **Parks and Squares:** Boston Public Garden and Copley Square have prime people-watching.

Contents

MAPS

Fodor's Features

Chapter 1

EXPERIENCE BOSTON

20 ULTIMATE EXPERIENCES

Boston offers terrific experiences that should be on every traveler's list. Here are Fodor's top picks for a memorable trip.

1 Ride a Swan Boat in the Public Garden

No warm weather visit to Boston is complete without taking a spin on one of these iconic, foot-pedal powered Swan Boats. Astonishingly, they've plied this 4-acre pond in America's oldest botanical garden since 1877. (Ch. 7)

2 Visit Faneuil Hall

Dedicated to the creation of a new nation, Faneuil Hall has seen it all, from protesting colonists to World Series celebrations. (Ch. 4)

3 Catch a Game at Fenway

The nation's oldest Major League Baseball ballpark, home to the Red Sox since 1912 and where Babe Ruth swung for the fences, is hallowed ground for most Bostonians. (Ch. 8)

4 Ice Skate on the Frog Pond

Ice-skating on the Boston Common Frog Pond is an iconic winter activity. With the golden dome of the State House as a backdrop, it's one for the memory books. (Ch. 3)

5 Visit the Isabella Stewart Gardner Museum

One of the city's most charming attractions is this small but lovely museum. It's a Venetian palazzo with an eclectic collection and gorgeous gardens. (Ch. 8)

6 Eat a Lobster Roll

Nothing says "New England" more than seafood, and nothing says it better—or tastier—than a lobster roll. Head to Boston's waterfront, where any number of restaurants beckons. (Ch. 6, 12)

7 Tour the USS Constitution

Better known as "Old Ironsides," the oldest commissioned ship in the U.S. fleet is docked at the Charlestown Navy Yard. Take a tour of the ship, and then head to the adjacent museum. (Ch. 5)

8 Spend the Day at the Museum of Fine Arts

With almost half a million carefully curated objects spanning the centuries, this massive museum is one of the most highly regarded in the world. (Ch. 8)

9 Get out on the Charles River (Kayak, Canoe, Duck Boat)

The watery border between Boston and Cambridge offers a wealth of activities, from kayaking and canoeing to one of the city's ubiquitous Duck Boat tours. (Ch. 3, 11)

10 Visit the Institute of Contemporary Art

Filled with cutting-edge art, the gorgeous glass-walled cantilevered museum sits right on the edge of the Boston waterfront, offering breathtaking views both inside and out. (Ch. 10)

11 Walk Down Acorn Street in Beacon Hill

This charming one-lane cobblestone street, complete with 19th-century row houses and gas lamps, is said to be the city's most photographed street. (Ch. 3)

12 Revisit the Boston Tea Party

This hands-on, family-friendly, interactive museum includes 3-D holograms, talking portraits, actors clad in Colonial period costumes, and two ship replicas. (Ch. 10)

13 Visit Boston's Little Italy

The North End almost has an embarrassment of food riches. Nearly every store has something to do with food, be it a coffee shop, café, gelateria, food store, restaurant, or bakery. (Ch. 4)

14 Walk the Freedom Trail

One of Boston's most famous (and free) attractions, this 2.5-mile line (painted red or paved in red brick) takes visitors to some of the city's most important sights. (Ch. 3, 4, 5, 6)

15 Walk Along the Emerald Necklace

This delightful string of six green spaces and parks—the Back Bay Fens, the Riverway, Olmsted Park, Jamaica Pond, Arnold Arboretum, and Franklin Park—runs from one end of the city to the other. (Ch. 7, 9)

16 Eat Oysters at the Union Oyster House

It gets a bad rap, but this National Historic Landmark—the National Park Service designated it the country's oldest continually run restaurant and oyster bar—is worth a visit. (Ch. 4)

17 Step Back in Time at the Mapparium

Located in the Mary Baker Eddy Library this three-story, stained-glass globe is one of Boston's more unusual attractions. It depicts the world as it was in 1935, offering a glimpse into another era. (Ch. 7)

18 Head Out to the Boston Harbor Islands

Don't miss the chance to hop on a ferry to explore old forts, beaches, hiking trails, and even the nation's oldest continually used light station. (Ch. 6)

19 Stroll Down Newbury Street in the Back Bay

Boston's version of New York's 5th Avenue is an eight-block-long street jam-packed with upscale shops, trendy cafés, quirky boutiques, and great people-watching. (Ch. 7)

20 Take the Architecture Tour at the Boston Public Library

The magnificent main branch of the city's library system is in an 1895 Renaissance Revival building that houses hidden treasures like murals by John Singer Sargent. (Ch. 7)

WHAT'S WHERE

1 Beacon Hill, Boston Common, and the West End. Beacon Hill's historic streets lined with Federal-style homes make this an atmospheric place to explore. Bordering the Hill, grassy Boston Common serves as the start of the Freedom Trail. The West End has the Museum of Science and the TD Garden, where the Bruins and Celtics play.

2 Government Center and the North End. Architecture buffs may admire Government Center's brutalist City Hall, but most scurry past en route to Faneuil Hall and Faneuil Hall Marketplace. Across the Greenway, the North End attracts huge crowds to its Italian-American eateries, a vestige of the Italian immigrants who settled here in the 19th century.

3 Charlestown. On the banks of Boston Harbor and the Mystic River, Charlestown's top sights —the towering Bunker Hill Monument and the USS *Constitution* at the Navy Yard— can't be missed.

4 Downtown and the Waterfront. Downtown has many Freedom Trail sights, including the Old South

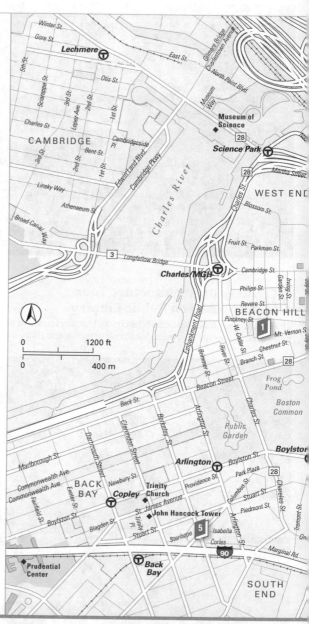

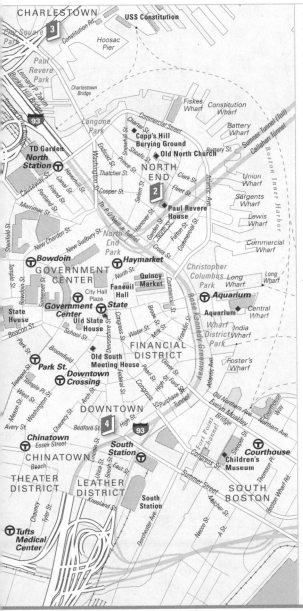

Meeting House and the
Old State House, as well
as a mish-mash of
shopping options. The
Theater District's home to
most of Boston's major
stages (dance, opera,
regional theater, and
national Broadway tours).
Chinatown—the
country's third largest—
offers a variety of authentic restaurants, while the
lofty Leather District
remains largely residen-
tial. The Financial
District bustles with
professionals during the
day, and the Waterfront
features wharves,
walking paths, and
Boston Harbor views.

**5 The Back Bay
and South End.** The Back
Bay—so called because it
was, once, a bay—
features Boston's iconic
brownstones, ritzy
Newbury Street
shopping, the city's tallest
buildings, a fair amount
of green space, and must-
see destinations like the
Boston Public Library
and Trinity Church. More
shopping awaits in the
South End, but it's a
different experience as
the boutiques are locally
owned and it has the
country's largest extant
Victorian row house
district. Today, it's
become home turf for
many of Boston's LGBTQ
community.

WHAT'S WHERE

6 Fenway and Kenmore Square. Baseball fans, tourists, and intellectuals meet in the Fens, a meandering green space that serves as the first "jewel" in Frederick Law Olmsted's intentional Emerald Necklace park system. To the northwest, Fenway Park—Major League Baseball's oldest ballpark—is home to the Boston Red Sox. The Museum of Fine Arts, Boston and the Isabella Stewart Gardner Museum offer lessons in art history.

7 Brookline and Jamaica Plain. Locals refer to Jamaica Plain as J.P., and as one of the first-ever streetcar suburbs, it still feels like a community enhanced by Olmsted's 19th-century landscaped parks, including Arnold Arboretum and Jamaica Pond. J.P. boasts a multicultural, though largely Latino, population, which is reflected in its main street restaurants and shops. Affluent Brookline boasts multimillion dollar homes and neighborhoods that just sound wealthy, like Chestnut Hill and Washington Square.

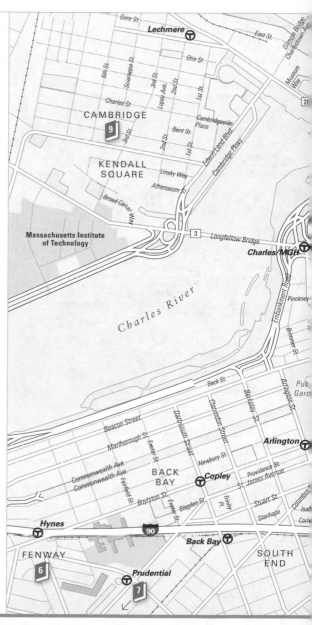

8 Seaport District, South Boston, and East Boston. Across from the Waterfront, the Seaport District is the poster child for revitalization, thanks to the continued development over the last 15 years, including the Boston Convention and Exhibition Center, the Institute of Contemporary Art, and swanky restaurants and hotels. Once a working-class Irish enclave, South Boston—very different from the South End—now mixes residential and commercial vibes for those who live there. Directly across Boston Harbor from Southie is the busy international Logan Airport in East Boston.

9 Cambridge and Somerville. While Cambridge is often lumped in when people refer to (air quotes) Boston, it's actually a much artsier, libertine city in its own right and has long been a haven for writers, academics, and iconoclasts. Harvard University plays a huge part in the personality of Harvard Square, while MIT asserts its tech and biotech leanings in Kendall and Central squares. The adjacent city of Somerville feels like a cousin with its collection of squares and indie airs.

Boston Today

Boston is the undisputed birthplace of American history. It's home to a number of firsts: first public park (Boston Common), first botanical garden (the Public Garden), and even the first phone call (made by Alexander Graham Bell in 1876). Much of the political ferment that spawned the nation happened here, and visitors are often awed by the dense concentration of landmarks. But this is a living city—not a museum—and, as such, its entrepreneurial spirit continues to evolve. Cambridge's Kendall Square, close to MIT, is a hotbed of technological progress, while Boston's Seaport District has a number of start-ups.

NEIGHBORHOOD DEVELOPMENTS

In a city as old as Boston, there's always room for reinvention, so it's no surprise that a few different parts of town are currently making themselves over. The Seaport District, formerly commercial buildings, parking lots, and working fish piers, is now home to high-res hotels and residences, water-facing, upscale restaurants, and purposeful green space. Across the harbor, developers are polishing up East Boston's waterfront, albeit on a smaller scale.

THE HISTORIC HARBOR

This city has long been defined by its harbor: The first colonists were largely drawn here because of it, and local commerce has been inextricably bound to the water ever since. See the amazing views for yourself along the Boston Harborwalk, a 43-mile-long path that skirts the coastline and passes by piers, parks, working wharves, hotel lounges, and urban beaches. It's also the launching pad for loads of harbor cruises, whale watches, and tall ship sails.

KENNEDY HONORS

The memory of Boston's beloved native son John F. Kennedy and his legendary family lingers. Tour historical collections dedicated to the 35th president at the John F. Kennedy Presidential Library & Museum; the legacy of his brother Ted is equally apparent next door at the Edward M. Kennedy Institute. Downtown's Rose Fitzgerald Kennedy Greenway features many diversions from the workday, including splash fountains, public art, beer gardens, and food trucks.

LIGHTS! CAMERA! ACTION!

The Massachusetts film tax subsidy program that was implemented in 2006 has continued to draw more productions to the Bay State. As a result, playing "spot the star" is a popular pastime. Big-screen names like Chris Evans, Johnny Depp, Jennifer Lawrence, Ryan Reynolds, Rosamund Pike, Ben Affleck, and Mark Wahlberg have all worked here.

FOOD SCENE SIZZLES

Boston lays claim to a long line of innovative chefs such as Karen Akunowicz, Jody Adams, Jamie Bissonnette, Tiffani Faison, Barbara Lynch, Ken Oringer, Ana Sortun, Ming Tsai, and Tony Maws, but it all started circa the 1960s when Julia Child launched a culinary revolution from her Cambridge kitchen. Today, it's getting harder to try traditional Yankee dishes like baked beans, codfish cakes, and Indian pudding—although Union Oyster House is a holdout on all accounts, and other restaurants may offer a modernized version of one or two. The Parker House still serves its signature Boston cream pie that was there in 1856. And, of course, the North End is an essential stop for Italian-American food.

THE AFTERMATH OF COVID-19

The U.S. (including Boston) was gravely impacted by COVID-19 in 2020. Restaurants, hotels, shops, bars, and even cultural institutions were forced to close. If you're planning a visit, remember to verify open hours, and to make sure that the property is still in operation.

Frugal Fun in Boston

WHEN FREEDOM RINGS FREE

Walking the **Freedom Trail** is free, as is entrance to 13 of its 16 attractions. For instance, the **Massachusetts State House** offers complimentary tours on weekdays. The spectacular views from the top of the Bunker Hill Monument, if you attempt to climb it, only depletes your energy, not your pocket change. In season (usually Memorial Day through Columbus Day), **Boston National Historical Park** hosts guided tours of portions of the trail for free—but you do need to reserve a ticket.

WALK BOSTON'S OTHER TRAILS

The Freedom Trail's success has spawned other no-cost, less formal pedestrian routes, including the **Black Heritage Trail** (⇨ *Box in the Beacon Hill, Boston Common, and West End chapter*) and the **Norman B. Leventhal Walk to the Sea** (⊕ *www.walktothesea.com*), which traces four centuries of civic development from Beacon Hill to the tip of Long Wharf. More niche options include **Irish Heritage Trail** (⊕ *www.irishheritagetrail. com/boston*) covering sites relating to Irish-American history in Boston, and the **Boston Women's Heritage Trail** (⊕ *www. bwht.org*) that pays tribute to ladies who gained fame as suffragettes and artists.

ARTSY ALTERNATIVES

Boston's cultural organizations consider the purse, especially for those who can be flexible. Most major museums waive admission during select time frames: the **Museum of Fine Arts, Boston** on Wednesday after 4 pm, most times for ages 17 and under, and anytime for members of the military; the **Institute of Contemporary Art/Boston** on Thursday after 5 pm, for ages 18 and under, and for families on the last Saturday of every month; the **Isabella Stewart Gardner Museum** for anyone named Isabella, and also for ages 17 and under; **Harvard Art Museums** on

Saturday 10 am–noon for Massachusetts residents, and always for ages 18 and under, students, and military families. As for performing arts, **Boston Symphony Orchestra** hosts free, informative lectures on Wednesdays at 5:30 pm followed by a free tour of Symphony Hall; **New England Conservatory** and **Berklee College of Music** both regularly offer free concerts and musical performances by rising stars. The **Boston Public Library,** filled with books, world-class art, and architecture, hosts free guided tours daily.

THE GREAT OUTDOORS

When you're ready for a rest, remember that the green in Boston's parks comes from Mother Nature herself. If you've already spent time exploring the **Public Garden** and **Boston Common,** you can check out the **Emerald Necklace,** a 7-mile string of pocket parks designed in 1878 by landscape architect Frederick Law Olmsted that includes gems like **Jamaica Pond** and **Arnold Arboretum.** Downtown, the **Rose Kennedy Greenway** features free diversions for the kids, including large-scale public art installations, interactive splash fountains, sitting areas, and a custom-made carousel. **Boston Harborwalk** offers visitors a bit of everything on its interconnected 43 miles of waterfront trails and pathways. Aside from scenic viewpoints (some with free binoculars), amenities range from interpretive panels to a pocket Maritime Museum at the **Fairmont Battery Wharf Hotel.**

HOLY GOOD MUSIC

In Copley Square, the architectural marvel that is **Trinity Church** hosts free, 30-minute Friday lunchtime organ recitals at 12:15 pm. Along the Freedom Trail, **King's Chapel** presents free weekly recitals on Tuesday at 12:15 pm, where the music ranges from jazz to folk to medieval and classical.

10 Best Museums in Boston

MUSEUM OF FINE ARTS, BOSTON
Home to more than half a million objects spanning from ancient Egyptian artifacts to contemporary artwork, the Museum of Fine Arts, Boston is one of the most highly regarded museums in the world and a must-visit site. Daily free one-hour guided tours give a good overview.

INSTITUTE OF CONTEMPORARY ART BOSTON
Inside the stunning glass-walled cantilevered building located on Boston's waterfront, you'll find cutting-edge art. Since 1936, the museum has shown the likes of Edvard Munch, Andy Warhol, Laurie Anderson, and Roy Lichtenstein. There's always something new to see.

ISABELLA STEWART GARDNER MUSEUM
This quirky museum, named for its owner, was built in the 19th century to mimic a Venetian palazzo. It's home to Gardner's impressive collection of art, with masterpieces like Titian's "Europa." As specified in her will, nothing has been changed since her death.

JFK MUSEUM
This library-museum pays homage to the life and presidency of John F. Kennedy and his family, with re-creations of his desk in the Oval Office and the TV studio in which he debated Richard M. Nixon, plus exhibits ranging from the Cuban missile crisis to his assassination.

MUSEUM OF SCIENCE, BOSTON
With more than 550 exhibits covering astronomy, astrophysics, anthropology, medical progress, computers, earth sciences, and much more, this is the place to ignite your imagination and curiosity. Also, the Charles Hayden Planetarium offers exciting astronomical programs.

MUSEUM OF AFRICAN-AMERICAN HISTORY
Established in 1964, this museum is composed of the Abiel Smith School, the first public school in the nation built specifically for black children, and the African Meeting House, both on Boston's Black Heritage Trail, plus the African Meeting House on Nantucket.

BOSTON TEA PARTY SHIPS & MUSEUM

This hands-on interactive museum lets you toss (fake) tea overboard in a reenactment of the Boston Tea Party. Exhibits include 3-D holograms, talking portraits, and replicas of two of the three ships on-hand that fateful night, the *Beaver II* and the *Eleanor*.

USS *CONSTITUTION* & MUSEUM

Better known as "Old Ironsides," the USS *Constitution* at the Charlestown Navy Yard, is the oldest commissioned ship in the U.S. fleet. After touring the ship, which was built in 1797 and is manned by navy personnel, head to the nearby USS *Constitution* Museum to learn more.

OLD STATE HOUSE

This colonial-era landmark, the seat of the colonial government from 1713 until the Revolution, is now an interactive museum. The Declaration of Independence was first read in public in Boston from the building's balcony, which also overlooks the site of the Boston Massacre.

HARVARD MUSEUM OF NATURAL HISTORY

With more than 12,000 specimens, including dinosaurs, rare minerals, hundreds of mammals and birds, and Harvard's world-famous and gorgeous Blaschka Glass Flowers, this museum offers both historic exhibits and new and changing exhibits.

Things to Eat and Drink in Boston

BOSTON BAKED BEANS

A nod to Native American and Pilgrims times, as well as Boston's rum-producing role in the late-1700s "triangle trade," beans are slow-baked with molasses and salt pork and served with brown bread. Find them at Beantown Pub or Rebel's Guild.

LOBSTER ROLL

What's your pleasure—cold lobster meat mixed with mayo or warm and drenched in melted butter? Whichever prep you decide on, one thing remains constant. Served on a toasted hot dog bun is the only acceptable way to eat this Boston classic. Find it at Pauli's North End and James Hook Lobster.

NEW ENGLAND CLAM CHOWDER

This New England soup-meets-stew is a rich, thick concoction of clams, potatoes, salt pork or bacon, and cream, topped with oyster crackers. While a few local places also add muscles or fish chunks, almost every local accent pronounces it chowdah. Find it at Island Creek Oyster Bar or Legal Seafood.

BOSTON CREAM PIE

More cake than pie, this dessert is a true Boston original. It was first served in 1856 in the Parker House Hotel, (also home to the Parker House Roll) and is made of sweet custard layered between yellow butter cake and topped with chocolate glaze. Find it at Omni Parker Hotel and Magnolia's Bakery.

CANNOLIS
Boston loves these masterpieces, as evidenced by the lines at North End Italian pastry shops like Mike's or Modern (there's an ever-lasting feud on who has the better ones). These crunchy tubes are stuffed with delicate ricotta or cream, sometimes dipped and covered in chocolate chips. Find it at Modern Pastry or Mike's Pastry.

TRADITIONAL CLAM BAKE
The typical clambake is a coastal and casual meal of lobster, clams, corn, and red potatoes steamed over a seaweed fire. Don't be surprised if it's served in the actual mesh steamer bag. Find it at Barking Crab and Summer Shack.

YANKEE POT ROAST
An homage to the patience and frugality of yesteryear's working class New Englanders, the dish is made from tough cuts of beef roasted for hours and served with onions, carrots, potatoes, parsnip, or turnips. Find it at Henrietta's Table and PARK.

FRAPPE
A milk shake is just milk and syrup. Bostonians take things up a notch by plopping in a scoop of ice cream. This addition turns it into thick, creamy dessert drink known as a frappe. Some go further with stir-in candies or booze. Find it at King's Dining and Entertainment and Boston Burger Company.

LOBSTER MAC AND CHEESE
This isn't a Boston original, but with tons of lobsters available from local waters, it makes sense this American classic is on the menus of several restaurants. Chefs mix in hunks of lobster to cheesy pasta goodness and top with browned and buttery breadcrumbs. Find it at Yankee Lobster and JM Curley.

ROAST BEEF SANDWICH
Boston's roast beef sandwiches are hearty, stacked with inches upon inches of roast beef. While tradition dictates slices are sandwiched into an onion roll, you'll also find them in sub rolls. Some places have their own special tangy sauce to accompany. Find it at Kelly's Roast Beef and Cutty's.

Boston's Historical Sites: Revolutionary and Beyond

MASSACHUSETTS STATE HOUSE
Famous for its golden dome, the Charles Bulfinch–designed State House has been the Commonwealth's seat of government since 1798. Today, visitors can tour the building while learning about the quirks of its political past.

BLACK HERITAGE TRAIL
During the late 18th- and early 19th-centuries, the abolition movement launched in Beacon Hill. This cultural trail explores sites relevant to the cause like the 1806 African Meeting House where Frederick Douglass spoke, and numerous private homes that served the Underground Railroad.

USS *CONSTITUTION* AND MUSEUM
The trip to Charlestown is worth it to see the still-commissioned USS *Constitution*, America's Ship of State; she's been in service since the War of 1812, but has never gone down in battle. Also, in the Navy Yard, the USS *Constitution* Museum features artifacts and interactive exhibits.

FREEDOM TRAIL
A conversation about history in Boston is never complete without mention of the Revolutionary War, and the Freedom Trail is at its heart. This self-guided walking path just more than 2 miles long, winds through Downtown, the North End and Charlestown, stopping at 16 sites like Old South Meeting House, Faneuil Hall, and the Paul Revere House.

OLD NORTH CHURCH HISTORIC SITE
The pivotal steeple where Robert Newman signaled to Paul Revere with two lanterns and launched him on his midnight ride to Concord and Lexington still stands. At the time, the congregation was, ironically, loyal to the British government, and today it remains Episcopal. Highlights include crypt and bell tower tours, a Colonial chocolate-making program at the Clough House, and five gardens.

BOSTON PUBLIC LIBRARY
One of the architectural marvels of Copley Square, Boston Public Library opened its McKim building in 1895. A century and a quarter later, visitors continue to gape at John Singer Sargent's triumphant murals, artwork by Chavannes, an open-air courtyard, and rare books including early Shakespearean folios and original writings by Copernicus and Newton.

HARVARD YARD

The campus of America's oldest university—at nearly 400 years old—has a lot of stories to tell. It's been a grazing ground for livestock, a place partly built by slavery, a protesting site, and a home to thousands of the world's brightest minds.

THE KENNEDYS ON COLUMBIA POINT

Boston's legendary clan holds court at the JFK Presidential Library and Museum, as well as at the Edward M. Kennedy Institute for the United States Senate.

MASS GENERAL HOSPITAL AND PAUL S. RUSSELL MUSEUM

Inside the world-renowned hospital's most historic building, the Ether Dome marks the site of the first public demonstration of the use of anesthesia. Around the corner, the Russell Museum delves into Mass General's medical legacy and its ongoing work, from targeted cancer therapies to deep brain stimulation.

THE EMERALD NECKLACE

Less known outside the city's history annals is the work of Frederick Law Olmsted, the visionary landscape architect who designed major green spaces from New York City's Central Park to the U.S. Capitol grounds. But before all that, Olmsted spent 20 years here in his hometown, building and linking six gorgeous parks that Bostonians know as the Emerald Necklace.

BOSTON TEA PARTY SHIPS & MUSEUM

Near the original site of the infamous "Tea Party," this museum honors the 18th-century protest with 21st-century holographic exhibits, a mock town meeting, and historic replicas of the actual ships.

Boston with Kids

FOLLOW THE REDBRICK ROAD

Travel back to the Revolutionary era and take the kids along while walking the Freedom Trail. Sign kids up for the free National Park Service Junior Ranger program, which uses fun and games to help them digest the history lesson. Most people follow the trail south to north, but reverse order actually works best for families; it allows you to start with "Old Ironsides" and the **Bunker Hill Monument** (star attractions in young eyes) in Charlestown and then end in Boston Common (an ideal place to unwind after a long trek). ⊕ *www.nps.gov/bost/learn/kidsyouth/beajuniorranger.htm*

MAKE A FOWL PLAY

In season (April through August), the **Swan Boats** take up residency in the **Public Garden** lagoon, and you can take a slow, peddle-powered ride for less than $4. Once you get your sea legs back, waddle over to the nearby bronze Make Way For Ducklings sculpture for a photo op with Mrs. Mallard and her quacking offspring written about in Robert McCloskey's 1941 book, *Make Way for Ducklings.*

KID AROUND

The multistory climbing structure that dominates the lobby of the **Boston Children's Museum** could be a tough act to follow, but the museum manages it with some seriously cool exhibits including an interactive dinosaur exploration, an authentic merchant's home from Japan, and, simply, bubbles. There is also a Play-Space just for kids under three.

YELL "EUREKA"

No place does gizmos and gadgets like the **Museum of Science,** where almost everything is meant to be pushed, pulled, or otherwise maneuvered.

FIND NEMO

The **New England Aquarium** features endless exhibits, including its central Giant Ocean Tank, and multiple live touch tanks (sharks, rays, sea stars). There are in-the-water animal encounters and behind-the-scenes tours for visitors willing to pay over and above admission— they're worth every penny. The aquarium also organizes whale-watching trips to Stellwagen Bank, late March to October.

EMBRACE ISLAND LIFE

Boston Harbor conceals 34 idyllic islands, and while most of them are open to the public they manage to fly under the radar. It's perfect for a fun family day of exploring nature, coastline, and abandoned military forts. A number of free resources help guide your adventures (⊕ *www.bostonharborislands.org/kids-and-families*).

HAVE A BALL

Major League Baseball's oldest ballpark, small but mighty Fenway Park has become a pilgrimage site for baseball fans of all ages and team preferences. Daily one-hour tours provide the ultimate insider's view to the Red Sox's home field with a look at the press box, the Green Monster (schedule permitting), and more. This is as close as anyone gets to the fabled field without being drafted.

TOUR THE TOWN

Boston By Foot (☎ *617/367–2345* ⊕ *www.bostonbyfoot.org*) features specialized "Boston By Little Feet" tours for 6- to 12-year-olds, May through October. **Boston Duck Tours** (☎ *617/267–3825* ⊕ *www.bostonducktours.com*) operates amphibious vehicles for a land and water journey around Boston—lucky kids get to captain the ship. And **Old Town Trolley** (☎ *888/910–8687* ⊕ *www.trolleytours.com*) offers hop-on, hop-off tours for anyone who would rather ride than walk.

What to Read and Watch

THE HEAT (2013)
Melissa McCarthy and Sandra Bullock show off their comedic chops in this hilarious film set in and around a blue-collar Boston neighborhood. As polished FBI agent Sarah Ashburn, Bullock butts heads with McCarthy's rough-around-the-edges Boston Police Department detective Shannon Mullins on their joint quest to take down a local drug lord.

THE GIVEN DAY
BY DENNIS LEHANE
Boston-born, mega-talented writer Lehane has famously set many of his novels in and around Boston. But this one takes a look at the city just after World War I through the lens of two families—one white and one black. It wades through an accurate depiction of the era's political and societal atmosphere, where fictitious members of a fractious community have varying allegiances and motivations. It's a Boston you won't recognize.

THE DEPARTED (2006)
Martin Scorsese's Academy Award–winning film tells the story of a South Boston mob boss and his protégé who infiltrates the Boston Police Department's special forces. If you're thinking this sounds a bit like real life, you're right.

MONDAY MORNING PODCAST
Boston-raised comedian Bill Burr has been doling out acerbic observations about the state of things in Hollywood, gender roles, sports, and other topics in his popular, opinionated podcast-slash-rant for more than a decade now.

JOHN ADAMS
BY DAVID MCCULLOUGH
In his Pulitzer Prize–winning biography of the United States' second president, historian David McCullough shares personal and political details of the brilliant lawyer, patriot, and founding father. Readers will get a sense of what Boston was like during Revolutionary times, what drove its people, and how America was built.

I SHIMMER SOMETIMES, TOO
BY PORSHA OLAYIWOLA
Poignant words written by Boston's current poet laureate and self-proclaimed hip-hop feminist-futurist croon from the pages of her 2019 release. In this book of verse, Olayiwola considers some of the challenges of living black, female, and queer.

LAST SEEN
Boston's most famous whodunnit—in 1991, 13 priceless works of art were stolen from the Isabella Stewart Gardner Museum—has yet to be solved and this true-crime podcast, presented by WBUR with The Boston Globe, takes a deep dive into what happened.

CHEERS (1982–93)
Gen Xers and Boomers surely wax nostalgic over this beloved sitcom that centers around a beer-loving cast of commiserating regulars in a Boston bar where "everybody knows your name." Cast includes some of acting's greats: Ted Danson, Shelley Long, Rhea Perlman, George Wendt, Woody Harrelson, Bebe Neuwirth, and Kelsey Grammer. The real bar that inspired the location of Cheers is still open on Beacon Hill today.

GOOD WILL HUNTING (1997)
This is the movie that launched Matt Damon and Ben Affleck into Hollywood's stratosphere. With scenes taking place across town, predominantly in South Boston and Cambridge, Good Will Hunting follows a young, working-class MIT janitor—and quiet genius—trying to navigate his way from a messy past to a promising future. Featured in the film, the L Street Tavern is still a popular place for a pint.

Boston Sports: Where and How to See Them

Everything you've heard about the zeal of Boston sports fanatics is true. Here, you root for the home team; you cheer, and you pray, and you root some more. How else can you explain how the Red Sox reversed the curse in 2004 for the team's first World Series victory since 1918?

BASEBALL

The Boston Red Sox may be New England's most storied professional sports team of all time. For 86 years, the club suffered a World Series drought, a streak of bad luck that fans attributed to the "Curse of the Bambino," spelled in 1920 when the Sox sold Babe Ruth to the New York Yankees. All that changed in 2004, when a maverick squad broke the curse in a thrilling seven-game semifinals series against the Yankees, followed by a four-game sweep of St. Louis in the finals. Repeat World Series wins in 2007, 2013, and 2018 have cemented Bostonians' sense that the universe is back in order.

Ticket-holding Sox fans can browse display cases mounted inside Fenway Park before and during a ball game; these shed light on and show off memorabilia from particular players and eras over the course of the team's history. Speaking of Fenway, it is Major League Baseball's oldest ballpark and has seen some stuff since its 1912 opening, including such events of this millennia as Curt Schilling's bloody sock in 2004, the 19–3 massacre of the Yankees during the 2019 season, and, well, the entire legacy of Big Papi, home run by home run.

The Red Sox play home games at Fenway Park from April to October, accessible from all parts of Boston by foot or the T's Green Line. It's typically not too difficult to get single tickets to a game (buy them online ⊕ *www.mlb.com/red-sox/tickets/single-game-tickets*) and many sell for as little as $10–$20. Although the team is officially tied to Boston, it has earned time-honored fans from across the country and all economic strata. There's nothing quite like sitting in the stands as "Sweet Caroline" plays during the eighth inning. For a most unique viewing experience, try to get tickets for the Monster Seats, aptly perched on top of the Green Monster in left-field. Do splurge for food inside the park—if you're gonna do it somewhere, it might as well be here. For a time-honored treat, order a Sam Adams beer, a Fenway Frank with all the fixings, a slice of Regina pizza, and—you know it's coming—some Cracker Jacks. But, for modern palates, the ballpark has taken its menu up a notch, featuring food by local kitchens including Tasty Burger and Yankee Lobster Co., as well as gluten-free, vegetarian and kosher options.

BASKETBALL

The Boston Celtics franchise has the most championship titles in the NBA, with 17 banners; rival Los Angeles Lakers come in second with 16, which is at least 10 more than any other team. It's a mind-blowing stat, yes, but today's fans will note that 11 of those wins were earned between 1957 and 1969 (thanks, Bill Russell), with the most recent coming in 2008 after a sweet victory over the Lakers. It's been a mixed journey, for sure.

So, what to expect at a Celtics game from today's squad? An all-around fun experience, a charged atmosphere and devotion, from the fans to the team and the team to the fans. You'll hear "Let's Go, Cel-tics" no matter the score. For a truly unique day, die-hard sports fans should take advantage of a Celtics–Bruins doubleheader, which means both pro teams play at the TD Garden on the same day, just hours apart. There's at least one per season, and it usually happens in November, on Black Friday.

From anywhere in Boston, it's easy to get to the Garden, since North Station (servicing Commuter Rail trains, and the MBTA's Orange and Green lines) is located within the complex. For pre- and postgame nourishment, the Hub on Causeway, also at North Station, opened in the fall of 2019, featuring a number of restaurants and bars, like the upscale Banners Kitchen & Tap, and a localized food court, Hub Hall. Or, take a walk down Canal, Friend, and Portland streets for a bar that's to your liking.

FOOTBALL

St. Patrick's Day 2020 was miserable for New England football fans who learned of Patriots' greatest-of-all-time quarterback Tom Brady's eminent departure after a historic 20-year run—and six Super Bowl wins—with this hometown team.

Over its entire history since 1959, the Pats have been successful and less-so. In fact, the franchise was one of the American Football League's eight original teams. They first played at Boston University Field, and intermittently at Harvard Stadium and Fenway Park, until building the team's first official arena, Schaefer Stadium, 20 miles outside the city in Foxboro, Massachusetts.

Today, the New England Patriots take the field at Robert Kraft's massive, 2002-built Gillette Stadium, also in Foxboro, from August through January. Since Brady and coach Bill Belichick partnered up in 2000 to create one helluva dynasty, it has been nearly impossible to get single game tickets through the Patriots' box office, so resellers like Ticketmaster and StubHub are your best bet; regardless of your point of purchase, tickets are expensive.

The MBTA Commuter Rail services Patriots trains to Gillette Stadium from both Boston and Providence before and after every home game; round-trip tickets are $20 (buy them in person at South Station or Back Bay, or via the mTicket app; find more information online ⊕ *www. mbta.com/destinations/gillette-stadium*). To take full advantage of the Patriots' pregame experience, drive to Gillette and bring some food and a grill (no open flames); parking lots ($30–$60) open four hours before kick-off.

HOCKEY

In 1924, the Boston Bruins became the first U.S. ice hockey team to enter the NHL. Fun fact: In looking for a name, team owner Charles Adams sought out something that would represent an "untamed animal embodied with size, strength, agility, ferocity, and cunning."

The Bruins have been playing at the Garden since 1928 (although the original Boston Garden was rebuilt in 1995) and have won six Stanley Cup titles over that time. Great players to skate for the Big Bad Bruins have included Bobby Orr and Phil Esposito in the early 1970s, Ray Bourque in the 1980s and 1990s, and current players six-foot-nine-inch Zdeno Chara and feisty left wing Brad Marchand. Spectators can watch the championship banners hanging in the rafters above the ice and the stands, which are packed for every home game, despite high ticket prices.

Fans are loud, vocal and extremely loyal, so ticket holders with delicate personalities may not feel comfortable. However, Saturday afternoon games are a win for the family. Single tickets are available at the TD Garden Box Office or through Ticketmaster. For a real pre-game experience, stop by a real dive, Sullivan's Tap on Canal Street for a few beers.

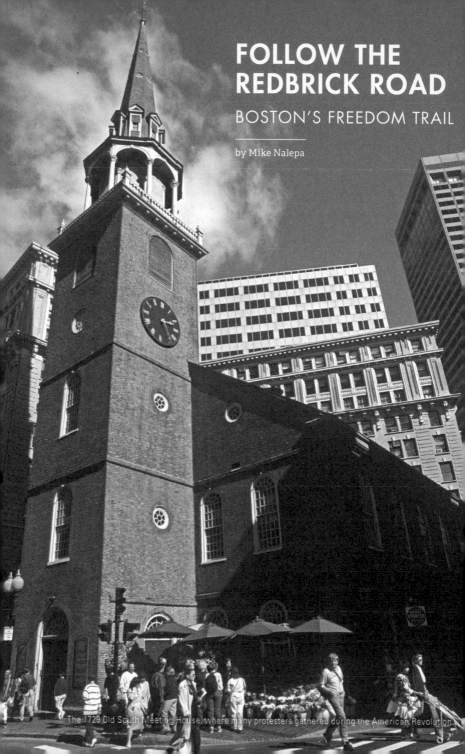

FOLLOW THE
REDBRICK ROAD

BOSTON'S FREEDOM TRAIL

by Mike Nalepa

The 1729 Old South Meeting House, where many protesters gathered during the American Revolution

Paul Revere
Benjamin Franklin
John Hancock

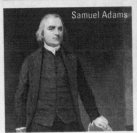

Samuel Adams

Paul Revere's ride

The Freedom Trail is more than a collection of historic sites related to the American Revolution or a suggested itinerary connecting Boston's unique neighborhoods. It's a chance to walk in the footsteps of our forefathers—literally, by following a crimson path on public sidewalks—and pay tribute to the figures all school kids know, like Paul Revere, John Hancock, and Ben Franklin. In history-proud Boston, past and present intersect before your eyes not as a re-creation but as living history accessible to all.

Boston played a key role in the dramatic events leading up to the American Revolution. Many of the founding fathers called the city home, and many of the initial meetings and actions that sparked the fight against the British took place here. In one day, you can visit Faneuil Hall—the "Cradle of Liberty"—where outraged colonial radicals met to oppose British authority; the site of the incendiary Boston Massacre; and the Old North Church, where lanterns hung to signal Paul Revere on his thrilling midnight ride. Colonists may have originally landed in Jamestown and Plymouth, but if you really want to see where America began, come to Boston.

Boston Common, Founder's Statue

⊕ www.nps.gov/bost
⊕ www.thefreedomtrail.org

☎ 617/242–5642

✉ Admission to the Freedom Trail itself is free. Several museum sites charge for admission. However, most attractions are free monuments, parks, and landmarks.

PLANNING YOUR TRAIL TRIP

THE ROUTE

The 2½-mi Freedom Trail begins at Boston Common, winds through Downtown, Government Center, and the North End, and ends in Charlestown at the USS *Constitution*. The entire Freedom Trail is marked by a red line on the sidewalk; it's made of paint or brick at various points on the Trail. ⇨ *For more information on Freedom Trail sites, see listings in Neighborhood chapters.*

GETTING HERE AND BACK

The route starts near the Park Street T stop. When you've completed the Freedom Trail, head for the nearby Charlestown water shuttle, which goes directly to the downtown area. For schedules and maps, visit ⊕ *www.mbta.com.*

TIMING

If you're stopping at a few (or all) of the 16 sites, it takes a full day to complete the route comfortably. ■TIP→ **If you have children in tow, you may want to split the trail into two or more days.**

VISITOR CENTERS

There are Freedom Trail information centers in Boston Common (Tremont Street), outside of Faneuil Hall (near the Old State House), and at the Charlestown Navy Yard Visitor Center (in Building 5).

TOURS

The National Park Service's free 90-minute Freedom Trail walking tours begin at the Boston National Historical Park Visitor Center outside of Faneuil Hall and cover sites from the Old South Meeting House to the Old North Church. Check online for times; it's a good idea to show up at least 30 minutes early, as the popular tours are limited to 30 people.

Half-hour tours of the USS *Constitution* are offered Tuesday through Sunday. Note that visitors to the ship must go through security screening.

FUEL UP

The trail winds through the heart of Downtown Boston, so finding a quick bite or a nice sit-down meal isn't difficult. Quincy Market, near Faneuil Hall, is packed with cafés and eateries. Another good lunch choice is one of the North End's wonderful Italian restaurants.

WHAT'S NEARBY

For a short break from revolutionary history, be sure to check out the major attractions nearby, including the Boston Public Garden, New England Aquarium, and Union Oyster House.

Above: In front of the Old State House a cobblestone circle marks the site of the Boston Massacre.

○ TOP SIGHTS

Boston Common

Benjamin Franklin Statue

The Granary Burial Grounds

Faneuil Hall

Park Street Church

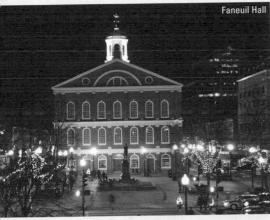

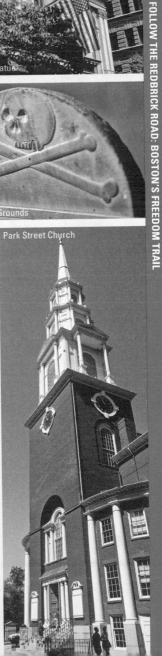

Old North Church

Bunker Hill Monument

BOSTON COMMON TO FANEUIL HALL

Old State House

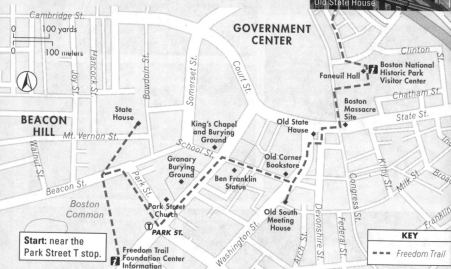

Cambridge St.

0 — 100 yards
0 — 100 meters

GOVERNMENT CENTER

Clinton

Faneuil Hall

Boston National Historic Park Visitor Center

Chatham St.

Boston Massacre Site

State St.

BEACON HILL

Mt. Vernon St.

State House

King's Chapel and Burying Ground

Old State House

Old Corner Bookstore

Granary Burying Ground

School St.

Walnut St.

Beacon St.

Ben Franklin Statue

Boston Common

Park St.

Park Street Church

PARK ST.

Old South Meeting House

Washington St.

Devonshire St.

Congress St.

Federal St.

Arch St.

Kilby St.

Milk St.

Franklin

Start: near the Park Street T stop.

Freedom Trail Foundation Center Information

KEY

- - - Freedom Trail

Many of the Freedom Trail sites between Boston Common and the North End are close together. Walking this 1-mile segment of the trail makes for a pleasant morning.

THE ROUTE
Begin at ★ **Boston Common,** then head for the **State House,** Boston's finest example of Federal architecture. Several blocks away is the **Park Street Church,** whose 217-foot steeple is considered to be the most beautiful in New England. The church was actually founded in 1809, and it played a key role in the movement to abolish slavery.

Reposing in the church's shadows is the ★ **Granary Burying Ground,** final resting place of Samuel Adams, John Hancock, and Paul Revere. A short stroll to Downtown brings you to **King's Chapel,** founded in 1686 by King James II for the Church of England.

Follow the trail past the **Benjamin Franklin statue** to the **Old Corner Bookstore** site, where Hawthorne, Emerson, and Longfellow were published. Nearby is the **Old South Meeting House,** where arguments in 1773 led to the Boston Tea Party. Overlooking the site of the Boston Massacre is the city's oldest public building, the **Old State House,** a Georgian beauty. In 1770 the Boston Massacre

occurred directly in front of here—look for the commemorative stone circle.

Cross the plaza to ★ **Faneuil Hall** and explore where Samuel Adams railed against "taxation without representation." ■TIP→ **A good mid-trail break is the shops and eateries of Faneuil Hall Marketplace, which includes Quincy Market.**

Old Corner Book Store Site

★ = **Fodor's**Choice ★ = Highly Recommended ☺ = Family Friendly

NORTH END TO CHARLESTOWN

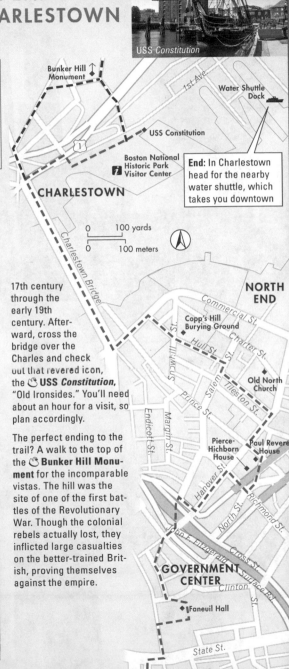

USS *Constitution*

Freedom Trail sites between Faneuil Hall and Charlestown are more spread out along 1½ miles. The sites here, though more difficult to reach, are certainly worth the walk.

THE ROUTE

When you depart Faneuil Hall, follow the red stripe to the North End, Boston's Little Italy.

The ☙ **Paul Revere House** takes you back 200 years—here are the hero's own saddlebags, a toddy warmer, and a pine cradle made from a molasses cask. It's also air-conditioned in the summer, so try to stop here in mid-afternoon to escape the heat. Next to the Paul Revere House is one of the city's oldest brick buildings, the **Pierce-Hichborn House**.

Next, peek inside a place guaranteed to trigger a wave of patriotism: the ★ **Old North Church** of "One if by land, two if by sea" fame. Then head toward **Copp's Hill Burying Ground,** where you can view graves from the late

17th century through the early 19th century. After-ward, cross the bridge over the Charles and check out that revered icon, the ☙ **USS *Constitution*,** "Old Ironsides." You'll need about an hour for a visit, so plan accordingly.

The perfect ending to the trail? A walk to the top of the ☙ **Bunker Hill Monument** for the incomparable vistas. The hill was the site of one of the first battles of the Revolutionary War. Though the colonial rebels actually lost, they inflicted large casualties on the better-trained British, proving themselves against the empire.

End: In Charlestown head for the nearby water shuttle, which takes you downtown

CHARLESTOWN

NORTH END

Bunker Hill Monument

Water Shuttle Dock

USS Constitution

Boston National Historic Park Visitor Center

1st Ave.

Charlestown Bridge

Commercial St.

Copp's Hill Burying Ground

Hull St.

Snowhill St.

Charter St.

Salem St.

Tileston St.

Old North Church

Prince St.

Margin St.

Endicott St.

Pierce-Hichborn House

Paul Revere House

Hanover St.

North St.

Richmond St.

John F. Fitzgerald

Cross St.

Surface Rd.

GOVERNMENT CENTER

Clinton St.

Faneuil Hall

State St.

0 100 yards
0 100 meters

Paul Revere House

Did You Know?

If the Freedom Trail leaves you eager to see more Revolutionary War sites, drive about 30 minutes to Lexington and Concord, where the "shot heard 'round the world" launched the first battles in 1775.

TRAVEL SMART

Updated by
Cheryl Fenton

👥 POPULATION:
685,094

💬 LANGUAGE:
English

$ CURRENCY:
U.S. Dollar

☎ AREA CODE:
617 and 857

⚠ EMERGENCIES:
911

🚗 DRIVING:
On the right

⚡ ELECTRICITY:
120–220 v/60 cycles;
plugs have two or three
rectangular prongs

🕐 TIME:
Same as New York

🌐 WEB RESOURCES:
🌐 Boston.gov
🌐 www.bostonusa.com

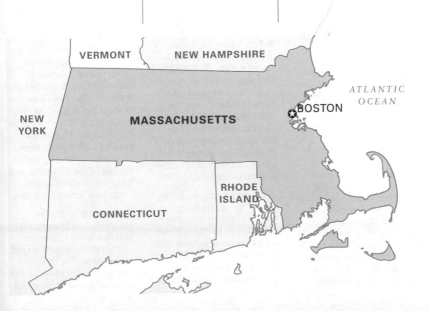

Know Before You Go

Are tips expected? What's the best way to see the city? When's the best time to visit? What should I wear? Is pot legal? Are sports really that important to the city? We've got answers and a few tips to help you make the most of your visit.

WHAT TO PACK

As the old joke goes: If you don't like the weather in New England, wait a minute. A chilly, overcast morning can become a sunny, warm afternoon—and vice versa. Try to layer your clothing so that you can remove or add garments as needed for comfort. Rain may appear with little warning, so pack a raincoat and umbrella if you have the room. Boston is a great walking city—despite picturesque but bumpy cobblestone streets, brick walkways, and uneven asphalt—so be sure to bring comfortable shoes. In all seasons, it's often breezier (and colder) along the coast; so bring a warm layer when touring the beach or harbor areas.

BE A SPORT

Everything you've heard about the zeal of Boston fans is true. Locals mark off seasons by checking the sports lineup. When the Boys of Summer play at home, "Red Sox Nation" is out braving Yawkey Way outside of legendary Fenway Park (the country's oldest ball park), munching on Fenway Franks or sausage subs from The Sausage Guy, and bellowing "Sweet Caroline" in the middle of the eighth inning. Sox aside, this city is also home to the six-time Stanley Cup Bruins, six-time champion New England Patriots, and 17 NBA champion Celtics.

If you can't score tickets to watch the Bruins hockey or Celtics basketball, you can still visit the Sports Museum at the TD Garden (true locals pronounce it "Gah-din"). Come early on game day and you might see players warming up. Football fans get a kick out of Gillette Stadium in Foxborough, the Pats' home turf and sprawling Patriot Place, with its restaurants, entertainment complex, and high-tech Hall of Fame. The city is also home to the Boston Marathon, New England's largest sporting event and the world's oldest annual marathon.

Bostonians' long-standing fervor for sports is equally evident in their leisure-time activities. Once harsh winters give way, Boston's extensive parks, paths, woods, and waterways teem with sun seekers and weekend warriors—until November's bitter winds bite again, and that energy is redirected toward white slopes and frozen rinks.

BOSTON WAS MADE FOR WALKING

"America's Walking City," with all its historic nooks and crannies, is best explored on foot. The most popular way to see all the city's notable sites is the Freedom Trail, an important page out of the city's history book. Follow the redbrick road, a 3-mile trail connecting most of Boston's National Historical Park sites including Granary Burial Ground, Kings' Chapel Cemetery, the Old State House, and the Boston Massacre Site. There's also the Black Heritage Trail, a 1.6-mile path winding through important African American history sights, and the Boston Women's Heritage Trail, which highlights the city's influential women.

BOOK IT TO THE LIBRARY

Boston has always been home to noted authors (John Updike, Junot Diaz, Robert Parker) and poets (Robert Pinsky, Sylvia Plath, Mary Oliver), and the city remains a haven for readers (tributes are seen throughout the city, including the Edgar Allan Poe and adorable "Make Way For Ducklings" bronze statues).

Bookworms adore the Boston Public Library, just as Ralph Waldo Emerson and his literary buddies did in the 1800s. The building stands proudly as America's first municipal library, and nyone can browse its vast ollection, reading halls, nd courtyard. A newly xpanded children's section s worth a visit with tots.

Among its books, the Mary Baker Eddy Library houses a **Mapparium** (a mammoth walk-in glass globe spanned by a 30-foot bridge) and a virtual fountain spewing famous quotes.

The John F. Kennedy Presidential Library & Museum at Dorchester's Columbia Point feels like hallowed ground for Boston's lost son, with memorabilia and multimedia on display.

JOIN THE FESTIVITIES

While the Brits who founded Boston get a lot of attention, they were only the first of many immigrant groups who helped shape this city. Locals applaud the others' colorful legacy through equally colorful celebrations. In America's third-largest Chinatown, dragon parades and firecrackers mark Chinese New Year, while the August Moon Festival features dancing lions, lanterns, and moon cakes around the Gateway Arch. And, Irish eyes are always smiling on the Sunday closest to March 17, when the famous St. Patrick's Day Parade passes through Southie, the city's infamous Irish neighborhood.

The North End hosts summer weekend street festivals, honoring Italy's patron saints on their name days with processions, brass bands, and Italian delicacies like *zeppole* (fried dough), pizza, and pasta. St. Anthony of Padua's is the biggie, going three days in late August.

DON'T WORRY. BE HAPPY.

Since 1984, Boston has banned the term "happy hour," but that doesn't mean restaurants and bars haven't found a way to keep you happy. Most places have discounted drinks and fare between 4 and 6 pm.

THIS CITY DOES SLEEP

While most large cities enjoy their nightlife way into the wee hours, Boston bar-goers must head home at 2 am. After the public transporation's last call (the last T is around 1 am, depending on the line and service), it's Uber, taxi, or foot to get home.

POT IS LEGAL

Don't be alarmed if you walk by a marijuana dispensary; recreational pot became legal in Masschuestts in mid-2017. Be sure to check into local purchasing and usage laws/ guidelines.

BOSTON ACTUALLY LOVES TEA

Despite its tea-stained past, Boston actually loves a good tea party. Several of the local high-end hotels like Mandarin Oriental Boston, Ritz Carlton Boston, Boston Harbor Hotel (with Rowes Wharf harbor views), and Taj Boston host afternoon teas, complete with finger sandwiches, scones, champagne toasts, and steaming pots. The Boston Public Library is also known for its Courtyard Tea Room settings Wednesday through Friday.

THE CITY OF FIRSTS

Boston is a special city. Just ask any of its residents. They're proud of its place as many of America's firsts and oldests—first public park, oldest restaurant, first public school, first subway system, oldest MLB park, first marathon, first post office, and first restaurant, to name a few.

TAKE TO THE SEAS

This city embraces its waterfront location. There are plenty of harbor cruises, whale watching tours, and water taxi experiences available throughout the spring, summer, and fall.

DINE ON TRADITION

With a rich colonial history, international influences, and a seaside locale, Boston certainly has a seat at the table as a culinary influencer. Taking a page out of history's cookbook, don't miss out on Boston Baked Beans or Yankee Pot Roast. And don't forget to visit the original home of the Boston Cream Pie—the Omni Hotel's Parker House.

BOSTON AND COVID-19

In the spring of 2020, the United States (including Boston) was gravely impacted by COVID-19. Restaurants, hotels, shops, bars, and even cultural institutions were forced to closed. If you're currently planning a visit, remember to call ahead to verify open hours, and to make sure the property is open.

Getting Here and Around

Boston's maze of old and new fuses together remarkably well with a little patience. Follow its endless array of narrow, twisting one-way streets radiating from Boston Harbor in the east, and you'll reach the bustle of the Italian-flavored North End. Go west and hit Faneuil Hall, the quaintly named streets of Downtown, and the bricky expanse of Government Center; head southwest toward the West End, the Garden—home of the Celtics and Bruins—and historic Beacon Hill. The Back Bay's orderly (and alphabetical) grid of streets runs southwest from the base of Beacon Hill, where you'll discover the retail wonderland near patrician Copley Square, Prudential Center, and high end boutique- and gallery-filled Newbury Street (known as the Rodeo Drive of the East). Beyond that, Fenway opens onto many art museums, the Emerald Necklace's skein of parkland and ponds, and Fenway Park, baseball field of the much-loved yet oft-reviled Red Sox. To the south spreads the eclectic, trendy South End with its streets lined with shops, eateries, and mimosa brunches.

The Charles River serves as a natural division between Boston and its northern neighborhoods and suburbs, including Charlestown and the cities of Cambridge and Somerville. The Fort Point Channel and its picturesque waterside Harbor Walk beneath the spectacularly suspended Zakim Bridge links Downtown with the lively Seaport and Fan Pier districts and South Boston.

Walking is by far the best way to explore, and in good weather, biking is also an option (*see Bike Travel*), as are pedicabs. But the next-best transport within Boston or its near environs is the MBTA system, aka "the T", which you can ride to nearly all of the city's major points of interest.

Air

More than 40 airlines operate at Logan International Airport (BOS), offering nonstop flights to 120 cities. Flying times to Boston from New York average 1 hour it's 1½ hours from Washington, D.C., 2¼ hours from Chicago, 3 hours from Miami 3½ hours from Dallas, 5½ hours from Los Angeles, 6½ hours from London, 13 hours from Tokyo, and 20 hours from Sydney. Delta, American Airlines, and Jet Blue run daily shuttle flights from New York and Washington, D.C.

■TIP➔ **The Boston Convention and Visitor Bureau's website (⊕ www.bostonusa. com, ☎ 888/733–2678) has direct links to worldwide airlines and national bus lines that service the city. You can book flights here, too.**

AIRPORTS

Boston's major airport, Logan International (BOS), is across the harbor, barely 2 miles from Downtown, and can be easily reached by taxi, water taxi, or bus/subway via MBTA's Silver or Blue line. Logan's four passenger terminals are identified by the letters A, B, C, and E. Some airlines use different terminals for international and domestic flights; most international flights arrive at Terminal E. There's a visitor center in Terminal C.

Worcester Regional Airport (ORH), T. F. Green Airport (PVD) in Providence, Rhode Island, and Manchester Boston Regional Airport (MHT) in New Hampshire are about an hour's drive from Boston.

GROUND TRANSPORTATION
BUSES OR SHUTTLE VANS

Free airport shuttles run between the terminals and airport hotels; most companies provide door-to-door service to Back Bay and Downtown hotels. Reservations are not required, because vans swing by all the terminals every 15 minutes.

One-way fares are $17 (less for additional people). The best deal is Logan Express, with buses from the airport to the suburbs of Braintree, Framingham, Peabody, Woburn, and the Back Bay. One-way fares are $12 to the suburbs and free from Logan Airport to Boston or $3 (by credit/debit card) to Logan; accompanied children under 10 ride free.

CAR

For recorded information about traveling to and from Logan Airport, as well as details about parking, contact the airport's ground-transportation hotline ☎ 800/235–6426. Traffic in the city can be maddening; it's a good idea to take public transportation on the Silver and Blue T lines (Airport Station).

When driving from Logan to Downtown Boston, the most direct route is the Sumner Tunnel ($2.05). On weekends, holidays, and after 10 pm weekdays, you can get around Sumner Tunnel backups by using the Ted Williams Tunnel ($2.05), which will steer you onto the Southeast Expressway south of Downtown Boston. Follow the signs to I–93 northbound to head back into the Downtown area.

Bicycle

The city has a growing number of stands for locking your bike, and they can be hitched to racks on the front of most buses or carried onto subway cars (with the exception of the Green Line) during nonpeak hours ("peak" is 7–10 am and 4–7 pm. "Pedal and Park" bike cages are available to cyclists at major transit hubs like Alewife and Forest Hills Stations.
■ TIP➜ Helmets are required for anyone 16 or younger.

BIKE RENTAL

The typical fee for a hybrid bike (with helmet and lock) is $40 per eight-hour day. Centrally located bike rental and repair shops include Papa Wheelies/Back Bay Bicycles, Landry's Bikes, and Urban AdvenTours; some bike shops offer guided tours. Helmets are available to rent.

BLUEBIKES

Boston's short-term bike rental program is primarily commuter-oriented, but it can also be a handy and fun way for travelers to cover relatively short distances. Members are able to unlock a bike from a dock, ride it for up to two hours at a time (45 minutes a trip if you choose a monthly membership), and then return it to any other dock. There's no additional charge for any ride that lasts less than 30 minutes, and the docks are in dozens of metro area locations.

The short-term Adventure Pass membership is available for 24 hours ($10) or by the month ($20), and you must be 18 or over to join. Sign up online or via one of the kiosks at each dock. Note that the prices don't include a helmet or a lock.

Before taking a bike out, plan your route to the next dock—Bluebikes' website and the free app show docks' locations, and how many bikes and empty spaces are available at each. If you don't manage to return a bike within the alloted time an overtime fee will be charged to your credit card. Such fees can be stiff, especially if you've kept the bike longer than an hour.

Getting Here and Around

Boat

Several boat companies make runs between the airport and Downtown destinations. Take the free Shuttle Bus 66 from any terminal to the airport's ferry dock to catch Boston's water taxis.

Rowes Wharf Water Taxi goes from Logan Airport to Rowes Wharf, Downtown, or other stops, for $15 per person ($35 round-trip with luggage storage). It operates daily year-round.

MBTA Harbor Express water taxis take passengers from Logan Airport to Long Wharf, Downtown, and to Hingham and Hull on the South Shore (one-way fares range from $3.70 to $9.75). Boats leave approximately every 40–45 minutes from 6:20 am to 10:30 pm on weekdays, and from 8:20 am to 10:30 pm on weekends.

Boston Harbor Cruises has an on-call boat service between the airport and several Downtown locations that operates year-round from 6:30 am to 10 pm Monday through Saturday and 6:30 am to 8 pm on Sunday. One-way fares to or from the airport are $15, and round-trip tickets are $20. One-way service to Charlestown or North Station is $20, and $18 to the Black Falcon Cruise Ship Terminal.

GETTING AROUND BY BOAT

MBTA commuter boat service operates weekdays between several Downtown harbor destinations, Charlestown, and quite a few locations on the South Shore. One-way fares range from $3.70 to $9.75 depending on destination; seniors and students ride half-price, children under 11 are free. Schedules change seasonally, so call ahead.

Bus

Greyhound has buses to Boston from all major cities in North America. Besides its main location at South Station, there are also suburban terminals in Newton and Framingham. Peter Pan Bus Lines connects Boston with cities elsewhere in Southern New England, New Jersey, New York, and Maryland.

Concord Coach runs buses between Boston and several cities in New Hampshire and Maine. C&J sends buses up the New Hampshire coast to Newburyport, Massachusetts; Dover, New Hampshire; Durham, New Hampshire; and Portsmouth, New Hampshire. Concord and C&J both leave from South Station (which is connected to the Amtrak station) and Logan Airport. BoltBus offers cheap fares in well-kept buses between Boston, New York City, Philadelphia, and Washington, D.C. (express service between Boston and New York City is also available). Megabus also offers low fares, and serves New York City and points south along the East Coast. Both companies leave from South Station.

GETTING AROUND BY BUS

Massachusetts Bay Transportation Authority (MBTA) buses crisscross the metropolitan area and travel farther into suburbia than the subway and trolley lines. Most bus routes run from 5:30 am to 12:30 am.

One-way fares within the city are $2 if paying in cash, or $1.70 if paying with a prepurchased CharlieCard (*see Public Transit*; fares are higher for longer suburban lines. Fare machines accept paper currency but do not return change.

Car

n a place where roads evolved from cow paths and colonial lanes, driving is not for the faint of heart. One-way streets, nconsistent signage, lack of parking, rotaries (traffic circles), and aggressive ocal drivers add to the confusion.

■ TIP➔ **When entering a rotary, the law states that cars entering traffic circles must yield to cars already in the circle, but don't expect all drivers to obey this rule.**

PARKING

Parking on Boston streets is tricky. Some neighborhoods have strictly enforced commercial plate or residents-only rules, with just a handful of two-hour visitors' spaces; others have meters, which cost 25¢ for 12 minutes, with a two-hour limit. On-street parking is free before 8 am and after 8 pm, and all day Sunday and most major holidays. Keep $5 in quarters handy, as some city meters take nothing else. Newer meters accept credit cards and issue receipts that you leave on your dashboard, on the street side. You may also be able to pay with the ParkBoston app on your smartphone.

The parking police are watchful and ruthless—it's not unusual to find a ticket on your windshield five minutes after your meter expires. Repeat offenders who don't pay fines may find the "boot" (an immovable steel clamp) secured to a wheel.

Major public lots are at Government Center, Quincy Market, beneath Boston Common (entrance on Charles Street), beneath Post Office Square, at Prudential Center, at Copley Place, and off Clarendon Street near the John Hancock Tower. Smaller lots and garages are scattered throughout Downtown, especially around the Theater District

and off Atlantic Avenue in the North End. Most are expensive; expect to pay up to $12 an hour. The few city garages are a comparative bargain, such as the large one beneath Boston Common. Theaters, restaurants, stores, and tourist attractions often provide patrons with discounted parking; ask your establishment to validate your receipt. Most Downtown restaurants offer valet parking.

RENTAL CARS

Rates in Boston begin at about $50 a day on a weekly rate for an economy car with unlimited mileage. This doesn't include gas, insurance, or the 6.25% tax and $10 surcharge. All major agencies have branches at Logan International Airport, even Zipcar.

◉ Pedicab

Pedicabs, human-powered three-wheeled bicycle rickshaws that hold two adults easily and three with difficulty, are popular in spring and summer around Boston and Cambridge. You can hail one on the street, or phone ☎ *(617) 266–2005* for one, with an average wait of 15–20 minutes. They are usually used to get from point A to a not-too-distant point B; on Red Sox game days, pedicabs swarm towards Fenway Park, usually arriving ahead of auto traffic.

There are no fixed fares, since the bikers work for tips; pay your biker (cash only) what you think the ride was worth, though be ready for a sour look if you pay much less than $10 a mile or so. Try to agree on a fee ahead of time. Most pedicabs also offer tours, with minimum fixed fees.

Getting Here and Around

🚇 Public Transit

The "T," as the subway system is affectionately nicknamed, is the cornerstone of a far-reaching public transit network that also includes aboveground trains, buses, and ferries. Its five color-coded lines will put you within a block of virtually anywhere. Subways operate from 5 am to 1 am (schedules vary by line). The same goes for buses, which crisscross the city and suburbia.

FARES AND THE CHARLIECARD

Retro music fans recall the 1959 Kingston Trio hit about a fellow named Charlie, who, unable to pay his fare, "never returned" from Boston's subway system. Charlie lives on as the mascot of the MBTA's ticketing scheme. There are two stored-value options: a plastic CharlieCard or paper CharlieTicket, both of which are reusable and reloadable with cash, or credit or debit cards. Getting a CharlieCard makes it easier to transfer between the subway and the bus, because such transfers are free and you don't need to keep track of individual tickets. At a station, obtain a CharlieCard from an attendant or a CharlieTicket from a machine. CharlieCards can't yet be used on commuter rail, commuter boats, or Inner Harbor ferries. A standard adult subway fare is $2.40 with a CharlieCard or $2.90 with a ticket or cash (children ages 11 and under ride free, while senior citizens and students with proper ID are discounted). For buses it's $1.70 with a CharlieCard or $2 with a ticket or cash (more for an Inner or Outer Express bus). Commuter rail and ferry fares depend on the route. For details on schedules, routes, and rates, visit the MBTA (Massachusetts Bay Transportation Authority) website. For most visitors, the best deal will be the unlimited one-day ($12.75) or one-week ($22.50).

GETTING AROUND ON THE "T"

"Inbound" trains head into the city center (Park Street Station) and "outbound" trains head away from it. If you get on the Red Line at South Station, the train heading toward Alewife (Cambridge) is inbound. But once you reach Park Street, the train becomes outbound. Similarly, the Green Line to Fenway Park would be the Boston College or Cleveland Circle train. Large maps prominently posted at each station show the line(s) that serve it, with each stop marked; small maps are overhead in each car. Free 24-hour shuttle buses connect Airport Blue Line Station with all airline terminals. Shuttle Bus 22 runs between the subway and Terminals A and B, and Shuttle Bus 33 runs between the subway and Terminals C and E.

The Red Line originates at Braintree and Quincy Center to the south; the routes join near South Boston at the JFK/UMass stop and continue to Alewife, the northwest corner of Cambridge by suburban Arlington. (The Mattapan high-speed line, or M-line, is considered part of the overall Red Line. Originating in Ashmont Station, it transports passengers via vintage yellow trolleys to Mattapan Square.)

The Green Line operates elevated trolleys that dip underground in the city center. The line originates at Cambridge's Lechmere, heads south, and divides into four westward routes: D ends at Boston College (Commonwealth Avenue); C ends at Cleveland Circle (Beacon Street, in Brighton); D ends at Riverside (Newton at Route 128); and E ends at Heath Street (Huntington Avenue in Jamaica Plain).

The Blue Line runs weekdays from Bowdoin Square (and weeknights and weekends from Government Center) to the Wonderland Racetrack in Revere, north of Boston. The Blue Line is best if you're heading to North Station, Faneuil

Hall, the North End/Waterfront, or the Back Bay (the Hynes Convention Center, Prudential Center area). The Orange Line runs from Oak Grove in north suburban Malden southwesterly to Forest Hills near the Arnold Arboretum in Jamaica Plain.

The Silver Line (a bus line with its own dedicated lanes) has four routes. SL1 connects South Station to Logan Airport; SL2 runs between South Station and the Design Center; SL4 connects Dudley Square and South Station; and SL5 runs between Downtown Crossing and Dudley Square, also stopping in Boylston.

Taxi

Cabs are available around the clock. You can find them outside most hotels and at designated cabstands around the city. Taxis generally line up around South Station, near Faneuil Hall Marketplace, at Long Wharf, near Massachusetts General Hospital, in the Theater District, and in Harvard Square. You can also call or use smartphone apps, such as Lyft or Uber to get a taxi or other hired car.

A taxi ride within the city of Boston costs $2.60 at entry for the first 1/7 mile, and 40¢ for each 1/7 mile thereafter. Licensed cabs have meters and provide receipts. If you're going to or from the airport or to the suburbs, ask about flat rates. Cab drivers may charge extra for multiple stops. One-way streets, and major traffic jams, make circuitous routes necessary, but also add to the fare.

Avoid "rogue taxis." These sleek black town cars (legitimate Boston taxis are white) aggressively offer rides on the street or at airports; their drivers often charge more than the agreed-upon rate, and may even be dangerous. Always

check for a valid taxi medallion plate and a posted photo ID of the driver.

Taxis can be hired outside each terminal at Logan Airport. Fares to and from Downtown should be about $20, including tip. Taxis must pay an extra toll of $5.25 and a $2.75 airport fee when leaving the airport, which will be tacked onto your bill at the end of the trip. On the way back to the airport, you'll pay the $2.75 fee again, but not the $5.25 toll.

Train

Boston is served by Amtrak at North Station, South Station, and Back Bay Station. North Station is the terminus for Amtrak's *Downeaster* service from Boston to New Hampshire and Maine. South Station and Back Bay Station, nearby, accommodate frequent Northeast Corridor departures to and arrivals from New York, Philadelphia, and Washington, D.C. Amtrak's Acela train cuts the travel time between Boston and New York to 3½ hours. South Station and Back Bay Station are the two stops in Boston for Amtrak's *Lake Shore Limited,* which travels daily between Boston and Chicago by way of Albany, Buffalo, and Cleveland.

The MBTA runs commuter trains to nearby points south, west, and north. Trains bound for Worcester, Needham, Forge Park, Providence (Rhode Island), and Stoughton leave from South Station and Back Bay Station; those to Fitchburg, Lowell, Haverhill, Newburyport, and Rockport operate out of North Station; those to Middleboro/Lakeville, Kingston/ Route 3, Plymouth, and Greenbush depart from South Station.

MBTA commuter-rail stations generally accept only cash. Buy your ticket in advance, or be ready to pay a $1–$2 surcharge in cash when you're on board.

Essentials

Activities

Whether it's taking advantage of being by the water with harbor strolls, riverfront Frisbee games, or logging in picturesque miles of jogging, active Bostonians love their extensive parks, paths, and waterways. Winter winds redirect that energy to white slopes, frozen rinks, and, for those who don't want to don down coats, sheltered gyms and pools.

BEACHES

After more than 20 years of massive cleanup efforts, the water in Boston Harbor is safe for swimming, though many locals and visitors still prefer to head to more traditional beaches that are a short drive or train ride away. The rocky North Shore—about an hour away—is studded with New England beach towns, each with its favorite swimming spot. Alternatively, if the traffic isn't too awful (and during the summer, that's a big if), you can reach the southern base of Cape Cod in a little over an hour.

Dining

In a city synonymous with tradition, Boston chefs have spent recent years rewriting culinary history. The stuffy, wood-paneled formality is gone; the endless renditions of *chowdah*, lobster, and cod have retired; and the assumption that true foodies better hop the next Amtrak to New York is also—thankfully—a thing of the past. Small, upscale neighborhood spots that use local New England ingredients—fresh fish and shellfish, locally grown fruits and vegetables, handmade cheeses, and humanely raised heritage game and meats—to delicious effect have taken their place. Traditional eats can still be found (Beantown Pub remains the best place for baked beans), but many diners now gravitate toward innovative food in understated environs. Whether you're looking for casual French, down-home Southern cooking, some of the country's best sushi, or Vietnamese banh mi sandwiches, Boston restaurants are ready to deliver.

RESERVATIONS

Reservations generally need to be made at least a few nights in advance, but this is easily done by your concierge, online at ⊕ *www.opentable.com* and ⊕ *www.resy.com* or by calling the restaurant directly. Tables can be hard to come by if you want to dine between 7 and 9 pm, or on Friday or Saturday night. But most restaurants will get you in if you show up and are willing to wait.

WHAT IT COSTS in U.S. Dollars			
$	$$	$$$	$$$$
RESTAURANT			
under $18	$18–$24	$25–$35	over $35

🛏 Lodging

Because of its status as a major college town, Boston students dictate the flow of hotel traffic. Commencement weekends in May and June book months in advance; prices can be triple the off-season rate, with minimum stays of two to four nights. Those returning students invade their city again for move-in months of August and September. Leaf-peepers arrive in early October, and fall conventions bring waves of business travelers, especially in the Seaport District. Events such as the Boston Marathon in April and the Head of the Charles in October are busy times for large hotels and small inns alike.

PRICES

The hotel tax in Boston adds 14.95% to your bill; some hotels also tack on energy, service, or occupancy surcharges. Though it's not an absolute necessity, many visitors prefer to bring a car, but then parking is another expense to consider. Almost all lodgings have parking, and most charge for the privilege—anywhere from $15 per day for self-garaging to $35 for valet. When looking for a hotel, don't write off the pricier establishments immediately. Price categories are determined by "rack rates"—the list price of a hotel room, which is usually discounted. Specials abound, particularly in Downtown on weekends. With so many new rooms in Boston, pricing is very competitive, so always check out the hotel website in advance for current special offers.

WHAT IT COSTS for Hotels			
$	$$	$$$	$$$$
HOTEL			
under $200	$200–$299	$300–$399	over $399

Money

Prices are generally higher in Beacon Hill, the Back Bay, and Harvard Square than other parts of town. You're more likely to find bargains in the North End, Kenmore Square, Downtown Crossing, and Cambridge's Central Square. Many museums offer free admission on one weekday evening, and reduced admissions at all times for children, students, and senior citizens.

Nightlife

Whether it's cheering on local sports at a watering hole, rocking out at an underground club, applauding a symphonic performance, or chilling with cocktails in an elegant lounge, Boston has a nightlife vibe to suit all types and moods. Consider it a Cinderella city, set aglow with energy that for some ends all too soon. With the T (subway and bus) making its final runs between midnight and 1 am, most nightspots follow accordingly, closing their doors typically by 2 am. Though night owls may be disappointed by the meager late-night options, except in Chinatown, visitors find plenty of possibilities for stepping out on the early side. The martini set may stroll Newbury and Boylston streets in the Back Bay or Downtown, selecting from swank restaurants, lounges, and clubs. Coffee and tea drinkers can find numerous cafés in Cambridge and Somerville, particularly Harvard and Davis squares. Microbrew enthusiasts find viable options at sports bars, pop-up beer gardens, and craft breweries, especially on the Rose Kennedy Greenway, along the water, near campuses and sports arenas. The thriving "lounge" scene in Downtown's cooler hybrid bar-restaurant-clubs provides a mellower, more mature alternative to the collegiate indie spots, and DJs spin the late night dance parties into a frenzy with house music at crowded clubs like The Grand in the Seaport. Tourists crowd Faneuil Hall for its pubs, comedy spots, and dance scenes. The South and North Ends cater to the "dinner-and-drinks" set. Several casual indie rock and music clubs abound with plenty of local bands on stage and cold beer behind the bar in Allston, Somerville, and Cambridge.

Where Should I Stay?

NEIGHBORHOOD	VIBE	PROS	CONS
Beacon Hill and Boston Common	Old brick and stone buildings host luxe boutique hotels and B&Bs in Beacon Hill; Boston Common has some skyscraper luxury lodging.	Safe, quaint area with lamp-lighted streets; chain-free upscale shopping and dining; outdoor fun abounds in the park; good T access.	Street parking is extremely hard to come by; not budget-friendly; close to noisy hospital; Boston Common can be sketchy at night.
Downtown Boston	Financial District hums with busy hotels during the week; new boutique lodging compete with big-box chains.	Great for business travelers; frequent low weekend rates; T and bus access; theaters and some museums walkable.	All but dead at night; expensive garage parking during the day; Downtown Crossing is mobbed at lunchtime and on weekends.
The Back Bay	High-priced hotels in the city's poshest neighborhood; Comm Ave is lined with historic brownstones.	Easy, central location; safe, beautiful area to walk around at night; ample T access; excellent people-watching.	Rooms, shopping, and eating can be ridiculously expensive; Newbury Street is overcrowded with tourists on weekends.
The South End	Small, funky lodgings in a hip and LGBTQ-friendly area; awesome independent restaurants and shops.	Great dining scene; easy T and bus access; easy walking to the Back Bay and Downtown; main avenues safe at night with foot traffic.	Some bordering blocks turn seedy after dusk; difficult street parking (and few garages); only a handful of hotel options.
Fenway and Kenmore Square	A sampling of large and small hotels and inns; a mix of students, young professionals, and diehard Sox fans.	Close to Fenway Park (home of the Red Sox); up-and-coming dining scene; less expensive than most 'hoods; accessible by the T.	No street parking on game days (and pricey garages); crowds for concerts and sporting events; some bars are loud and tacky.
Seaport	Modern and massive; tons of dining and entertainment; excellent water views.	Lots of bustling restaurants; waterfront location; younger crowds.	Opposite of Boston's historical charm; parking is expensive; traffic congested.
Brookline and Jamaica Plains	Mid-size chain hotels in student neighborhoods; coffee shops, convenience stores, and rowdy college bars; Brookline has lovely inns.	Cheap rates on rooms in Brighton and parts of Brookline; easier driving than in Downtown.	No overnight street parking in Brookline; far from city center; some areas get dicey at night; T ride into city can be an hour.
Cambridge	A mix of hotels pepper the hip, multiuniversity neighborhood; young freethinkers and efficient (if laid-back) service.	Hallowed academia; verdant squares; good variety of eating and lodging; few chain anythings.	Spotty T access; less of a city feel; a few areas can be slightly dodgy at night; difficult driving and parking.

Essentials

GETTING INFORMED

The best source of arts and nightlife information is the *Boston Globe*'s "Arts & Entertainment" section (⊕ *www.boston. com/thingstodo*). Also worth checking out are the Thursday "Calendar" section of the *Boston Globe*; the Friday "Scene" section of the *Boston Herald*; and the calendar listings in free magazines in drop boxes around town, like *DigBoston* (⊕ *www.digboston.com*). The *Globe, Dig,* and specialized sites as diverse as the thoroughly classical *Boston Musical Intelligencer* (⊕ *www.classicalscene. org*) and the scruffy indie-rock broadside *Boston Hassle* (⊕ *www.bostonhassle. com*), provide up-to-the-minute information online. Other reliable websites include the comprehensive ⊕ *artsfuse. org* and The ARTery at ⊕ *wbur.org* the radio station of Boston University.

🎭 Performing Arts

MUSEUMS

Boston's compilation of art museums is a bracing mix of old-world aesthetics and new-world experimentation. At the classical end of the spectrum, revered institutions like the Museum of Fine Arts (MFA) and the Isabella Stewart Gardner Museum offer refined experiences, while the edgy Institute of Contemporary Art (ICA) features electronic concerts, graffiti and multimedia exhibitions, and a less reverential attitudes toward the arts. All these institutions have one thing in common—they also host special shows, events, and festivals in strikingly handsome performance spaces. *See the Sights section of each chapter for more information on Boston's museums.*

MUSIC

For its size, Boston has a great diversity and variety of live music choices. Supplementing appearances by nationally known artists are performers from the area's many colleges and conservatories, which also provide music series, performing spaces, and audiences. Berklee College of Music has made itself especially visible, with student (and/or faculty) ensembles popping up at formal and informal venues far and wide, especially in summer months, playing mainly jazz, blues, rock, indie, pop, and world music. Other college-owned concert halls, such as Harvard University's Sanders Theatre, New England Conservatory's Jordan Hall, MIT's Kresge Auditorium, and Agganis Arena at Boston University, regularly host homegrown and visiting ensembles.

For live shows, head to the compact Theater District to see traveling Broadway revues, national comedy, opera companies, rock bands, and premiere previews headed to New York.

Classical music aficionados love the Boston Symphony Orchestra, which performs at Symphony Hall October through early May and at Tanglewood Music Center in Lenox, Massachusetts, from late June through August. A favorite of TV audiences, the Boston Pops presents concerts of "lighter music" from May to July (their outdoor July 4 concert at the Hatch Shell is legendary) and during December. Throughout the year choose from an active roster of orchestral, chamber, and choral ensembles that enrich Boston's musical ambience.

Boston also has emerged as the nation's capital of early-music performance. Dozens of small groups, often made up of performers who have one foot in the university and another on the concert stage, play pre-18th-century music on period instruments, often in small churches where the acoustics resemble the venues in which some of this music was first performed.

Essentials

THEATER

In the 1930s Boston had no fewer than 50 performing-arts theaters; by the 1980s the city's Downtown Theater District had all but vanished. Happily, since the 1990s several historic theaters, extensively restored, have reopened to host pre-Broadway shows, visiting artists, comedy, jazz, and local troupes. The glorious renovation of the Opera House in 2004 added new light to the district. Established companies, such as the Huntington Theatre Company and the American Repertory Theater in Cambridge, stage classic and modern repertory, premiere works by major writers like David Mamet, August Wilson, Tom Stoppard, and Don DeLillo, and pieces by new talents like Lydia Diamond and Diane Paulus. ArtsEmerson provides the city with contemporary world theater in the Emerson Cutler Majestic Theatre and the Emerson Paramount Center.

🛍 Shopping

Shopping in Boston in many ways mirrors the city itself: a mix of classic and cutting-edge, the high-end and the handmade, and international and local sensibilities. There is a strong network of idiosyncratic gift stores, handicrafts shops, galleries, and a growing number of savvy, independent fashion boutiques. Boston's shops and department stores lie concentrated in the area bounded by Quincy Market, the Back Bay, and Downtown, with plenty of bargains in the Downtown Crossing area. The South End's gentrification creates its own kind of consumerist milieus, from housewares shops to avant-garde art galleries. In Cambridge you can find many shops around Harvard and Central squares, with independent boutiques migrating west along Massachusetts Avenue ("Mass Ave.") toward Porter Square and beyond. There's no state sales tax on clothing. However, there's a 6.25% sales tax on clothes priced higher than $175 per item; the tax is levied on the amount in excess of $175.

Most major shopping neighborhoods are easily accessible on the T: Boston's Charles Street and Downtown Crossing and Cambridge's Harvard, Central, and Porter squares are on the Red Line; Copley Place, Faneuil Hall, and Newbury Street are on the Green Line; the South End is an easy trip on the Orange Line.

📍 Visitor Information

Contact the city and state tourism offices for general information, details about seasonal events, discount passes, trip planning, and attraction information. The National Park Service office screens an entertaining and informative eight-minute slide show on Boston's historic sites and supplies you with maps and directions. The Welcome Center, Boston Common Visitor Information Center, and the Cambridge Tourism Office offer general information.

ONLINE RESOURCES

Boston.com, home of the *Boston Globe* online, has news and feature articles, ample travel information, and links to towns throughout Massachusetts. Revolutionary Spaces (formerly The Bostonian Society) answers frequently asked questions about Boston history on its website. The iBoston page posts wonderful photographs of buildings of architectural and historical importance. *WickedLocal* provides a more relaxed (and somewhat irreverent) take on Boston and suburban news and information.

Contacts

✈ Air

AIRPORT INFORMATION Logan International Airport (Boston). ✉ *I–90 East to Ted Williams Tunnel* ☎ *800/235–6426* ⊕ *www.massport.com/logan-airport* Ⓜ *Airport.* **Manchester Boston Regional Airport.** ✉ *Off I–293N/Rte. 101W, Exit 13, Manchester* ☎ *603/624–6539* ⊕ *www.flymanchester.com.* **T. F. Green Airport.** ✉ *2000 Post Rd., off I–95, Exit 13, Warwick* ☎ *401/691–2000* ⊕ *www.pvdairport.com.*

GROUND TRANSPORTATION Easy Transportation. ☎ *617/869–7760.* **Logan Express.** ☎ *800/235–6426* ⊕ *www.massport.com/logan-airport.*

🚲 Bicycle

BICYCLE INFORMATION Back Bay Bicycles. ✉ *362 Commonwealth Ave., Back Bay* ☎ *617/247–2336* ⊕ *papa-wheelies.com.* **Bluebikes.** ☎ *855/948–2929* ⊕ *www.bluebikes.com.* **Landry's Bicycles.** ✉ *1048 Commonwealth Ave., Allston* ☎ *617/232–0446* ⊕ *www.landrys.com.* **MassBike. Massachusetts Bicycle Coalition** ✉ *50 Milk St., 16th fl., Downtown* ☎ *617/542–2453* ⊕ *massbike.org.*

🚢 Boat

BOAT INFORMATION Boston Harbor Cruises. ☎ *617/227–4321* ⊕ *www.bostonharborcruises.com.* **MBTA Harbor Express.** ☎ *617/222–6999, 617/222–3200* ⊕ *www.mbta.com/schedules/ferry.* **Rowes Wharf Water Taxi.** ☎ *617/406–8584 pick-up line, 617/261–6620 questions* ⊕ *www.roweswharfwatertaxi.com.*

🚌 Bus

BUS CONTACTS Bolt-Bus. ☎ *877/265–8287* ⊕ *www.boltbus.com.* **C&J.** ☎ *800/258–7111* ⊕ *www.ridecj.com.* **Concord Coach.** ☎ *800/639–3317* ⊕ *www.concordcoachlines.com.* **Greyhound.** ☎ *800/231–2222 nationwide, 617/526–1801 South Station* ⊕ *www.greyhound.com.* **Megabus.** ☎ *877/462–6342* ⊕ *www.megabus.com.* **Peter Pan Bus Lines.** ☎ *800/343–9999* ⊕ *www.peterpanbus.com.*

🎭 Performing Arts

CONTACTS BosTix. ⊕ *www.bostix.org.* **Broadway Across America-Broadway in Boston.** ☎ *866/523–7469* ⊕ *boston.broadway.com.*

◉ Pedicabs

CONTACT Boston Pedicab. ☎ *617/266–2005* ⊕ *www.bostonpedicab.com.*

🚍 Public Transportation

CONTACT MBTA. ☎ *800/392–6100, 617/222–3200, 617/222–5146 TTY* ⊕ *www.mbta.com.*

◉ Visitor Information

CONTACTS Boston Common Visitor Information Center. ✉ *Downtown* ☎ *617/536–4100* ⊕ *www.bostonusa.com/visit/planyourtrip/resources/vic.* **Greater Boston Convention and Visitors Bureau.** ✉ *2 Copley Pl. Suite 105, Back Bay* ☎ *888/733–2678, 617/536–4100* ⊕ *www.bostonusa.com.* **iBoston.** ⊕ *www.iboston.org.* **National Parks Service Visitor Center.** ✉ *Faneuil Hall, Downtown* ☎ *617/242–5601* ⊕ *www.nps.gov/bost.* **Revolutionary Spaces.** ✉ *310 Washington St.* ⊕ *www.revolutionaryspaces.org.*

Great Itineraries

Boston in 4 Days

Clearly every traveler moves at a different pace. One might be content to snap a pic of the Bunker Hill Monument and push on; another might insist on climbing the obelisk's 294 spiraling steps and studying the adjacent museum's military dioramas. Nevertheless, in four days you should be able to see the city highlights without feeling rushed. With more time, explore nearby communities.

DAY 1: HIT THE TRAIL
About 3 million visitors walk the Freedom Trail every year—and there's a good reason why: taken together, the route's 16 designated sites offer a crash course in colonial history. That makes the trail a must, so tackle it sooner rather than later. Linger wherever you like, leaving ample time to lunch amid magicians and mimes in Faneuil Hall Marketplace. Next, cross into the North End via the Rose F. Kennedy Greenway. Though hemmed in by water on three sides, this bustling neighborhood is crammed full of history and Italian heritage. Don't miss Old North Church and Paul Revere's former home (Boston's oldest house, constructed almost 100 years prior to his arrival); then, after wandering the narrow Italianate streets, fortify yourself with espresso or gelato and cross the Charlestown Bridge. See the currently drydocked USS *Constitution* and climb the Bunker Hill Monument (a breathtaking site in more ways than one) before catching the MBTA water shuttle back to Downtown.

DAY 2: HEAD FOR THE HILL
Named for the signal light that topped it in the 1800s, Beacon Hill originally stood a bit taller until locals dug earth off its summit and used it as landfill nearby. Now its shady, gas-lighted streets, brick sidewalks, tidy mews, and stately Brahmin brownstones evoke a bygone Boston. (Lovely Mt. Vernon Street opens onto leafy Louisburg Square, where Louisa May Alcott once lived.) Be sure to snap a photo on Acorn Street, the most photographed street in the nation. When soaking up the ambience, take in some of Beacon Hill's major sites from Boston's various theme trails: gold-domed Massachusetts State House, Boston Athenaeum, Granary Burying Ground, and the African Meeting House. Afterward, stroll to the Common and Public Garden. Both promise greenery and great people-watching. If shopping's your bag, cruise for antiques along Charles Street, the thoroughfare that separates them. In the evening, feast on dumplings or dim sum in pan-Asian Chinatown or go upscale at an ubertrendy restaurant (Ostra, Teatro) in the Theater District where restorations in recent years have been, well, dramatic.

DAY 3: TAKE IT ALL IN
From the Back Bay you can cover a lot of Boston's attractions in a single day. Plot a route based on your interests. Architecture aficionados can hit the ground running at the neoclassical Public Library (the nation's first) and Romanesque Trinity Church. Shoppers can opt for stores along Newbury Street and in Copley Place, a high-end mall anchored by Neiman Marcus. Farther west in the Fens, other choices await. Art connoisseurs might view the collections at the Museum of Fine Arts or Isabella Stewart Gardner Museum. Carnival-like Fenway Park beckons baseball fans to the other side of the Fens. Depending on your taste—and ticket availability—cap the day with a Symphony Hall concert or a Red Sox game.

DAY 4: ON THE WATERFRONT

A spate of openings and reopenings in recent years has transformed the Seaport District into a magnet for museum hoppers. Begin your day artfully at the Institute of Contemporary Art (ICA) on Fan Pier. The mod museum's bold cantilevered design makes the most of its waterside location. It makes the most of its art collection, too, by offering programs and exhibits that appeal to little tykes and hard-to-please teens. Keep tiny tots engaged with a run to the Children's Museum and its innovative exhibits; then relive a turning point in American history at the Boston Tea Party Ships & Museum's authentic-looking vessels and interpretive center. From there, continue on to that waterfront favorite, the New England Aquarium, where you can watch the sea lions and penguins frolic. On the wharf, sign up for a harbor cruise, whale-watch boat trip, or ferry ride to the beckoning Boston Harbor Islands.

Beyond Boston Proper

DAY 1: EXPLORE CAMBRIDGE

From pre-Revolutionary times, Boston was the region's commercial center and Cambridge was the burbs: a retreat more residential than mercantile, with plenty of room to build the nation's first English-style, redbrick university. The heart of the community—geographically and practically—is still Harvard Square. It's easy enough to while away a day here browsing the shops, lounging at a café, then wandering to the riverbank to watch crew teams practice. But Harvard Square is also the starting point for free student-led campus tours, as well as for strolls along Brattle Street's "Tory Row" (No. 105 was occupied by both Washington and Longfellow!). Fine museums include the family-friendly Harvard

Museum of Natural History, loaded with dinosaur bones, gemstones, and 21 million stuffed critters. The newly remodeled Harvard Art Museum is another must. End your day in true Cantabrigian style by taking in a concert or lecture at Harvard's Sanders Theatre or with a show at the American Repertory Theater, helmed by noted artistic director Diane Paulus.

DAY 2: STEP BACK IN TIME

You only have to travel a short distance to visit historic places you read about in grade school. For a side trip to the 17th century, head 35 miles south to Plymouth. The famed rock doesn't live up to its hype in terms of its size, but Plimoth Plantation (an open-air museum re-creating life among Pilgrims) and the *Mayflower II* are well worth the trip. A second option is to veer northwest to explore Revolutionary-era sites in handsome, suburban Lexington. Start at the National Heritage Museum for a recap of the events that kicked off the whole shebang; then proceed to Battle Green, where "the shot heard round the world" was fired. After stopping by Minute Man National Historical Park, continue to Concord to tour the homes of literary luminaries like Ralph Waldo Emerson, Louisa May Alcott, and Nathaniel Hawthorne. Conclude your novel excursion with a walk around Walden Pond, where transcendentalist Henry David Thoreau wrote one of the founding documents of the environmental movement, "Walden."

DAY 3: A SHORE THING

Anyone eager to taste the salt air or feel the surge of the sea should take a day trip to the North Shore towns of Salem and Gloucester. The former has a Maritime National Historic Site—complete with vintage wharves and warehouses that proves there is more to the notorious town than just witchcraft. Or, hop on the 90-minute ferry ride to Provincetown for a taste of Cape Cod.

Back Bay Art and Architecture Walk

In the folklore of American neighborhoods, Boston's Back Bay stands alongside New York's Park Avenue as a symbol of chic. In the 1850s, Boston's power brokers built Victorian mansions amid lush green spaces and by the time the Great Depression hit, the Back Bay was the city's poshest address.

COPLEY SQUARE

The Back Bay's hub embraces a range of architectural styles from Romanesque Revival to Bauhaus-inspired skyscrapers. The Fairmont Copley Plaza Hotel's Oak Long Bar + Kitchen, with its catbird seats, offers a perfect place to begin your walk. Designed in 1912 by Henry Hardenbergh, five years after his famed Plaza Hotel in Manhattan, the hotel underwent a $20-million centenary renovation. Boston Public Library, housing 9 million books, was conceived by architects Mead, McKim, and White, who opted for an Italian Renaissance palazzo. Modern architect Philip Johnson's 1972 wing respectfully reflects the original.

THE PRU AND COMMONWEALTH AVENUE

Heading up Boylston Street with the library on your left, you'll find the 52-story Prudential Tower, built in the 1960s, and affectionately dubbed "The Pru" and today is a retail mecca. With the Pru behind you, take Gloucester Street across Newbury to Commonwealth Avenue, where if you look to the right, you will see the Mall—a linear park that stretches all the way to the edge of the Public Garden. The Mall's 32 acres were designed in the French boulevard style by Arthur Gilman in 1856. Turn left, and cross Massachusetts Avenue to 395 Commonwealth, where you'll see Louis Comfort Tiffany's famous Ayer Mansion.

Back Bay Art and Architecture Walk

HIGHLIGHTS
Copley Square's handsome ensemble of church, park, library, and skyscraper; Boston Public Garden

WHERE TO START
Oak Bar in Fairmont Copley Square Hotel

LENGTH
1.6 miles or about 1½ hours with brief stops

WHERE TO END
Back where you started, people-watching from an Oak Bar settee or a bench facing the Boston Public Library or Trinity Church

BEST TIME TO GO
Any time when you can see all the sights in daylight

WORST TIME TO GO
Rush hour or when it's raining or very cold

EDITOR'S CHOICE
Strolling the Comm. Ave Mall in the snow, tiny cloister garden behind Trinity Church, George Washington with his attendant pigeons

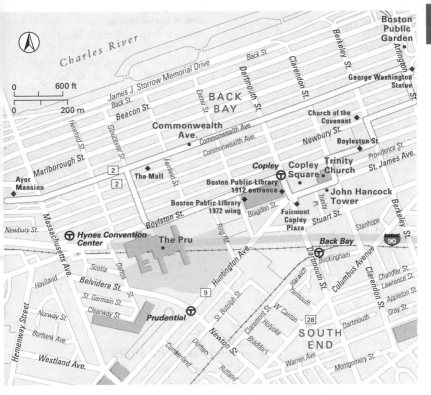

BOSTON PUBLIC GARDEN

At the bronze statue of George Washington at the foot of Commonwealth Avenue, enter Boston Public Garden, America's oldest botanical garden sheltering 24 acres of weeping willow, elm, spruce, and dawn redwood. The garden pond is spanned by a faux-suspension bridge while the garden itself abuts Boston Common. Exit with Washington behind you, walk one block to Newbury Street, turn right and head toward the Gothic Revival Church of the Covenant, on Newbury Street at Berkeley, built in 1867.

TRINITY CHURCH AND HANCOCK TOWER

Take Berkeley one block to Boylston Street then head back up Boylston to Copley Square to visit its crowning centerpiece, Trinity Church. This 1877 Romanesque Revival masterpiece conceived by Henry Hobson Richardson exhibits sumptuously carved interior woodwork, ornamented ceilings, and intricate stained glass. Another architectural award winner is the John Hancock Tower, behind Trinity Church on St. James Street. Architect Henry Cobb managed to construct this modernist 58-story building without disrupting the square's scale and proportion in part by having the glass panels mirror Trinity Church.

Best Tours

Bike Tours

★ Urban AdvenTours

BICYCLING | A variety of themed excursions run throughout Boston and Cambridge, with most covering about 10 to 12 miles. They leave from Urban AdvenTours's Atlantic Avenue headquarters and are offered almost every day; in winter, the tours depend on the weather—call to confirm. The main tours start at $55 per person, and tickets are available for purchase through the website; bike, helmet, and water are all included. A variety of rental bikes are also available, including the new electric-assist. ⊠ *103 Atlantic Ave., Downtown* ☎ *617/670–0637 for rentals and tours* ⊕ *www.urbanadventours.com* Ⓜ *Aquarium.*

Boat Tours

Boston Duck Tours

BOAT TOURS | **FAMILY** | Paul Revere would have trouble calling this one, since this city tour is by land and by sea. Hop aboard and discover Boston as your conDUCKtor weaves through streets and harbor waterways on one of its famed WWII-style amphibious landing vehicles. There are three departure locations: the Museum of Science, Prudential Center, and New England Aquarium. You'll enjoy a fully narrated, historic tour of Boston, as you cruise by all the places that highlight Boston's prominent place in the country's history, from the golden domed State House to the Boston Common, the historic North End to fashionable Newbury Street. Then it's time for a Big Splash as you head straight into the Charles River for breathtaking views of the Boston and Cambridge skylines. ⊠ *4 Copley Pl., , Suite 4155* ☎ *617/267–3825* ⊕ *bostonducktours.com* ⌛ *$46.*

Boston Harbor Cruises

PARK—SPORTS-OUTDOORS | Take to the seas to see the city from a new vantage point with Boston Harbor Cruises. They offer ferries to the Harbor Islands from Long Wharf (Downtown) with limited service in spring and fall, as well as expanded service in June with additional departures from Hingham and Hull to six island destinations. High-speed catamarans run daily from May through mid-October and cost $19.95 round-trip. Other islands can be reached by the free inter-island water shuttles that depart from Georges Island. The boat touring company also offers leisurely sunset and brunch harbor cruises, as well as narrated historical sightseeing ventures. Thrill seekers love a get-wet trip on their Codzilla, a turbo-charged craft. ⊠ *Long Wharf, Waterfront* ☎ *617/227–4321* ⊕ *www.bostonharborcruises.com* Ⓜ *Aquarium.*

Food Tours

Boston Food Tours

GUIDED TOURS | To eat like an Italian, you've got to know your sfogliatelle from your amaretti. Local foodie Michele Topor schools visitors on the "right" kind of olive oil and the primo places to buy Italian pastries during three-hour culinary market of the North End, which get off the beaten Hanover Street path and include a few sample noshes. The $69 tours are held Wednesday, Friday, and Saturday morning and afternoon and can be booked online or by phone. ⊠ *6 Charter St.* ☎ *617/523–6032, 888/774–8303 tour bookings* ⊕ *www.bostonfoodtours.com.*

⚬ Specialty Tours

Boston Women's Heritage Trail

TOUR—SIGHT | Boston Women's Heritage Trail has several self-guided walks that highlight more than 200 remarkable women who played an integral role in shaping the history of Boston and the nation as patriots, intellectuals, abolitionists, suffragists, artists, and writers. In addition, there are various trails through different Boston neighborhoods and themed trails, such as a women artist trail in the Back Bay. View maps on the organization's website. Guided tours available upon request. ⊠ *Back Bay* ☎ ⊕ *www.bwht.org.*

On Location Tours

TOUR—SIGHT | On Location Tours takes you to Boston's TV and movie hot spots like the South Boston of *The Departed,* the *Ally McBeal* building, the L Street tavern from *Good Will Hunting, American Hustle'*s big deal site, the chase scene from *The Town,* the *Cheers* bar, and Red Sox home base Fenway Park, filming location for movies like *Field of Dreams* and *Fever Pitch.* Guides share filming secrets and trivia from movies like *Legally Blonde* and *Mystic River* along with the best celeb spots in town. The "theater-on-wheels" bus tour takes two to three hours, depending on traffic ($48 plus $2.96 ticket fee), and you can get out and explore at some sites. Exact pick-up location is sent once you purchase tickets. ⊠ *Downtown* ☎ *617/379–6770 to purchase tickets* ⊕ *onlocationtours.com/tour/boston-tv-movie/* ⊠ *$48* ⊗ *Tours run every other Sat., Apr.–Oct.* Ⓜ *Park.*

⊕ Trolley Tours

Old Town Trolley Tours

GUIDED TOURS | **FAMILY** | Talk about flexible. With these state-of-the-art stadium trolleys, you have unlimited hop-on and hop-off options as often as you like all day long. Live guides ride along with you, as passengers learn as much (or as little) as they want about Boston. Enjoy double-decker height views while protected from the elements. There are 18 trolley stops, including Faneuil Hall, Historic North End, Charles Street Meeting House, the Cheers bar, Prudential Center. and *U.S.S. Constitution* and Museum. ⊠ *Boston* ☎ *855/396–7433* ⊕ *www.trolleytours.com/boston* ⊠ *From $48.*

On the Calendar

January

Boston Wine Festival. Created by Chef Daniel Bruce, the country's longest running food and wine festival features an all-star lineup of hosted dinners, seminars and receptions January through March at the Boston Harbor Hotel. ⊕ *www.bostonwinefestival.net*

February

Beanpot Hockey Tournament. Boston College, Boston University, Harvard, and Northeastern face off in this annual, fiercely contested tournament. ⊕ *www.beanpothockey.com*

March

St. Patrick's Day Parade. Bands, floats, and veterans groups all walk proudly along the main streets of Boston's robust Irish Southie neighborhood, lined with rowdy revelers. ⊕ *southbostonparade.org*

April

Boston Marathon. Every Patriots' Day (the third Monday in April), fans gather along the Hopkinton-to-Boston route of the Boston Marathon to cheer on more than 25,000 runners from all over the world. ⊕ *www.baa.org*

Esplanade Summer Events. From April through September, the art deco Hatch Shell on the Esplanade is abuzz with free concerts, movie showings, and more. ⊕ *www.mass.gov*

Paul Revere's Ride. This live reenactment on Patriot's Day follows the horse-back route of this famed activist, beginning in the North End and culminating at the Battle Green in Lexington. ⊕ *www.nationallancers.org*

May

Lilac Sundays. This day-long celebration includes tours of the lilacs, family activities, and is the only day picnicking is permitted at the Arnold Arboretum. ⊕ *www.arboretum.harvard.edu*

June

Boston Pride. Showing the city's positive support of the LGBTQ community, this month-long celebration is full of activities, seminars, movies, dance parties, and the decked out and bedazzled Boston Pride Parade. ⊕ *www.bostonpride.org*

Jimmy Fund Scooper Bowl. The nation's largest all-you-can-eat ice cream festival, located at the DCR Hatch Memorial Shell on Boston's Charles River Esplanade, includes a 21+ Scoop at Night with Harpoon beer, local wines, music, and entertainment. ⊕ *www.jimmyfund.org*

July

Boston Pops Fireworks Spectacular. Independence Day is capped off with world-renowned pyrotechnics, celebrity musical guests, and live performances from the Boston Pops along the Charles River. ⊕ *bostonpopsjuly4th.org*

Harborfest. Boston's four-day July 4 celebration sponsors more than 200 events, including Revolutionary War reenactments, curated art festivals, special museum exhibits, and free concerts.

Most popular is the Chowderfest, during which thousands gather at City Hall Plaza for the annual chowder cook-off. ⊕ *www.bostonharborfest.com*

Shakespeare on the Common. On July and August evenings, the Commonwealth Shakespeare Company produces free performances of Shakespeare on the Boston Common, such as *Cymbeline* (2019) and *The Tempest* (2020). ⊕ *commshakes.org*

Summer in the City at Boston Harbor Hotel. Each weeknight of summer, dazzling things happen at Rowes Wharf—soul-bros and sisters enjoy Motown on Tuesday, Rat-Packers salute Frankie and Sammy on Wednesday, blues lovers get on that Blue Barge on Thursday, and cinephiles catch starry silver-screen classics on Friday. Boston Harbor Hotel hosts these events along Harborwalk from 6 to 10 pm. ⊕ *www.bhh.com*

September

Boston Film Festival. Get "reel" at the weeklong fall Boston Film Festival, a forum for evolving filmmakers to express their artistic visions. This is where top independent films premiere, many with Massachusetts ties. The festival offers audiences first-hand access to the filmmakers and filmmaking process during the Q&A sessions with the director and talent following every screening. ⊕ *www.bostonfilmfestival.org*

October

Haunted Happenings. Salem hosts witch trial reenactments and other haunted happenings. ⊕ *www.hauntedhappenings.com*

Head of the Charles Regatta. In October, sculling crew teams compete in the world-famous Head of the Charles Regatta, a tradition for more than 50 years. The world's largest two-day rowing event draws athletes from their teens to their 80s, collegians and clubbers, from England, Australia, and worldwide. Food, beer, and clothing vendors set up tents, and hordes gather atop the Charles River's many bridges to watch the races. ⊕ *www.hocr.org*

November

America's Hometown Thanksgiving Celebration. Celebrated the weekend before Thanksgiving in Plymouth, the holiday's birthplace, this event focuses on history, Americana, Pilgrims, and Native Americans. ⊕ *usathanksgiving.com*

Nutcracker Ballet. Under the artistic direction of Mikko Nissinen, this Christmas-time classic is performed in the historic Boston Opera House by the world-renowned Boston Ballet. Show times are scheduled annually, beginning the Friday after Thanksgiving through December 31. ⊕ *www.bostonballet.org*

December

Blink! This is Faneuil Hall Marketplace's extravaganza of 350,000 sparkling LEDs synchronized to holiday music that continues all month. ⊕ *www.faneuilhallmarketplace.com*

Boston Holiday Pops. These seasonal performances find beloved conductor Keith Lockhart and the Boston Pops celebrating with holiday music favorites, sing-alongs, and Santa's visit in Historic Symphony Hall. ⊕ *www.bso.org*

How to Speak Boston

Boston vocab can be interesting to follow if you're visiting for the first time. Frappes are milk shakes (with ice cream). Grinders are sandwiches (on sub rolls). And wicked? Well, that's how you describe almost everything to the extreme (usually good things).

There's also a strong accent to be aware of. Many Bostonians drop the final "r" in a word, as in the pronunciation of the famous sports arena, "the Gahden." Bostonians also lengthen their vowels, so chowder sounds like "chowdah." Town names in Massachusetts are often spoken very differently than they are spelled; Gloucester, for example, becomes "Glawstuh." Bostonians also rush their speech, so "Hi, how are you?" is "hihawaya?" and "Did you eat?" sounds like "Jeet?"

VOCABULARY AND PRONUNCIATIONS

■ **Bang a U-ey.** Make a U turn.

■ **Beantown.** Announces that you're a visitor, don't use it.

■ **Bubbler.** Water fountain.

■ **The Cape.** Short for Cape Cod.

■ **Chowder.** Pronounced *chowdah*; always New England–style, never Manhattan-style.

■ **Comm Ave.** Commonwealth Avenue in Boston.

■ **The Dot.** Dorchester.

■ **Dunks.** Locals run on coffee from Dunkin' Donuts (aka Dunkies or Dunks). Order like a native by asking for a coffee regular—that's cream and sugar (two of each for a small, three for a medium, and so on).

■ **Eastie.** East Boston.

■ **Fens.** Fenway, the neighborhood not the ball park.

■ **Frappes.** Milk shakes but with a scoop of ice cream blended in.

■ **Grinder.** Pronounced *grindah*; also known as heros, hoagies, or subs in other parts of the country, these are sandwich fillings served on a sub roll.

■ **The Hub.** Boston's nickname.

■ **Jimmies.** Chocolate sprinkles on ice cream.

■ **Mass Ave.** Massachusetts Avenue in Boston.

■ **Nor'easter.** Pronounced *Nor'eastah*; strong winter storm on the East Coast.

■ **Packie/Package store.** Liquor store.

■ **The Pats.** Nickname for the New England Patriots, the most revered NFL team.

■ **The Pike.** Nickname for the Massachusetts Turnpike.

■ **The Pru.** The Prudential Center.

■ **Regular coffee.** Pronounced *regulah*; coffee with with cream and sugar, not black

■ **Rotary.** Traffic circle or roundabout.

■ **Southie.** South Boston, refers to neighborhood south of Boston. Not to be confused with the South End.

■ **Statie.** State trooper.

■ **The T.** The only accepted term used to refer to the MBTA transit system.

■ **Wicked.** A synonym for "very" or "extremely" when describing something (usually something good), for example, a wicked good time, a wicked tasty burger, and so on.

Chapter 3

BEACON HILL, BOSTON COMMON, AND THE WEST END

3

Updated by
Leigh Harrington

◉ Sights	🍴 Restaurants	🏨 Hotels	🛍 Shopping	🍸 Nightlife
★★★★☆	★★★☆☆	★★★☆☆	★★★★☆	★★★☆☆

NEIGHBORHOOD SNAPSHOT

TOP EXPERIENCES

■ **Discover the Black Heritage Trail:** At sanctuaries, schools, and Underground Railroad sites, this self-guided historical walk visits early Boston's African American community.

■ **Start the Freedom Trail:** From Boston Common, follow the red-painted and brick path to knock off four of its 16 stops.

■ **Window shop:** Shop Charles Street for antiques, clothing, and contemporary gifts.

■ **Embrace your inner science nerd:** Explore space, the human body, electricity and more at the Museum of Science.

■ **See picturesque history:** One of Boston's most photographed locales, Acorn Street features elements from the Colonial era through the Victorian period.

■ **Gear up for game day:** Visit the TD Garden to root for the Boston Celtics or Boston Bruins, or take a spin around The Sports Museum.

GETTING HERE

Beacon Hill is best experienced on foot. Bounded by Cambridge Street, Beacon Street, and Bowdoin Street, the neighborhood is an array of short, tight, winding roads, and street parking (free on Sunday) is at a minimum. To reach Beacon Hill via the T, take the Green Line to Park Street and walk through the Common toward Beacon Street; or take the Red Line to Charles/MGH for access to Charles Street. The Blue Line's Bowdoin stop offers access to both Beacon Hill and the West End.

Across Cambridge Street, the West End is home to Massachusetts General Hospital, the TD Garden, the Museum of Science, and residential high-rises. There's plenty of garage parking; street parking is limited. To access by T, take the Red Line to Charles/MGH for the hospital and Charlesbank Park; the Green Line to Science Park for the Museum of Science, or to North Station for the TD Garden.

QUICK BITES

■ **Anna's Taqueria.** Locals love this Mexicali takeout. ✉ *242 Cambridge St., Beacon Hill* ⊕ *www.annastaque-ria.com* Ⓜ *Charles/MGH, Bowdoin.*

■ **The Paramount.** There's usually a line at this cafeteria-style standout, but it moves quickly. ✉ *44 Charles St., Beacon Hill* ⊕ *www.paramountboston.com* Ⓜ *Charles/MGH.*

■ **Sevens Ale House.** Tasty pub grub and beer in a no-frills bar setting. ✉ *77 Charles St., Beacon Hill* ⊕ *www.facebook.com/SevensAle* Ⓜ *Charles/MGH.*

PLANNING YOUR TIME

■ From top to bottom, historic Beacon Hill can easily be explored in half a day. Shoppers will want to visit Charles Street after noon, when shops are more likely to be open. Add an extra few hours if you wish to linger on Boston Common, visit the State House or other historical sites. The West End is larger in area, so you'll walk more between attractions. The Museum of Science is worth a full day; smaller museums about an hour each.

Beacon Hill is Boston at its most Bostonian. Redbrick row houses dressed with black shutters and the occasional violet-hued windowpane filter into view, and narrow streets return you to the 19th century just as surely as if you had stumbled into a time machine. Across Beacon Street from Beacon Hill, the wide expanse of Boston Common has provided green space for locals since 1634.

Its history dates to the Colonial Era; in ensuing years, Beacon Hill achieved a narrative that includes the abolitionist movement, politics, and, even, prostitution. Blue-blood Brahmins, with surnames like Cabot and Shaw, are perpetual residents, but the Hill gets a consistent influx of the contemporary, at pricey boutiques on its main thoroughfare, Charles Street.

Boston Common had its start as a place for cattle to graze, then as an encampment for British regulars during the Revolutionary War, as a place for public assembly, and today, as a wonderful recreation area.

Beacon Hill and Boston Common

Once the seat of the Commonwealth's government, Beacon Hill was called "Tri-mountain" and later "Tremont" by early colonists because of its three summits:

Pemberton, Mt. Vernon Hill, and Beacon Hill (named for the warning light set on its peak in 1634). In 1799, settlers leveled out the ground for residences, using it to create what is now Charles Street. By the early 19th century, the crests of the other two hills had also been lowered.

When the Hill's fashionable families decamped for the new development of the Back Bay starting in the 1850s, enough residents remained to ensure that the south slope of the Hill never lost its wealthy Brahmin character. By the mid-20th century, most of the multistory single-family dwellings on Beacon Hill had been converted to condominiums and apartments, which are today among the most expensive in the city.

A good place to begin an exploration of Beacon Hill is at the Boston Common Visitor Information Center (below), where you can buy a map or a complete guide to The Freedom Trail.

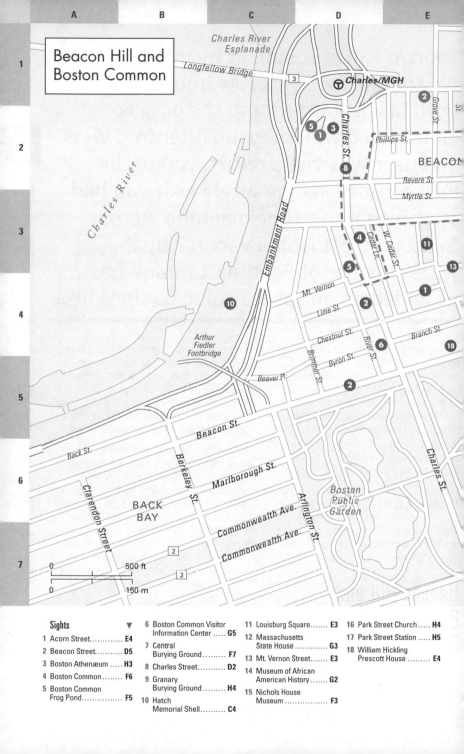

Beacon Hill and Boston Common

Charles River
Esplanade

Longfellow Bridge

Charles River

Charles/MGH

Embankment Road

Phillips St.

BEACON

Revere St.

Myrtle St.

Grove St.

W. Cedar St.

Cedar Ln.

Mt. Vernon

Lime St.

Chestnut St.

River St.

Branch St.

Byron St.

Beaver Pl.

Brimmer St.

Arthur
Fiedler
Footbridge

Back St.

Beacon St.

Berkeley St.

Marlborough St.

BACK
BAY

Clarendon Street

Commonwealth Ave.

Commonwealth Ave.

Arlington St.

Boston
Public
Garden

Charles St.

0   500 ft

0   150 m

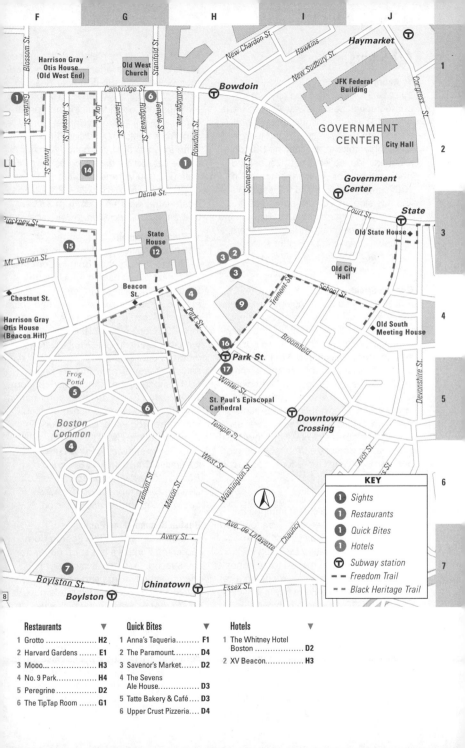

KEY

①	Sights
①	Restaurants
①	Quick Bites
①	Hotels
Ⓣ	Subway station
– –	Freedom Trail
– –	Black Heritage Trail

Restaurants ▼
1 Grotto **H2**
2 Harvard Gardens **E1**
3 Mooo.... .... **H3**
4 No. 9 Park............... **H4**
5 Peregrine **D2**
6 The TipTap Room **G1**

Quick Bites ▼
1 Anna's Taqueria......... **F1**
2 The Paramount.......... **D4**
3 Savenor's Market....... **D2**
4 The Sevens
   Ale House............... **D3**
5 Tatte Bakery & Café **D3**
6 Upper Crust Pizzeria.... **D4**

Hotels ▼
1 The Whitney Hotel
   Boston **D2**
2 XV Beacon.............. **H3**

Sights

★ Acorn Street

BUILDING | Often called the city's most photographed passageway, Acorn Street offers its visitors an iconic image of "historic Boston." Short, steep, and narrow, the cobblestone street may be Boston's roughest ride, so leave your car behind. Brick row houses—once the homes of 19th-century artisans and tradespeople—line one side, and on the other, doors lead to Mt. Vernon's hidden gardens. Find American flags, creative door knockers, window boxes, and gas lights aplenty. ⊠ *Between W. Cedar and Willow Sts., Beacon Hill* Ⓜ *Park.*

Beacon Street

BUILDING | Some New Englanders believe that wealth is a burden to be borne with a minimum of display. Happily, the early residents of Beacon Street were not among them. They erected many fine architectural statements, from the magnificent State House to grand patrician mansions. Here are some of the most important buildings of Charles Bulfinch, the ultimate designer of the Federal style in America: dozens of bowfront row houses, the Somerset Club, and the glorious Harrison Gray Otis House. ⊠ *Beacon Hill* Ⓜ *Park.*

Boston Athenaeum

LIBRARY | One of the oldest libraries in the country, the Athenæum was founded in 1807 from the seeds sown by the Anthology Club (headed by Ralph Waldo Emerson's father). It moved to its imposing, present-day quarters—modeled after Palladio's Palazzo da Porta Festa in Vicenza, Italy—in 1849. Membership in this cathedral of scholarship has been passed down for generations, but the Athenæum is open in part to the public. The first floor houses an art gallery with rotating exhibits, marble busts, porcelain vases, lush oil paintings, and books. The children's room features secluded nooks overlooking the Granary Burying Ground. To see one of the most marvelous sights in the world of Boston academe, take a guided tour, which visits the fifth-floor Reading Room. Among the Athenæum's holdings are most of George Washington's private library, as well as King's Chapel Library, sent from England by William III in 1698. With a nod to the Information Age, an online catalog contains records for more than 600,000 volumes. ⊠ *10½ Beacon St., Beacon Hill* ☎ *617/227–0270* ⊕ *www.bostonathenaeum.org* 🎫 *From $10* ⊘ *Closed Sun. and Mon.* Ⓜ *Park.*

★ Boston Common

CITY PARK | **FAMILY** | Nothing is more central to the city than Boston Common, the oldest public park in the United States Dating from 1634, the Common started as 50 acres where freemen could graze their cattle. (Cows were banned in 1830.) Don't confuse the Common with its sister park, the Public Garden, where the Swan Boats glide. Around the park, visit-worthy sites include Brewer Fountain Plaza, the start of The Freedom Trail, Boston Common Visitor Information Center, the Soldiers and Sailors Monument, the Frog Pond, Central Burying Ground and the Robert Gould Shaw 54th Regiment Memorial. ◼**TIP→ This is Freedom Trail stop 1.** ⊠ *Bounded by Beacon, Charles, Tremont, and Park Sts., Beacon Hill* ⊕ *www.boston.gov/parks/boston-common* Ⓜ *Park, Boylston.*

Boston Common Frog Pond

ICE SKATING | **FAMILY** | The Boston Common Frog Pond is a hot spot, no matter the season. In winter (November to March), city dwellers and visitors alike can skate around the man-made pool (skate rentals available), which vibes an atmosphere reminiscent of a Currier & Ives painting. In warm weather, the Frog Pond transforms into a shallow spray pool, free to all. Nearby, a carousel opens in April and a large playground is open year-round. ⊠ *Boston Common, Beacon Hill* ☎ *617/635–2120* ⊕ *www.bostonfrog-pond.com* Ⓜ *Park.*

Touring Beacon Street

After the **Boston Athenaeum**, Beacon Street highlights begin at No. 34, originally the Cabot family residence and, until 1996, the headquarters of Little, Brown and Company, once a mainstay of Boston's publishing trade. At 33 Beacon, **George Parkman House** shows off a gracious facade hiding more than a few secrets. One of the first sensational "trials of the century" involved the murder of Dr. George Parkman, a wealthy landlord and Harvard benefactor. He was bludgeoned to death in 1849 by Dr. John Webster, a Harvard medical professor and neighborhood acquaintance. He allegedly became enraged by Parkman's demands that he repay a personal loan. At the conclusion of the trial, the professor was hanged; he's buried in an unmarked grave on Copp's Hill in the North End. Parkman's son lived in seclusion in this house overlooking the Common until he died in 1908. The building is now used for civic functions.

Notice the windows of the twin **Appleton-Parker Houses**, built by the pioneering textile merchant Nathan Appleton and a partner at Nos. 39 and 40. These are the celebrated purple panes of Beacon Hill; only a few buildings have them, and they are incredibly valuable. Their amethystine color was the result of the action of the sun's ultraviolet light on imperfections in a shipment of glass sent to Boston circa 1820. The mansions aren't open to the public.

The quintessential snob has always been a Bostonian—and the **Somerset Club**, at 42 Beacon, has always been the inner sanctum of blue-blood Cabots, Lowells, and Lodges. The mansion is a rare intrusion of the granite Greek Revival style into Beacon Hill. The older of its two buildings was erected in 1819 by David Sears and designed by Alexander Parris, the architect of Quincy Market.

A few doors down at No. 45 resides the grandest of the three homes Harrison Gray Otis, a U.S. senator and Boston's third mayor, built for himself. They are also the city's most splendidly ostentatious Federal-era houses, all designed by Charles Bulfinch and all still standing. Otis moved in circa 1805, and stayed until his death in 1848. The **Otis House** was once freestanding and surrounded by English-style gardens; today, it's the headquarters of the American Meteorological Society.

Boston Common Visitor Information Center
INFO CENTER | FAMILY | Run by the Greater Boston Convention and Visitors Bureau this visitor information center not only serves as a well-staffed source of things to see and do, it is a frequent meeting spot for walking tours around town and is the first stop on Boston's historic Freedom Trail. ■**TIP→ Find it on the Tremont Street side of Boston Common, equidistant between the Green Line's Boylston and Park Street T stops.** ⊠ *139 Tremont St., Beacon Hill* ☎ *617/536–4100* ⊕ *www.bostonusa. com* Ⓜ *Park, Boylston.*

Central Burying Ground
CEMETERY | The Central Burying Ground may seem an odd feature for a public park, but remember that in 1756, when the land was set aside, this was a lonely corner of Boston Common. It's the final resting place of Tories and Patriots alike, as well as many British casualties of the Battle of Bunker Hill. The most famous

person buried here is Gilbert Stuart, the portraitist best known for his likenesses of George and Martha Washington. ⊠ *Boston Common, along Boylston St., Downtown* ⊕ *www.boston.gov/cemeteries/central-burying-ground* Ⓜ *Boylston.*

★ Charles Street

COMMERCIAL CENTER | You won't see any glaring neon, in keeping with the historic character of the area, but Charles Street more than makes up for the general lack of commercial development on Beacon Hill with a plethora of antiques shops, clothing boutiques, small restaurants, and cafés. Once the home of Oliver Wendell Holmes and the publisher James T. Fields (of the famed Bostonian firm of Ticknor and Fields), Charles Street sparkles at dusk from gas-fueled lamps, making it a romantic place for an evening stroll. ⊠ *Between Beacon and Cambridge Sts., Beacon Hill* Ⓜ *Charles/MGH.*

Granary Burying Ground

CEMETERY | Boston's cemeteries are among the most historic in America, and the Granary, established in 1660, is no exception. Headstones are elaborately ornamented with skeletons and winged skulls among other carved Colonial folk art. Samuel Adams, John Hancock, Paul Revere, and Benjamin Franklin's parents are among the impressive list of the estimated 5,000 folks interred here; there hasn't been a new burial since 1880. Note the winged hourglasses carved into the stone gateway of the burial ground; they are a 19th-century addition. ■**TIP➜ This is Freedom Trail stop 4.** ⊠ *95 Tremont St., Beacon Hill* ⊕ *www.thefreedomtrail.org/trail-sites/granary-burying-ground* Ⓜ *Park.*

Hatch Memorial Shell

ARTS VENUE | **FAMILY** | Situated on the wonderfully scenic Charles River Esplanade, this acoustic and artful concert venue—100 feet wide and wood inlaid—annually hosts the Boston Pops' famous July 4 concert and dozens of other free, summer classical-orchestra performances, music festivals, film screenings, and other events. It's called a shell because it looks like one. ⊠ *Beacon Hill* ✛ *Access Hatch Shell from Arthur Fiedler Footbridge, at Arlington and Beacon Sts.* ☎ *617/626–1250* ⊕ *www.hatchshell.com* Ⓜ *Charles/MGH, Arlington.*

Louisburg Square

HISTORIC SITE | Charming Louisburg Square (proper Bostonians *always* pronounce the "s") was an 1840s model for a town-house development that was never built on the Hill because of space restrictions. Today, it features a central grassy square enclosed by a wrought-iron fence and a history of famous tenants, including former U.S. Secretary of State John Kerry. ⊠ *Between Mt. Vernon and Pickney Sts., Beacon Hill* Ⓜ *Charles/MGH, Park.*

★ Massachusetts State House

BUILDING | **FAMILY** | On July 4, 1795, the surviving fathers of the Revolution were on hand to enshrine the ideals of their new Commonwealth in a graceful seat of government designed by Charles Bulfinch. Governor Samuel Adams and Paul Revere laid the cornerstone; Revere would later roll the copper sheathing for the dome. Inside the building, visitors can check out Doric Hall, with its statuary and portraits; the Hall of Flags, where an exhibit shows the battle flags from all the wars in which Massachusetts regiments have participated; the Great Hall, an open space used for state functions that houses 351 flags from the cities and towns of Massachusetts; the governor's office; and the chambers of the House and Senate. Free guided tours; call for reservation. ■**TIP➜ This is Freedom Trail stop 2.** ⊠ *24 Beacon St., Beacon Hill* ☎ *617/727–3676* ⊕ *www.sec.state.ma.us/trs/trsidx.htm* ▨ *Free* ۞ *Closed weekends* Ⓜ *Park.*

The Black Heritage Trail

Until the end of the 19th century, a vibrant, free, black community—more than 8,000 at its peak—settled on the north slope of the otherwise opulent Beacon Hill. Here, black-owned businesses lined the streets, and the community built houses, schools, and churches that stand to this day. For example, you can visit the African Meeting House, once called the Black Faneuil Hall, where orators rallied against slavery. The black community has since shifted to other parts of Boston, but visitors can rediscover this 19th-century legacy on the Black Heritage Trail.

Established in the late 1960s, the self-guiding trail stitches together 14 sites along a 1½-mile walk. To tour on your own, pick up brochures from the **Museum of African American History** (✉ 46 Joy St.) or download one online at ⊕ maah.org/trail.htm. National Park rangers give daily guided tours Memorial Day through Columbus Day (⊕ www.nps.gov/boaf/planyourvisit/hours.htm).

Start at the stirring **Robert Gould Shaw 54th Regiment Memorial** in Boston Common. Shaw, a young white officer from a prominent Boston abolitionist family, led the first black regiment to be recruited in the North during the Civil War. From here, walk up Joy Street to 5–7 Pinckney Street to see the 1797 **George Middleton House**, Beacon Hill's oldest existing home built by blacks. Nearby, the **Phillips School** at Anderson and Pinckney streets was one of Boston's first integrated schools. The **John J. Smith House**, at 86 Pinckney, was a rendezvous point for abolitionists and escaping slaves, and the **Charles Street Meeting House**, at Mt. Vernon and Charles streets, was once a white Baptist church and later a black church and community center. In 1876 the building became the site of the **African Methodist Episcopal Church**, which was the last black institution to leave Beacon Hill, in 1939. The **Lewis and Harriet Hayden House** at 66 Phillips Street, the home of freed slaves turned abolitionists, was a stop on the Underground Railroad. Harriet Beecher Stowe, author of *Uncle Tom's Cabin*, visited here in 1853 for her first glimpse of fugitive slaves. The Haydens reportedly kept a barrel of gunpowder under the front step, saying they'd blow up the house before they'd surrender a single slave. At **2 Phillips Street**, John Coburn, cofounder of a black military company, ran a gaming house, described as a "private place for gentlemen."

The five residences on **Smith Court** are typical of African American Bostonian homes of the 1800s, including No. 3, the 1799 clapboard house where William C. Nell, America's first published black historian and a crusader for school integration, boarded from 1851 to 1865. At the corner of Joy Street and Smith Court is **Abiel Smith School**, the city's first public school for black children. The school's exhibits interpret the ongoing struggle started in the 1830s for equal school rights. Next door is the venerable **African Meeting House**, which was the community's center of social, educational, and political activity. The ground level houses a gallery; in the airy upstairs, you can imagine the fiery sermons that once rattled the upper pews.

Several Founding Fathers rest at the Granary Burial Ground, a picturesque Freedom Trail stop.

Mt. Vernon Street

NEIGHBORHOOD | Mt. Vernon Street runs from the flat of the Hill, past Louisburg Square, and all the way up the Massachusetts State House. Along with Chestnut Street, it has some of Beacon Hill's most distinguished addresses, but Mt. Vernon is the grander of the two, with houses set back farther and rising taller. Henry James once wrote that Mt. Vernon Street was "the only respectable street in America," and he must have known, as he lived with his brother William at No. 131 in the 1860s. James was just one of many literary luminaries who resided here, including Julia Ward Howe, who composed "The Battle Hymn of the Republic" and lived at No. 32, and the poet Robert Frost, who lived at No. 88. ⊠ *Beacon Hill* Ⓜ *Park.*

Museum of African American History

MUSEUM | FAMILY | The Museum of African American History was established in 1964 to recognize Boston's African American community, from slavery through the abolitionist movement. The Abiel Smith School, the first public school in the nation built specifically for black children, now serves as the museum's main building, filled with exhibits. The African Meeting House was built in 1806 entirely by black labor; in 1832, William Lloyd Garrison formed the New England Anti-Slavery Society here, and in 2011 the building completed a $9.5 million restoration. ⊠ *46 Joy St., Beacon Hill* ☎ *617/725–0022* ⊕ *maah.org* ⊠ *$10* ⊘ *Closed Sun.* Ⓜ *Park.*

Nichols House Museum

HISTORIC SITE | The only Mt. Vernon Street home open to the public, the Nichols House was built in 1804 and is attributed to Charles Bulfinch. It became the lifelong home of Rose Standish Nichols (1872–1960), Beacon Hill eccentric, philanthropist, peace advocate, and one of the first female landscape designers. Nichols inherited the Victorian furnishings, but she added a number of Colonial-style pieces to the mix, and the result is a delightful mélange of styles. To see the house, you must take a guided tour. ⊠ *55 Mt. Vernon St., Beacon Hill* ☎ *617/227–6993* ⊕ *www.nicholshousemuseum.org* ⊠ *$10* ⊗ *Closed Sun.–Wed.* Ⓜ *Park.*

Park Street Church

HISTORIC SITE | If this Congregationalist church at the corner of Tremont and Park streets could sing, you'd hear Samuel Smith's iconic hymn "America," which was first sung here in 1831. But that's only one fun fact about this historic site. It was designed by Peter Banner and erected in 1810. The Handel & Haydn Society was founded here in 1815. William Lloyd Garrison began his long public campaign for the abolition of slavery in 1829. Just outside the church is Brimstone Corner, and whether the name refers to the fervent thunder of the church's preachers, the gunpowder that was once stored in the church's crypt, or the burning sulfur that preachers once scattered on the pavement to attract potential churchgoers, we'll never know—historians simply can't agree. Summer travelers get the rare treat of exploring Park Street Church from the inside, the only few months it's open to the public. ■ TIP→ **This is Freedom Trail stop 3.** ⊠ *1 Park St., Beacon Hill* ☎ *617/523–3383* ⊕ *www.parkstreet.org* ⊗ *Closed Sept.–mid-June.* Ⓜ *Park.*

Park Street Station

HISTORIC SITE | FAMILY | One of the first four stops on the first subway in America, Park Street Station opened for service in 1897, against the warnings of those convinced it would make buildings along Tremont Street collapse. The copper-roof kiosks are National Historic Landmarks—outside them cluster vendors, street musicians, and partisans of causes and beliefs ranging from Irish nationalism to Krishna Consciousness. The station is the heart of Boston's subway system; "inbound" trains are always traveling toward Park Street. ⊠ *Park St. at Tremont St., Beacon Hill* ⊕ *www.mbta.com* Ⓜ *Park.*

William Hickling Prescott House

BUILDING | Now a modest but engaging house museum, this 1808 Federal-style structure was designed by Asher Benjamin. From 1845 to 1859, it was the home of noted historian William Hickling Prescott, and today it's the headquarters for the Massachusetts Society of Colonial Dames of America. Guided tours venture through rooms furnished with period furniture, including the Prescott's former study with his desk and "noctograph," which helped the nearly blind scholar write. Fun fact: Prescott's secret staircase allowed him to escape into his study when bored by guests in the parlor. ⊠ *55 Beacon St., Beacon Hill* ☎ *617/742–3190* ⊕ *nscdama. org/william-hickling-prescott-house* ⊠ *$8* ⊗ *Closed Oct.–May for guided tours, unless by appointment.* Ⓜ *Park, Arlington.*

🍴 Restaurants

Eminently walkable, this is one of Boston's smallest and most historic neighborhoods filled with brick sidewalks, shimmering gas lamps, and 19th-century row houses with brass knockers and flower boxes. On the food front you'll find an appealing blend of fancy and casual restaurants, as well as cafés, along the main pedestrian path of Charles Street, where you'll see mothers with strollers, young professionals, and patrician elderly couples, who live right around the corner, all going about their day.

Grotto

$$$ | ITALIAN | Intimate, romantic, and tucked away, this small, Italian-inspired restaurant makes for a great date spot, which may have something to do with the "candle-lit" chandeliers, the rustic brick walls, the fabulous wine list, and the handmade pasta. Owner Scott Herritt uses his imagination to create contemporary Italian cuisine. **Known for:** a three-meat Bolognese sauce that would rival any Sunday supper; a well-curated menu of intentional dishes; nookish, cozy space.

$ *Average main: $28* ⊠ *37 Bowdoin St., Beacon Hill* ☎ *617/227–3434* ⊕ *www. grottorestaurant.com* Ⓜ *Bowdoin.*

Harvard Gardens

$ | **AMERICAN** | A Beacon Hill legend, this was the first bar in the city to get its liquor license after the repeal of Prohibition. It opened in 1930, and was owned by the same family until the 1990s. **Known for:** a killer, house-made Bloody Mary mixed with the bar's own peppercorn vodka; a reuben sandwich stuffed with corned beef that's made in-house; casual, comfortable vibe that's a little bit different from a typical Beacon Hill experience. $ *Average main: $17* ⊠ *316 Cambridge St., Beacon Hill* ☎ *617/523–2727* ⊕ *www. harvardgardens.com* Ⓜ *Charles/MGH.*

Mooo....

$$$$ | **STEAKHOUSE** | Do dress nicely for a visit to Mooo..., a luxurious, refined steak house inside the swanky XV Beacon hotel that remains civilized despite the restaurant's somewhat whimsical name. Prime dry-aged steaks are served à la carte, and, although the Japanese A5 Wagyu sirloin will set you back $185, portions are as exaggerated as the prices. **Known for:** unbelievably delicious steaks served in a dining room with "cow" art; delightful, attentive service; hefty prices. $ *Average main: $65* ⊠ *XV Beacon Hotel, 15 Beacon St., Beacon Hill* ☎ *617/670–2515* ⊕ *www. mooorestaurant.com* Ⓜ *Park.*

★ No. 9 Park

$$$$ | **EUROPEAN** | Welcome to the first and now flagship restaurant in acclaimed chef Barbara Lynch's empire. Even after 20 years, No. 9 Park continues to win rave reviews for Lynch's stellar, unique interpretation of fine French and Italian cuisine. **Known for:** a chef's six-course, wine-paired tasting menu, served for the whole table; polished service; Lynch's memorably rich, prune-stuffed gnocchi drizzled with bits of foie gras, which is always offered, even if you don't see it on the menu. $ *Average main: $46* ⊠ *9 Park St., Beacon Hill* ☎ *617/742–9991* ⊕ *www. no9park.com* Ⓜ *Park.*

Peregrine

$$$ | **MEDITERRANEAN** | Owner and chef Josh Lewin serves up a sophisticated take on rustic, coastal Mediterranean food and diners are meant to rest, order slowly, and enjoy a meal in multiple stages. Everything is made from scratch in the kitchen, and although the preparations are Italian-based, there's a nod to New England ingredients and seasonality. **Known for:** plated meals as pretty as they are delicious; curated wine selection from small vineyards that complement the cuisine; not taking gratuities, tips or any other kind of cash handout at the end of your meal. $ *Average main: $35* ⊠ *The Whitney Hotel, 170 Charles St., Beacon Hill* ☎ *617/826–1762* ⊕ *www.peregrineboston.com* Ⓜ *Charles/MGH.*

The TipTap Room

$$ | **AMERICAN** | **FAMILY** | Befitting its name, Chef Brian Poe's casual Beacon Hill restaurant focuses on two main things: meat and interesting beers on tap. But, Poe's menu of meat goes beyond steak and chicken staples, and depending on the season and what's readily available from purveyors, dinner entrees may feature bison, camel, ostrich, emu, kangaroo, snake, yak, elk, or antelope. **Known for:** a half-dozen-plus styles of meat tips, from steak to swordfish, and even tofu; exotic meat specials, like kangaroo and ostrich; Nick's Deep Stash secret-ish menu of exclusive, hard-to-find (and kind of expensive) meat. $ *Average main: $24* ⊠ *138 Cambridge St., Beacon Hill* ☎ *857/350–3344* ⊕ *www.thetiptaproom. com* Ⓜ *Bowdoin, Charles/MGH.*

☕ Coffee and Quick Bites

Anna's Taqueria

$ | **MEXICAN** | **FAMILY** | Inspired by the authentic Mexican take-out readily available in West Coast cities, Anna's owner moved to Boston and opened shop more than 25 years ago. This small, local chain has been a hit ever since for its burritos, tacos, and quesadillas. **Known**

for: Tacos al pastor—marinated, rotisserie cooked pork with pineapples and onions; fat, flavorful burritos; bringing the heat with really spicy sauces you can add on. $\boxed{s}$ *Average main: $8* ✉ *242 Cambridge St., Beacon Hill* ☎ *617/227–8822* ⊕ *www.annastaqueria.com* Ⓜ *Charles/MGH.*

★ The Paramount

$ | **AMERICAN** | **FAMILY** | Don't be surprised to see a queue at this neighborhood hot spot, no matter the time of day. Regulars happily line up for waffles topped with fresh fruit, caramel and banana french toast, huge salads, and hefty sandwiches, all made to order as you do from the counter. **Known for:** long, but quick-moving, lines; decadent, all-day breakfast items; Old Bay-seasoned homefries. $\boxed{s}$ *Average main: $12* ✉ *44 Charles St., Beacon Hill* ☎ *617/720–1152* ⊕ *www.paramountboston.com* Ⓜ *Charles/MGH.*

Savenor's Market

$ | **DELI** | When they need snacks for a cocktail party or something for the grill, Beacon Hill residents pop over to this market famous for being Julia Child's favorite butcher and known for procuring exotic game meats. Tamer choices include sandwiches, prepared salads, outstanding cheeses, breads, tinned fish, hummus, dips and more—this place is a foodie's nirvana. **Known for:** supplying established and emerging chefs with inspiration; delicious sandwiches to-go; exotic meat and game selections at its butcher counter. $\boxed{s}$ *Average main: $10* ✉ *160 Charles St., Beacon Hill* ☎ *617/723–6328* ⊕ *www.savenors-market.com* Ⓜ *Charles/MGH.*

The Sevens Ale House

$ | **AMERICAN** | This classic dive bar has been serving beer and wine (no liquor) since 1933. Today, it's pleasantly untrendy and an easygoing alternative to Beacon Hill's tony stuffiness, with its battered dark wood bar and booths, simple setup, dartboard, perfectly poured pints, and great pub food. **Known for:** great selection of small producer craft beers in addition

to the usual suspects; a tasty French dip; a no-frills environment. $\boxed{s}$ *Average main: $11* ✉ *77 Charles St., Beacon Hill* ☎ *617/523–9074* Ⓜ *Charles/MGH.*

★ Tatte Bakery & Café

$ | **ISRAELI** | Tzurit Or's upscale bakery and café takes pastries to the next level with items like kouign-amann, pistachio croissants, and Jerusalem bagels. While these items are staples, the majority of the menu changes frequently, but you can expect hearty plates all day, from breakfast sandwiches and tartines to salads, bowls, and shakshuka (an egg dish with tomatoes and peppers), all with a Middle Eastern spin. **Known for:** Or's take on traditional North African shakshuka, served with challah bread; signature nut tarts that are as pretty as they are tasty; convivial atmosphere. $\boxed{s}$ *Average main: $12* ✉ *70 Charles St., Beacon Hill* ☎ *617/723–5555* ⊕ *www.tattebakery.com* Ⓜ *Charles/MGH.*

Upper Crust Pizzeria

$$ | **PIZZA** | Walk into Upper Crust's first location and you'll see the kitchen staff pulling scratch-made dough in the open kitchen. The Neapolitan-style pizza—you can order by the slice (they're huge) or by the pie—is really tasty, and toppings go creatively beyond a classic cheese or pepperoni. **Known for:** deliciously thin, Neapolitan-style pizza crust; creative topping combinations; limited seating options. $\boxed{s}$ *Average main: $20* ✉ *20 Charles St., Beacon Hill* ☎ *617/723–9600* ⊕ *www.theuppercrustpizzeria.com* Ⓜ *Charles/MGH.*

Hotels

If you want calm, serenity, and class, then stay on Beacon Hill, one of the poshest neighborhoods in Boston. Its streets are lined with elegant brick buildings holding unique shops and restaurants, within close proximity to many other neighborhoods, including the Back Bay, Downtown, and Government Center.

The Whitney Hotel Boston

$$$$ | **HOTEL** | This brand new luxury boutique hotel fits right in with its Beacon Hill surroundings, views of which you can enjoy while you relax in-room in a plush Frette bathrobe with a cup of Nespresso coffee. **Pros:** excellent location within walking distance of the Back Bay, West End, and Downtown; easy access to sophisticated Mediterranean fare at the hotel's restaurant, Peregrine; complimentary bicycles. **Cons:** high rates; high noise levels from traffic in Storrow Drive-facing rooms; long wait for the valet. [$] *Rooms from: $600* ✉ *170 Charles St., Beacon Hill* ☎ *617/367–1866* 🌐 *www.whitneyhotelboston.com* 🛏 *68 rooms* 🍴 *No meals* [M] *Charles/MGH.*

★ XV Beacon

$$$$ | **HOTEL** | The 1903 Beaux Arts exterior of this intimate, luxury boutique hotel is a study in sophistication and elegance. **Pros:** rooftop deck with amazing city views; complimentary Lexus car service; dogs of any size welcome for no fee. **Cons:** some rooms are small; can be expensive on weekends during peak months; no view from classic rooms. [$] *Rooms from: $575* ✉ *15 Beacon St., Beacon Hill* ☎ *617/670–1500, 877/982–3226* 🌐 *www.xvbeacon.com* 🛏 *63 rooms* 🍴 *No meals* [M] *Park.*

Nightlife

There are no dance clubs in this leafy, patrician enclave. In fact, nightlife options are scarce, but not altogether missing, and most live on Charles Street or up by the State House.

BARS

Cheers

BARS/PUBS | The pub—dismantled in England, shipped to Boston, and reassembled—and formerly known as the Bull & Finch, later became the inspiration for the now-classic TV series, *Cheers*. Enjoy a burger at the model bar of the Hollywood set and imagine Sam and Diane walking in the door and calling your name. The crowd tends to be heavily tourists, so locals stay away. ✉ *84 Beacon St., Beacon Hill* ☎ *617/227–9605* 🌐 *www.cheersboston.com* [M] *Park, Arlington.*

Shopping

Most of the commerce that happens in Beacon Hill today happens on its main thoroughfare, Charles Street. Until recently, Charles Street was a premier destination for antiques shopping, but over the last decade, posh, independently owned gift, jewelry, and women's clothing boutiques have moved in and taken over the expensive commercial real estate of this upper class neighborhood.

ANTIQUES

Boston Antique Company

ANTIQUES/COLLECTIBLES | This flea market–style collection of dealers has been in business since 1981. The shop focuses on art, including sculpture, paintings and old master drawings, china and silver, and jewelry. ✉ *119 Charles St., Beacon Hill* ☎ *617/367–9000* 🌐 *www.bostonartsandantiques.com* [M] *Charles/MGH.*

Danish Country European & Asian Antiques

ANTIQUES/COLLECTIBLES | Antiques hunters with more casual, comfortable sensibilities will adore this Charles Street showroom that features an intriguing mix of antique Scandinavian furniture, red-lacquered Chinese pieces and Royal Copenhagen porcelain. ✉ *138 Charles St., Beacon Hill* ☎ *617/227–1804* [M] *Charles/MGH.*

Upstairs Downstairs

ANTIQUES/COLLECTIBLES | This Beacon Hill standout features furniture and home decor in a variety of styles, from Federal and Asian to art deco and midcentury modern. While antiques are the focus here, shoppers can also find new, vintage, and reproduction pieces among the stash. Artwork, sterling silver, and china round out the selection. ✉ *93 Charles S, Beacon Hill* ☎ *617/367–1950* 🌐 *www.upstairsdownstairsboston.com* [M] *Charles/MGH.*

CLOTHING

Crush Boutique

CLOTHING | Step down to this subterranean shop to find weekend casual outfits, jeans, silky shifts, and even party-girl attire. You'll also find affordable jewelry and handbags to dress up any ensemble. Crush's Newbury Street shop (between Fairfield and Gloucester Streets) has a more LA vibe to it. ⊠ *131 Charles St., Beacon Hill* ☎ *617/720–0010* ⊕ *www. shopcrushboutique.com* Ⓜ *Charles/MGH.*

December Thieves

CLOTHING | Definitely the edgiest clothing boutique on the Hill, December Thieves stocks contemporary, emerging designers and brands from Europe, Asia, and Latin America. Find a curious, curated and wildly fun array of apparel, scarves, handbags, jewelry, beauty products, and home decor. ⊠ *51 Charles St., Beacon Hill* ☎ *857/239–9149* ⊕ *decemberthieves. com* Ⓜ *Charles/MGH.*

Dress

CLOTHING | True to its name, this 15-year-old specialty store owned locally curates designer party dresses, but the selection doesn't end there. Women will also find tops and pants, shoes, accessories, handbags, and even a few home goods items. ⊠ *70 Charles St., Beacon Hill* ☎ *617/248–9910* ⊕ *www.dressboston. com* Ⓜ *Charles/MGH.*

French + Italian

CLOTHING | Exquisite European fabric and design comes to this upscale neighborhood boutique that spotlights emerging designers from Paris, Milan, and New York. Pieces can be expensive, but they're meant to be versatile wardrobe staples. ⊠ *119 Charles St., Beacon Hill* ☎ *857/990–3141* ⊕ *www.frenchitalian. com* Ⓜ *Charles/MGH.*

Helen's Leather Shop

SHOES/LUGGAGE/LEATHER GOODS | Channel your inner cowgirl (or-boy) at this family-owned shop specializing in Western wear, including hand-tooled boots embroidered, dyed, and crafted from leather and exotic skins. Browse leather sandals, jackets, briefcases, luggage, and other accessories from top quality brands, including Lucchese, Dan Post, Frye and Schott. ⊠ *110 Charles St., Beacon Hill* ☎ *617/742–2077* ⊕ *www. helensleather.com* Ⓜ *Charles/MGH.*

Sara Campbell

CLOTHING | Women who identify with the style aesthetic of pretty, preppy places like Newport, RI, Charleston, SC, and Nantucket Island will feel at home dressed in the upscale apparel created by veteran Boston fashion designer Sara Campbell. Each seasonal collection includes dresses, tops, pants, shorts, jackets and cardigans. ⊠ *84 Chestnut St., Beacon Hill* ☎ *617/377–4054* ⊕ *www. saracampbell.com* Ⓜ *Charles/MGH.*

GIFTS

Black Ink Boston

GIFTS/SOUVENIRS | This smart and whimsical shop has had a foothold on Charles Street for the last quarter century, and yet, its stash of unexpected home accessories, knicknacks, toys, and gifts continues to stay ahead of the trends ⊠ *101 Charles St., Beacon Hill* ☎ *617/723–3883* ⊕ *www.blackinkboston.com* Ⓜ *Charles/ MGH.*

Blackstone's of Beacon Hill

GIFTS/SOUVENIRS | If you've shopped Charles Street in the last 40 years, you'll recognize this long-standing gift shop that puts an upscale spin on gifts and souvenirs. Many items are made in the United States or even more locally. Hardcover books, exquisite hand towels, cocktail napkins, vases, blankets, collectible Christmas ornaments, and candles are among the selection. After the recent closure of its sister store KitchenWares, Blackstone's now offers professional quality culinary utensils, too. ⊠ *46 Charles St., Beacon Hill* ☎ *617/227–4646* ⊕ *www.blackstonesbeaconhill.com* Ⓜ *Charles/MGH.*

Flat of the Hill

GIFTS/SOUVENIRS | Look for the lifelike golden retriever that guards the entrance to this shop named for its location at the base—or, flat—of Beacon Hill, rather than any lack of pluck in its semi-preppy selection of skin care creams, vases and platters, pillows, wall art, baby gifts, and whatever else catches the fancy of its owner. ⊠ *60 Charles St., Beacon Hill* ☎ *617/619–9977* ⊕ *www.flatofthehill.com* ⊙ *Closed Mon.; Sun. in Jan. and Aug.* Ⓜ *Charles/MGH.*

HOUSEHOLD ITEMS

E. R. Butler & Co. Manufacturers

HOUSEHOLD ITEMS/FURNITURE | This museum-like store shows off historical collections of original architectural hardware designs, as well as brand new restoration pieces. Along with luxury lighting pieces and home furnishings, new trinkets, and objects by New York City–based jewelry designer Ted Muehling. ⊠ *38 Charles St., Beacon Hill* ☎ *617/722–0230* ⊕ *www.erbutler.com* ⊙ *Closed Sun. and Mon.* Ⓜ *Charles/MGH.*

JEWELRY

Persona Jewelry

JEWELRY/ACCESSORIES | Using precious metals and a variety of gemstones, Gary Shteyman crafts gorgeous, unique pieces from his in-store workshop for Persona's own line of fine jewelry. Elsewhere in the store, necklaces, earrings, bangles, and bold cocktail rings by a few local designers fill the cases, and shoppers can browse a small selection of Miller leather bags by Paris-based brand Les Cuirs Fournier. ⊠ *62 Charles St., Beacon Hill* ☎ *617/266–3003* ⊕ *www.personastyle.com* ⊙ *Closed Sun.* Ⓜ *Charles/MGH.*

The West End

One of Boston's less-traveled neighborhoods, the West End features primarily recent construction—the brick tenements housing myriad ethnic groups and tangled web of streets of the old West End were razed in 1960s in the name of urban renewal. A few structures survived, namely Massachusetts General Hospital and the former Suffolk County Jail, which is today known as the luxurious Liberty Hotel. If you've attended a Celtics or Bruins game at the TD Garden, you've been in this 'hood and probably not realized it. In 2019, the Garden underwent a face lift and the addition of The Hub on Causeway, nearly three acres of mixed-use space that puts a bounce back in the West End's step.

Where the Charles River separates the West End in Boston from the city of Cambridge, the Museum of Science puts a cool spin on technology, earth sciences, and more. And, on the skyline one can spy the Leonard P. Zakim Bunker Hill Bridge, a majestic and modern piece of transportation architecture.

 ## Sights

Boston Bruins

SPORTS VENUE | **FAMILY** | In 1924, the Boston Bruins became the first U.S. ice hockey team to enter the NHL. The Bruins have been playing at the Garden since 1928 (although the original Boston Garden was rebuilt in 1995) and have won six Stanley Cup titles over that time. Spectators can watch the championship banners hanging in the rafters above the ice and the stands, which are packed for every home game, despite high ticket prices. Fans are loud, vocal and extremely loyal, so spectators with delicate personalities won't feel comfortable. Saturday afternoon games are a win for the family. Seasons run from October until April; playoffs last through early June. ⊠ *TD Garden, 100 Legends Way, West End* ☎ *617/624–2327* ⊕ *www.nhl.com/bruins* Ⓜ *North Station.*

Overlooking the Charles River, the Museum of Science—sitting half in Cambridge and half in Boston—focuses on science, technology, and hands-on learning.

Boston Celtics

SPORTS VENUE | FAMILY | The Boston Celtics franchise has the most championship titles in the NBA, with 17 banners; rival Los Angeles Lakers come in second with 16, which is at least 10 more than any other team. So, what to expect at a Celtics game from today's squad? An all-around fun experience, a charged atmosphere and devotion, from the fans to the team and the team to the fans. You'll hear "Let's Go, Cel-tics" no matter the score. Season runs from late October to April, and playoffs last until mid-June. ⊠ *TD Garden, 100 Legends Way, West End* ☎ *866/423–5849* ⊕ *www.nba.com/celtics* Ⓜ *North Station.*

The Ether Dome at Mass General Hospital

COLLEGE | FAMILY | Tiny, but well worth the 15 minutes you'll spend here if you're already in the neighborhood, this operating theater is now open to the public because of its historical significance. In fact, it served as Mass General Hospital's first operating room, in use from 1821 to 1867, and it was here where the world witnessed the first public demonstration of surgical anesthesia, in 1846. Today, the room contains two 19th-century operating chairs complete with red velvet to mask patients' blood, a teaching skeleton, and, interestingly, an authentic Egyptian mummy. ⊠ *Mass General's Bulfinch Bldg., 55 Fruit St., West End* ✛ *Enter historic gray Bulfinch Bldg. at its main door, Ether Dome is on 4th floor* ☎ *617/724–9557* ⊕ *www.mass-general.org/museum/exhibits/ether-dome* ⊗ *Closed weekends* Ⓜ *Charles/MGH.*

The Hub On Causeway

STORE/MALL | FAMILY | This massive, multiuse, 1.9 million-square-foot complex is the West End's newest and biggest attraction, and it's attached to the TD Garden. It's easy to get here from anywhere in the city, since the Hub incorporates North Station, which is serviced by both the subway (Orange and Green lines) and the commuter rail. Travelers can stay at bold and bustling citizenM hotel; ArcLight Cinema entertains with movies on 15 screens; and Boston-based Big

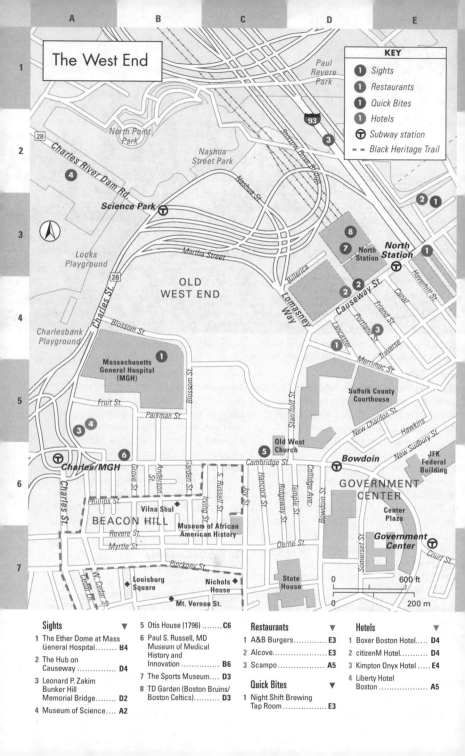

The West End

Paul Revere Park

93

North Point Park

Nashua Street Park

28

Charles River Dam Rd.

4

Science Park Ⓣ

2 1

8

7 North Station

North Station Ⓣ

1

Locks Playground

Martha Street

28

OLD WEST END

Billerica St.

2 2 Causeway St.

Lomasney Way

Friend St.

Portland St.

Lancaster

1

3

Traverse

Merrimac St.

Charlesbank Playground

Blossom St.

4

Massachusetts General Hospital (MGH)

1

Blossom St.

Suffolk County Courthouse

New Chardon St.

Hawkins

5

Fruit St.

Parkman St.

New Sudbury St.

JFK Federal Building

3 4

6

Charles/MGH Ⓣ

Grove St.

Anderson St.

Garden St.

S. Russell St.

Irving St.

Joy St.

Hancock St.

Old West Church

5 Cambridge St.

Cutridge Ave.

Ridgeway St.

Temple St.

Bowdoin Ⓣ

Bowdoin St.

GOVERNMENT CENTER

Center Plaza

6

Charles St.

Phillips St.

Vilna Shul

Museum of African American History

BEACON HILL

Revere St.

Myrtle St.

Derne St.

Somerset St.

Government Center Ⓣ

Court St.

7

Pinckney St.

Louisburg Square

Nichols House

Mt. Vernon St.

State House

W. Cedar St.

Cedar Ln.

0   600 ft
0   200 m

Sights ▼

1 The Ether Dome at Mass General Hospital........ **B4**
2 The Hub on Causeway **D4**
3 Leonard P. Zakim Bunker Hill Memorial Bridge........ **D2**
4 Museum of Science.... **A2**
5 Otis House (1796) **C6**
6 Paul S. Russell, MD Museum of Medical History and Innovation **B6**
7 The Sports Museum.... **D3**
8 TD Garden (Boston Bruins/ Boston Celtics).......... **D3**

Restaurants ▼

1 A&B Burgers............. **E3**
2 Alcove.................... **E3**
3 Scampo **A5**

Quick Bites ▼

1 Night Shift Brewing Tap Room **E3**

Hotels ▼

1 Boxer Boston Hotel..... **D4**
2 citizenM Hotel........... **D4**
3 Kimpton Onyx Hotel **E4**
4 Liberty Hotel Boston **A5**

Night Live features a sexy, modern live music and concert space with DJs and bottle service, plus, its resident restaurant, Guy Fieri's Tequila Cocina (order the trash-can nachos). There are plenty of other dining options, including American sports bar Banners Kitchen & Tap, which has a truly massive LED TV screen and shows all types of sports games. Iron Chef Masaharu Morimoto's Momosan Ramen is adjacent to the Hub Hall food hall, which features a dozen and a half local vendors. ⊠ *Causeway St., West End* Ⓜ *North Station.*

Leonard P. Zakim Bunker Hill Memorial Bridge

BRIDGE/TUNNEL | Dedicated in 2002, the Zakim Bridge is the crown jewel of Boston's legendary Big Dig construction project. The Zakim rings in at 1,432 feet, is one of the widest cable-stayed hybrid bridges ever built, and is the first to use an asymmetrical design. At night, the illuminated bridge glows blue. ⊠ *West End* ⊕ *www.leonardpzakimbunkerhill-bridge.org.*

★ Museum of Science

COLLEGE | FAMILY | From its perch above the Charles River, the Museum of Science sits half in Cambridge and half in Boston. This unique trait is the first of many at this 70-plus-year-old institution that's focused on science, technology, and hands-on learning. Diverse permanent exhibits explore dinosaurs, the electromagnetic spectrum, modern conservation, math, motion, nanotechnology, the natural world, space travel, and more. The Theater of Electricity hosts explosive daily lightening shows. Add-ons to admission include: the live Butterfly Garden; the multisensory 4-D Theater; Thrill Ride 360 dynamic simulator; and the Charles Hayden Planetarium. The Mugar Omni Theater with IMAX programming reopened in spring 2020 after a complete renovation. ⊠ *Science Park, West End* ☎ *617/723–2500* ⊕ *www.mos.org* ⊡ *$29* Ⓜ *Science Park.*

Duck Boats 👁

Have you noticed the unusual looking, boatlike vehicles touring around Boston's streets? While carrying more than half a million people every year, these **Boston Duck Tours** (☎ *617/267–3825* ⊕ *www.bostonducktours.com*) are amphibious journeys that venture into the Greenway and the Back Bay, Downtown and the West End to explore the city's many points of interest before coasting into the Charles River. You might even get to captain for awhile; 80-minute tours ($46) depart from the Prudential Center, Museum of Science, and, seasonally, New England Aquarium.

Otis House (1796)

HISTORIC SITE | The stately Federal-style manor on Cambridge Street was designed by Charles Bulfinch for former Boston mayor and lawyer Harrison Gray Otis. Today, it serves as the headquarters for Historic New England, and visitors can stop in for guided tours that offer insight into wealthy domestic life during the early 1800s. ⊠ *141 Cambridge St., West End* ☎ *617/994–5920* ⊡ *$15* ⊙ *Closed Mon. and Tues. and Dec.–Mar.* Ⓜ *Charles/MGH, Bowdoin.*

Paul S. Russell, MD Museum of Medical History and Innovation

LOCAL INTEREST | The campus of Mass General Hospital is a fitting site for this small museum dedicated to the hallowed medical institution's past, present, and future discoveries. Shiny copper and glass walls enfold interesting exhibits on topics like patient care, fMRI development, depression and dementia, and targeted cancer therapy. Interactive displays ask visitors to try out mirror therapy and train for laproscopic surgery like a doctor would. Historical artifacts—some quite terrifying—are peppered around

3

Beacon Hill, Boston Common, and the West End   THE WEST END

Hunt for Hidden History

When you hear the moniker "Massachusetts General Hospital" visions of doctors, patients, surgeries, sickness, and treatment likely come to mind. But did you know that the Commonwealth's hallowed medical institution has plenty of historic points of interest for healthy folk? Try an informal scavenger hunt across the hospital's campus to find them.

Sights include a **poster exhibit** in the Yawkey Building, video and photography about **proton therapy** at the

Burr Proton Therapy Center, **1830 and 1980 models of the MGH campus** at the Warren Building, and a real **horse-drawn ambulance** at the Thier Building.

Mass General's historic Bulfinch Building—incidentally, named for the famous Boston architect who designed it—houses both a gallery of historical MGH photographs and the **Ether Dome**, site of the first successful public demonstration of surgical anesthesia.

the space for an eye-opening lesson in our forefathers' medical techniques. A few temporary exhibits and films rotate in and out. ⊠ *2 N. Grove St., West End* ☎ *617/724–8009* ⊕ *www.massgeneral. org/museum* ⊗ *Closed Sun. and Nov–Mar., Sat.* Ⓜ *Charles/MGH.*

The Sports Museum

MUSEUM | FAMILY | The fifth and sixth levels of the TD Garden house The Sports Museum, where displays of memorabilia and photographs showcase New England–based amateur and pro sports history and legends. Test your sports knowledge with interactive games, see how you stand up to life-size statues of heroes Carl Yastrzemski and Larry Bird, and take an hour-long tour of the museum. ⊠ *100 Legends Way, West End* ⊹ *Use TD Garden's The Hub on Causeway grand entrance for access* ☎ *617/624–1234* ⊕ *www.sportsmuseum. org* 🎟 *$15* ⊗ *Closed during games and TD Garden events* Ⓜ *North Station.*

TD Garden

SPORTS VENUE | FAMILY | This mammoth, modern facility opened in 1995 to the chagrin of diehard local sports fans who occasionally still grieve the crusty, old

Boston Garden. Today, the home arena of the Boston Celtics (basketball) and Boston Bruins (hockey) seats nearly 20,000 patrons and also hosts headlining musical acts, Disney on Ice, wrestling events, and Boston's iconic Beanpot tourney. TD Garden Arena Tours depart from the ProShop daily during summer only; get tickets ($15) at ProShop. ⊠ *100 Legends Way, West End* ⊹ *Use The Hub on Causeway grand entrance for access to TD Garden* ☎ *617/624–1050* ⊕ *www. tdgarden.com* ⊗ *Closed during events.* Ⓜ *North Station.*

🍴 Restaurants

A&B Burgers

$ | AMERICAN | FAMILY | Burgers, of course, are the staple of the menu here, featuring all-natural, farm-raised beef (or all-natural, farm-raised Wagyu, if you're feeling fancy); there are also renditions made with lamb, turkey, salmon, and veggies. If burgers aren't your thing, the menu at this light and airy modern spot does feature a few other options. **Known for:** top-quality, tasty burgers; hot spot before Bruins and Celtics games; expensive prices. 💲 *Average main: $16* ⊠ *115*

Beverly St., West End ☎ 857/449–2251 ⊕ *anbburgers.com* Ⓜ *North Station.*

Alcove

$$$ | **CONTEMPORARY** | A mix of New England seafood dishes, European-style charcuterie, and an international flair to most everything else describes what you'll see on the menu at this West End restaurant with a view; you're meant to share plates with your guests, but you can also order solo if that's your preference. Meals here are comfortable with coastal vibes and spectacular views of the Zakim Bridge. **Known for:** sharing plates; fantastic, small producer wine program, with hands-on customer approach; fantastic views. $ *Average main: $28* ⊠ *50 Lovejoy Wharf, West End* ☎ *617/248–0050* ⊕ *www.alcoveboston. com* Ⓜ *North Station.*

★ Scampo

$$$$ | **ITALIAN** | The Italian word "scampo" translates to "escape" in English, and that's what this restaurant at the Liberty Hotel—the former site of the Charles Street Jail—is: an escape into chef-owner Lydia Shire's delectable, buttery take on Italian-American cuisine. Everything is made from scratch, down to the bread and cheese options, and including a dozen different exceptional pastas and nearly as many crusty pizzas. **Known for:** the house-made-mozzarella bar feature at least a half-dozen creamy options; Tandoori-oven cooked, crusty pizzas (the lamb is a classic) and breads; one hearty Sunday supper special, served weekly, like at Nonna's house. $ *Average main: $41* ⊠ *The Liberty Hotel, 215 Charles St., West End* ☎ *617/536–2100* ⊕ *www. scampoboston.com* Ⓜ *Charles/MGH.*

☕ Coffee and Quick Bites

Night Shift Brewing Tap Room

$ | **AMERICAN** | **FAMILY** | This place is hard to classify, and satisfies a variety of different needs, although beer is at the forefront. There's a small breakfast menu of sandwiches and pastries to go with great coffee options using Night Shift's own signature roasted beans, and the lunch and dinner menu has items made from scratch like salads, sandwiches, flatbreads, and main dishes, about half of which have beer as an ingredient in some way. **Known for:** brews its own beers; roasts its own coffee beans; tasty food. $ *Average main: $17* ⊠ *1 Lovejoy Wharf, West End* ☎ *617/294–4233* ⊕ *www.nightshiftbrewing.com* Ⓜ *North Station.*

Hotels

Boxer Boston Hotel

$$ | **HOTEL** | This lovely boutique hotel in one of Boston's only flatiron buildings and it features a freshly renovated, crisp, contemporary look. **Pros:** premium alcohol in minibar; Peloton machines in fitness center; newly renovated. **Cons:** small rooms; far from Back Bay shopping; area can be rowdy at night by the TD Garden. $ *Rooms from: $220* ⊠ *107 Merrimac St., West End* ☎ *617/624–0202* ⊕ *www. theboxerboston.com* ⤳ *80 rooms* ❤️ *No meals* Ⓜ *North Station.*

citizenM Hotel

$$ | **HOTEL** | At present, Boston's citizenM hotel is only the third of its kind in the United States (and the first outside of New York City); it's a brand that keeps the jet-setting traveler in mind, but not necessarily one who is overly wealthy, just one who appreciates the finer things in life. **Pros:** free Wi-Fi; attached to North Station; open kitchen filled with snacks and drinks, 24/7. **Cons:** small rooms; if traveling with more than two people (including children), must book additional rooms; no pets. $ *Rooms from: $200* ⊠ *70 Causeway St., West End* ☎ *617/861–4360* ⊕ *www. citizenm.com* ⤳ *272 rooms* ❤️ *No meals* Ⓜ *North Station.*

Kimpton Onyx Hotel

$$ | HOTEL | A sexy, supper-club atmosphere oozes from this contemporary Kimpton Group hotel, located a block from North Station. **Pros:** good location for catching a sporting event or concert at the Garden; near North Station commuter rail and T stop; near several inexpensive restaurants and bars. **Cons:** smallish rooms and bathrooms; small gym; neighborhood can get noisy at night. [$] *Rooms from: $300* ✉ *155 Portland St., West End* ☎ *617/557–9955, 866/660–6699* 🌐 *www.onyxhotel.com* 🛏 *112 rooms* 🍴 *No meals* [M] *North Station.*

★ Liberty Hotel Boston

$$$ | HOTEL | Since it opened in late 2007, the buzz surrounding the chic Liberty—formerly Boston's Charles Street Jail—was at first deafening, with bankers, tech geeks, foreign playboys, and fashionistas all scrambling to call it their own; more than a decade later, the Liberty has evolved into what is part retreat, part nightclub. **Pros:** Lydia Shire's popular restaurant Scampo; exclusive daily events including art exhibits, live music, and yoga sessions; proximity to the Esplanade and Beacon Hill. **Cons:** loud in-house nightlife; long waits at bars and restaurants; parking is expensive. [$] *Rooms from: $350* ✉ *215 Charles St., West End* ☎ *617/224–4000* 🌐 *www.libertyhotel.com* 🛏 *298 rooms* 🍴 *No meals* [M] *Charles/MGH.*

🍸 Nightlife

The Fours

BARS/PUBS | Sports fans/historians must visit this popular gathering place for imbibers—appropriately located near the TD Garden—and appreciate the authentic sports memoribilia tacked all over the walls. Food is casual but excellent, and the buffalo chicken nachos are a favorite of regulars. ✉ *166 Canal St., West End* ☎ *617/720–4455* 🌐 *www.thefours.com* [M] *North Station.*

McGann's Irish Pub

BARS/PUBS | FAMILY | With its bright red and light blue facade, polished wooden tabletops, and stools, McGann's feels like a bar right out of Ireland. Food is what you might find in an Irish pub—sandwiches, fish and chips, stews, and curries—but there are also burgers. The huge beer list is a mix of usual suspects, as well as some local craft and imports. The vibe is casual, and the place can get busy on game days. For rugby and football (not the American kind) fans, the bar shows all the matches, and favors Manchester United. ✉ *197 Portland St., West End* ☎ *617/227–4059* 🌐 *www.mcgannsirishpub.com* [M] *North Station.*

Chapter 4

GOVERNMENT CENTER AND THE NORTH END

4

Updated by
Cheryl Fenton

👁 Sights	🍴 Restaurants	🛏 Hotels	🛍 Shopping	🍸 Nightlife
★★★★☆	★★★★★	★★★☆☆	★★★★☆	★★★★★

NEIGHBORHOOD SNAPSHOT

TOP EXPERIENCES

■ **Shop 'til you drop:** Visit the countless shops and kiosks of Quincy Marketplace, the country's oldest pushcart market.

■ **Take a history lesson:** Imagine the debates of old during a tour of historic Faneuil Hall.

■ **Smell the roses:** Stroll the Rose Kennedy garden dedicated to the matriarch of the beloved local family.

■ **Ride a sea turtle:** The hand-carved characters on the Greenway Carousel are inspired by realistic and mythical air, sea, and land animals.

■ **Come hungry, leave happy:** Visit the North End, Boston's take on Little Italy.

GETTING HERE

While Government Center is best explored on foot, nearby Green Line stops include Park Street and Haymarket. On the Blue Line, the nearest stations are State and Bowdoin. All of these stations are within a five-minute walk of Government Center Station. The T is your best bet for accessing the North End. Get off the Orange Line at Haymarket and walk southeast to Hanover Street; take a left there to enter the North End. Alternatively, exit the Blue Line at Aquarium and walk northeast on Atlantic Avenue, past Christopher Columbus Park, to access the North End.

PLANNING YOUR TIME

Plan to spend several hours hitting the eateries, boutiques, and historic sites of the Faneuil Hall and Quincy Market complex. On Friday and Saturday join crowds at Haymarket farmers' market; wear good walking shoes, as the cobblestones get slippery with trampled produce.

Allow two hours for a walk through the North End, longer if you plan on stopping in a café. This part of town is made for strolling, day or night. Many people like to spend part of a day at Quincy Market, then head over to the North End for dinner.

QUICK BITES

■ **Mike's Pastry.** Expect crowds at this bustling North End café for cappuccino and worth-the-wait cannoli. ⊠ *300 Hanover St., North End* ⊕ *www.mikespastry.com.*

■ **Quincy Market.** Filled with stalls of every imaginable food—lobster rolls to Indian to ice cream—grab your grub and enjoy it outside on the benches between the North and South markets. ⊠ *Bordered by Clinton, Commercial, and Chatham Sts., Government Center* ⊕ *www.quincy-market.com* Ⓜ *Government Center, Aquarium, State.*

■ **Saus.** Grab a Frik (their specialty sausage) and choose from 15 homemade sauces to douse it with. ⊠ *33 Union St.* ⊕ *www.sausboston.com* Ⓜ *Government Center, State.*

FREEDOM TRAIL SIGHTS

■ The Freedom Trail snakes through the city; within Government Center and North End you'll find the Boston Massacre Site, Copp's Hill Burying Ground, Faneuil Hall, Old North Church, Old State House, Paul Revere House.

This is a section of town Bostonians love to hate. While it's not Boston's prettiest locale (it's home to some of the city's bleakest architecture), it does have plenty of feathers in its tricorn cap, including City Hall Plaza (the site of feisty political rallies, summer concerts, and festivals), the country's oldest pushcart market (cobble-stoned Quincy Market), and the site where speeches were held encouraging independence from Great Britain (18th-century Faneuil Hall).

Just a short stroll across the Rose Kennedy Greenway sits the North End, Boston's proud Italian community and oldest neighborhood. It can be summed up in one word—*mangia*. This is where you find a good meal, along with a little city history including Paul Revere's House.

Government Center

The curving six-story Center Plaza building, across from the newly redone glass entrance of the Government Center T stop and the broad brick desert of City Hall Plaza, echoes the much older Sears Crescent, a curved commercial block next to the Government Center T stop. The Center Plaza building separates Tremont Street from Pemberton Square and the old and "new" courthouses to the west.

The warren of small streets on the northeast side of Government Center is the North End. For visitors, Government Center is usually just a way station to get to Faneuil Hall, Quincy Market, and other downtown attractions, unless there happens to be a festival scheduled. Come during the annual Jimmy Fund Scooper Bowl ice cream event in June or during the city's July 4 festival, and you'll find bleak City Hall Plaza a bustling, jubilant spot.

◉ Sights

Blackstone Block
NEIGHBORHOOD | Between North and Hanover streets, near the Haymarket, lies the Blackstone Block, now visited mostly for its culinary landmark the **Union Oyster House.** Named for one of Boston's first settlers, William Blaxton, or Blackstone, it's the city's oldest commercial block, for decades dominated by the butcher

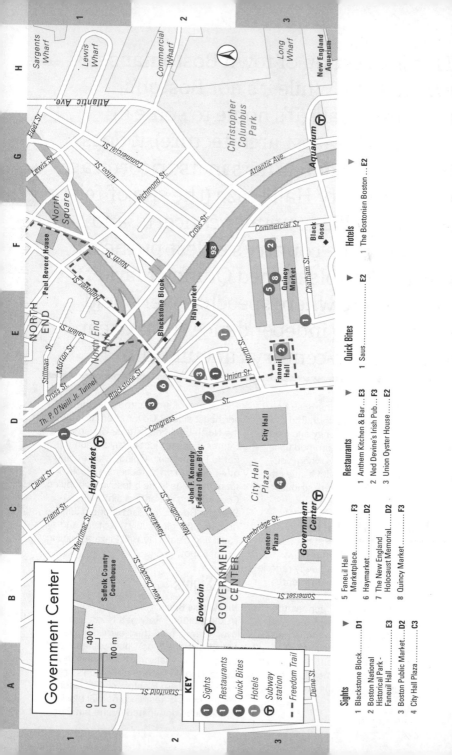

Government Center

KEY

- 1 Sights
- 1 Restaurants
- 1 Quick Bites
- 1 Hotels
- ⊖ Subway station
- --- Freedom Trail

0 ___ 400 ft
0 ___ 100 m

Sights ▶

1 Blackstone Block **D1**
2 Boston National Historical Park - Faneuil Hall **E3**
3 Boston Public Market... **D2**
4 City Hall Plaza **C3**
5 Faneuil Hall Marketplace **F3**
6 Haymarket **D2**
7 The New England Holocaust Memorial...... **D2**
8 Quincy Market **F3**

Restaurants ▶

1 Anthem Kitchen & Bar... **E3**
2 Ned Devine's Irish Pub... **F3**
3 Union Oyster House **E2**

Quick Bites ▶

1 Saus................. **E2**

Hotels ▶

1 The Bostonian Boston ... **E2**

trade. As a tiny remnant of Old Boston, the Blackstone Block remains the city's "family attic"—to use the winning metaphor of critic Donlyn Lyndon: more than three centuries of architecture are on view, ranging from the 18th-century Capen House to the modern Bostonian Hotel. A colonial-period warren of winding lanes surrounds the block.

Facing the Blackstone Block, in tiny **Union Park,** framed by Congress Street and Dock Square, are two bronze figures, one seated on a bench and the other standing eye-to-eye with passersby. Both represent James Michael Curley, the quintessential Boston pol and a questionable role model for urban bosses. It's just as well that he has no pedestal. Also known as "the Rascal King" or "the Mayor of the Poor," and dramatized by Spencer Tracy in *The Last Hurrah* (1958), the charismatic Curley was beloved by the city's dominant working-class Irish for bringing them libraries, hospitals, bathhouses, and other public-works projects. His career got off to a promising start in 1903, when he ran—and won—a campaign for alderman from the Charles Street Jail, where he was serving time for taking someone else's civil-service exam.

Over the next 50 years he dominated Boston politics, serving four nonconsecutive terms as mayor, one term as governor, and four terms as congressman. No one seemed to mind the slight glitch created when his office moved, in 1946, to the federal penitentiary, where he served five months of a 6- to 18-month sentence for mail fraud: he was pardoned by President Truman and returned to his people a hero. ⊠ *Blackstone St., Government Center* Ⓜ *Haymarket.*

Boston National Historical Park–Faneuil Hall

INFO CENTER | FAMILY | A 7,400-square-foot NPS visitor center at Faneuil Hall features history exhibits, a film-screening area, and a bookstore. It's the starting point for NPS rangers' two different 60-minute Freedom Trail tours and other talks; there's a sister site at Charlestown's Navy Yard. It's open daily from 9 to 6. There's also the Boston African American historic site on Beacon Hill, home to guided tours of the Black Heritage Trail, and the Boston Harbor Islands national recreation area, with trails, forts, wildlife, and camping on 34 islands. ⊠ *Faneuil Hall Visitor Center, Government Center* ☎ *617/242–5642* ⊕ *www.nps.gov/bost.*

Boston Public Market

MARKET | FAMILY | Open year-round, the indoor Boston Public Market offers a great place to grab a sandwich, sample local foods, and even pick up a souvenir. The New England–centric marketplace has more than three-dozen vendors, selling everything from fresh herbs and fruit to meat and seafood. Everything sold at the market is produced or originates in New England. There's also a food demonstration kitchen, where visitors might be able to catch a live cooking class (with samples). The Kids' Nook is a designated area to gather and play, and there are kids activities during the week. ⊠ *100 Hanover St., Government Center* ☎ *617/973–4909* ⊕ *www.bostonpublic-market.org* Ⓜ *Haymarket.*

City Hall Plaza

GOVERNMENT BUILDING | Over the years, various plans—involving gardens, restaurants, music, and hotels—have been floated to make this a more people-friendly site. Possibly the only thing that would ameliorate Bostonians' collective distaste for the chilly Government Center is tearing it down. City Hall itself is an upside-down ziggurat design on a brutalist redbrick plaza. The design, by Kallman, McKinnell, and Knowles, confines administrative functions to the upper floors and places offices that deal with the public at street level. As one of the largest civil spaces in Boston, City Hall Plaza plays host to festivals and outdoor concerts. ⊠ *1 City Hall Sq., Government Center* Ⓜ *Government Center.*

In 1772 Samuel Adams stood on the steps of Faneuil Hall and stoked the fires of revolution; today it's the center of Boston's main marketplace.

★ Faneuil Hall Marketplace

HISTORIC SITE | FAMILY | Faneuil Hall has always sat in the middle of Boston's main marketplace and, to be clear, the single building facing Congress Street is the real Faneuil Hall, though locals often give that name to all five buildings in this shopping complex. Bostonians pronounce it *Fan*-yoo'uhl or *Fan*-yuhl. It was erected in 1742, the gift of wealthy merchant Peter Faneuil, who wanted the hall to serve as both a place for town meetings and a public market. It burned in 1761 and was immediately reconstructed according to the original plan of its designer, the Scottish portrait painter John Smibert (who lies in the Granary Burying Ground). In 1763 the political leader James Otis helped inaugurate the era that culminated in American independence when he dedicated the rebuilt hall to the cause of liberty.

In 1772 Samuel Adams stood here and first suggested that Massachusetts and the other colonies organize a Committee of Correspondence to maintain semiclandestine lines of communication in the face of hardening British repression. In later years the hall again lived up to Otis's dedication when the abolitionists Wendell Phillips and Charles Sumner pleaded for support from its podium. The tradition continues to this day: in presidential-election years the hall is the site of debates between contenders in the Massachusetts primary.

Faneuil Hall was substantially enlarged and remodeled in 1805 according to a Greek Revival design of the noted architect Charles Bulfinch; this is the building you see today. Its purposes remain the same: the balconied Great Hall is available to citizens' groups on presentation of a request signed by a required number of responsible parties; it also plays host to regular concerts.

Inside Faneuil Hall are dozens of paintings of famous Americans, including the mural *Webster's Reply to Hayne* and Gilbert Stuart's portrait of Washington at Dorchester Heights. Park rangers give informational talks about the history and importance of Faneuil Hall every half hour. There are interactive displays about Boston sights and National Park Service rangers at the visitor center on the first floor can provide maps and other information.

On the building's top floors are the headquarters and museum and library of the **Ancient & Honorable Artillery Company of Massachusetts,** which is free to visit (but a $3 donation is welcome). Founded in 1638, it's the oldest militia in the Western Hemisphere, and the third oldest in the world, after the Swiss Guard and the Honorable Artillery Company of London. The museum is open weekdays 9 am to 3:30 pm.

When such men as Andrew Jackson and Daniel Webster debated the future of the Republic here, the fragrances of bacon and snuff—sold by merchants in **Quincy Market** across the road—greeted their noses. Today the aroma of coffee wafts through the hall from a snack bar. The shops at ground level sell New England bric-a-brac. ⊠ *Faneuil Hall Sq., Government Center* ☎ *617/523–1300* ⊕ *www.nps.gov/bost/learn/history-culture/fh.htm* 🎫 *Free* Ⓜ *Government Center, Aquarium, State.*

Haymarket

MARKET | Loud, self-promoting vendors pack this exuberant maze of a marketplace at Marshall and Blackstone Streets on Friday and Saturday from dawn to dusk (most vendors are usually gone by 5). As they have since 1829, pushcart vendors hawk fruits and vegetables against a backdrop of fish, meat, and cheese shops. The accumulation of debris left every evening has been celebrated in a whimsical 1976 public-arts project—Mags Harries's *Asaroton,* a Greek word meaning "unswept floors"— consisting of bronze fruit peels and other detritus smashed into pavement. Another Harries piece, a bronze depiction of a gathering of stray gloves, tumbles down between the escalators in the Porter Square T station in Cambridge. At Creek Square, near the Haymarket, is the

Boston Stone. Set into a brick wall, this was allegedly a marker used as milepost zero in measuring distances from Boston. ⊠ *Blackstone St., between Hanover St. and North St., Government Center* ⊕ *www.haymarketboston.org* ⊗ *Closed Sun.–Thurs.* Ⓜ *Government Center.*

The New England Holocaust Memorial

MEMORIAL | Located at the north end of Union Park, the Holocaust Memorial is the work of Stanley Saitowitz, whose design was selected through an international competition; the finished memorial was dedicated in 1995. During the day the six 50-foot-high glass-and-steel towers seem at odds with the 18th-century streetscape of Blackstone Square behind it; at night, they glow like ghosts while manufactured steam from grates in the granite base makes for a particularly haunting scene. Recollections by Holocaust survivors are set into the glass-and-granite walls; the upper levels of the towers are etched with 6 million numbers in random sequence, symbolizing the Jewish victims of the Nazi horror. ⊠ *Union St. near Hanover St., Government Center* ☎ *617/457–8755* ⊕ *www.nohm.org* Ⓜ *Haymarket, Government Center, State.*

★ Quincy Market

MARKET | FAMILY | Quincy Market, also known as Faneuil Hall Marketplace, is not everyone's cup of tea; some people prefer grit to polish, and disdain the shiny cafés and boutiques. But there's no denying that this pioneer effort at urban recycling set the tone for many similar projects throughout the country, and that it has brought tremendous vitality to a once-tired corner of Boston. Quincy Market attracts huge crowds of tourists and locals throughout the year. In the early '70s, demolition was a distinct possibility for the decrepit buildings. Fortunately, with the participation of the Boston Redevelopment Authority, architect Benjamin Thompson planned a renovation of Quincy Market,

The haunting New England Holocaust Memorial sits at the north end of Union Park; at night, the six 50-foot-high glass-and-steel towers glow.

and the Rouse Corporation of Baltimore undertook its restoration, which was completed in 1976. Try to look beyond the shop windows to the grand design of the market buildings themselves; they represent a vision of the market as urban centerpiece, an idea whose time has certainly come again.

The market consists of three block-long annexes: **Quincy Market, North Market,** and **South Market,** each 535 feet long and across a plaza from Faneuil Hall. The structures were designed in 1826 by Alexander Parris as part of a public-works project instituted by Boston's second mayor, Josiah Quincy, to alleviate the cramped conditions of Faneuil Hall and clean up the refuse that collected in Town Dock, the pond behind it. The central structure, made of granite, with a Doric colonnade at either end and topped by a classical dome and rotunda, has kept its traditional market-stall layout, but the stalls now purvey international and specialty foods: sushi, frozen yogurt, bagels, calzones, sausage-on-a-stick, Chinese

noodles, barbecue, and baklava, plus all the boutique chocolate-chip cookies your heart desires. ■TIP➔ **In between Quincy Market and South Market colonnades, be sure to stop and take a seat next to the sculpture of legendary Boston Celtics coach, Red Auerbach, smoking one of his famous stogies.**

Along the arcades on either side of the Central Market are vendors selling sweatshirts, photographs of Boston, and arts and crafts—some schlocky, some not—alongside a couple of patioed bars and restaurants, including the new Sam Adams Brewery (perfectly poised within sight of his famous statue). The North and South markets house a mixture of chain stores and specialty boutiques.

Faneuil Hall provides a splash of color; during the winter holidays, trees along the cobblestone walks are strung with thousands of sparkling lights and Blink! brings holiday music to the large Christmas tree. In summer up to 50,000 people a day descend on the market; the outdoor cafés are an excellent spot to watch the hordes if you can find a seat. Year-round the pedestrian walkways draw street performers, and rings of strollers form around magicians and musicians. ✉ *Bordered by Clinton, Commercial, and Chatham Sts., Government Center* ☎ *617/523–1300* 🌐 *www.quincy-market.com* [M] *Government Center, Aquarium, State.*

🍴 Restaurants

Government Center is home to touristy Faneuil Hall Marketplace and Quincy Market, both packed with grab-and-go concessions as well as some more serious sit-down alternatives.

Anthem Kitchen & Bar

$$$ | AMERICAN | FAMILY | With its tavern vibe and prime location (just steps from historic Faneuil Hall in the South Market Building), a meal at Anthem conjures up visions of patriots dining on traditional New England fare. Day-time appetites are satisfied with lobster mac n' cheese, Cape Cod fish reubens, wood-fired pizzas, and stacked burgers, while dinner gets serious by serving up plates of short rib gnocchi, New England lobster rolls, and Boston baked haddock. **Known for:** views of historic Faneuil Hall; New England fare; New England Clam Chowder. [$] *Average main: $26* ✉ *101 S. Market St., South Market Bldg., Government Center* ☎ *617/720–5570* 🌐 *www.anthem-boston.com* [M] *Government Center.*

Ned Devine's Irish Pub

$$ | IRISH | A trifecta of Celtic celebration, this Quincy Market hotspot is part Irish pub, part lounge, and part live music hall. A destination for tourists and townies, the menu is mix of classic Irish dishes like chicken curry, warm Jameson bread pudding, and beef stew, alongside New England favorites such as chowder fries, Samuel Adams chicken tenders, and clam chowder. **Known for:** Irish eats; live music; great location. [$] *Average main: $23* ✉ *1 Fanueil Hall Marketplace, Government Center* ☎ *617/248–8800* 🌐 *www.neddevinesboston.com* [M] *Government Center, Aquarium.*

Union Oyster House

$$$ | SEAFOOD | Opening its door in 1826 and earning a place on the National Historic Landmark list, Union Oyster House is Boston's oldest restaurant. Dine like Daniel Webster (alongside his nightly hangover-heavy tumbler of brandy and water) and order oysters on the half shell at the ground-floor raw bar in the oldest part of the restaurant. **Known for:** oldest Boston restaurant; long waits on weekends; oysters. [$] *Average main: $28* ✉ *41 Union St., Government Center* ☎ *617/227–2750* 🌐 *www.unionoysterhouse.com* [M] *Haymarket.*

☕ Coffee and Quick Bites

Saus

$ | CAFÉ | With 15 unique sauces on the menu, including homemade hot beer mustard, truffle ketchup, cheddar ale, smoky chipotle mayo, and gravy, Saus believes in the power of the condiment, which accompany its made-from-scratch sandwiches. The hand-cut fries are house-aged and twice fried, and they're known for their Friks, hand-rolled beef and pork sausages. **Known for:** Frik sausages; large variety of dipping sauces; tiny space. [$] *Average main: $9* ✉ *33 Union St., Government Center* 🌐 *www.sausboston.com* [M] *Government Center.*

🛏 Hotels

The Bostonian Boston

$$$ | HOTEL | FAMILY | Near historic Faneuil Hall, the Bostonian has guest rooms featuring Frette linens, pillowtop mattresses, and 40-inch TVs—many also have French doors with step out balconies showcasing city views and the popular North End. Warmed up with red wall coverings, the lobby provides sofas and arm chairs, perfect for relaxing with a book chosen from one of the floor-to-ceiling bookshelves. **Pros:** updated fitness center; great location for sightseeing; free Wi-Fi. **Cons:** some rooms get street noise; Faneuil Hall can get clogged with tourists; parking is expensive. $ *Rooms from: $309* ✉ *Faneuil Hall Marketplace, 26 North St., Downtown* ☎ *617/523–3600, 866/866–8086* ⊕ *www.millennium-hotels.com* ⇌ *201 rooms* ⦿ *No meals* Ⓜ *Haymarket, Aquarium.*

Ⓨ Nightlife

The seat of Boston's city hall and financial center, the Center hosts concerts and circuses on its plaza, shelters popular food trucks serving sidewalk gourmet grub, and overlooks those historic brick beehives of activity, Old State House and Faneuil Hall, and the haunting, transparent New England Holocaust Memorial. The Rose F. Kennedy Greenway, a mile-long parkland built over the depressed central artery, links the North End to Chinatown with gardens and trees, and parallels the hotel-rich stretch of the Harborwalk.

BARS

Bell in Hand Tavern

BARS/PUBS | America's oldest continuously operating pub (founded 1795) is named after its original owner, town crier Jimmy Wilson, whose bell-ringing wooden sign still hangs on the wall. On the edge of the Freedom Trail, this glassed-in flatiron pub serves fried haddock sandwiches, burgers, and New England's favorite entrées, against a background of live music. Bands play each night downstairs, and DJs spin Top 40 for dancers Thursday through Saturday upstairs; there's karaoke every Tuesday. ■**TIP**→ **Expect long lines of twentysomethings on the weekends.** ✉ *45–55 Union St., Government Center* ☎ *617/227–2098* ⊕ *www.bellinhand.com* Ⓜ *Haymarket.*

Black Rose

BARS/PUBS | Hung with 20 bright county banners, decorated with pictures of Ireland and portraits of Samuel Beckett, Lady Gregory, and James Joyce, the Rose draws as many tourists as Irish-loving locals. Friendly Irish bartenders serve up pints, blarney, and far more Irish whiskies (42) than Scotches (14). Nightly shows by traditional Irish and contemporary musicians confirm its abiding Gaelic good cheer, or *craic*. Dine on Guinness beef stew and fish n' chips—all served by staffers with authentic brogues. ✉ *160 State St., Government Center* ☎ *617/742–2286* ⊕ *www.blackroseboston.com* Ⓜ *Aquarium, State.*

Green Dragon Tavern

BARS/PUBS | Less rowdy than its Faneuil Hall neighbors, this now-Irish bar claims to have housed the "Headquarters of the Revolution" and was the inn where silversmith Paul Revere overheard plans for a British assault on Lexington and Concord, prompting his famous ride. While yesteryear found John Hancock (whose brother lived next door) strolling past its doors, today the Green Dragon is known for a great Guinness pour and Irish music—soloists play in the evenings from 5 to 9 Wednesday through Friday, and bands bring it on nightly beginning at 9. There's comedy night every Monday and a selection of Top 40's cover bands playing Tuesday through Sunday. ■**TIP**→ **College kids and young professionals tend to crowd the bar in the evenings.** ✉ *11 Marshall St., Government Center* ☎ *617/367–0055* ⊕ *www.somerspubs.com* Ⓜ *Haymarket, Government Center.*

Hennessy's

BARS/PUBS | Grab a seat by the windows overlooking Faneuil Hall on hot summer days, or cozy up to a coal fireplace in winter, and enjoy your pint (or a pick from one of the largest selections of single malt whiskies in Boston). There's lots of ive music in Hennessy's seven nights a week, as well as plenty of rowdy crowds that overrun the yellow-and-black confines for Top 40 cover bands mixed with DJs on weekends from 9 pm to 1 am at Upstairs at Hennessy's. ⊠ *25 Union St., Government Center* ☏ *617/742–2121* ⊕ *www.somerspubs.com* Ⓜ *Haymarket, Government Center.*

Sam Adams Tap Room

BREWPUBS/BEER GARDENS | Aptly overlooking its namesake's statue, the 15,000-square-feet Samuel Adams Tap Room boasts three floors, including a rooftop outdoor deck with views over Faneuil Hall. Drink like a local, by choosing a flight of innovative styles and rotating experimental beers from the nano-brewery as well as fan favorites such as Boston Lager and seasonal brews like Summer Ale. Wednesdays' #CheesyHour serves up samples of artisan cheese paired with a flight of four R&D beers. And on Thursday, they have newly introduced drafts to try. ⊠ *60 State St., Government Center* ☏ *617/466–6418* ⊕ *samueladams.com* Ⓜ *State Street, Government Center.*

MUSIC CLUBS

Hard Rock Cafe

MUSIC CLUBS | This famed global chain draws rock music and memorabilia fans to its large space with a double bar—decorated with hundreds of Zildjian cymbals—dance floor, bandstand, restaurant (wall art of signed photos, LPs, guitars, and gear), and private party room. The Cavern Club welcomes name (think Psychedelic Furs and Charlie Puth) or tribute bands (Doors, Aerosmith, and Pixies) occasionally on weekends for ticketed entry, while the Rock Shop sells iconic and collectible merchandise. Fuel up on their legendary burgers. ⊠ *22–24 Clinton St., Government Center* ☏ *617/424–7625* ⊕ *www.hardrock.com/location/boston* Ⓜ *Haymarket, Government Center.*

🛍 Shopping

The heart of Government Center is the Shops at Faneuil Hall Marketplace, where approximately 18 million people come each year to stroll through the pushcarts, farm stands, and kiosk shops since 1742. There are also plenty of indoor storefronts along the promenades on either side of the marketplace.

FOOD

★ Boston Public Market

FOOD/CANDY | Open year-round, the indoor Boston Public Market offers a great place to grab a sandwich, sample local foods, and even pick up a tasty souvenir. The New England–centric marketplace has more than three-dozen vendors, selling everything from fresh herbs and fruit to meat and seafood, as well as plenty of food stalls. Everything sold at the market is produced or originated in New England including nonperishables like wool and carved wooden bowls. There's also a food demonstration kitchen, where visitors might be able to catch a live cooking class (with samples). Since it's all about staying with the season, the exciting about visiting the BPM is that no two days are the same. The Kids' Nook is a designated area for kids to gather and play, with activities throughout the week. ⊠ *100 Hanover St., Government Center* ⊕ *bostonpublicmarket.org* Ⓜ *Haymarket/ Government Center.*

SHOPPING CENTERS

Faneuil Hall Marketplace

SHOPPING NEIGHBORHOODS | This complex is both huge and hugely popular (drawing 18 million people a year), but not necessarily unique—most of its independent shops have given way to Banana Republic, Uniqlo, Urban Outfitters, and other chains. Founded in 1742 as a market for crops and livestock, the place has plenty of history and offers one of the area's great à la carte casual dining experiences (Quincy Market). Pushcarts sell everything from apparel to jewelry to candy to Boston souvenirs. Live bands set up gigs throughout the weekend days, while buskers perform crowd-pleasing feats such as break dancing and juggling routines. Have your dollar bills ready for when the hat gets passed around. ⊠ *Bounded by Congress St., Atlantic Ave., the Waterfront, and Government Center, Government Center* ☎ *617/523–1300* ⊕ *www.faneuilhallmarketplace.com* Ⓜ *Government Center.*

The North End

On the northeast side of Government Center is the North End, Boston's Little Italy. In the 17th century the North End *was* Boston, as much of the rest of the peninsula was still under water or had yet to be cleared. Here the town bustled and grew rich for a century and a half before the birth of American independence. Now visitors can get a glimpse into Revolutionary times while filling up on some of the most scrumptious pastries and pastas to be found in modern Boston.

Today's North End is almost entirely a creation of the late 19th century, when brick tenements began to fill up with European immigrants—first the Irish, then Central European Jews, then the Portuguese, and finally the Italians. For more than 60 years, the North End attracted an Italian population base, so much so that one wonders whether wandering Puritan shades might scowl at the concentration of Mediterranean verve, volubility, and Roman Catholicism here. This is Boston's haven not only for Italian restaurants but also for Italian groceries, bakeries, boccie courts, churches, social clubs, cafés, and street-corner debates over home-team soccer games. ■TIP➔ **July and August are highlighted by a series of street festivals, or feste, honoring various saints, and by local community events that draw people from all over the city. A statue of St. Agrippina di Mineo—which is covered with money when it's paraded through the streets—is a crowd favorite.**

Though small, only 0.36 square miles, the neighborhood has nearly 100 businesses and a variety of tourist attractions. Although hordes of visitors follow the redbrick ribbon of the Freedom Trail through the North End, the jumbled streets retain a neighborhood feeling, from the grandmothers gossiping on fire escapes to the laundry strung on back porches. Gentrification diluted the quarter's ethnic character some, but linger for a moment along Salem or Hanover street and you can still hear people speaking with Abruzzese accents. If you wish to study up on this fascinating district, head for the North End branch of the Boston Public Library on Parmenter Street, where a bust of Dante acknowledges local cultural pride.

Sights

Christopher Columbus Park (*Waterfront Park*)

CITY PARK | This green space bordering the harbor and several of Boston's restored wharfs is a pleasant oasis of benches and a long arborlike shelter twinkling with colorful strands of lights at night. Lewis Wharf and Commercial Wharf (north of the park), which long lay nearly derelict, had been transformed into condominiums, offices, restaurants, and upscale shops by the mid-1970s. There are sprinklers, lawn games, summer outdoor movie nights, a playground, and even free Wi-Fi. The Rose Kennedy Rose Garden is enclosed by a wrought-iron fence in the center of the park. ⊠ *Atlantic Ave., bordered by Atlantic Ave., Commercial Wharf, and Long Wharf, North End* ☎ *617/635–4505* ⊕ *www.foccp.org* Ⓜ *Aquarium.*

Two Ways to Explore the North End

La Dolce Vita

Known as Boston's Little Italy, the North End has, in addition to an abundance of top-notch Italian eateries, many deliciously authentic Italian bakeries and cafés. Take a stroll down **Hanover Street**, the main thoroughfare, and you'll find all the cannoli and cappuccinos your heart could desire. On this street alone you'll find Caffe Paradiso at 255, Caffe Vittoria at 290, and Caffe dello Sport at 308. Have a seat in any of these to relax, have a small snack, and take in the scene. Hanover Street is almost always crowded on weekend afternoons and nights, so it's an excellent place to people-watch. If you're looking to take a piece of the North End home with you in a little cardboard box tied up with string, visit one of Hanover's excellent bakeries: Modern Pastry Shop at 257, Mike's Pastry at 300, or Bova's Bakery at 134 Salem Street.

Bova's claim to fame is that it is open 24 hours a day, so it is at your service no matter when the craving strikes.

Relive Revolutionary History

Because the North End was Boston at the time of the Revolution, some of the city's most historic buildings reside here. Visit the **Paul Revere House,** the oldest home in Boston, and learn how this legendary patriot made his historic midnight ride to warn of the oncoming British troops. The **Pierce-Hitchborn House** next door was owned by some of Revere's relatives and provides a peek into 18th-century middle-class life. Also in the North End is **Old North Church,** where Paul Revere hung two lanterns to signal that the British troops would depart by sea. Finally, stroll the **Prado,** or Paul Revere Mall, to see the bronze statue that commemorates Revere's famous ride.

Clough House at Old North

HOUSE | FAMILY | Built in 1712, this house (whose name rhymes with "fluff") is now the only local survivor of its era aside from Old North Church, which stands nearby. Picture the streets lined with houses such as this, with an occasional grander Georgian mansion and some modest wooden-frame survivors of old Boston's many fires—this is what the North End looked like when Paul Revere was young. Today, the lower rooms serve as the Old North gift shop and Captain Jackson's Colonial Chocolate Shop, which offers an interactive look into the past. Watch daily hands-on chocolate making demonstration (and get a taste) accompanied by stories of local chocolate merchants. ⊠ 21 Unity St., North End ☎ 617/523–4848 ⊕ www.oldnorth. com/chocolate-exhibit/.

Copp's Hill Burying Ground

CEMETERY | An ancient and melancholy air hovers like a fine mist over this Colonial-era burial ground. The North End graveyard incorporates four cemeteries established between 1660 and 1819. Near the Charter Street gate is the tomb of the Mather family, the dynasty of church divines (Cotton and Increase were the most famous sons) who held sway in Boston during the heyday of the old theocracy. Also buried here is Robert Newman, who crept into the steeple of the Old North Church to hang the lanterns warning of the British attack the night of Paul Revere's ride. Look for the tombstone of Captain Daniel Malcolm; it's pockmarked with musket-ball fire from British soldiers, who used the stones for target practice. Across the street is 44 Hull (Boston's historic

The statue of Paul Revere outside the Old North Church commemorates his famous ride.

Skinny House), the city's **narrowest house,** measuring at just a mere 10 feet wide. ✉ *Intersection of Hull St. and Snowhill Rd., North End* ☎ *617/635–7361* ⊕ *www. cityofboston.gov/parks/hbgi/CoppsHill. asp* Ⓜ *North Station.*

Hanover Street

NEIGHBORHOOD | FAMILY | This is the North End's main thoroughfare, along with the smaller and narrower Salem Street. It was named for the ruling dynasty of 18th- and 19th-century England; the label was retained after the Revolution, despite a flurry of patriotic renaming (King Street became State Street, for example). Hanover's business center is thick with restaurants, pastry shops, and cafés, all celebrating the cuisine of the Old Country and most offering valet parking to combat the lack of parking. Hanover is one of Boston's oldest public roads, once the site of the residences of the Rev. Cotton Mather and the Colonial-era patriot Dr. Joseph Warren, as well as a small dry-goods store run by Eben D. Jordan—who went on to launch the

now defunct Jordan Marsh department stores. ✉ *Between Commercial and Congress Sts., North End* Ⓜ *Haymarket, North Station.*

★ Old North Church

BUILDING | At one end of the **Paul Revere Mall** is a church famous not only for being the oldest standing church building in Boston (built in 1723) but for housing the two lanterns that glimmered from its steeple on the night of April 18, 1775. This is Christ, or Old North, Church, where Paul Revere and the young sexton Robert Newman managed that night to signal the departure by water of the British regulars to Lexington and Concord. Newman, carrying the lanterns, ascended the steeple, while Revere began his clandestine trip by boat across the Charles.

Although William Price designed the structure after studying Christopher Wren's London churches, Old North—which still has an active Episcopal congregation (including descendants of the Reveres)—is an impressive building in its own right. Inside, note the gallery and the graceful arrangement of pews; the bust of George Washington, pronounced by the Marquis de Lafayette to be the truest likeness of the general he ever saw; the brass chandeliers, made in Amsterdam in 1700 and installed here in 1724; and the clock, the oldest still running in an American public building. Try to visit when changes are rung on the bells, after the 11 am Sunday service; they bear the inscription, "We are the first ring of bells cast for the British Empire in North America." The steeple itself is not the original—the tower was destroyed in a hurricane in 1804 and was replaced in 1954. On the Sunday closest to April 18, descendants of the patriots reenact the raising of the lanterns in the church belfry during a special ticketed evening service, which also includes readings of Longfellow's renowned poem, "Paul Revere's Ride" and Revere's first-person account of that fateful night. Visitors are welcome to drop in, but to see the bell-ringing chamber and the crypts, take the 30-minute behind-the-scenes tour.

Behind the church is the **Washington Memorial Garden,** where volunteers cultivate a plot devoted to plants and flowers favored in the 18th century. ✉ *193 Salem St., North End* ☎ *617/858–8231* ⊕ *www. oldnorth.com* ✉ *$3 suggested donation; $6 behind-the-scenes tour* Ⓜ *Haymarket, North Station.*

Paul Revere House

HOUSE | FAMILY | Originally on the site was the parsonage of the Second Church of Boston, home to the Rev. Increase Mather, the Second Church's minister. Mather's house burned in the great fire of 1676, and the house that Revere was to occupy was built on its location about four years later, nearly 100 years before Revere's 1775 midnight ride through Middlesex County. Revere owned it from 1770 until 1800, although he lived there for only 10 years and rented it out for the next two decades. Pre-1900 photographs show it as a shabby warren of store-fronts and apartments. The clapboard sheathing is a replacement, but 90% of the framework is original; note the Elizabethan-style overhang and leaded windowpanes. A few Revere furnishings are on display here, and just gazing at his silverwork—much more of which is displayed at the Museum of Fine Arts—brings the man alive. Special events are scheduled throughout the year, many designed with children in mind, such as role play by characters dressed in period costume serving apple-cider cake and other colonial-era goodies, a silversmith practicing his trade, a dulcimer player entertaining a crowd, or a military-reenactment group in full period regalia.

The immediate neighborhood also has Revere associations. The little cobbled stoned park in North Square is named after Rachel Revere, his second wife, and the adjacent brick **Pierce-Hichborn House** once belonged to relatives of Revere and is open for $4 guided tours only. The garden connecting the Revere house and the Pierce-Hichborn House is planted with flowers and medicinal herbs favored in Revere's day. ✉ *19 North Sq., North End* ☎ *617/523–2338* ⊕ *www.paulreverehouse.org* ✉ *$5 (cash only)* ☉ *Closed Mon. Jan.–Mar.* Ⓜ *Haymarket, Aquarium, Government Center.*

Paul Revere Mall (*Prado*)

PLAZA | FAMILY | This makes a perfect time-out spot from the Freedom Trail. Bookended by two landmark churches—Old North and St. Stephen's—the mall is flanked by brick walls lined with bronze plaques bearing the stories of famous North Enders. An appropriate centerpiece for this enchanting cityscape is Cyrus Dallin's equestrian **statue of Paul Revere.** Despite his depictions in such statues as this, the gentle Revere was stocky and of medium height—whatever manly dash he possessed must have been in his eyes rather than his physique. That physique served him well enough,

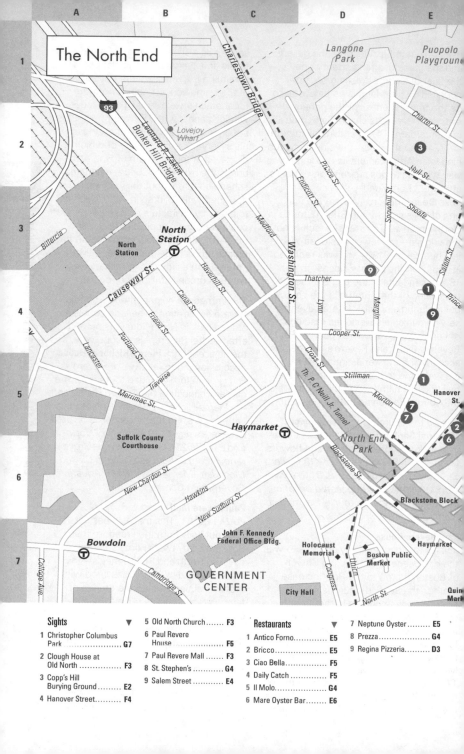

The North End

Sights ▼	
1 Christopher Columbus Park	**G7**
2 Clough House at Old North	**F3**
3 Copp's Hill Burying Ground	**E2**
4 Hanover Street	**F4**
5 Old North Church	**F3**
6 Paul Revere House	**F5**
7 Paul Revere Mall	**F3**
8 St. Stephen's	**G4**
9 Salem Street	**E4**

Restaurants ▼	
1 Antico Forno	**E5**
2 Bricco	**E5**
3 Ciao Bella	**F5**
4 Daily Catch	**F5**
5 Il Molo	**G4**
6 Mare Oyster Bar	**E6**
7 Neptune Oyster	**E5**
8 Prezza	**G4**
9 Regina Pizzeria	**D3**

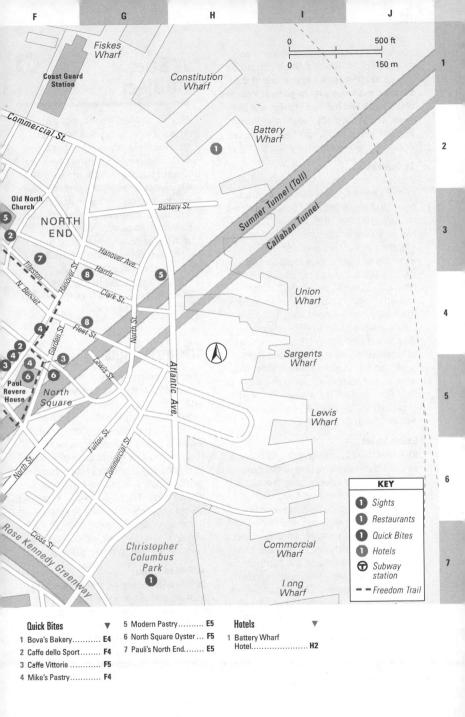

KEY

- 1 Sights
- 1 Restaurants
- 1 Quick Bites
- 1 Hotels
- 🅣 Subway station
- – – Freedom Trail

Quick Bites ▼

1 Bova's Bakery........... **E4**
2 Caffe dello Sport........ **F4**
3 Caffe Vittoria **F5**
4 Mike's Pastry............ **F4**

5 Modern Pastry.......... **E5**
6 North Square Oyster ... **F5**
7 Pauli's North End........ **E5**

Hotels ▼

1 Battery Wharf
Hotel..................... **H2**

however, for he lived to be 83 and saw nearly all of his Revolutionary comrades buried. ■ TIP→ **Take a seat at one of the benches and enjoy your to-go treat from any of the North End Italian trattorias and bakeries.** ✉ *Bordered by Tileston, Hanover, and Unity Sts., North End* Ⓜ *Haymarket, Aquarium, Government Center.*

St. Stephen's

RELIGIOUS SITE | Rose Kennedy, matriarch of the Kennedy clan, was christened here; 104 years later, St. Stephen's held mourners at her 1995 funeral. This is the only Charles Bulfinch church still standing in Boston, and a stunning example of the Federal style to boot. Built in 1804, it was first used as a Unitarian Church; since 1862 it has served a Roman Catholic parish. When the belfry was stripped during a major 1960s renovation, the original dome was found beneath a false cap; it was covered with sheet copper and held together with hand-wrought nails, and later authenticated as being the work of Paul Revere. ✉ *401 Hanover St., North End* ☎ *617/523–1230* Ⓜ *Haymarket, Aquarium, Government Center.*

Salem Street

NEIGHBORHOOD | This ancient and constricted thoroughfare, one of the two main North End streets, cuts through the heart of the neighborhood and runs parallel to and one block west of Hanover. Between Cross and Prince Streets, Salem Street contains numerous restaurants and shops. One of the best is Shake the Tree, one of the North End's trendiest boutiques, selling stylish clothing, gifts, and jewelry. The rest of Salem Street is mostly residential, but makes a nice walk to the Copp's Hill Burying Ground. ✉ *Between Cross and Prince Sts., North End* Ⓜ *Haymarket.*

A Sticky Subject

Boston has had its share of grim historic events, from massacres to stranglers, but on the sheer weirdness scale, nothing beats the Great Molasses Flood. In 1919 a steel container of molasses exploded on the Boston Harbor waterfront, killing 21 people and 20 horses and injuring 150 people. More than 2.3 million gallons of goo oozed onto unsuspecting citizenry, a veritable tsunami of sweet stuff that reached speeds up to 35 mph. The smell of the molasses lasted for decades and its memory lives on.

🍴 Restaurants

Third-generation Italians may have decamped to the suburbs, yet today's North End still echoes with brass parades in summer street fairs honoring saints. The friendly neighborhood attracts resident young professionals with convenient and safe housing, and entices all by wafting aromas of bitter espresso, pastries, fish specialties, red-sauce pasta, and pizza. Most, if not all, restaurants have a populated bar scene; while even the smaller locales serve beer and wine and let you linger over your casual counter-service meal to enjoy a drink.

★ Antico Forno

$$ | ITALIAN | Many of the menu choices here come from the eponymous wood-burning brick oven, which turns out surprisingly delicate thin-crust pizzas simply topped with tomato and buffalo mozzarella or complicated combos like pistachio pesto, fresh mozzarella,

Paul Revere's Ride

Test: Paul Revere was (1) a patriot whose midnight ride helped ignite the American Revolution; (2) a part-time dentist; (3) a silversmith who crafted tea services; (4) a printer who engraved the first Massachusetts state currency; (5) a talented metallurgist who cast cannons-and bells; or (6) all of the above. The correct response is (6). But there's much more to this outsize Revolutionary hero—bell ringer for the Old North Church, founder of the copper mills that still bear his name, and father of 16 children.

Although his life spanned eight decades (1734–1818), Revere is most famous for that one night, April 18, 1775, when he became America's most celebrated Pony Express rider. *"Listen, my children, and you shall hear / Of the midnight ride of Paul Revere"* are the opening lines of Henry Wadsworth Longfellow's poem, which placed the event at the center of American folklore. Longfellow may have been an effective evangelist for Revere, but he was an indifferent historian.

Revere wasn't the only midnight rider. As part of the system set in motion by Revere and William Dawes Jr., also dispatched from Boston, there were at least several dozen riders, so that the capture of any one of them wouldn't keep the alarm from being sounded. It's also known that Revere never looked for the lantern signal from Charlestown. He told Robert Newman to hang two lanterns from Old North's belfry since the redcoats were on the move by water, but by that time Revere was already being rowed across the Charles River to begin his famous ride.

Revere and Dawes set out on separate routes, but had the same mission: to warn patriot leaders Samuel Adams and John Hancock that British regular troops were marching to arrest them, and alarm the countryside along the way. The riders didn't risk capture by shouting the news through the streets—and they never uttered the famous cry "The British are coming!," since Bostonians still considered themselves British. When Revere arrived in Lexington a few minutes past midnight and approached the house where Adams and Hancock were lodged, a sentry challenged him, requesting that he not make so much noise. "Noise!" Revere replied. "You'll have noise enough before long."

Despite Longfellow's assertion, Revere never raised the alarm in Concord, because he was captured en route. He was held and questioned by the British patrol, and eventually released, without his horse, to walk back to Lexington in time to witness part of the battle on Lexington Green.

Poetic license aside, this tale has become part of the collective American spirit. Americans dote on hearing that Revere forgot his spurs, only to retrieve them by tying a note to his dog's collar, then awaiting its return with the spurs attached. The resourcefulness he showed in using a lady's petticoat to muffle the sounds of his oars while crossing the Charles is greatly appreciated. Little wonder that these tales resonate in the hearts and imagination of America's citizenry, as well as in Boston's streets on the third Monday of every April, Patriots' Day, when Revere's ride is reenacted—in daylight—to the cheers of thousands of onlookers.

and sausage. While the name, which translates to "old oven" gives the pizzas top billing, Antico excels at a variety of Italian country dishes that harken back to the Old Country, like veal parmigiana, osso buco with pork shanks, chicken saltimbocca, and handmade pastas; the specialty, gnocchi, is rich and creamy but light. **Known for:** wood-fired, brick-oven pizza; Italian country classics; casual, jovial atmosphere. [$] *Average main: $22* ✉ *93 Salem St., North End* ☎ *617/723–6733* 🌐 *www.anticofornoboston.com* [M] *Haymarket.*

Bricco

$$$$ | **ITALIAN** | A sophisticated but unpretentious enclave of nouveau Italian, Bricco has carved out quite a following, which is no wonder because the handmade pastas alone are reasons for reservations. Simple but well-balanced main courses such as veal osso buco, roast chicken marinated in seven spices and a brimming *brodetto* (fish stew) with half a lobster and a pile of seafood may linger in your memory. **Known for:** sophisticated Italian classics; dark, elegant atmosphere; pillowy homemade pastas. [$] *Average main: $38* ✉ *241 Hanover St., North End* ☎ *617/248–6800* 🕓 *No lunch* [M] *Haymarket.*

Ciao Bella

$$$ | **ITALIAN** | Located on the Freedom Trail and overlooking the country's oldest public square, the vintage-looking facade of Ciao Bella is owner Nick Frattaroli's elevated alternative to dining old-school in the North End. Classics are simple in nature but complex in taste, with dishes such as squid ink spaghetti fra diavolo, chicken piccata, scallop risotto, and classic antipasto vying for your attention. **Known for:** beautifully displayed crudo; Italian classics; white tablecloth. [$] *Average main: $30* ✉ *5 North Sq., North End* ☎ *617/829–4975* 🌐 *www.ciaobellanorth-end.com* [M] *Haymarket.*

The Rose Kennedy Greenway

The one linear mile of winding parks known as the Rose Fitzgerald Kennedy Greenway starts in the North End and goes thru Chinatown and Government Center.
⇨ *For more information about the Greenway, see the complete listing in the Downtown and the Waterfront chapter.*

★ Daily Catch

$$ | **SEAFOOD** | You've just got to love this shoebox-size place—for the noise, the intimacy, the complete absence of pretense, and, above all, the Sicilian-style seafood, which proved so popular, it spawned two other locations (one in Brookline and another in Boston's Seaport area). With garlic and olive oil forming the foundation for almost every dish, this cheerful, bustling spot specializes in calamari, black squid-ink pastas, and linguine with clam sauce, all served in the skillets in which they were cooked, hot from the stove. **Known for:** garlic-rich preparations; luscious seafood skillet pastas; intimate, elbow-to-elbow dining. [$] *Average main: $24* ✉ *323 Hanover St., North End* ☎ *617/523–8567* 🌐 *thedailycatch.com* 💳 *No credit cards* [M] *Haymarket.*

Il Molo

$$$$ | **ITALIAN** | Step down a few stairs and open the door to renowned restaurateur Donato Frattaroli's intimate sea-centric restaurant along the waterfront side of the North End. Coastal charm is seen not only in the way the food—pan-seared diver scallops with lobster crema, grilled Spanish octopus, and pasta arrabbiata with mussels—is prepared, but also in the unparalleled decor of white leather library chairs, dark green velvet backed banquettes, coral and glass pendant lights resembling sea glass, and beautiful turquoise and white tiles. **Known for:** fresh seafood dishes; spectacular ocean decor; Italian coast specialties. $ *Average main: $37* ✉ *326 Commercial St., North End* ☏ *857/277–1895* ⊕ *www.ilmoloboston. com* Ⓜ *Haymarket.*

Mare Oyster Bar

$$$$ | MODERN ITALIAN | When a restaurant's very name conjures up images of the ocean waters, its menu choices should follow suit. Mare does exactly that, focusing on a locally sourced oyster program, fresh and innovative crudo dishes, and simple yet elegant entrées highlighting the natural flavors of its fresh, sustainable seafood. **Known for:** fresh crudo and oysters; dark intimate setting; whole grilled fish. $ *Average main: $45* ✉ *3 Mechanic St., North End* ☏ *617/723–6273* ⊕ *www.mareoysterbar.com* ⊙ *Closed Mon. in winter* Ⓜ *Haymarket.*

★ Neptune Oyster

$$$ | SEAFOOD | This *piccolo* oyster bar, the first of its kind in the neighborhood, has only 22 chairs, but the long marble bar adorned with mirrors has extra seating for 15 more patrons, who can watch the oyster shuckers deftly undo handfuls of more than a dozen different kinds of bivalves to savor as an appetizer or on a *plateau di frutti di mare,* a gleaming tower of oysters and other raw-bar items piled over ice that you can order from the slip of paper they pass out listing each day's crustacean options. Daily specials run the gamut, from lobster spaghetti to scarlet prawns to sea urchin bucatini. **Known for:** casual setting; Italian-style seafood; generously packed lobster roll. $ *Average main: $34* ✉ *63 Salem St., North End* ☏ *617/742–3474* ⊕ *www.neptuneoyster. com* Ⓜ *Haymarket.*

Prezza

$$$$ | MODERN ITALIAN | Chef Anthony Caturano pays homage to his Italian grandmother at this warm, convivial eatery by naming it after the tiny Abruzzese village where she was born and then putting a modern twist on the rustic dishes she would have cooked. An emphasis on garden-fresh ingredients means appetizers like baby kale ricotta salata with pistachios and persimmons and wood-grilled squid and octopus with white beans, while "Gravy Sunday" specials translate to heaping plates of traditional dishes like veal saltimbocca and chicken parm. **Known for:** scrumptious country-style Italian; generous portions; impressive Italian wine list. $ *Average main: $37* ✉ *24 Fleet St., North End* ☏ *617/227–1577* ⊕ *www.prezza.com* ▭ *No credit cards.*

Regina Pizzeria

$$ | ITALIAN | This North End institution has been doing what it does best since the Polcari family took over in 1956—creating thin-crusted, brick-oven-charred pizzas with fresh toppings, excellent sauce, and just the right amount of cheese. With 15 locations, they only offer what they excel in: incredibly well-made pies, like the Margherita, which contains fresh basil leaves baked into the cheese so they don't burn; try a combo from their Old Time Favorites menu, such as the Old World Style Anchovy or the St. Anthony's, a white pizza with sausage, cheese, and peppers. **Known for:** excellent thin-crust pizzas; good prices; no-frills atmosphere. $ *Average main: $24* ✉ *11½ Thatcher St., North End* ☏ *617/227–0765* ⊕ *www.pizzeriaregina.com.*

😀 Coffee and Quick Bites

Café culture is alive and well in the North End.

Bova's Bakery

$ | ITALIAN | FAMILY | The allure of Bova's Bakery, a neighborhood institution since 1926, lies not only in its takeaway Italian breads, calzones, and pastries, but also in its hours: 24 a day (the deli closes at 1 am, however). Family owned and operated, this is where you can not only satisfy a hunger with their homemade Italian breads, oversized subs, Sicilian pizza and calzones, but also a sweet tooth with their famed Sicilian chocolate dipped cannoli, award-winning tiramisu, raspberry and blueberry turnovers, and lobster tails. **Known for:** open 24/7; tiramisu; fresh baked bread. $ *Average main: $10 ⊠ 134 Salem St., North End* ☎ *617/523–5601* ⊕ *bovabakeryboston.net* Ⓜ *Haymarket.*

Caffe dello Sport

$ | **ITALIAN** | An Italianate version of a sports bar, Caffe dello Sport has two wide screens transmitting live soccer. The buzz is not only from the world games excitement but also the espressos, pastries, beer, wine, cordials, and gelato. **Known for:** soccer games; full espresso bar; gelato. $ *Average main: $8 ⊠ 308 Hanover St., North End* ☎ *617/523–5063* ▤ *No credit cards.*

★ Caffe Vittoria

$ | **ITALIAN** | **FAMILY** | Established in 1929, Caffe Vittoria—Boston's oldest Italian café—is rightfully known as Boston's most traditional Italian café, which is one of the reasons why the place packed with locals. With gleaming brass, marble tabletops, four levels of seating, three bars that serve aperitifs, one of the city's best selections of grappa, and one massive, ancient espresso maker, this old-fashioned café will make you want to lose yourself in these surroundings. **Known for:** specialty coffee drinks; grapa; gelato. $ *Average main: $10 ⊠ 290–296 Hanover St., North End* ☎ *617/227–7606* ⊕ *www.caffevittoria. com* ▤ *No credit cards.*

Mike's Pastry

$ | **BAKERY** | Every local knows the white box with the blue and white string as a to-go treasure chest of Italian delicacies. Known for their cannoli, Mike's has been bringing the best in pastries and cookies to the North End (and presidential patrons like Bill Clinton) since 1946. **Known for:** cannolis; long lines; cases of Italian cookies. $ *Average main: $9 ⊠ 300 Hanover St., North End* ☎ *617/742–3050* ⊕ *www. mikespastry.com.*

Mike's vs. Modern

Welcome to Boston's long-standing cannoli war. Mike's Pastry and Modern Pastry are widely considered to be the North End's two best cannoli spots, but locals can't seem to agree on which is better, splitting their strong allegiance right down the center. Modern's cannoli are smaller and more delicate than Mike's, while Mike's are crunchier, sweeter, and boast more flavors (18 to be exact). Which will you choose?

Modern Pastry

$ | **ITALIAN** | The North End's other favorite cannoli king, Modern is a hit with the locals. Using old world recipes that were relied on for more than 150 years, their crusts are flaky, their fillings rich, and they have a selection of torrone nougat confections, cookies, French horns, and Napoleons. **Known for:** dainty cannolis; deliciously moist cakes; handmade Italian candies. $ *Average main: $8 ⊠ 257 Hanover St., North End* ☎ *617/523–3783* ⊕ *www.modernpastry.com* ▤ *No credit cards.*

North Square Oyster Bar

$$ | **SEAFOOD** | Adjacent to the Ciao Bella restaurant, you'll find bubbles and bivalves at the North Square Oyster and Wine Bar. Quite the opposite of its sister spot's light and bright florals, this slick and small 10-seat wine and raw bar serves fresh oysters, creative takes on local seafood, gorgeous rotating crudo options, and small production natural, organic, and biodynamic wines. **Known for:** freshly shucked oysters; intimate setting; organic wines. $ *Average main: $20 ⊠ 5 North Sq., North End* ☎ *617/829–4975* ⊕ *www.northsquareoyster.com* Ⓜ *haymarket.*

Pauli's North End

$ | **CAFÉ** | In this North End nook, the lobster roll—in 7 ounces, 14 ounces, and the biggest lobster roll in Boston 28-ounce "U.S.S. Lobstitution"—reigns supreme. **Known for:** Boston's largest lobster roll; fresh sandwich fixings; pasta entrées to go. [$] *Average main: $13* ✉ *65 Salem St., North End* ☎ *857/284–7064* 🌐 *www.paulisnorthend.com* [M] *Haymarket.*

Hotels

Battery Wharf Hotel

$$$$ | **HOTEL** | **FAMILY** | One of the growing number of lodgings clustered along Boston's ever-expanding Harborwalk—a pretty pedestrian path that runs from Charlestown to Dorchester—the Battery Wharf Hotel looks more like a gated community than a chain hotel. **Pros:** walking distance to more than 80 world-class restaurants; on-site Exhale Spa has discounted spa services and fitness classes for hotel guests; great North End location; water taxi stand on-site. **Cons:** far from Newbury Street and South End shopping; 15- to 20-minute walk to nearest T stations; hotel is in two separate buildings. [$] *Rooms from: $400* ✉ *3 Battery Wharf, North End* ☎ *617/657–1834* 🌐 *www.batterywharfhotelboston.com* 🛏 *166 rooms* 🍴 *No meals* [M] *Haymarket, North Station.*

Shopping

This has to be one of Boston's best neighborhoods for shopping. Browse through the Italian greengrocers and butchers, inhaling the tantalizing aromas. Or get yourself a little bling at one of the stylish shops lining the crooked streets.

BOOKS

I Am Books

BOOKS/STATIONERY | Once you've eaten your fill of pasta and cannoli, nourish your noggin at this independent, Italian American bookstore, where you'll find more than 1,200 titles in English and Italian. In addition to books written in Italian, including many children's books like Dr. Seuss, you'll find books devoted to Italian cooking, art, history, language, literature, and more, along with Italian comic books, card games, magazines, ceramics, and fragrances. ✉ *189 North St., North End* ☎ *857/263–7665* 🌐 *www.iambooksboston.com.*

CLOTHING

★ Shake the Tree

SPECIALTY STORES | Irresistible defines this one-stop shop, brimming with an eclectic array of floral dresses and tops, wide-legged pants, letterpress greeting cards, small brand apothecary, craft cocktail supplies, global cookbooks, woven baskets, and mixed media jewelry that you never knew you needed. Owner Marian Klausner creates an inspiring award-winning selection from her global travels. ✉ *67 Salem St., North End* ☎ *617/742–0484* 🌐 *www.shakethetreeboston.com* [M] *Haymarket.*

FOOD

Happy Pills

FOOD/CANDY | **FAMILY** | Nothing will make you happier than this tiny candy shop filled with 88 bins of pick-your-own colorful gummies. The North End location of Happy Pills' is the Barcelona-based sweet treat purveyor's first U.S. location and the largest of any in the world (which doesn't mean much since it's still a tight spot). The fun begins with the selection of a bottle to fill, each reminiscent of a pill bottle and playfully named—the sizes range from the smallest at 75-milliliter bottled called "Asymptomatic" to an enormous 1,500-milliliter canister aptly named "Chronic." What's your pleasure: little marshmallows, champagne bears, mojito-flavored fruits, or licorice? Once the jar is filled, a label is selected for the finishing touch with a variety of artwork designs. ✉ *121 Salem St., North End* ☎ *208/ 502–1131* 🌐 *www.happypills.es/en/* ⏲ *Closed Mon.*

Polcari's Coffee

$$ | | If you're not able to kill a whole afternoon sipping cappuccino, this circa 1932 spot sells dried goods by the pound—coffees, teas, herbs, and spices (their secret dipping oil mix is well-known) displayed in antique brass bins—as well as a variety of nuts and Italian delicacies and candies. ⊠ *105 Salem St., North End* ☎ *617/227–0786* ⊕ *www. polcariscoffee.com.*

Chapter 5

CHARLESTOWN

Updated by
Cheryl Fenton

 Sights
★★★☆☆

 Restaurants
★★★☆☆

 **Hotels**
★☆☆☆☆

 Shopping
★☆☆☆☆

 Nightlife
★★☆☆☆

NEIGHBORHOOD SNAPSHOT

TOP EXPERIENCES

■ **Get vertical:** Climb 294 steps to the Bunker Hill Monument top and enjoy city views while imagining battles of the past.

■ **Step aboard a 1700s naval vessel:** Tour the USS *Constitution*, and discover why the world's oldest commissioned warship still afloat is nicknamed "Old Ironsides."

■ **Raise a glass to the patriots:** Grab a pint at Warren Tavern, the same pub frequented by George Washington and Paul Revere.

■ **Cityscape views:** The Harbor Walk is a raised section along the water that affords miles of peaceful Boston views.

■ **Stroll through a park with purpose:** Visit the Charlestown Navy Yard, a National Park Service site complete with its own gift shop and museum.

■ **Freedom Trail sights:** Bunker Hill Monument and USS *Constitution*.

QUICK BITES

■ **Emack & Bolio's.** This funky ice cream and smoothie shop boast crazy flavors and a rock n' roll vibe. ⊠ *100 City Sq., Charlestown* ⊕ *www.emackandbolios.com.*

■ **Sorelle Bakery & Cafe.** This neighborhood spot is known for delicious sandwiches and refreshing iced coffees. ⊠ *100 City Sq., Charlestown* ⊕ *www.sorellecafe.com.*

■ **Zume's Coffeehouse.** A cheerful vibe and friendly service accompany great coffee and housemade burritos at this local spot. ⊠ *221 Main St., Charlestown* ⊕ *www.zumescoffeehouse.com.*

GETTING HERE

The closest subway stop to the Charlestown Navy Yard is North Station (on the Green and Orange lines), about a 15-minute walk. Take Causeway Street northeast and make a left to walk over the Charlestown Bridge. Take a right on Chelsea Street and right again on Warren Street. Constitution Road will be your next left. From here you can enter the Navy Yard. From Downtown Crossing, take the 93 Bus, which drops you at the Navy Yard. If you're coming from Downtown, try the water shuttle from Long Wharf near the Aquarium. Boats run on the hour and half hour for the 10-minute ride.

PLANNING YOUR TIME

■ This little tight-knit community (Boston's oldest neighborhood) is only one square mile. Give yourself two to three hours for a Charlestown walk. A daytime visit affords the best Harbor views. You may want to save Charlestown's stretch of the Freedom Trail, which adds considerably to its length, for a second-day outing. If you drive yourself, be mindful of weekday resident-only parking spots.

■ This area of Boston has a rough reputation, but overall the Charlestown Navy Yard is generally a safe area.

This is Boston's beginning. Charlestown was a thriving settlement a year before colonials headed across the Charles River at William Blaxton's invitation to found the city proper. Today the district's attractions include two of the most visible—and vertical—monuments in Boston: the Bunker Hill Monument, which commemorates the grisly battle that became a symbol of patriotic resistance against the British, and the USS *Constitution*, whose masts continue to tower over the waterfront where it was built more than 200 years ago.

The blocks around the Bunker Hill Monument are a good illustration of how gentrification has changed the neighborhoods. Along streets lined with gas lamps are impeccably restored Federal and mid-19th-century town houses; cheek by jowl are working-class quarters of similar vintage but more modest recent pasts. Near the Navy Yard along Main Street is City Square, the beginning of Charlestown's main commercial district, which includes City Square Park, with brick paths and bronze fish sculptures. On Phipps Street is the grave marker of John Harvard, a minister who in 1638 bequeathed his small library to the fledgling Cambridge College, thereafter renamed in his honor. The precise location of the grave is uncertain, but a monument from 1828 marks its approximate site.

Sights

★ Bunker Hill Monument

MEMORIAL | Two misunderstandings surround this famous monument. First, the Battle of Bunker Hill was actually fought on Breed's Hill, which is where the monument sits today. (The real Bunker Hill is about ½ mile to the north of the monument.) In truth, Bunker was the originally planned locale for the battle, and for that reason its name stuck. Second, although the battle is generally considered a Colonial success, the Americans lost. It was a Pyrrhic victory for the British Redcoats, who sacrificed nearly half of their 2,200 men; American casualties numbered 400 to 600. One thing is true: the Battle of Bunker Hill put the British on notice that were up against a formidable opponent. According to history books, this is also

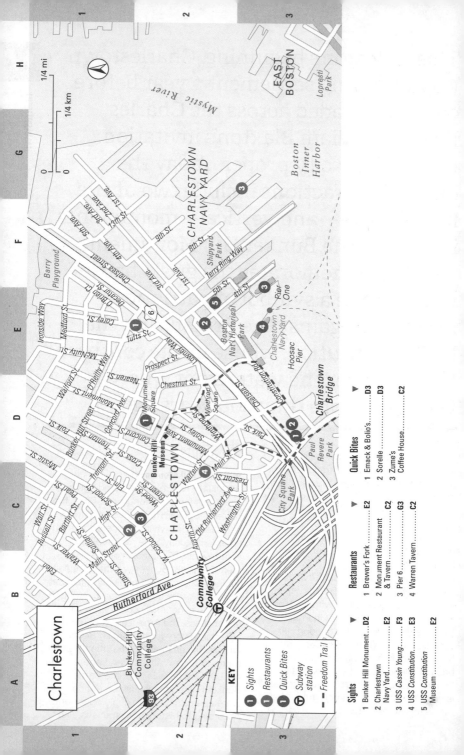

Charlestown

KEY

- ① Sights
- ① Restaurants
- ① Quick Bites
- ⊕ Subway station
- – – Freedom Trail

▶ **Sights**

1 Bunker Hill Monument...**D2**
2 Charlestown Navy Yard...........**E2**
3 USS Cassin Young........**F3**
4 USS Constitution............**E3**
5 USS Constitution Museum............**E2**

▶ **Restaurants**

1 Brewer's Fork............**E2**
2 Monument Restaurant & Tavern............**C2**
3 Pier 6............**G3**
4 Warren Tavern............**C2**

▶ **Quick Bites**

1 Emack & Bolio's........**D3**
2 Sorelle **D3**
3 Zume's Coffee House............**C2**

Mystic River

Boston Inner Harbor

EAST BOSTON

Lopresti Park

CHARLESTOWN NAVY YARD

Shipyard Park

Terry Ring Way

Boston Nat'l Historical Park

Charlestown Navy Yard Pier

Hoosac Pier

Pier One

Charlestown Bridge

Paul Revere Park

City Square Park

CHARLESTOWN

Bunker Hill Museum

Monument Square

Winthrop Square

Community College

Bunker Hill Community College

Barry Playground

Rutherford Ave.

1/4 mi
1/4 km

the location of the famous war cry, "Don't fire until you see the whites of their eyes," uttered by American colonel William Prescott or General Israel Putnam (there's still debate on who gave the actual command). This was a shout out to an 18th-century Prussian warning to soldiers that lack of ammunition and notorious musket inaccuracy meant every shot needed to count. The Americans did employ a deadly delayed-action strategy on June 17, 1775, and conclusively proved themselves capable of defeating the forces of the British Empire.

Among the dead were the brilliant young American doctor and political activist Joseph Warren, recently commissioned as a major general but fighting as a private, and the British major John Pitcairn, who two months prior had led the Redcoats into Lexington. Pitcairn is believed to be buried in the crypt of Old North Church.

In 1823 the committee formed to construct a monument on the site of the battle chose the form of an Egyptian obelisk. Architect Solomon Willard designed a 221-foot-tall granite obelisk, a tremendous feat of engineering for its day. The Marquis de Lafayette laid the cornerstone of the monument in 1825, but because of a lack of funds, it wasn't dedicated until 1843. Daniel Webster's stirring words at the ceremony commemorating the laying of its cornerstone have gone down in history: "Let it rise! Let it rise, till it meets the sun in his coming. Let the earliest light of the morning gild it, and parting day linger and play upon its summit."

The monument's zenith is reached by a flight of 294 tightly spiraled steps. There's no elevator, but the views from the observatory are worth the effort of the arduous climb. From April through June, due to high numbers, all visitors who wish to climb must first obtain a pass from the Bunker Hill Museum at 43 Monument Square. Climbing passes are free, but limited in number and can be either reserved up to two weeks in advance or on a first-come, first-served basis. The museum's artifacts and exhibits tell the story of the battle, while a detailed diorama shows the action in miniature. ✉ *Monument Sq., Charlestown* ☎ *617/242–5641* ⊕ *www.nps.gov/bost/historyculture/bhm.htm* ✈ *Free* Ⓜ *Community College.*

Charlestown Navy Yard

HISTORIC SITE | FAMILY | A National Park Service Historic Site since it was decommissioned in 1974, the Charlestown Navy Yard was one of six established to build warships. For 174 years, as wooden hulls and muzzle-loading cannons gave way to steel ships and sophisticated electronics, the yard evolved to meet the Navy's changing needs. Here are early-19th-century barracks, workshops, and officers' quarters; a ropewalk (an elongated building for making rope, not open to the public), designed in 1834 by the Greek Revival architect Alexander Parris and used by the Navy to turn out cordage for more than 125 years; and one of the oldest operational naval dry docks in the United States. The USS *Constitution* was the first to use this dry dock in 1833. In addition to the ship itself, check out the *Constitution* Museum, the collections of the Boston Marine Society, and the USS *Cassin Young,* a World War II Fletcher class destroyer typical of the ships built here during that era. At the entrance of the Navy Yard is the **Charlestown Navy Yard Visitors Information Center,** with exhibits on ships and a fun little souvenir shop. A 10-minute movie about the Navy Yard runs every 15 minutes in a small theater. ✉ *55 Constitution Rd., Charlestown* ☎ *617/242–5601* ⊕ *www.nps.gov/bost/historyculture/cny.htm* Ⓜ *North Station; MBTA Bus 92 to Charlestown City Sq. or Bus 93 to Chelsea St. from Haymarket; or Boston Harbor Cruise water shuttle from Long Wharf to Pier 4.*

Did You Know?

The USS *Constitution* is a bit of an anachronism on the Freedom Trail. Though it is the oldest ship in the Navy, "Old Ironsides" wasn't launched until 1797— well after the American Revolution had been won.

USS *Cassin Young*

MILITARY SITE | From a later date than the *Constitution,* this Fletcher-class U.S. Navy destroyer survived action in Asian waters during World War II (including seven Pacific battles and two Kamikaze hits). She served the Navy until 1960. Walk beside her and take in her size, explore her top deck, or go below deck for a guided tour offered by the National Park Service. She is the namesake of Captain Cassin Young, who was awarded the Medal of Honor for his heroism at the Japanese attack on Pearl Harbor; he was killed in the Naval Battle of Guadalcanal in the fall of 1942. Check the website for special opening hours. ⊠ *Charlestown Navy Yard, 55 Constitution Rd., Charlestown* ☎ *617/242–5601* ⊕ *www.nps.gov/ bost/historyculture/usscassinyoung. htm* 🖾 *Free* 🕙 *Closed Nov.–Apr.* Ⓜ *North Station; MBTA Bus 92 to Charlestown City Sq. or Bus 93 to Chelsea St. from Haymarket; or Boston Harbor Cruise water shuttle from Long Wharf to Pier 4.*

★ USS *Constitution*

MILITARY SITE | FAMILY | Affectionately known as "Old Ironsides," the USS *Constitution* rides proudly at anchor in her berth at the Charlestown Navy Yard. The oldest commissioned ship in the U.S. fleet is a battlewagon of the old school, of the days of "wooden ships and iron men"—when she and her crew of 200 succeeded at the perilous task of asserting the sovereignty of an improbable new nation. Every July 4, she's towed out for a celebratory turnabout in Boston Harbor, the very place her keel was laid in 1797.

The venerable craft has narrowly escaped the scrap heap several times in her long history. She was launched on October 21, 1797, as part of the nation's fledgling navy. Her hull was made of live oak, the toughest wood grown in North America; her bottom was sheathed in copper, provided by Paul Revere at a nominal cost. Her principal service was during Thomas Jefferson's campaign against the Barbary pirates, off the coast of North Africa, and in the War of 1812. In 42 engagements her record was 42–0.

The nickname "Old Ironsides" was acquired during the War of 1812, when shots from the British warship *Guerrière* appeared to bounce off her hull. Talk of scrapping the ship began as early as 1830, but she was saved by a public campaign sparked by Oliver Wendell Holmes's poem "Old Ironsides." She underwent a major restoration in the early 1990s. Today she continues, the oldest commissioned warship afloat in the world, to be a part of the U.S. Navy. In 2015, she was dry docked for a 26-month restoration that included replacement of select hull planks, the 1995 copper sheathing, and deck beams, returning to the water in 2017.

The navy personnel who look after the *Constitution* maintain a 24-hour watch. Instead of taking the T, you can get closer to the ship by taking MBTA Bus 93 to Chelsea Street from Haymarket. Or you can take the Boston Harbor Cruise water shuttle from Long Wharf to Pier 4. ⊠ *Charlestown Navy Yard, 55 Constitution Rd., Charlestown* ☎ *617/242–7511* ⊕ *ussconstitutionmuseum.org* 🖾 *Free* Ⓜ *North Station.*

★ USS *Constitution* Museum

MUSEUM | FAMILY | With nearly 2,000 artifacts and more than 10,000 archival records pertaining to the USS *Constitution* on display, exhibits spark excitement about maritime culture and naval service. All ages enjoy "All Hands on Deck: A Sailor's Life in 1812," complete with opportunities to scrub decks, scramble aloft to furl a sail, eat a meal of salted meat and ship's biscuit, and crawl into a hammock. History buffs get a stem-to-stern look at the ship's history, from its creation to battles. ⊠ *Charlestown* ✛ *Adjacent to USS Constitution, Charlestown Navy Yard* ☎ *617/426–1812* ⊕ *www.ussconstitutionmuseum.org* 🖾 *Suggested donation from $5* Ⓜ *North Station; MBTA Bus 92* *to Charlestown City Sq. or Bus 93 to Chelsea St. from Haymarket; or Boston Harbor Cruise water shuttle from Long Wharf to Pier 4.*

🍴 Restaurants

English colonists founded this little neighborhood across the Harbor before they established Boston. Known for its brick town houses and war-time history, including the Bunker Hill Monument and the USS *Constitution,* it also contains a vibrant mix of affordable eateries and taverns, mainly along Main Street and in City Square, that cater to the area artists, working families, and young couples.

Brewer's Fork
$ | **AMERICAN** | With the Bunker Hill Monument in your sights, relax with a wood-fired pizza and a pint. Brewer's Fork's list of 30 draft cider and craft beers is impressive (yet approachable), its wine list massive, and their pizzas beyond basic with toppings like spicy clam, bacon jam, and smoked chicken, and the pie is served straight out of a gigantic fiery oven, the restaurant's only cooking method. **Known for:** creative pizzas; lively brunch; beer program. [$] *Average main: $15* ✉ *7 Moulton St., Charlestown* ☎ *617/337–5703* 🌐 *www.brewersfork.com.*

Monument Restaurant & Tavern
$ | **AMERICAN** | **FAMILY** | A "gastropub meets bistro," Monument Restaurant & Tavern is as quintessential as it comes for dining in cozy Charlestown with a brownstone vibe of brick and weathered woods, 16-foot ceilings, and 40-foot bar. The pizza is the menu's superstar, coming out piping and bubbly from the 900-degree oven in the extremely open kitchen, but the other dishes on the menu are designed to share with groups; there are also a few hearty entrées for bigger appetites, including slow-braised short ribs and seared skirt steak. **Known for:** piled-high sandwiches; brunch prosecco pails; wood-fired pizza. [$] *Average main: $16* ✉ *251 Main St., Charlestown* ☎ *617/337–5191* 🌐 *www.monumentcharlestown.com.*

Pier 6
$$$ | **SEAFOOD** | For a meal on the waterfront, try Pier 6 in the Charlestown Navy Yard just steps from the USS *Constitution.* You'll be treated to requisite New England seafood dishes coupled with outstanding harbor views right on the marina. Plates are piled high with fresh seafood such as fried calamari, seared octopus, lobster rolls, and the giant shellfish platter of local oysters, clams, shrimp and lobster, which will draw all eyes to your table. **Known for:** waterfront location; lively cocktail scene; fresh shellfish dishes. [$] *Average main: $27* ✉ *1 8th St., Pier 6, Charlestown* ☎ *617/337–0054* 🌐 *pier6boston.com.*

Warren Tavern
$ | **AMERICAN** | Built in 1780 and reportedly one of the country's oldest taverns, this restored colonial neighborhood pub in the quaint and historic gaslight district was once frequented by George Washington and Paul Revere. After a blustery walk through the Navy Yard, grab a seat

A Good Walk

If you choose to hoof it to Charlestown, follow Hull Street from Copp's Hill Burying Ground to Commercial Street; turn left on Commercial and, two blocks later, right onto the bridge. The entrance to the **Charlestown Navy Yard** is on your right after crossing the bridge. Just ahead is the Charlestown Navy Yard Visitors Information Center; inside the park gate are the **USS *Constitution*** and the associated **USS *Constitution* Museum.** From here, the Red Line of the Freedom Trail takes you to the **Bunker Hill Monument.**

by the fireplace and warm yourself with a hearty chowder or short rib shepherd's pie and Sam Adams draft. **Known for:** historical atmosphere; beer selection; short rib shepherd's pie. [$] *Average main: $14* ✉ *2 Pleasant St., Charlestown* ☎ *617/241–8142* 🌐 *www.warrentavern.com* [M] *Community College.*

Coffee and Quick Bites

Emack & Bolio's

$ | CAFÉ | Originally started as a late-night place for local musicians to chill with ice cream after a set, Emack & Bolio's has been rocking the Boston frozen treat scene since the mid-1970s. Diet meets decadence at this smoothie bar/ice-cream parlor that serves in-house microbrewed soda and floats, ice-cream pizzas, and chocolate confections like the chocolate-dipped Twinkie. **Known for:** decadent frozen treats; vegan ice cream; outrageous cones. [$] *Average main: $5* ✉ *100 City Sq., Charlestown* ✣ *On Freedom Trail near Old Iron Sides* ☎ *617/337–3571* 🌐 *www.emackandbolios.com.*

Sorelle

$ | BAKERY | When you need a break, duck into this hot little bakery for piping hot coffees, teas, and cocoa, or you can take yours chilled to perfection. If you're hungry, dig into one of their well-known bagel sandwiches, nutella and banana panini, filled pastries, or a chop-chop (a croissant-meets-danish treat). **Known for:** bagel sandwiches; iced coffees; pastries. [$] *Average main: $10* ✉ *100 City Sq., Charlestown* ☎ *617/242–5980* 🌐 *www.sorellecafe.com* [M] *North Station.*

Zume's Coffee House

$ | CAFÉ | This welcoming locally owned coffee shop has plenty of cozy chairs, local art-filled walls, cheerful purple ceilings and piping hot mugs of freshly brewed coffee served up by friendly baristas. The breakfast and lunch crowds love the grab-and-go sandwiches, such as the house-made burritos and English muffins, but there are plenty of sweet treats like made-to-order tea cakes, energy bars, brownies, and decorated sugar cookies to fulfill your sweet tooth. **Known for:** nitrobrew; tea cakes; homemade English muffin sandwiches. [$] *Average main: $5* ✉ *221 Main St., Charlestown* ☎ *617/242–0038* 🌐 *www.zumescoffeehouse.com* [M] *Community College.*

Nightlife

The historic waterfront along the harbor and Mystic River affords Charlestown sweeping views of the USS *Constitution*, the Navy Yard and Admiralty, and Boston itself, to which Charlestown is linked by bike paths and Prison Point and Zakim bridges. Bunker Hill's needle monument presides over a quiet, elegant neighborhood, while Main Street and City Square attract visitors to casual restaurants and lively taverns.

BARS

Blackmoor Bar & Kitchen

BARS/PUBS | Watch the sun set over the Zakim Bridge as you peruse the extensive list of 34 rotating draughts, elite bottled beers, cask ale, draught wine, craft spirits, and custom cocktails. Located along the Freedom Trail at the end of the Charlestown Bridge, this watering hole is a favorite among locals to hang out and watch the game on the big screen while throwing back a drink or two. Drinks like Old Colony Mule or Navy Yard Old Fashioned have ties to history, while their Bloody Mary list is unparalleled with nine tasty options. The eclectic menu is full of tavern favorites like burgers, chicken wings and flatbread pizzas, along with interesting twists like short rib poutine, Rock N' Roll Bowls, and fried seafood. ✉ *1 Chelsea St., Charlestown* ☎ *617/580–8166* 🌐 *www.blackmoorbar.com.*

Tavern at the End of the World

BARS/PUBS | At the end of your Charlestown trip, hit up this pub that keeps Irish eyes smiling with a 50-plus beer list and classic pub fare with an Irish flare. With a backdrop of live music and traditional Irish seisiún, grab a lager with a snack of curry fries or calamari, or satisfy a huge hunger with a bowl of piping hot stew and the perfect Guinness pour. Weekend brunch Bloody Marys sit sidecar to traditional Irish breakfasts. Bonus points for the Airbnb right above the tavern that sleeps maximum 18. ⊠ *108 Cambridge St., Charlestown* ☎ *617/241–4999* ⊕ *www.tavernattheendoftheworld.com* Ⓜ *Sullivan.*

Shopping

GIFTS

Place & Gather

GIFTS/SOUVENIRS | Tucked between two charming and colorful triple decker houses in Winthrop Square, this home and boutique shop is the perfect stop along the Freedom Trail for gifts galore. Treat yourself to home accents like candles and vases, or bring home a little something for someone special. Channel a little New England by filling your basket with items such as seashell frames, oyster plates, and pillow cases decorated with Charlestown zip code typography. The shelves are also stocked with fashion-forward items like bracelets, rings, and headbands for an accessory shopping spree. ⊠ *26 Common St., Charlestown* ☎ *617/580–8362* ⊕ *www.placeandgather.com.*

Chapter 6

DOWNTOWN AND THE WATERFRONT

Updated by
Leigh Harrington

◉ Sights	🍴 Restaurants	🛏 Hotels	🛍 Shopping	🍸 Nightlife
★★★★★	★★★★☆	★★★★☆	★★☆☆☆	★★★☆☆

NEIGHBORHOOD SNAPSHOT

TOP EXPERIENCES

■ **Swim with sea life:** Touch a shark, watch Myrtle the Turtle feed, and see many of the ocean's creatures at New England Aquarium.

■ **Revolutionary history:** Explore some of The Freedom Trail's most interactive sites, including Old South Meeting House and the Old State House.

■ **Savor Asia's authentic flavors:** Whether you prefer Cambodian, Vietnamese, or Cantonese, Chinatown is a great place to dine.

■ **Splendid waterfront views:** Stroll along the Harborwalk for gorgeous panoramas of Charlestown and East Boston, as well as fancy yachts, ferries, and maybe a harbor seal.

■ **See a show:** Most of the city's stages occupy Downtown's Theater District, and there's always something playing, from opera to Broadway musicals.

GETTING HERE AND AROUND

Travelers can access Downtown Boston very easily, as it is centrally situated. Each of the T's four main subway lines run through it: take the Orange Line to Downtown Crossing or State, the Blue Line to State or Aquarium, the Red Line to South Station or Downtown Crossing, or the Green Line to Park. If you're up for burning calories over a few hours, walking can be a great way to explore the neighborhood, with all its winding roads and historic sites to see along the way.

For the waterfront, get off at Aquarium and walk southeast, or South Station and walk northeast. You can also use the waterfront as a departure and arrival point when traveling by sea. A few ferry and water taxi services operated out of Rowes Wharf (**Rowes Wharf Water Taxi** ☎ 617/406–8584) and Long Wharf (**BHC Water Taxi** ☎ 617/227–4320), and feature dozens of stops around Boston Harbor.

Driving downtown is not recommended unless absolutely necessary. Parking is nonexistent, and traffic can crawl no matter the time of day.

QUICK BITES

■ **Clover Food Lab.** Famous for its meat-free menu and eco-conscious approach, Clover is an easy pitstop for food along the Freedom Trail. Expect local, organic ingredients in ever-changing options, but the chickpea fritters are a must-sample staple. ⊠ 27 School St., Downtown ⊕ www.cloverfoodlab.com Ⓜ Park, State.

■ **Dewey Square Food Trucks.** On weekday mornings and afternoons, locally operated food trucks congregate at Dewey Square plaza on the Rose Kennedy Greenway, ready to serve Financial District professionals an eat-it-while-you-walk-or-picnic meal. Typically, eight to 10 different options offer variety from curry to Korean. ⊠ Summer St. at Congress St., Financial District ⊕ www.rosekennedygreenway.org/foodtrucks Ⓜ South Station.

■ **Tradesman.** Hang out here for one or more of the three Cs: coffee, cocktails, and decadently stuffed croissants. A steampunk-meets-chic vibe is served up with quick bites like avocado toast, chia pudding, house-made pastries, and juice shots. ⊠ 58 Batterymarch St., Downtown ⊕ www.tradesmanboston.com Ⓜ Aquarium Station

Boston's commercial and financial districts are concentrated in a maze of streets laid out with little logic. They are, after all, only village lanes that happen to be lined with modern, 40-story office buildings. That's not to say the past has been erased; Downtown is one of the city's most historic 'hoods, and here beats the heart of the Freedom Trail.

Take the Green Line to Park and walk east, or take the Red Line to South Station and walk west. Downtown is bordered by State Street to the north, Chinatown to the south, Tremont Street and Boston Common on the west, and Boston Harbor wharves on its eastern edge. Be prepared: the tangle of streets can be confusing. If you get lost, don't worry. Downtown's windy streets are also typically short, so you'll be able to reorient yourself quickly. And in the mean time, you just might stumble upon something fun and historic.

Here's an interesting fact about Downtown: It's Boston's original landmass, along with the North End. Back in 1630, when Boston's founder John Winthrop sailed through, the place looked nothing like it does today. Look at an old map of the then-called Shawmut Peninsula, and you'll understand. Boston was a low laying, swampy mess, before landfill projects created the Back Bay and significant portions of Chinatown, the South End, and South Boston, in the 19th century.

Washington Street (aka Downtown Crossing) is Downtown's main commercial thoroughfare. The block reeks of history—and sausage carts. Street vendors, flower sellers, and gaggles of teenagers, businesspeople, and shoppers throng the pedestrian mall. Shops like Primark and new eateries have been helping to revitalize the area after a dormant period.

Downtown

Sights

Benjamin Franklin Statue/Boston Latin School

PUBLIC ART | **FAMILY** | This stop on the Freedom Trail, in front of Old City Hall, commemorates the noted revolutionary, statesman, and inventor. His likeness also marks the original location of Boston Latin School, the country's oldest public school (founded in 1635), which still molds young minds, albeit from the Fenway neighborhood today. Franklin attended Boston Latin with three other signers of the Declaration of Independence—Samuel Adams, John Hancock, and Robert Treat Paine—but he has the dubious distinction of being the only one of the four not to graduate. ■**TIP→** This

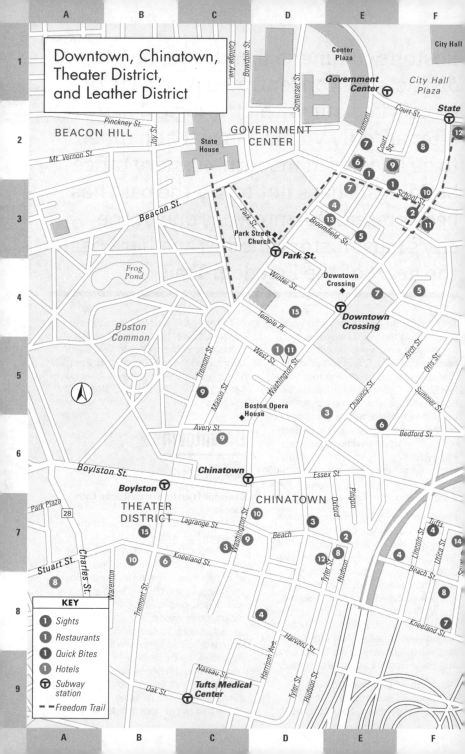

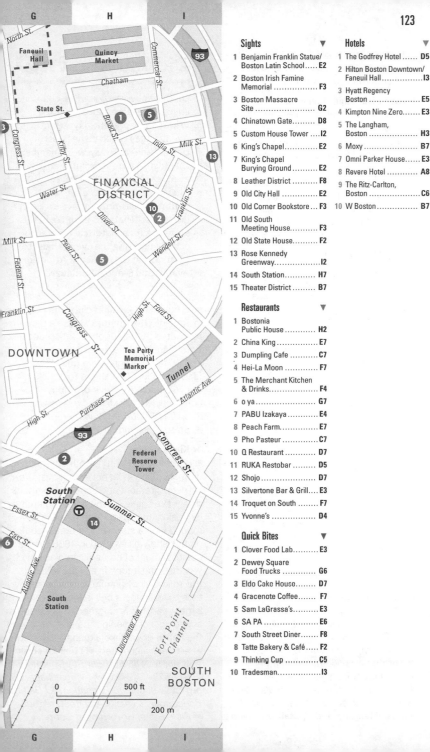

Sights ▼

1 Benjamin Franklin Statue/
   Boston Latin School **E2**
2 Boston Irish Famine
   Memorial **F3**
3 Boston Massacre
   Site **G2**
4 Chinatown Gate **D8**
5 Custom House Tower **I2**
6 King's Chapel **E2**
7 King's Chapel
   Burying Ground **E2**
8 Leather District **F8**
9 Old City Hall **E2**
10 Old Corner Bookstore ... **F3**
11 Old South
    Meeting House **F3**
12 Old State House **F2**
13 Rose Kennedy
    Greenway **I2**
14 South Station **H7**
15 Theater District **B7**

Restaurants ▼

1 Bostonia
   Public House **H2**
2 China King **E7**
3 Dumpling Cafe **C7**
4 Hei-La Moon **F7**
5 The Merchant Kitchen
   & Drinks **F4**
6 o ya **G7**
7 PABU Izakaya **E4**
8 Peach Farm **E7**
9 Pho Pasteur **C7**
10 Q Restaurant **D7**
11 RUKA Restobar **D5**
12 Shojo **D7**
13 Silvertone Bar & Grill **E3**
14 Troquet on South **F7**
15 Yvonne's **D4**

Quick Bites ▼

1 Clover Food Lab **E3**
2 Dewey Square
   Food Trucks **G6**
3 Eldo Cake House **D7**
4 Gracenote Coffee **F7**
5 Sam LaGrassa's **E3**
6 SA PA **E6**
7 South Street Diner **F8**
8 Tatte Bakery & Café **F2**
9 Thinking Cup **C5**
10 Tradesman **I3**

Hotels ▼

1 The Godfrey Hotel **D5**
2 Hilton Boston Downtown/
   Faneuil Hall **I3**
3 Hyatt Regency
   Boston **E5**
4 Kimpton Nine Zero **E3**
5 The Langham,
   Boston **H3**
6 Moxy **B7**
7 Omni Parker House **E3**
8 Revere Hotel **A8**
9 The Ritz-Carlton,
   Boston **C6**
10 W Boston **B7**

is **Freedom Trail stop 6.** ⊠ *45 School St., Downtown* ☎ *617/635–3911* ⊕ *www. thefreedomtrail.org* Ⓜ *Park.*

Boston Irish Famine Memorial

MEMORIAL | Dedicated in 1998 with this memorial and a small park, artist Robert Shure's two sculptures—one depicting an anguished family on the shores of Ireland, the other a determined and hopeful Irish family stepping ashore in Boston—are a tribute to the rich immigrant past of this most Irish of American cities. ⊠ *School St. at Washington St., Downtown* Ⓜ *State, Downtown Crossing.*

Boston Massacre Site

MEMORIAL | **FAMILY** | A circle of cobblestones in front of the Old State House marks the site of the Boston Massacre. To recap: it was on the snowy evening of March 5, 1770, that nine British soldiers fired in panic upon a taunting mob of more than 75 colonists who were upset over British occupation and taxation. Five townsmen died. In the legal action that followed, the defense of the accused soldiers was undertaken by John Adams and Josiah Quincy, both of whom vehemently opposed British oppression but were devoted to the principle of fair trial. All but two of the nine regulars charged were acquitted; the others were branded on the hand for the crime of manslaughter. Paul Revere lost little time in capturing the "massacre" in a dramatic engraving that soon became one of the Revolution's most potent images of propaganda. ■**TIP→ This is Freedom Trail stop 10.** ⊠ *206 Washington St., Downtown* ⊕ *www.thefreedomtrail.org* Ⓜ *State.*

Custom House Tower

BUILDING | **FAMILY** | One of Boston's most recognizable buildings, the gorgeous 1847 Custom House resembles a Greek Revival temple and features an iconic tower that was added much later, in 1915. This addition gave the building notoriety at the time as the city's tallest. Where the skyscraper once operated as a federal building, today, Marriott owns it

as a hotel and vacation club. The public is invited into the Custom House's recently renovated 26th-floor observation deck—for unparalleled views of Downtown and Boston Harbor—on a guided tour for a small fee. Call ahead for a ticket, but you still must arrive promptly to be admitted. ⊠ *3 McKinley Sq., Downtown* ☎ *617/310–6300* ⊕ *www.marriot.com* Ⓜ *State, Aquarium.*

★ King's Chapel

RELIGIOUS SITE | **FAMILY** | Both somber and dramatic, King's Chapel looms over the corner of Tremont and School streets. Its distinctive shape wasn't achieved entirely by design; for lack of funds, it was never topped with a steeple. The first chapel on this site was erected in 1688 for the establishment of an Anglican place of worship, and it took five years to build the solid Quincy-granite structure seen today. The chapel's bell is Paul Revere's largest and, in his judgment, his sweetest sounding. For a behind-the-scenes look at the bell or crypt, take a guided tour. You won't be disappointed. ■**TIP→ Freedom Trail stop 5.** ⊠ *58 Tremont St., Downtown* ☎ *617/523–1749* ⊕ *www.kings-chapel. org* ⌨ *$4 suggested donation; $7 Bell & Bones tour; $5 Art & Architecture tour* Ⓜ *Park, State, Government Center.*

King's Chapel Burying Ground

CEMETERY | FAMILY | Legends linger in this oldest of the city's cemeteries, its first proper burying ground. A handy map of famous grave sites is posted a short walk down the left path. Notable people buried here include Elizabeth Pain, the model for Hester Prynne in Nathaniel Hawthorne's *The Scarlet Letter*, William Dawes Jr. who rode out to warn of the British invasion the night of Paul Revere's famous ride, John Winthrop, Massachusetts' first governor, and several generations of his descendants. ■TIP➜ This is Freedom Trail stop 5. ⊠ *50 Tremont St., Downtown* ☏ *617/523–1749* ⊕ *www. kings-chapel.org* Ⓜ *Park, State, Government Center.*

Old City Hall

BUILDING | Built in 1865, Old City Hall is a historic site and served as the municipal seat of government for 38 of Boston's mayors, including famous ones like John "Honey Fitz" Fitzgerald, James Curley, and Kevin White. In its courtyard, find Richard S. Greenough's bronze statue of Benjamin Franklin and a mural marking the original site of the Boston Latin School. Today, Old City Hall is an office building. While you can't really venture too far inside the building, do go up and check out the murals around its entrance. ⊠ *45 School St., Downtown* ⊕ *www. oldcityhall.com* Ⓜ *State, Park.*

Old Corner Bookstore

BUILDING | Through these doors, between 1845 and 1865, passed some of the century's literary lights: Henry David Thoreau, Ralph Waldo Emerson, and Henry Wadsworth Longfellow—even Charles Dickens paid a visit. Many of their works were published here by James T. "Jamie" Fields, who in 1830 had founded the influential firm Ticknor and Fields. In the 19th century, the graceful, gambrel-roof, early-Georgian structure—built in 1718 on land once owned by religious rebel Anne Hutchinson—also housed the city's leading bookstore. There's a plaque on the wall to read more about its history, but today, somewhat sadly, the building is home to a fast-food joint. ■TIP➜ This is Freedom Trail stop 7. ⊠ *1 School St., Downtown* ⊕ *www.thefreedomtrail.org* Ⓜ *State.*

★ Old South Meeting House

HISTORIC SITE | FAMILY | This is the second-oldest church building in Boston, and were it not for Longfellow's celebration of the Old North in "Paul Revere's Ride," it might well be the most famous. Today, visitors can learn about its history through exhibits and audio programs. Some of the fiercest of the town meetings that led to the Revolution were held here, culminating in the gathering of December 16, 1773, which was called by Samuel Adams to confront the crisis of three ships, laden with dutiable tea, anchored at Griffin's Wharf. The activists wanted the tea returned to England, but the governor would not permit it—and the rest is history. The Voices of Protest exhibit celebrates Old South as a forum for free speech from Revolutionary days to the present. ■TIP➜ This is Freedom Trail stop 8. ⊠ *310 Washington St., Downtown* ☏ *617/720–1713* ⊕ *www.revolution aryspaces.org* ⊠ *$6* Ⓜ *State, Downtown Crossing.*

★ Old State House

BUILDING | FAMILY | This colonial-era landmark has one of the most recognizable facades in Boston, with its gable adorned by a brightly gilded lion and silver unicorn, symbols of British imperial power. This was the seat of the colonial government from 1713 until the Revolution, and after the evacuation of the British from Boston in 1776 it served the independent Commonwealth until its replacement on Beacon Hill was completed in 1798. The Declaration of Independence was first read in public in Boston from its balcony. John Hancock was inaugurated here as the first governor under the new state constitution. Today, it's an interactive museum with exhibits, artifacts, and

The Old South Meeting House is Boston's second-oldest church building; it's also where the spark was lit for the infamous Boston Tea Party.

18th-century artwork, and tells the stories of Revolutionary Bostonians through costumed guides. ■TIP➜ **This is Freedom Trail stop 9.**

✉ *206 Washington St., Downtown* ☎ *617/720–1713* ⊕ *www.revolutionaryspaces.org* 🎟 *$12* Ⓜ *State, Government Center.*

Rose Kennedy Greenway

CITY PARK | FAMILY | This one linear mile of winding parks marks the path the highway once took through the city (the Big Dig project is legendary for not the best of reasons, as the most expensive highway project in the United States), adds much-needed flora and fauna to the area and has turned into a delightful backyard playground that stretches from the North End to Chinatown. Lawn furniture and games, seasonal farmers and artist markets, art installations, water features, live performances, free Wi-Fi, and more make it a lively spot, especially in warmer months. There's a one-of-a-kind, hand-carved carousel; and the food truck scene has grown into a bustling lunchtime destination (not to mention the seasonal Trillium Beer Garden hotspot). The park's website has a map of its 17 acres; a pleasant stroll through all of them will take you from the North End to Chinatown. ✉ *Downtown* ✛ *Between New Sudbury St. in North End and Beach St. in Chinatown; along Atlantic Ave.* ⊕ *www.rosekennedygreenway.org* Ⓜ *State, Haymarket, Chinatown, Aquarium.*

🍽 Restaurants

In Downtown, professionals and execs keep the lunch business booming. While 15 to 20 years ago, the streets would get quiet after 6 pm, it's not so today. Dinner and drinks have become a thing, and the neighborhood has followed suit featuring a number of social hot spots with fantastic culinary options after dark.

★ Bostonia Public House

$$$ | AMERICAN | FAMILY | Airy and classic in atmosphere, this modern restaurant focuses on two things: food and local history (it is, after all, situated in a historic

1902 building). The menu features elevated takes on comfort food; at lunch expect more sandwiches. **Known for:** weekend brunch set to live music; long bar with lots of seating; really, really good food. $ *Average main: $30* ⊠ *131 State St., Downtown* ☎ *617/948–9800* ⊕ *www.bostoniapublichouse.com* Ⓜ *Aquarium.*

The Merchant Kitchen & Drinks
$$$ | **CONTEMPORARY** | Dig into grilled and seared fish, great burgers, and snacky items with global flourishes at this dark-wood and leather-dressed restaurant. You may need to use your phone to light up the menu before ordering—it can get pretty dark inside. **Known for:** signature buffalo cauliflower; extensive local beer selection; Sunday jazz brunch. $ *Average main: $28* ⊠ *60 Franklin St., Downtown* ☎ *617/482–6060* ⊕ *www.themerchantboston.com* Ⓜ *Downtown Crossing, State.*

PABU Izakaya
$$$$ | **JAPANESE** | Internationally renowned chefs Ken Tominaga and Michael Mina teamed up to offer Bostonians a place to experience top-quality Japanese izakaya food, from sashimi and sushi to grilled meats robata-style. Cold and hot small plates, grilled skewers, makimono rolls please foodies, travelers, and residents of the modern Millennium Tower residences in which this restaurant holds court on the second floor. **Known for:** seafood imported fresh daily from Tsukiji Market in Japan; more than two-dozen Japanese whiskies; limited-batch and rare sake. $ *Average main: $50* ⊠ *3 Franklin St., Downtown* ☎ *857/327–7228* Ⓜ *Downtown Crossing, Park.*

RUKA Restobar
$$ | **FUSION** | If you've never heard of *chifa* cuisine (yeah, it's a real thing), you'll wonder why not after having a meal at RUKA in Downtown Crossing, where the kitchen creates dishes inspired by Cantonese–Peruvian and Japanese culinary traditions. Menu features bountiful sushi options, raw bar items, snacks, and wok-prepared dishes. **Known for:** Cantonese–Peruvian–Japanese fusion cuisine; colorful, artful vibes; interesting sushi options. $ *Average main: $20* ⊠ *The Godfrey Hotel, 505 Washington St., Downtown* ☎ *617/266–0102* ⊕ *www.rukarestobar.com* Ⓜ *Downtown Crossing.*

Silvertone Bar & Grill
$ | **AMERICAN** | Devotees of this retro-cool basement restaurant with strong cocktails and reasonable prices swear by the no-fuss menu options, such as a truly addictive macaroni and cheese topped with crispy bacon, meat loaf with mashed potatoes, and steak tips. The wine list is compact but varied and has one of the lowest markups in the city. **Known for:** strong cocktails; comfort food; laid-back feel. $ *Average main: $17* ⊠ *69 Bromfield St., Downtown* ☎ *617/338–7887* ⊕ *www.silvertone-downtown.com* Ⓜ *Park.*

Yvonne's
$$$ | **CONTEMPORARY** | For a big, brassy, bountiful night out in an iconic Boston building, head to this glamorous reimagined supper club inside the former 1862 Locke-Ober restaurant, now a wildly ornate setting where the buffed and beautiful sink into plush chairs in the book-packed library or at the original mahogany mirrored bar to swill down ice-cold martinis and large format whiskey drinks. Should cocktails morph into dinner, white-clothed tables glowing with votives behind the boisterous bar provide a cushy place to share plates of globally inspired comfort food. **Known for:** glamorous supper club concept; historic setting; large-format cocktails and shared feasts. $ *Average main: $35* ⊠ *2 Winter Pl., Downtown* ☎ *617/267–0047* ⊕ *www.yvonnesboston.com.*

☕ Coffee and Quick Bites

Clover Food Lab

$ | **VEGETARIAN** | After more than a decade, locals still love this vegetarian restaurant's chickpea fritters, not to mention the daily changing menu of freshly prepared sustainable and local veg- and vegan-friendly sandwiches and plates. Boston and Cambridge feature a number of Clover locations, but this one, in Downtown Crossing, is bright and airy with huge windows that open onto School Street, making for great people watching. **Known for:** chickpea fritter sandwich; house-made juice sodas and George Howell coffee; sourcing ingredients locally and sustainably. $ Average main: $10 ✉ 27 School St., Downtown ⊕ www.cloverfoodlab.com Ⓜ Park, State.

Dewey Square Food Trucks

$ | **FAST FOOD** | **FAMILY** | On weekday mornings and afternoons, locally operated food trucks congregate at Dewey Square plaza on the Rose Kennedy Greenway, ready to serve Financial District professionals an eat-it-while-you-walk-or-picnic meal. Typically, 8 to 10 different options offer variety from curry to Korean. **Known for:** multiple local food trucks in a gorgeous park location; always changing options; easily accessible outdoor seating. $ Average main: $10 ✉ Rose Kennedy Greenway, Dewey Sq., Financial District ⊕ www.rosekennedygreenway. org/foodtrucks Ⓜ South Station.

Sam LaGrassa's

$ | **DELI** | **FAMILY** | It's unlikely you'll simply happen upon this iconic Boston sandwich joint, tucked away as it is, but the hefty sandwiches (they weigh pounds) are worth the trouble of looking. The line typically snakes out the door, but while you're standing in it, you can savor the deli-like smells and browse the meats behind the counter. **Known for:** pastrami and corned beef made in-house; huge portions; a long line that moves fast. $ Average main: $15 ✉ 44 Province St., Downtown ☎ 617/357–6861 ⊕ www.samlagrassas. com ⊘ Closed weekends Ⓜ Park.

SA PA

$ | **VIETNAMESE** | A former hedge fund manager left his career to open SA PA, his Downtown lunch spot inspired by the Vietnamese food he ate as a child. SA PA takes the authentic and makes it approachable for Boston diners, offering pho (Vietnamese soup), bowls, banh mi, and banh mi burritos, in a really casual yet cool setting. **Known for:** banh mi sandwiches—get the spicy sriracha mayo; fresh pho, made in small batches every day; chili mint limeade. $ Average main: $10 ✉ 92 Bedford St., Downtown ☎ 617/303–7000 ⊕ www.sa-pa.com Ⓜ South Station.

★ Tatte Bakery & Café

$ | **ISRAELI** | Tzurit Or's upscale bakery and café takes pastries to the next level with items like kouign-amann, pistachio croissants, and Jerusalem bagels. While these items are staples, the majority of the menu changes with the season or even more frequently. **Known for:** Or's take on traditional North African shakshuka, served with challah bread; signature nut tarts that are as pretty as they are tasty; convivial atmosphere. $ Average main: $12 ✉ 201 Washington St., Downtown ☎ 617/723–5555 ⊕ www.tattebakery. com Ⓜ State, Government Center.

★ Thinking Cup

$ | **CAFÉ** | Across Tremont Street from Boston Common, Thinking Cup caters to a mixed crowd of area professionals and comm students from nearby Emerson College. Rarely is the coffeehouse not packed with caffeine addicts looking for their next fix of Stumptown coffee, whether it's in the form of a single origin pour over or a macchiato. **Known for:** signature lattes: the hazelnut is made with roasted hazelnut paste, and the honey-cinnamon with a house-made syrup; awesome sandwiches, especially the Jittery Hen, made with coffee-braised chicken; no Wi-Fi access. $ *Average main: $10* ✉ *165 Tremont St., Downtown* ☎ *617/482–5555* 🌐 *www.thinkingcup.com* [M] *Boylston, Park.*

Tradesman

$ | **CAFÉ** | A magnet for hipsters in the Financial District, this coffee shop and lounge offers a quiet scene for business folk who want a place to settle in with their laptops and a perfect cold brew, But, they're not the only patrons: Instagrammers come for the decadent stuffed croissants, while guests of the Hilton Hotel next door stop in for an afternoon cocktail. Fare is mostly sandwiches and baked goods. **Known for:** stuffed croissants in flavors like red velvet and Valrhona chocolate; house-made pop tarts; Barrington Coffee Company's award-winning gold blend. $ *Average main: $12* ✉ *58 Batterymarch St., Downtown* ☎ *617/348–1230* 🌐 *www.tradesmanboston.com* [M] *State, Aquarium.*

Hotels

Business travelers tend to congregate at Downtown hotels near the Financial District, since that's where the work is. Hotels closer to the Freedom Trail are better suited for Boston's abundance of leisure travelers.

The Godfrey Hotel

$$$ | **HOTEL** | This chic, bustling boutique hotel is popular with business folk, who appreciate the ease of walking to the nearby Financial District. **Pros:** Frette linens; complimentary bikes and yoga mats; ideal for business travelers. **Cons:** added daily "urban fee" of $25; expensive valet parking; no airport shuttle. $ *Rooms from: $300* ✉ *505 Washington St., Downtown* ☎ *617/804–2000, 855/649–4500* 🌐 *www.godfreyhotelboston.com* 🛏 *242 rooms* 🍴 *No meals* [M] *Downtown Crossing.*

Hilton Boston Downtown/Faneuil Hall

$$$ | **HOTEL** | If you're looking for comfortable downtown lodging, you'll find it at this classic business hotel with a 1920s, art deco vibe, complete with mahogany paneling and soft gold lighting. **Pros:** 24-hour fitness and business centers; clean, quiet, and 100% smoke-free; ideal for business travelers. **Cons:** $15 daily Wi-Fi fee, or free on first floor; pets welcome for $75 nonrefundable fee; doesn't have a Hilton Honors lounge. $ *Rooms from: $300* ✉ *89 Broad St., Downtown* ☎ *617/556–0006* 🌐 *www.hilton.com* 🛏 *403 rooms* 🍴 *No meals* [M] *State.*

Hyatt Regency Boston

$$$ | **HOTEL** | **FAMILY** | Hyatt Regency Boston sits amid the colorful Downtown Crossing neighborhood, just steps away from world-renowned cultural attractions, businesses, and universities like Suffolk and Emerson. **Pros:** steps from Financial District and historic Downtown; 52-foot heated, indoor saline swimming pool; good for business travelers, with a 24-hour business center and free Wi-Fi. **Cons:** views of office buildings from guest rooms; thin walls; $25 daily "destination fee". $ *Rooms from: $379* ✉ *1 Ave. de Lafayette, Downtown* ☎ *617/912–1234, 800/233–1234* 🌐 *www.hyatt.com/en-US/hotel/massachusetts/hyatt-regency-boston/bosto* 🛏 *502 rooms* 🍴 *No meals* [M] *Downtown Crossing.*

★ Kimpton Nine Zero

$$$ | **HOTEL** | **FAMILY** | This Kimpton boutique hotel is sleek, sleek, sleek—all smooth lines, neutral tones, wood, and leather, and then bam! sudden bursts of vibrant color and pop art. **Pros:** in-room spa therapy available; late-afternoon hosted lobby wine reception (daily, 5–6 pm); in-room yoga mats. **Cons:** smallish rooms; fee for Wi-Fi; no airport shuttle. $ *Rooms from: $350* ✉ *90 Tremont St., Downtown* ☎ *617/772–5800, 866/906–9090* 🌐 *www.ninezero.com* 🛏 *190 rooms* 🍴 *No meals* [M] *Park, Government Center.*

The Langham, Boston

$$$$ | **HOTEL** | Its 1922 Renaissance Revival building and the former Federal Reserve Bank of Boston is a historic juxtaposition for The Langham's brand new, contemporary luxury retreat. **Pros:** all-new, private Club Lounge; glass-enclosed indoor pool; lavish rooms boast a homey feel. **Cons:** not close to Beacon Hill or the Back Bay; luxury pricing; a bit of a walk to public transportation. [$] *Rooms from: $399* ✉ *250 Franklin St., Downtown* ☎ *617/451–1900* 🌐 *www.boston.langhamhotels.com* 🛏 *312 rooms* 🍴 *No meals* [M] *South Station.*

Omni Parker House

$$ | **HOTEL** | **FAMILY** | There's more than a century and a half of rich and varied history within these walls, where JFK proposed to Jackie, and Charles Dickens gave his first reading of "A Christmas Carol." Though it's America's longest, continuously operating hotel, its lobby, restaurant, and bar received a makeover in 2016, so you can steep yourself in Boston history while enjoying today's modern conveniences. **Pros:** overflowing with history; great location on the Freedom Trail; in-room fitness kits. **Cons:** small rooms, some of which are a bit dark; thin-walled rooms can be noisy; area parking is very expensive. [$] *Rooms from: $200* ✉ *60 School St., Downtown* ☎ *617/227–8600, 800/843–6664* 🌐 *www.omniparkerhouse.com* 🛏 *551 rooms* 🍴 *No meals* [M] *Park.*

The Ritz-Carlton, Boston

$$$$ | **HOTEL** | **FAMILY** | Warm wood complements an extensive art collection in the lobby of The Ritz-Carlton Boston, where modern furnishings provide seating at check-in (no front desk here!), and lights are made of hand-blown Murano glass. **Pros:** excellent service; giant marble soaking tubs; spacious rooms and suites. **Cons:** fee to access Equinox Sports Club, unless you're staying on Club Level; food service is expensive; steep valet parking costs. [$] *Rooms from: $700* ✉ *10 Avery St., Downtown* ☎ *617/574–7100, 800/542–8680* 🌐 *www.ritzcarlton.com* 🛏 *193 rooms* 🍴 *No meals* [M] *Boylston.*

🍸 Nightlife

BARS

Avery Bar

BARS/PUBS | Whether you're staying at The Ritz or just stopping by for a drink, the decadent and modern Avery Bar serves some serious, handcrafted cocktails, including a few *sans* alcohol. While this is a hotel lobby bar to be sure, the experience is anything but. The warm ambiance attracts a 40-something crowd. ✉ *The Ritz-Carlton Boston, 10 Avery St., Downtown* ☎ *617/574–7176* [M] *Downtown Crossing, Chinatown.*

Beantown Pub

BARS/PUBS | Beantown Pub cleverly posits, "The only pub in the world where you can drink a cold Sam Adams' while viewing a cold Sam Adams." And, it's true, since this casual bar sits on The Freedom Trail across Tremont Street from Granary Burying Ground where the Founding Father is interred. The bar is a fine place to watch multiple sports events on television, shoot pool, or people-watch. There's also a standard pub menu, available until 2 am. ✉ *100 Tremont St., Downtown* ☎ *617/426–0111* 🌐 *www.beantownpub.com* [M] *Park St., Downtown Crossing.*

Good Life

BARS/PUBS | This funky bar in a heritage flatiron building mixes exotic martinis and fresh-juice cocktails, and boasts a whopping selection of international vodkas. The menu is broad, reasonable, and healthy. The basement level lounge draws eclectic crowds for dancing and the occasional live band. ✉ *28 Kingston St., Downtown* ☎ *617/451–2622* 🌐 *www.goodlifebar.com* 🕒 *Closed Sun.* [M] *Downtown Crossing, South Station.*

Last Hurrah

BARS/PUBS | Whiskey, champagne, desserts: they're all staples within this historic bar at the Omni Parker House where mahogany club chairs and silver-tray service might make you feel like a Boston Brahmin, even if only for a martini or two. ✉ *60 School St., Downtown* ☎ *617/305–1888* ⊕ *www.omnihotels. com/hotels/boston-parker-house/dining/ the-last-hurrah* ☉ *Closed Sun.* Ⓜ *Park.*

Mariel

BARS/PUBS | Fitzgerald's "The Beautiful and Damned" meets the breezy tropics within this Havana-inspired, recent addition to Boston's dining and nightlife scene. Mariel best serves those who appreciate good food and drink, and a vivacious atmosphere. Think arepas, plantain dumplings, gulf shrimp, Cuban-style pizza, fresh juices, mojitos, and an extensive list of rums. Fun vibe; gets louder as it gets later. ✉ *10 Post Office Sq., Downtown* ☎ *617/333–8776* ⊕ *www. marielofficial.com* Ⓜ *State.*

🛍 Shopping

Historically, shopping has been the biggest reason to visit the Downtown Crossing area of the Downtown neighborhood, although its heyday was in the early part of the 20th century. Then and now, stores collect where Washington and Summer streets meet, and disperse from there. International retailers like Macy's and Primark dominate the area, mingling with discount retailers, hundreds of local jewelers in the Boston Jewelers Building, and specialty shops.

BOOKS

★ Brattle Book Shop

BOOKS/STATIONERY | Bibliophiles can't get enough of this old-timey book store that is, literally, chockablack with books—floor to ceiling and stuffed into corners. The store has been in operation since 1825, and today, owner Ken Gloss (a fixture on PBS' *Antiques Road Show*) fields queries from passionate book lovers about out-of-print, rare, antique and foreign language tomes, and also last year's used best-seller. If you're in need of a read for the ride home, browse the rolling carts in Brattle's adjacent outdoor lot, where books of all genres go for $5, $3, or just $1. ✉ *9 West St., Downtown* ☎ *617/542– 0210* ⊕ *www.brattlebookshop.com* ☉ *Closed Sun.* Ⓜ *Downtown Crossing.*

SPECIALTY SHOPS

Bromfield Pen Shop

SPECIALTY STORES | Dedicated to the fine art of writing since 1948, this small store carries more than 40 different brands of pens, ranging in price from two bucks to thousands. The friendly, knowledgeable staff guides you through the selection of fountain, rollerball, and ballpoint pens, as well as pencils, in gold, silver, wood, and plastic from makers such as Cross, Visconti, and Faber-Castell. The store also stocks refills, inks, leather gifts, desk accessories, watches, and Swiss Army knives and offers on-site engraving within 24 hours. ✉ *5 Bromfield St., Downtown* ☎ *617/482–9053* ⊕ *www.bromfieldpen-shop.com* ☉ *Closed Sun.* Ⓜ *Park.*

Chinatown, Theater District, and Leather District

The heart of Asian-American life in Boston beats in Chinatown, with its authentic restaurants, cultural festivals, markets, and, of course, thousands of residents. Reportedly, it's the third largest Chinatown in the United States, after those in San Francisco and Manhattan, although today's neighborhood runs the spectrum of many Far East cultures, from Thai to Taiwanese, Korean to Cambodian. Before the 1870s, the area was resettled a few times as immigrant groups moved in and out: Syrian, Irish, Jewish, Italian. Chinese laborers arrived and settled here after 1870, and their families kept coming through the 1950s. Today, Beach Street serves as Chinatown's main street. The neighborhood is bounded by Essex, Washington, Lincoln and Marginal streets; Tufts Medical Center complex occupies approximately one third of the area.

Just west of Chinatown, the majority of Boston's historic stages reside in the Theater District, which means the area is a hot spot for ballet, opera, Broadway tours, stand-up comedy, and other performing arts productions. Emerson College students keep the vibe young.

And, then, to the east of Chinatown, a very small enclave known as the Leather District is bounded by Kneeland Street, Essex Street, Atlantic Avenue, and Lincoln Street. Before its 19th-century brick warehouses (now residential lofts) boomed with leather and textile merchants, it was known as South Cove, a soggy area that was filled in with land during the 1830s. Today, the Leather District features a few destination standouts, including the city's best sushi restaurant and South Station.

 Sights

Chinatown Gate
BUILDING | Two foo lions ward off evil for those who pass through the massive, traditional paifang gate that signals your entrance to Chinatown. It was donated to the Asian residents of Boston by Taiwan, in the early 1980s. You'll likely see red lanterns hanging from it; they signify good luck. The main square around the gate acts as a gathering place for the neighborhood's residents, who meet to socialize or play games. The gate is situated at Beach Street, and it also marks the end of the Greenway. ⊠ *Beach St. at Hudson St., Chinatown* Ⓜ *South Station.*

Leather District
NEIGHBORHOOD | Opposite South Station and inside the angle formed by Kneeland Street and Atlantic Avenue is a corner of Downtown that has been relatively untouched by high-rise development: the old Leather District. For those who like to get a sense of history through place, this is probably the best place in downtown Boston to get an idea of what the city's business center looked like in the late 19th century as the wholesale supply area for raw materials in the days when the shoe industry was a regional economic mainstay. Today, a few leather firms remain, but most warehouses now contain expensive loft apartments. ⊠ *Bordered by Kneeland St., Atlantic Ave., and Lincoln St., Chinatown* Ⓜ *South Station.*

South Station
TRANSPORTATION SITE (AIRPORT/BUS/FERRY/TRAIN) | This gorgeous colonnaded granite structure is to Boston what Grand Central Station is to New York. Behind its grand 1900s facade, you'll find an airy, modern transit center that services the MBTA commuter rail for lines originating west and south of the city, the Red and Silver subway lines, and regional Amtrak trains. Thanks to its eateries, coffee bars, newsstand, and other shops, waiting for a train here can actually be a pleasant experience. South Station's bus terminal for Greyhound, Peter Pan, and other bus lines, is right next door. ■**TIP➜ South Station is a great launching point for exploring a variety of neighborhoods, including Downtown, Chinatown, and the Seaport.** ⊠ *700 Atlantic Ave., Downtown* ⊕ *www.south-station.net* Ⓜ *South Station.*

Theater District
NEIGHBORHOOD | Bounded by Washington and West streets, Marginal Road, and Charles Street South, the Theater District is fertile ground for Boston's performing arts scene—traditional, avant-garde, and otherwise. Each theater—the Wang, the Shubert, the Majestic, the Colonial, the Wilbur, the Paramount, the Modern,

the Charles Playhouse, and the Opera House—has a history all its own and most have been restored within the last two decades. Emerson College and its campus occupy a large part of the neighborhood, and student-interest brings in some interesting acts from around the world. Night owls can enjoy stand-up shows at a few comedy clubs or feel the beat at a variety of dance and nightclubs. ✉ *Theater District* [M] *Boylston.*

🍴 Restaurants

When it comes to cuisine, Old World and New World traditions mingle in Chinatown, although the emphasis is definitely on the former. Restaurants are a big draw for this neighborhood, and today, Chinese establishments are interspersed with Vietnamese, Cantonese, Korean, Japanese, Thai, Taiwanese, and Malaysian eateries, to name a few. Many places are open after midnight. On Sunday, Bostonians often head here for dim sum.

China King

$ | **CHINESE** | **FAMILY** | This friendly, family owned Chinese restaurant serves crave-worthy, modern-ish takes on classic Chinese dishes. China King is not large, and it can get busy with diners clamoring for scallion pie, homemade Shanghai chow mein noodles, hot and spicy lamb, and more. **Known for:** owner and chef Doris Mei's cooking; the three-course Peking duck—order a day in advance; attentive service. [$] *Average main: $14* ✉ *60 Beach St., Chinatown* ☎ *617/542–1763* 🌐 *www.chinakingbostonma.com* 🕓 *Closed Mon.* [M] *Chinatown.*

Dumpling Cafe

$ | **TAIWANESE** | **FAMILY** | Discerning diners stream into this no-frills Taiwanese eatery to slurp down the house specialty—wobbly, *xiaolongbao* (soup dumplings) filled with a rich, flavorful broth; be careful, they'll scald your chin if you drip! For those in the mood for other items, an extensive menu features authentic dishes and crowd favorites. **Known for:** Taiwanese/Szechuan dishes; soup dumplings; hard-to-find ingredients, like intestine, liver, and kidney. [$] *Average main: $14* ✉ *695 Washington St., Chinatown* ☎ *617/338–8858* 🌐 *www.dumplingcafe.com* [M] *Chinatown.*

★ Hei-La Moon

$ | **CHINESE** | **FAMILY** | Hei-La Moon is located on Beach Street, but don't get lost looking for it; you have to put Chinatown at your back and cross Surface Road, almost into the Leather District. But once you do locate this Cantonese dim sum palace, you will be glad for it—locals fill the large, ornately decorated dining room pretty early in the morning, drinking tea and noshing on small plates brought around by waitstaff on carts. **Known for:** endless dim sum; inexpensive prices; few English-speaking staff. [$] *Average main: $10* ✉ *88 Beach St., Chinatown* ☎ *617/338–8813* [M] *South Station.*

★ o ya

$$$$ | **SUSHI** | If you want to experience the best sushi you've ever tasted—and you have the purse for it—eat at upscale Tim and Nancy Cushman's Leather District restaurant (this was the first, but there's also Manhattan and Mexico City locations). Despite o ya's tucked away location and hidden door, the place isn't exactly a secret: critics from the *New York Times, Bon Appetit,* and *Food & Wine* have all named this improvisational sushi spot among the best in the country. **Known for:** delicate, beautiful, sophisticated sushi; spectacular omakase tasting menu: 17 courses ($185) or 21 courses ($285); expensive prices. [$] *Average main: $60* ✉ *9 East St., Chinatown* ☎ *617/654–9900* 🌐 *o-ya.restaurant/o-ya-boston* 🕓 *Closed Sun. and Mon.* [M] *South Station.*

★ Peach Farm

$ | **CANTONESE** | **FAMILY** | It may look a bit worse for wear, but this authentic Cantonese restaurant is a Chinatown landmark among locals and neighborhood visitors.

What's really special is the live fish tank where diners can select the fish they want to eat—and it's cooked to order fresh—while the extensive menu offers perhaps too many options, but the waitstaff is happy to give recommendations. **Known for:** incredibly fresh seafood; house-fried rice with sweet Chinese sausage and scallops; late-night hours—until 3 am. $ Average main: $12 ⊠ 4 Tyler St., Chinatown ☎ 617/482–3332 ⊕ www.peachfarmboston.com Ⓜ Chinatown, South Station.

Pho Pasteur

$ | **VIETNAMESE** | Day or night, patrons pack this Vietnamese staple of the Chinatown neighborhood known for its steaming bowls of pho. A lengthy menu offers plenty of alternatives, vermicelli dishes, traditional Vietnamese preparations, and about 20 options for vegetarians. **Known for:** traditional Vietnamese pho; unique espresso, ades, and soda beverages; millennial crowd. $ Average main: $11 ⊠ 682 Washington St., Chinatown ☎ 617/482–7467 ⊕ www.phopasteurboston.net Ⓜ Chinatown, Boylston.

Q Restaurant

$ | **ASIAN FUSION** | For a more upscale Chinatown experience, look no farther than this sleek Asian outpost with a full cocktail menu, extensive sushi bar, and addictive Mongolian-style hot pot menu featuring rich, robust broths served with a fleet of herbs, chilis, and ginger for further seasoning to taste. Order whatever vegetables, seafood, meats, and noodles you want to cook at the table, from paper-thin slices of Wagyu rib eye to shelled shrimp. **Known for:** flavorful, Mongolian-style hot pot; good cocktails; long wait times for tables. $ Average main: $15 ⊠ 660 Washington St., Chinatown ☎ 857/350–3968 ⊕ www.thequsa.com Ⓜ Chinatown.

Shojo

$ | **ASIAN FUSION** | Fun, lively, and contemporary, Shojo puts a shine on its little corner of Chinatown. Owner Brian Moy may be a millennial, but he's no stranger to running a restaurant or Asian cuisine—it's his family's business. **Known for:** a killer bao bun burger; from sake to rice beer, a big selection of Japanese spirits; tats and grafitti. $ Average main: $10 ⊠ 9 Tyler St., Chinatown ☎ 617/423–7888 ⊕ www.shojoboston.com ⊙ Closed Sun. Ⓜ Chinatown.

★ Troquet on South

$$$$ | **FRENCH FUSION** | Despite having what might well be Boston's longest wine list, with nearly 500 vintages (more than 50 of which are available by the glass), plus an interactive champagne cart, this French fusion spot flies somewhat under the radar. Still, locals know that Troquet offers all the ingredients for a lovely and delectable evening: a generous space for drinking and dining, a knowledgeable yet unpretentious staff, and decadent fare, beginning with chewy rolls and farm-churned butter scooped from a bucket, and dishes like seared Hudson Valley foie gras and decadent duck a l'Orange. **Known for:** exceptional wine selection; mouthwatering bistro fare; excellent cheese cart. $ Average main: $45 ⊠ 107 South St., Theater District ☎ 617/695–9463 ⊕ troquetboston.com ⊙ No lunch Sat. Closed Sun. Ⓜ Boylston.

☕ Coffee and Quick Bites

Eldo Cake House

$ | **BAKERY** | Devotees of this Chinese bakery's Hong Kong–style egg tarts travel from miles around to get them—and it's no wonder; they are really good. Eldo presents baked buns, fluffy fresh fruit cakes, Swiss rolls and other authentic treats in a self-service manner, so you can pick what you like and pay at the counter. **Known for:** the best egg tarts; light-as-air cake layered with strawberries and cream; Swiss rolls. $ Average main: $10 ⊠ 36 Harrison Ave., Chinatown ☎ 617/350–7977 Ⓜ Chinatown.

★ Gracenote Coffee

$ | CAFÉ | Gracenote roasts top-shelf coffee beans using its own unique process here in Massachusetts, and then serves it in a teeny Leather District storefront just across the border from Chinatown. The flavor is well worth the slightly out-of-the-way jaunt to this hipster haven for pour-overs and espresso drinks that are the focus of the menu. **Known for:** unmatched coffee; extensive variety of milk alternatives; really friendly baristas. $ *Average main: $5* ⊠ *108 Lincoln St., Chinatown* ⊕ *www.gracenotecoffee.com* Ⓜ *South Station.*

South Street Diner

$ | AMERICAN | FAMILY | With its oversized coffee cup signage perched on its roof and decor that seemingly hasn't changed since this Leather District joint first opened in 1943, South Street Diner looks the part. Belly up to the counter for breakfast food, burgers, and sandwiches, all served all day—and we do mean all day, since South Street is open 24 hours. **Known for:** open 24/7; laid-back vibe; one of the only places in town you can get an old-fashioned ice-cream soda. $ *Average main: $14* ⊠ *178 Kneeland St., Chinatown* ☎ *617/350–0028* ⊕ *www.southstreetdiner.com* Ⓜ *South Station.*

 ## Hotels

Moxy

$$ | HOTEL | One of Boston's newest hotels—it opened in October 2019—Moxy is an Instagrammer's dream come true with its sleek exterior and artful flair (say, like custom murals by well-known street artists). **Pros:** 24th-floor rooftop lounge for guest-only use; floor-to-ceiling windows and viewfinders in every room; Bar Moxy work-fun space featuring board games, free Wi-Fi, coffee, cocktails, and food. **Cons:** not good for families; lots of street noise; small rooms. $ *Rooms from: $280* ⊠ *240 Tremont St., Theater District* ☎ *617/793–4200* ⊕ *www.marriott.com/hotels/travel/bosox-moxy-boston-downtown/* ⤴ *340 rooms* ⭘ *No meals* Ⓜ *Boylston, Chinatown.*

Revere Hotel

$$$$ | HOTEL | This stylish spot embraces New England history with a twist—you'll notice artwork tied to Paul Revere throughout the hotel, whether as a steampunk sculpture constructed out of recycled metals by a local artist, or a mural of his famous Boston Massacre engraving on the wall of the hotel bar. **Pros:** rooftop pool and bar has amazing city views; balconies in every room; dog-friendly hotel, complete with bedding and a puppy menu of snacks. **Cons:** $25 guest amenity fee per day; elevators can get congested; for less mobile folks, it's a bit of a walk to Freedom Trail sites. $ *Rooms from: $400* ⊠ *200 Stuart St., Theater District* ☎ *617/482–1800* ⊕ *www.reverehotel.com* ⤴ *356 rooms* ⭘ *Free Breakfast* Ⓜ *Arlington, Boylston.*

W Boston

$$$ | HOTEL | This 238-room tower is fronted by a metal-and-glass "awning" that is outfitted with soft, color-changing neon lights that cast a cheeky glow on passersby. **Pros:** expansive on-site Bliss spa; signature W feather-top beds; free electric-car charging stations. **Cons:** lobby can be loud; late-night street noise; expensive parking. $ *Rooms from: $350* ⊠ *100 Stuart St., Theater District* ☎ *617/261–8700* ⊕ *www.whotels.com/boston* ⤴ *238 rooms* ⭘ *No meals* Ⓜ *Boylston, Tufts Medical Center.*

 ## Nightlife

BARS
4th Wall

BARS/PUBS | This local hangout tries to be seen as a dive bar, but it's much nicer and too new to be called one. The menu features bar bites, hearty entrées, and a burger of the week, all made from scratch in the kitchen, while the bar serves craft beers on draft, craft cocktails, and vodka-soaked gummy bears. To find the 4th Wall from Tremont Street, look for the small, brick building with a gable roof squeezed in by much taller surrounding buildings. ⊠ *228 Tremont St., Theater District* ☎ *857/957–0909* ⊕ *www.4thwallrestaurant.com* Ⓜ *Chinatown, Boylston.*

W Lounge

BARS/PUBS | Vibrant purples and metallics set the tone at this chic, but accessible, bar and lounge in the W Hotel. The resident DJ—and he's legit—curates music (Thursday through Saturday) based on the crowd, while patrons warm up by the fireplace and nosh on charcuterie, flatbreads, charred veggies and signature cocktails. The scotch list is informed and extensive. On Sunday, the Brass Brunch, complete with a live band, is a must. ■**TIP→ Don't wear a hoodie here.** ⊠ *W Hotel, 100 Stuart St., Theater District* ☎ *617/261–8700* Ⓜ *Boylston, Chinatown.*

COMEDY

Nick's Comedy Stop

COMEDY CLUBS | Boston's oldest comedy club has been yukking it up since 1977—Jay Leno reportedly got his start here. The lineup is always funny, whether you catch a local comic on the weekend, or, occasionally, a well-known one. ⊠ *100 Warrenton St., Theater District* ☎ *617/963–6261* ⊕ *www.nickscomedystop.com* 🎟 *$20, reservations advised* Ⓜ *Boylston.*

The Wilbur

COMEDY CLUBS | Inside this 1914-built, American style stage, some of the country's funniest comics—like Tracy Morgan, Whitney Cummings, and Jenny Slate—get audiences laughing and laughing. On nights when comedy is off the bill, The Wilbur hosts more intimate musical perfomances by some serious talent, including Melissa Etheridge, Tanya Tucker, and The Hollies. ⊠ *246 Tremont St., Theater District* ☎ *617/248–9700* ⊕ *www.thewilbur.com* Ⓜ *Boylston.*

Performing Arts

THEATER

Boch Center Wang Theatre and Shubert Theatre

CONCERTS | The historic Wang Theatre, which opened in 1925 and holds an audience of 3,500, and its 1910 little sister, the Shubert Theatre, partner up to create this performance-space complex dedicated to national and international productions, dance companies, concerts, and headlining comics. ■**TIP→ Check out the schedule online, and order your tickets before you come to town.** ⊠ *265 and 270 Tremont St., Theater District* ☎ *800/982–2787 Wang Theatre, 866/348–9738 Shubert Theatre* ⊕ *www.bochcenter.org* Ⓜ *Boylston.*

Charles Playhouse

THEATER | The Charles Playhouse celebrated its 175th anniversary in 2014 with a $2 million renovation. The vintage stage—also formerly serving as a church, Prohibition-era speakeasy, and jazz club—has been hosting two long-running local favorites: *Blue Man Group* since 1995 ,and the zany whodunit *Shear Madness* since 1980. Blue Man Group's uniquely exhilarating production features a trio of deadpan performance artists painted vivid cobalt as they pound drums, share eureka moments, spray sloppy good will, and freely dispense toilet paper. ■**TIP→ First-timer alert: dress casual, especially if you're seated down front.** ⊠ *74 Warrenton St., Theater District* ☎ *617/426–6912 general box office, 800/258–3626 Blue Man Group tickets, 617/426–5225 Shear Madness tickets* ⊕ *www.charlesplayhouse.com* Ⓜ *Boylston.*

★ Citizens Bank Opera House

DANCE | FAMILY | The 2,700-seat, meticulously restored, vaudville-era beaux arts building has been lavished with $35 million worth of gold leaf, lush carpeting, and rococo ornamentation, and it reopened to the public in 2004 after being dormant and neglected for about 12 years. Since then, it has been Boston's premiere destination for touring Broadway companies as well as the home theater for Boston Ballet and all its productions, including its famous *The Nutcracker*. ■**TIP→ The Opera House offers really cool one-hour, guided historical tours, and 25-minute backstage tours, which must be reserved online in advance.** ✉ *539 Washington St., Theater District* ☎ *617/695–6955 Boston Ballet tickets, 800/982–2787 Broadway show tickets* ⊕ *www.bostonoperahouse.com* ⊠ *$17 historical tour; $10 backstage tour* Ⓜ *Boylston, Chinatown, Downtown Crossing.*

Cutler Majestic Theatre at Emerson College

OPERA | This gorgeous beaux arts theater and historic landmark was built with opera performances in mind, so it's fitting that Boston Lyric Opera calls it home today. Also, it's owned by Emerson College, which uses the stage for ArtsEmerson, its presenting arm that focuses on contemporary theater from around the globe. ✉ *219 Tremont St., Theater District* ☎ *617/824–8000 for tickets* ⊕ *www. emersontheatres.org* Ⓜ *Boylston.*

Emerson Colonial Theater

CONCERTS | Welcome to Boston's oldest, continuously operated theater, where musical magic was created, performed and transformed by the likes of Stephen Sondheim, Ethel Merman, and George and Ira Gershwin, before traveling to Broadway to become "official"—tryouts included *Porgy and Bess, Follies, Grand Hotel*, and *La Cage aux Folles*. Today, the Colonial continues to present Broadway tours and headline bands and musicians. ■**TIP→ The Colonial hosts historical tours typically once monthly; reserve tickets online.** ✉ *106 Boylston St., Theater District* ☎ *888/616–0272 for tickets* ⊕ *www. emersoncolonialtheatre.com* ⊠ *$17 historical tours* Ⓜ *Boylston.*

Tip: Boston Harborwalk Bit by Bit 👁

For the last 30-plus years, a number of agencies and organizations have been collaborating to create a walking path along Boston's shoreline—currently, it stretches 43 miles. In the North End, Downtown, the Waterfront, the Seaport, and South Boston, marked signs point the way—plus you can find maps online. The public can hop on and off at their leisure, using the Harborwalk for exercise and other types of recreation. In the Waterfront, the trail navigates the city's many wharves; its also features art exhibits, educational panels, stationary viewfinders, and open green space. ⊕ *www.bostonharborwalk.org*

Emerson Paramount Center

CULTURAL TOURS | Look for the orange-, red-, and yellow-lit marquee, and you'll find the Paramount. Three performance spaces make up this 1930s-era complex owned by Emerson College. Its main stage features an art deco vibe and performing artists from all over. Smaller, alternative productions—think classic and art films, professional puppet shows, circus arts—can also take place in a black box theater or a screening room. ArtsEmerson schedules all events here. ✉ *559 Washington St., Theater District* ☎ *617/824–8400* ⊕ *www.emersontheatres.org* Ⓜ *Downtown Crossing, Boylston, Park.*

Located in the Harbor Islands National Recreation Area, the 105-acre Spectacle Island is just 4 miles offshore of downtown Boston and accessible by ferry.

Waterfront

You won't hear the sound of crashing waves thanks to Boston's protected and relatively calm inner harbor, but the lean stretch of coastline running from South Station to the North End is one of the prettiest, most serene escapes you'll encounter in this city. And, it manages to slow the pace of the bustling, driven Financial District behind it.

Along the Waterfront, you'll encounter wharf after wharf of harbor activity: private vessels, luxury yachts, harbor cruises, ferries, and more. Long Wharf, Central Wharf with the New England Aquarium, and Rowes Wharf are the three most prominent. Other attractions in this neighborhood include Boston Harborwalk, the Rose Kennedy Greenway, and the lesser-known gem just offshore, the Boston Harbor Islands. Many upscale hotels and restaurants make the most of the expansive water views.

Sights

★ Boston Harbor Islands National Recreation Area

BUILDING | FAMILY | Comprising 34 tiny islands and peninsulas, this is a one of the city's best hidden gems—and it's literally out of sight. Stretching from South Boston (Castle Island) to the coastlines of South Shore towns Hingham and Hull, each island is different, but most feature abundant nature with miles of lightly traveled trails, shoreline, sea life and wild plants. The focal point of the national park is 39-acre Georges Island and its partially restored pre–Civil War Fort Warren that once held Confederate prisoners. Other islands worth visiting include Peddocks Island, which holds the remains of Ft. Andrews, and Spectacle Island, a popular destination for swimming (with lifeguards). Lovells, Peddocks, Grape, and Bumpkin islands all allow camping with a permit, from late June through Labor Day. Pets and alcohol are not allowed on the Harbor Islands. ■ TIP→ Ferries shuttle visitors from Boston to Georges and Spectacle islands daily during summer months. Plan to spend a whole day exploring! ⊠ *Boston Harbor Islands National and State Park Welcome Center, 191 W. Atlantic Ave., Waterfront* ☎ *617/223–8666* ⊕ *www. bostonharborislands.org* ⊗ *Closed mid-Oct.–mid–May* Ⓜ *Aquarium.*

Long Wharf

HISTORIC SITE | Stand in front of Faneuil Hall and you'll see lines on the ground marking Boston's original waterfront. Find State Street to your right and look straight down all the way to Boston Harbor. Where you're standing is where Long Wharf originally started, and in Colonial days it was, in fact, the city's longest wharf. Today, Long Wharf starts east of Atlantic Avenue, and it serves as the launching point for many of the city's water tours, sails, and cruises. Halfway down the wharf, you can have dinner at The Chart House, a nice seafood restaurant, but note that the historic building it houses was once John Hancock's counting house and still contains his vault. The New England Aquarium sits next door, at Central Wharf. ⊠ *Long Wharf, Waterfront* Ⓜ *Aquarium.*

★ New England Aquarium

ZOO | **FAMILY** | As interesting and exciting as it is educational, this aquarium is a must for those who are curious about what lives in and around the sea. The building's glass-and-steel exterior is constructed to mimic fish scales, and seals bark and swim in the outdoor tank. Inside the main facility, more than 30,000 animals of 800 different species frolic in simulated habitats. Penguins, hands-on creature touch tanks, and sea lions, are a few star exhibits. The real showstopper, though, is the four-story, 200,000-gallon ocean-reef tank. Ramps winding around the tank lead to the top level and allow you to view the inhabitants from many vantage points. Don't miss the five-times-a-day feedings; each lasts nearly an hour and takes divers 24 feet into the tank. ⊠ *1 Central Wharf, Waterfront*

☎ *617/973–5200* ⊕ *www.neaq.org* ⊠ *$32; $10 IMAX; $55 whale watch* Ⓜ *Aquarium.*

Rowes Wharf

MARINA | Get a feel for *Lifestyles of the Rich and Famous* at Rowes Wharf, where a six-story arched rotunda frames gorgeous views of Boston Harbor complete with mega-yachts and a water-set gazebo. Well-heeled patrons stay and dine at Boston Harbor Hotel and its upscale restaurants. ■**TIP→ During summer months, stop by any weekday night for free live music performances or film screenings, hosted by the hotel.** ⊠ *Rowes Wharf, Waterfront* Ⓜ *Aquarium.*

🍴 Restaurants

Legal Sea Foods

$$$ | **SEAFOOD** | **FAMILY** | What began as a tiny restaurant adjacent to a Cambridge fish market has grown to important regional status, with more than 30 East Coast locations, including almost a dozen in Boston. The hallmark is the freshest possible seafood, whether you have it wood-grilled, in New England chowder, or doused in an Asia-inspired sauce. **Known for:** classic, supertresh New England seafood; family-friendly setting; locations all over town. Ⓢ *Average main: $30* ⊠ *Long Wharf, 255 State St., Waterfront* ☎ *617/742–5300* ⊕ *www.legalseafoods.com* Ⓜ *Aquarium.*

Nebo Cucina & Enoteca

$$$ | **ITALIAN** | **FAMILY** | Its name, Nebo, is an acronym for "North End Boston," which is the neighborhood where the first iteration of this local restaurant operated for a time. Today, it serves rustic Italian dishes from the owners' Nonna in a classy, corner spot on the waterfront. **Known for:** zucchini lasagne that beat Bobby Flay in his own game on Food Network's *Throwdown*; 10 different styles of pizza on house-made dough; all-Italian wine list, many by the glass. Ⓢ *Average main: $27* ⊠ *520 Atlantic Ave., Waterfront* ☎ *617/723–6326* ⊕ *www.neborestaurant. com* ⊗ *Closed Sun.* Ⓜ *South Station.*

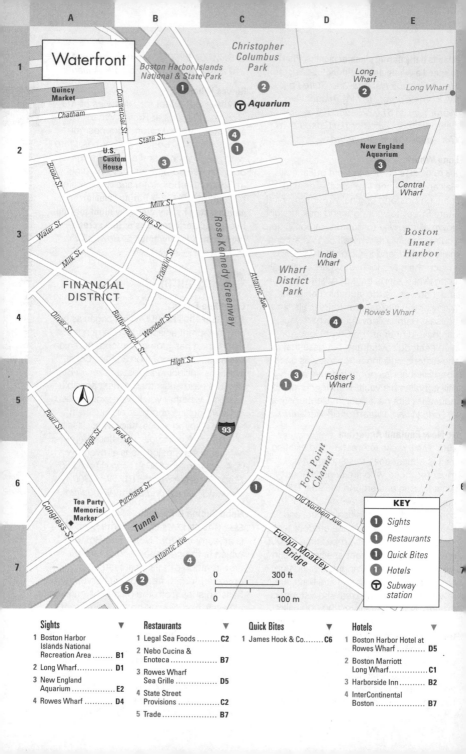

Waterfront

A B C D E

1

Christopher
Columbus
Park

Quincy
Market

Boston Harbor Islands
National & State Park

Long
Wharf

Long Wharf

Chatham

🅣 Aquarium

State St.

U.S.
Custom
House

New England
Aquarium

Central
Wharf

Broad St.

Milk St.

Water St.

Milk St.

India St.

Franklin St.

Boston
Inner
Harbor

FINANCIAL
DISTRICT

Rose Kennedy Greenway

India
Wharf

Atlantic Ave.

Wharf
District
Park

Oliver St.

Batterymarch St.

Wendell St.

Rowe's Wharf

High St.

5

Pearl St.

High St.

Ford St.

Foster's
Wharf

93

6

Tea Party
Memorial
Marker

Purchase St.

Tunnel

Fort Point
Channel

Congress St.

Atlantic Ave.

Old Northern Ave.

Evelyn Moakley
Bridge

KEY	
①	Sights
①	Restaurants
①	Quick Bites
①	Hotels
🅣	Subway station

0 — 300 ft
0 — 100 m

Rowes Wharf Sea Grille

$$$ | **SEAFOOD** | Sophisticated, pristine, and yet unpretentious, this restaurant pairs nautical flair with light preparations of fresh seafood, fitting for its setting overlooking Boston Harbor. Seafood selections are mainly, but not exclusively, from nearby Atlantic waters, and diners who prefer meatier meals can select from roast duck, lamb, and filet mignon. **Known for:** lovely views of Boston Harbor beyond Rowes Wharf; fantastic wine-by-the-glass list; outdoor summer dining accompanied by live music or classic cinema. [$] *Average main: $35* ✉ *70 Rowes Wharf, Waterfront* ☎ *617/856–7744* 🌐 *www.roweswharfseagrille.com* [M] *Aquarium, South Station.*

State Street Provisions

$$$ | **AMERICAN** | Although this restaurant is a relatively recent addition to Boston's waterfront, its overall spirit harkens back to an earlier era, one that's laced with the city's Colonial character. This is reflected in a menu that highlights locally sourced ingredients in nostalgic, scratch-cooked dishes like Boston baked beans, seared scallops, sausages, and salt-cod fritters—even the pickles are pickled on-site. **Known for:** scratch cooking; the bartender's special hot grog, a drink that changes weekly; raw bar featuring East Coast oysters, little neck clams, and lobster tail. [$] *Average main: $25* ✉ *255 State St., Waterfront* ☎ *617/863–8363* 🌐 *www.statestreetprovisions.com* [M] *Aquarium.*

Trade

$$$ | **MEDITERRANEAN** | Financial District and Downtown professionals fill James Beard Award–winning chef-owner Jody Adams's lofty, white windowed space, eager to unwind over cocktails and small plates inspired by the Mediterranean region. Think spreads, salads, roasted vegetables, as well as Adams's signature, perfectly charred flatbreads that fly out of the open-hearth pizza oven. **Known for:** lemon-thyme roasted half-chicken; flavorful small plates; boisterous after-work, professional crowd. [$] *Average main: $27* ✉ *540 Atlantic Ave., Waterfront* ☎ *617/451–1234* 🌐 *www.trade-boston.com* [M] *South Station.*

Exploring with a View

Not only does Rowes Wharf Water Transport make trips across Boston Harbor to and from Logan Airport in under eight minutes, it does so with spectacular views. The water taxi also services about 20 other locations along the Waterfront, the Seaport, the North End, Charlestown, and East Boston. 🌐 *www.roweswharfwatertransport.com*

Coffee and Quick Bites

James Hook & Co.

$$$ | **SEAFOOD** | **FAMILY** | This Waterfront seafood shanty in the heart of Downtown leaves all its frills for its lobster-loaded rolls; they're served with mayo or with butter, in a bun, and wrapped with foil so you can sit for a minute or eat it on the go. Other specialties include lobster mac and cheese, whole boiled lobster, stuffed clams, and the shrimp and corn chowder. **Known for:** lobster rolls; whole-cooked lobsters; rustic vibe and no-frills seating. [$] *Average main: $35* ✉ *440 Atlantic Ave., Waterfront* ☎ *617/423–5501* 🌐 *www.jameshooklobster.com* [M] *South Station.*

Hotels

Boston Harbor Hotel at Rowes Wharf

$$$$ | **HOTEL** | Boston has plenty of iconic landmarks, but none are as synonymous with uber-hospitality as the Boston Harbor Hotel. **Pros:** free Wi-Fi and in-room tablet; premier views of Boston Harbor or the city; water shuttle to Logan Airport. **Cons:** pricey; the spa books up early, so

make an advance reservation; not convenient to the Back Bay, South End, and Fenway neighborhoods. $ *Rooms from: $700* ✉ *70 Rowes Wharf, Waterfront* ☎ *617/439–7000, 800/752–7077* 🌐 *www.bhh.com* 🛏 *232 rooms* 🍴 *No meals* [M] *Aquarium, South Station.*

Boston Marriott Long Wharf

$$$ | HOTEL | FAMILY | Families favor this spot that looks like a big brick ship docked in Boston Harbor for its proximity to New England Aquarium, Faneuil Hall Marketplace, and the North End. Guest rooms open to a five-story atrium, and some have views of the park, harbor, or the aquarium. **Pros:** beautiful upper level swimming pool with harbor views; centrally located to family interests; free Wi-Fi. **Cons:** surrounding area is packed with tourists; buffet breakfast is $29 per person; parking is difficult to find. $ *Rooms from: $350* ✉ *296 State St., Waterfront* ☎ *617/227–0800* 🌐 *www.marriott.com* 🛏 *415 rooms* 🍴 *No meals* [M] *Aquarium.*

Harborside Inn

$$ | HOTEL | With rates that are considerably lower than most Waterfront hotels, this hotel with an understated charm is an exceptional value. **Pros:** free Wi-Fi; close to key tourist sites; inexpensive. **Cons:** no on-site restaurant; no turndown service; no valet. $ *Rooms from: $260* ✉ *185 State St., Downtown* ☎ *617/723–7500, 888/723–7565* 🌐 *www.harborsideinnboston.com* 🛏 *116 rooms* 🍴 *No meals* [M] *Aquarium.*

InterContinental Boston

$$$ | HOTEL | Notice the two opulent, 22-story towers wrapped in blue glass facing Boston's waterfront, and you'll have found the InterContinental hotel. **Pros:** rooms have panoramic views; Miel restaurant and its seasonal waterfront dining terrace; close to the Financial District and South Station. **Cons:** no airport shuttle service; far from Newbury Street and Back Bay shopping; soundproofing needs improvement. $ *Rooms from: $325* ✉ *510 Atlantic Ave., Waterfront* ☎ *617/747–1000, 866/493–6495* 🌐 *www.icbostonhotel.com* 🛏 *424 rooms* 🍴 *No meals* [M] *South Station.*

🍸 Nightlife

RumBa

BARS/PUBS | Inside the InterContinental hotel, RumBa highlights two disparate spirited beverages: rum (more than 70 varieties) and champagne (two dozen). Bar offerings go above and beyond creative cocktails—although there are them—to flights and exclusive and rare rums, whiskies, and cognacs. Slip into the hidden champagne lounge area behind sliding mahogany doors for quieter, secluded celebrations—you must book in advance. ✉ *510 Atlantic Ave., Waterfront* ☎ *617/747–1000* 🌐 *www.icbostonhotel.com/boston-waterfront-restaurants* [M] *South Station.*

Trillium Garden

BREWPUBS/BEER GARDENS | FAMILY | BYOF (F is for food) for an afternoon or evening spent at Trillium Brewing Company's seasonal beer garden smack dab in the middle of the Rose Kennedy Greenway and directly across from Boston Harbor Hotel rotunda. The place is generally mobbed, especially considering it's both dog and kid friendly, leaving hardly an excuse to stay away. On tap: a rotating variety crafted by the Boston-based brewery. ✉ *High St. at Atlantic Ave., Waterfront* 🌐 *www.trilliumbrewing.com/locations/trillium-garden* [M] *Aquarium.*

Chapter 7

THE BACK BAY AND SOUTH END

Updated by
Kim Foley MacKinnon

⊙ Sights	🍴 Restaurants	🛏 Hotels	🛍 Shopping	🍸 Nightlife
★★★★★	★★★★☆	★★★★☆	★★★★★	★★★★☆

NEIGHBORHOOD SNAPSHOT

TOP EXPERIENCES

■ **Stroll down Newbury Street:** Join the throngs of students, locals, and visitors window-shopping on Newbury Street.

■ **Tour the Boston Public Library:** Admire the architecture, revel in the artistry, and even enjoy an excellent lunch at the Boston Public Library—all without taking out a single book.

■ **Ride a Swan Boat:** Visit the Public Garden on a sunny, late-spring day and take in the scenery from your seat on the Swan Boats. Don't forget to check out the bronze statues of the ducklings from Robert McCloskey's Boston classic *Make Way for Ducklings*.

■ **Embrace the arts:** Enjoy a play, concert, or art installation at the "people's" art-and-culture complex, the Boston Center for the Arts.

■ **Shop 'til you drop:** Shop Columbus Avenue and Tremont Street for the perfect additions to your home decor and head to the artsy SoWa Open Market on the weekends.

■ **See South End architecture:** Walk the streets around Rutland Square, Union Park, and Bay Village. Architecture buffs will love the Victorian and Italianate row houses harking back to the neighborhood's 19th-century roots.

GETTING HERE

There are myriad parking garages in the Back Bay. Take the Orange Line to the Back Bay station or the Green Line to Copley for the heart of the shopping areas. The Arlington stop on the Green Line is the most convenient to the Public Garden. ■**TIP→ To stay oriented, remember that the north–south streets are arranged in alphabetical order, from Arlington to Hereford.**

The South End is easily accessible by the T; take the Orange Line to Back Bay and head south on Dartmouth Street to Columbus Avenue, or jump off the Silver Line at Union Park Street or East Berkeley Street to access the neighborhood.

QUICK BITES

■ **J.P. Licks.** Stop in for a tasty scoop of ice cream or a freshly brewed cup of joe. ✉ *1106 Boylston St., Back Bay* ⊕ *jplicks.com* Ⓜ *Back Bay.*

■ **Pavement Coffeehouse.** Grab a homemade bagel and coffee at this hip spot. ✉ *286 Newbury St., Back Bay* ⊕ *pavementcoffeehouse.com* Ⓜ *Hynes, Copley.*

■ **Trident Booksellers & Cafe.** You can enjoy breakfast all day and pick up a bestseller or magazine at this bookstore café. ✉ *338 Newbury St., Back Bay* ⊕ *www.tridentbookscafe.com* Ⓜ *Hynes.*

PLANNING YOUR TIME

■ If you're not a shopper, you can cover the Back Bay in about two hours. If you are, allow at least half a day to cover Newbury Street and the shops at Copley Place and the Pru Center. Around the third week of April, magnolias arrive and the flowers are magnificent along Comm Ave. In May the Public Garden bursts with color, thanks to its flowering dogwood trees and thousands of tulips.

■ A few hours is perfect to explore the South End; add a few more hours for a show at the Boston Center of the Arts or to dine at one of the area's excellent restaurants.

In the roster of famous American neighborhoods, the Back Bay stands with New York's Park Avenue and San Francisco's Nob Hill as a symbol of propriety and high social standing. Before the 1850s it truly was a bay, a tidal flat that formed the south bank of a distended Charles River. The filling in of land along the isthmus that joined Boston to the mainland (the Neck) began in 1850, and resulted in the creation of the South End.

Though the name says it, it's hard to believe that this broad street grid running from Boston Public Garden up elegant Beacon Street and Commonwealth Avenue, divided by a center strip of statues and magnolia trees, was, until the 1850s, landfilled dockland. Anchored by the John Hancock Tower and the Prudential, the Back Bay is studded with beautiful churches around Copley Square and lively Newbury Street.

Today, the Back Bay is a mix of the historic and the new, happily coexisting in one of the city's loveliest areas, with everything from landmarks, like Trinity Church, and green spaces, such as the Esplanade, to a multitude of hip bars and fine-dining restaurants. Adjacent to the Back Bay, the South End nonetheless has its own identity, with stunning Victorian row houses, art galleries galore, Boston's largest gay community, and plenty of unique shops and restaurants of every type.

The Back Bay

To the north a narrow causeway called the Mill Dam (later Beacon Street) was built in 1814 to separate the Back Bay from the Charles. By the late 1800s, Bostonians had filled in the shallows to as far as the marshland known as Fenway, and the original 783-acre peninsula had been expanded by about 450 acres. Thus the waters of the Back Bay became the neighborhood of the Back Bay.

Heavily influenced by the then-recent rebuilding of Paris according to the plans of Baron Georges-Eugène Haussmann, the Back Bay planners created thoroughfares that resemble Parisian boulevards. The thorough planning included service alleys behind the main streets to allow provisioning wagons to drive up to basement kitchens. (Now they're used for waste pickup and parking.)

The Swan Boats have been an iconic part of Boston Public Garden since 1877.

Today the area retains its posh spirit, but mansions are no longer the main draw. Locals and tourists alike flock to the commercial streets of Boylston and Newbury to shop at boutiques, galleries, and the usual mall stores. Many of the bars and restaurants have patio seating and bay windows, making the area the perfect spot to see and be seen while indulging in ethnic delicacies or an invigorating coffee. The Boston Public Library, Symphony Hall, and numerous churches ensure that high culture is not lost amid the frenzy of consumerism.

Sights

Arlington Street Church

RELIGIOUS SITE | Opposite the Park Square corner of the Public Garden, this church was erected in 1861—the first to be built in the Back Bay. Though a classical portico is a keynote and its model was London's St. Martin-in-the-Fields, Arlington Street Church is less picturesque and more Georgian in character. Note the 16 Tiffany stained-glass windows.

During the year preceding the Civil War the church was a hotbed of abolitionist fervor. Later, during the Vietnam War, this Unitarian-Universalist congregation became famous as a center of peace activism. ⊠ 351 Boylston St., Back Bay ☎ 617/536–7050 ⊕ www.ascboston. org 🎫 Guided and self-guided tours $5 ⊗ Closed Tues. Ⓜ Arlington.

★ Boston Public Garden

NATIONAL/STATE PARK | FAMILY | America's oldest botanical garden is replete with gorgeous formal plantings; a 4-acre lagoon, famous since 1877 for its foot-pedal-powered (by a captain) Swan Boats (⊕ swanboats.com); and the Make Way for Ducklings bronzes sculpted by Nancy Schön, a tribute to the 1941 classic children's story by Robert McCloskey.

Keep in mind that the Boston Public Garden and Boston Common are two separate entities with different histories and purposes and a distinct boundary between them at Charles Street. The Common has been public land since Boston was founded in 1630, whereas the Public Garden belongs to a newer Boston, occupying what had been salt marshes on the edge of the Common. By 1837 the tract was covered with an abundance of ornamental plantings donated by a group of private citizens. Near the Swan Boat dock is what has been described as the world's smallest suspension bridge, designed in 1867 to cross the pond at its narrowest point. The beds along the main walkways are replanted every spring. The tulips during the first two weeks of May are especially colorful, and there's a sampling of native and European tree species. ⊠ *Bounded by Arlington, Boylston, Charles, and Beacon Sts., Back Bay* ☎ *617/522–1966 Swan Boats* ⊕ *friendsofthepublicgarden. org* ⛵ *Swan Boats $4* Ⓜ *Arlington.*

★ **Boston Public Library**

LIBRARY | FAMILY | This venerable institution is a handsome temple to literature and a valuable research library, as well as an art gallery of sorts and you don't need a library card to enjoy it. At the main entrance hall of the 1895 Renaissance Revival building, take in the immense stone lions by Louis St. Gaudens, the vaulted ceiling, and marble staircase. The corridor at the top of the stairs leads to Bates Hall, one of Boston's most sumptuous interior spaces. This is the main reference reading room, 218 feet long with a barrel-arch ceiling 50 feet high. The murals at the head of the staircase, depicting the nine muses, are the work of the French artist Puvis de Chavannes; those in the room to the right are Edwin Abbey's interpretations of the Holy Grail legend. Upstairs, in the public areas, is John Singer Sargent's mural series on the Triumph of Religion. The library offers free art and architecture tours daily. The corridor leading from the annex opens onto the Renaissance-style courtyard—an exact copy of the one in Rome's Palazzo della Cancelleria—around which the original library is built. A covered arcade furnished with chairs rings a fountain; you can bring books or lunch into the peaceful courtyard. ⊠ *700 Boylston St., at Copley Sq., Back Bay* ☎ *617/536–5400* ⊕ *www.bpl.org* Ⓜ *Copley.*

Boylston Street

NEIGHBORHOOD | Less posh than Newbury Street, this broad thoroughfare is the southern commercial spine of the Back Bay, lined with interesting restaurants and shops, and where you'll find the Boston Marathon Finish Line. Also located here is the Boston Marathon Bombing Memorial, composed of light spires and stone pillars, which pays homage to the Boston Marathon bombing victims at the sites where they were killed on April 15, 2013. ⊠ *Back Bay.*

Charles River Reservation

PARK—SPORTS-OUTDOORS | FAMILY | Runners, bikers, and in-line skaters crowd the Charles River Reservation at the Esplanade along Storrow Drive, the Memorial Drive Embankment in Cambridge, or any of the smaller and less-busy parks farther upriver. Here you can cheer a crew race, rent a canoe or a kayak, or simply sit on the grass, sharing the shore with packs of hard-jogging university athletes, in-line skaters, moms with strollers, dreamily entwined couples, and intense academics, often talking to themselves as they sort out their intellectual—or perhaps personal—dilemmas. ⊠ *Back Bay* ☎ *617/727–4708* ⊕ *www.mass.gov/eea/ agencies/dcr/massparks/region-boston/ charles-river-reservation.html* Ⓜ *Charles/ MGH, Chinatown, Copley.*

Church of the Covenant

RELIGIOUS SITE | This 1867 Gothic Revival church, a National Historic Landmark at the corner of Newbury and Berkeley streets, has one of the largest collections of liturgical windows by Louis Comfort Tiffany in the country. It's crowned by a 236-foot-tall steeple—the tallest in Boston—that Oliver Wendell Holmes called "absolutely perfect." Inside, a 14-foot-high Tiffany lantern hangs from a breathtaking 100-foot ceiling. The church is now Presbyterian and United Church

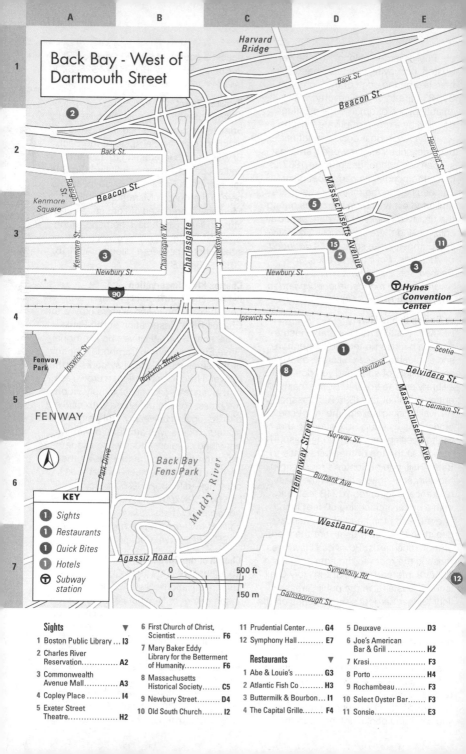

Back Bay - West of Dartmouth Street

Harvard Bridge

Kenmore Square

Fenway Park

FENWAY

Back Bay Fens Park

Muddy River

Hynes Convention Center

Back St.

Beacon St.

Back St.

Raleigh St.

Beacon St.

Kenmore St.

Newbury St.

Charlesgate W.

Charlesgate

Charlesgate E.

Newbury St.

Massachusetts Avenue

Hereford St.

90

Ipswich St.

Ipswich St.

Boylston Street

Park Drive

Haviland

Scotia

Belvidere St.

St. Germain St.

Massachusetts Ave.

Hemenway Street

Norway St.

Burbank Ave.

Westland Ave.

Agassiz Road

Symphony Rd.

Gainsborough St.

KEY

1 Sights
1 Restaurants
1 Quick Bites
1 Hotels
T Subway station

| 0 | | 500 ft |
| 0 | | 150 m |

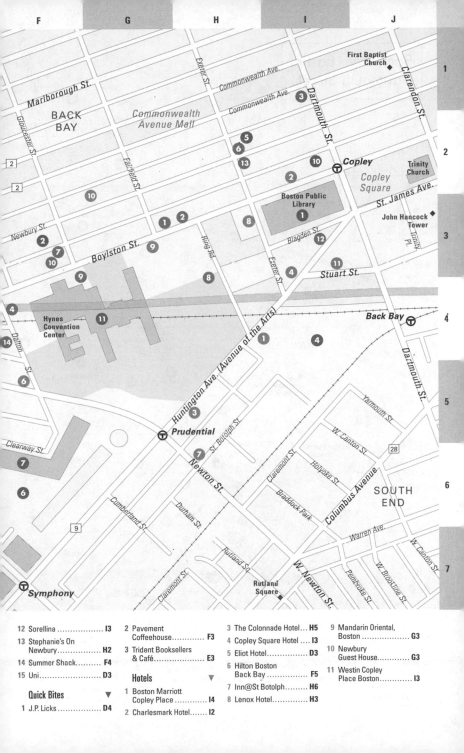

Back Bay - East of Dartmouth Street

Charles River

Arthur Fiedler Footbridge

0 — 500 ft
0 — 150 m

Beaver Pl.

Beacon Street

Arlington

James J. Storrow Memorial Drive

Back St.

Beacon St.

Dartmouth St.

Clarendon St.

Berkeley St.

Exeter St.

BACK BAY

Marlborough St.

Commonwealth Ave.

Commonwealth Ave.

Commonwealth Avenue Mall

Newbury St.

Boylston St.

Fairfield St.

Newbury St.

Exeter Street Theater

Old South Church

Copley

Copley Square

Providence St.

St. James Ave.

Berkeley St.

Boylston St.

Ring Rd.

Boston Public Library

Blagden St.

Copley Place

Trinity Pl.

Stuart St.

Stanhope St.

Prudential Center

Huntington Ave. (Avenue of the Arts)

Dartmouth St.

Columbus Avenue

90

Back Bay

The Boston Public Library is a stunning cathedral of books.

of Christ. ✉ *67 Newbury St., enter at church office, Back Bay* ☎ *617/266–7480* 🌐 *www.cotcbos.org* Ⓜ *Arlington.*

Commonwealth Avenue Mall
PROMENADE | The mall that extends down the middle of the Back Bay's Commonwealth Avenue, which serves as the green link between the Public Garden and the public parks system, is studded with statuary. One of the most interesting memorials, at the Exeter Street intersection, is a portrayal of naval historian and author Samuel Eliot Morison seated on a rock as if he were peering out to sea. The **Boston Women's Memorial,** installed in 2003, sculpted by Meredith Bergmann, is between Fairfield and Gloucester streets. Statues of Abigail Adams, Lucy Stone, and Phillis Wheatley celebrate the progressive ideas of these three women and their contributions to Boston's history.

A dramatic and personal memorial near Dartmouth Street is the **Vendome Monument,** dedicated to the nine firemen who died in a 1972 blaze at the Back Bay's Vendome Hotel, which, now office space, is across the street. The curved black-granite block, 29 feet long and waist high, is etched with the names of the dead. A bronze cast of a fireman's coat and hat is draped over the granite. ✉ *Commonwealth Ave. between Arlington St. and Massachusetts Ave., Back Bay* Ⓜ *Arlington, Copley.*

Copley Place
STORE/MALL | Two modern structures dominate Copley Square—the **John Hancock Tower** off the southeast corner and the even more assertive Copley Place skyscraper on the southwest. An upscale, glass-and-brass urban mall built between 1980 and 1984, Copley Place includes two major hotels: the high-rise Westin and the Marriott Copley Place. Dozens of shops, restaurants, and offices are attractively grouped on several levels, surrounding bright, open indoor spaces. ✉ *100 Huntington Ave., Back Bay* 🌐 *www.simon.com/mall/copley-place* Ⓜ *Copley.*

The Boston Marathon

The Boston Marathon is held on the third Monday of April, which is also known as Patriots' Day in Massachusetts, a state holiday that commemorates the first battles of the Revolutionary War in 1775. Though it missed being the country's first marathon by a year (the first, in 1896, went from Stamford, Connecticut, to New York City), the Boston Marathon is arguably the nation's most prestigious. Why? It's the only marathon in the world for which runners have to qualify; it's the world's oldest continuously run marathon; and it's been run on the same course since it began.

The marathon passes through Hopkinton, Ashland, Framingham, Natick, Wellesley, Newton, Brookline, and Boston; only the last few miles are run in the city proper, which has a festival atmosphere. Throngs of supporters and fans come out to cheer on the racers and eat and drink at restaurants and bars along the route. Some spectators have returned to the same spot for generations, bringing their lawn chairs and barbecues.

In 2013, a horrific bombing near the race's finish line killed three people and injured scores of others. The tragic event shocked Boston and the nation, but runners and supporters have returned in even bigger numbers. Located near the finish line is the poignant Boston Marathon Bombing Memorial, composed of light spires and stone pillars, which pays homage to the victims. Security, however, has gotten tighter during the race, especially in Boston proper. Driving is impossible anywhere near the route and the T is packed, so plan accordingly.

Copley Square

PLAZA | FAMILY | Every April thousands find a glimpse of Copley Square the most wonderful sight in the world: this is where the runners of the Boston Marathon end their 26.2-mile race. The civic space is defined by three monumental older buildings. One is the stately, bowfront 1912 **Fairmont Copley Plaza Hotel,** which faces the square on St. James Avenue and serves as a dignified foil to its companions, two of the most important works of architecture in the United States: Trinity Church—Henry Hobson Richardson's masterwork of 1877—and the Boston Public Library, by McKim, Mead & White. The John Hancock Tower looms in the background. To honor the runners who stagger over the marathon's finish line, bronze statues of the Tortoise and the Hare engaged in their mythical race were cast by Nancy Schön, who also did the much-loved *Make Way for Ducklings* group in the Boston Public Garden. From May through October, a popular farmers' market draws crowds. ⊠ *Bounded by Dartmouth, Boylston, and Clarendon Sts. and St. James Ave., Back Bay* Ⓜ *Copley.*

Emmanuel Church

RELIGIOUS SITE | Built in 1860, this Back Bay Gothic Episcopal church is popular among classical music lovers—every Sunday morning at 10, from September to May, as part of the liturgy, a Bach cantata, and music by Schütz, Mendelssohn, and others, including music written by living composers, is performed; guest conductors have included Christopher Hogwood and Seiji Ozawa. From May to September, the Chapel Choir, comprised of both professional and volunteer singers, performs. ⊠ *15 Newbury St., Back Bay* ☎ *617/536–3355* ⊕ *www.emmanuel-boston.org* Ⓜ *Arlington.*

Back Bay Mansions

If you like nothing better than to imagine how the other half lives, you'll suffer no shortage of old homes to sigh over in Boston's Back Bay. Most, unfortunately, are off-limits to visitors, but there's no law against gawking from the outside. Stroll Commonwealth, Beacon, and Marlborough streets for the best views. Of particular note are the Burrage Mansion (⊠ 314 Commonwelath Ave.); the Oliver Ames Mansion (⊠ 355 Commonwealth Ave.); and the Ames-Webster House (⊠ 306 Dartmouth St.), which can all be admired from the outside, at a respectable distance, of course. For details on lectures, films, and other events offered in some mansions that are now home to respected institutions, such as the French Library and Cultural Center (⊠ 53 Marlborough St.) and the Goethe Institute (⊠ 170 Beacon St.), check out the Boston Globe's art section or calendar listings.

Esplanade

PROMENADE | FAMILY | Near the corner of Beacon and Arlington Streets, the Arthur Fiedler Footbridge crosses Storrow Drive to the 3-mile-long Esplanade and the **Hatch Memorial Shell.** The free concerts here in summer include the Boston Pops' immensely popular televised July 4 performance. For shows like this, Bostonians haul lawn chairs and blankets to the lawn in front of the shell; bring a takeout lunch from a nearby restaurant, find an empty spot—no mean feat, so come early—and you'll feel right at home. An impressive stone bust of the late maestro Arthur Fiedler watches over the walkers, joggers, picnickers, and sunbathers who fill the Esplanade's paths on pleasant days. Here, too, is the turn-of-the-20th-century **Union Boat Club Boathouse,** headquarters for the country's oldest private rowing club. ⊠ Back Bay ⊕ www.esplanadeassociation.org.

Exeter Street Theater

BUILDING | This massive Romanesque structure was built in 1884 as a temple for the Working Union of Progressive Spiritualists. Beginning in 1914, it enjoyed a long run as a movie theater, then served a turn as a bookstore. Today, it's home to a private school. ⊠ 26 Exeter St., at Newbury St., Back Bay ⊕ www.fst.org/exeter.htm Ⓜ Copley.

First Baptist Church

RELIGIOUS SITE | This 1872 structure, at the corner of Clarendon Street and Commonwealth Avenue, was architect Henry Hobson Richardson's first foray into Romanesque Revival. It was originally erected for the Brattle Square Unitarian Society, but Richardson ran over budget and the church went bankrupt and dissolved. In 1882, the building was bought by the Baptists. The figures on each side of its soaring tower were sculpted by Frédéric Auguste Bartholdi, the sculptor who designed the Statue of Liberty. The friezes represent four points at which God enters an individual's life: baptism, communion, marriage, and death. If you phone ahead for an appointment on a weekday, you may be given an informal tour. ⊠ 110 Commonwealth Ave., Back Bay ☎ 617/267–3148 ⊕ www.firstbaptist-boston.org ⊠ Free Ⓜ Copley.

First Church of Christ, Scientist

RELIGIOUS SITE | The world headquarters of the Christian Science faith mixes the traditional with the modern—marrying Bernini to Le Corbusier by combining an old-world basilica with a sleek office complex designed by I. M. Pei & Partners and Araldo Cossutta, Associated Architects. Mary Baker Eddy's original granite First Church of Christ, Scientist

(1894) has since been enveloped by a domed Renaissance Revival basilica, added to the site in 1906, and both church buildings are now surrounded by the offices of the Christian Science Publishing Society, where the *Christian Science Monitor* is produced, and by Cossutta's complex of church-administration structures completed in 1973. You can hear all 13,000-plus pipes of the church's famed Aeolian-Skinner organ during services. Free tours are offered Tuesday through Sunday on the hour and half-hour and last about 20 minutes. ⊠ *275 Massachusetts Ave., Back Bay* ☎ *617/450–2000* ⊕ *www.christianscience.com/church-of-christ-scientist/the-mother-church-in-boston-ma-usa* ⊠ *Free* Ⓜ *Hynes, Symphony.*

Gibson House

HOUSE | Through the foresight of an eccentric bon vivant, this house provides an authentic glimpse into daily life in Boston's Victorian era. One of the first Back Bay residences (1859), the Gibson House is relatively modest in comparison with some of the grand mansions built during the decades that followed; yet its furnishings, from its 1795 Willard clock to the raised and gilded wallpaper to the multipiece faux-bamboo bedroom set, seem sumptuous to modern eyes. Unlike other Back Bay houses, the Gibson family home has been preserved with all its Victorian fixtures and furniture intact. The house serves as the meeting place for the New England chapter of the Victorian Society in America; it was also used as an interior for the 1984 Merchant-Ivory film *The Bostonians.* ■TIP→ **The museum is only open to the public by guided tour Wednesday through Sunday at 1 pm, 2 pm, and 3 pm; arrive 15 minutes early to get a ticket.** ⊠ *137 Beacon St., Back Bay* ☎ *617/267–6338* ⊕ *www.thegibsonhouse.org* ⊠ *$10* ☉ *Closed Mon. and Tues.* Ⓜ *Arlington.*

Hatch Memorial Shell

FESTIVAL | FAMILY | On the Esplanade, the Hatch Memorial Shell hosts free concerts and outdoor events all summer. ⊠ *Esplanade, 47 David G. Mugar Way, Back Bay* ☎ *617/277–0365* ⊕ *esplanade.org/projects-programs/hatch-shell* Ⓜ *Charles/MGH.*

John Hancock Tower

LOCAL INTEREST | In the early 1970s, the tallest building in New England became notorious as the monolith that rained glass from time to time. Windows were improperly seated in the sills of the blue rhomboid tower, designed by I. M. Pei. Once the building's 13 acres of glass were replaced and the central core stiffened, the problem was corrected. Bostonians originally feared the Hancock's stark modernism would overwhelm nearby Trinity Church, but its shimmering sides reflect the older structure's image, actually enlarging its presence. The tower is closed to the public. ⊠ *200 Clarendon St., Back Bay* ⊕ *www.200clarendon.com* Ⓜ *Copley.*

Mary Baker Eddy Library for the Betterment of Humanity

LIBRARY | FAMILY | One of the largest single collections by and about an American woman is housed at this library, located on the Christian Science Plaza. The library also includes two floors of exhibits, which celebrate the power of ideas and provide context to the life and achievements of Mary Baker Eddy (1821–1910).

The library is also home to the fascinating **Mapparium,** a huge stained-glass globe whose 30-foot interior can be traversed on a footbridge, where you can experience a unique sound-and-light show while viewing an accurate representation of the world from 1935. The Hall of Ideas showcases quotes from the world's greatest thinkers, which travel around the room and through a virtual fountain. In the Quest Gallery, explore how Mary Baker Eddy founded a church and a college, and at the age of 87, launched

The Christian Science Monitor newspaper. ✉ *200 Massachusetts Ave., Back Bay* ☎ *617/450–7000* ⊕ *www.marybakereddylibrary.org* 🚇 *Hall of Ideas and 3rd-fl. library free, exhibits $6* Ⓜ *Prudential.*

Massachusetts Historical Society

LIBRARY | The first historical society in the United States (founded in 1791) has paintings, a library, and a 12-million-piece manuscript collection from 17th-century New England to the present. Among these manuscripts are the Adams Family Papers, which comprise more than 300,000 pages from the letters and diaries of generations of the Adams family, including papers from John Adams and John Quincy Adams. Casual visitors are welcome, but if you'd like to examine the papers in depth, call ahead. The Society also offers a variety of programs and special exhibits. ✉ *1154 Boylston St., Back Bay* ☎ *617/536–1608* ⊕ *www.masshist. org* 🚇 *Free* ⊘ *Closed Sun.* Ⓜ *Hynes.*

Newbury Street

NEIGHBORHOOD | Eight-block-long Newbury Street has been compared to New York's 5th Avenue, and certainly this is the city's poshest shopping area, with branches of Chanel, Diane von Furstenberg, Burberry, Barbour, Fred Perry, and other top names in fashion. But here the pricey boutiques are more intimate than grand, and people live above the trendy restaurants and ubiquitous hair salons, giving the place a neighborhood feel. Toward the Massachusetts Avenue end, cafés proliferate and the stores get funkier, ending with Newbury Comics and Urban Outfitters. ✉ *From Arlington St. to Massachusetts Ave., Back Bay* ⊕ *www.newbury-st.com* Ⓜ *Hynes, Copley.*

New England Historic Genealogical Society

LIBRARY | Are you related to Miles Standish or Priscilla Alden? The answer may lie here. If your ancestors were pedigreed New Englanders—or if you're just interested in genealogical research of any kind—you can trace your family tree with the help of the society's collections.

The society dates from 1845, and is the oldest genealogical organization in the country. ✉ *101 Newbury St., Back Bay* ☎ *888/296–3447* ⊕ *www.americanancestors.org* 🚇 *$20 for a day pass for nonmembers to use facility* ⊘ *Closed Sun. and Mon.* Ⓜ *Copley.*

Old South Church

RELIGIOUS SITE | Members of the Old South Meeting House, of Tea Party fame, decamped to this new site in 1873, a move not without controversy. In an Italian Gothic style inspired by the art critic John Ruskin and an interior decorated with Venetian mosaics and stained-glass windows, the "new" structure could hardly be more different from the plain meetinghouse they vacated. The sanctuary is free and open to the public seven days a week. ✉ *645 Boylston St., Back Bay* ☎ *617/536–1970* ⊕ *www.oldsouth. org* Ⓜ *Copley.*

Prudential Center

STORE/MALL | **FAMILY** | The 52-story Prudential Tower, or the "Pru," dominates the acreage between Boylston Street and Huntington Avenue. Its enclosed shopping mall is connected by a glass bridge to the more upscale Copley Place. The popular food emporium, Eataly, located in the Pru, offers a great spot for a quick bite. As for the Prudential Tower itself, the architectural historian Bainbridge Bunting made an acute observation when he called it "an apparition so vast in size that it appears to float above the surrounding district without being related to it." Later modifications to the Boylston Street frontage of the Prudential Center effected a better union of the complex with the urban space around it, but the tower itself floats on, vast as ever. **Prudential Center Skywalk Observatory,** a 50th-floor observatory atop the Prudential Tower, offers panoramic vistas of Boston, Cambridge, and the suburbs to the west and south—on clear days, you can even see Cape Cod. Your ticket includes an audio tour, admission to the Dreams of Freedom Museum, and the multimedia theater.

✉ 800 Boylston St., Back Bay ☎ 800/746–7778, 617/859–0648 for Skywalk ⊕ www.prudentialcenter.com ⊠ Skywalk $21 Ⓜ *Prudential Center, Copley Station.*

Symphony Hall
ARTS VENUE | While Boston's Symphony Hall—the home of the Boston Symphony Orchestra and the Boston Pops—is considered among the best in the world for its sublime acoustics, it's also worth visiting to enjoy its other merits. The stage is framed by an enormous organ facade and an intricate golden proscenium. Above the second balcony are 16 replicas of Greek and Roman statues, which, like the rest of the Hall, marry the acoustic and aesthetic by creating niches and uneven surfaces to enhance the acoustics of the space. Although acoustical science was a brand-new field of research when Professor Wallace Sabine planned the interior, not one of the 2,500 seats is a bad one—the secret is the box-within-a-box design. ✉ *301 Massachusetts Ave., Back Bay* ☎ *888/266–1200 box office, 617/638–9390 tours ⊕ www.bso.org* Ⓜ *Symphony.*

★ Trinity Church
RELIGIOUS SITE | In his 1877 masterpiece, architect Henry Hobson Richardson brought his Romanesque Revival style to maturity; all the aesthetic elements for which he was famous come together magnificently—bold polychromatic masonry, careful arrangement of masses, sumptuously carved interior woodwork—in this crowning centerpiece of Copley Square. A full appreciation of its architecture requires an understanding of the logistical problems of building it here. The Back Bay is a reclaimed wetland with a high water table. Bedrock, or at least stable glacial till, lies far beneath wet clay. Like all older Back Bay buildings, Trinity Church sits on submerged wooden pilings. But its central tower weighs 9,500 tons, and most of the 4,500 pilings beneath the building are under that tremendous central mass. The pilings are checked regularly for sinkage by means of a hatch in the basement.

Richardson engaged some of the best artists of his day—John LaFarge, William Morris, and Edward Burne-Jones among them—to execute the paintings and stained glass that make this a monument to everything that was right about the pre-Raphaelite spirit and the nascent aesthetic of Morris's Arts and Crafts movement. Along the north side of the church, note the Augustus Saint-Gaudens statue of Phillips Brooks—the most charismatic rector in New England, who almost single-handedly got Trinity built and furnished. Shining light of Harvard's religious community and lyricist of "O Little Town of Bethlehem," Brooks is shown here with Christ touching his shoulder in approval. For a nice respite, try to catch one of the Friday organ concerts beginning at 12:15. The 11:15 Sunday service is usually followed by a free guided tour. ✉ *206 Clarendon St., Back Bay* ☎ *617/536–0944 ⊕ trinitychurchboston.org ⊠ Entrance free, guided and self-guided tours Tues.–Fri., $10 ⊗ Closed Mon.* Ⓜ *Copley.*

🍴 Restaurants

Easily the ritziest section of Boston, the Back Bay is where you'll find historic landmarks such as Copley Square and the Boston Public Library rubbing shoulders with stylish boutiques like Valentino and Max Mara. The restaurant scene follows suit with landmark steak houses and seafood spots sharing sidewalk space with more chic, more global options. But don't feel like you have to win the lottery to eat in this area. While lots of fine-dining establishments dot the neighborhood, you'll also find plenty of affordable spots including Irish taverns, burrito and burger joints, and Eataly, a massive Italian food emporium in the Prudential Center with groceries, bakeries, seafood, cheese, and meat markets, a dozen eateries, and public café tables to sit at and enjoy takeout.

Abe & Louie's

$$$$ | **STEAKHOUSE** | Go ahead: live the fantasy of the robber baron feasting in a setting of cavernous fireplaces and deep-textured, plush mahogany booths of this steak house. Abe & Louie's may be a tad Disney-esque in its decor, but its menu lives up to the promise with gorgeous, two-tiered raw seafood platters and juicy rib-eye steaks under velvety hollandaise. **Known for:** excellent meats; top-brass service; business-style setting. [$] *Average main: $50* ✉ *793 Boylston St., Back Bay* ☎ *617/536–6300* 🌐 *www.abeandlouies.com* [M] *Copley.*

★ Atlantic Fish Co

$$$ | **SEAFOOD** | Designed to look like an ocean vessel with gorgeous wood finishes and nautical artwork, this local seafood restaurant delivers first-class fish, so fresh that the extensive menus are printed daily to reflect the day's catch, served broiled, baked, blackened, fried, grilled, or pan-seared. Unsnap your starched napkin and begin with a platter of chilled seafood (lobster, littlenecks, oysters, crab, and shrimp), followed by any one of the specialties ranging from whole-bellied fried Ipswich clams to pan-seared bass with lobster ravioli in an unctuous lobster cream sauce. **Known for:** elegant seafood; solicitous service in a lux atmosphere; great outdoor patio. [$] *Average main: $35* ✉ *761 Boylston St., Back Bay* ☎ *617/267–4000* 🌐 *www.atlanticfish.com* [M] *Copley.*

Buttermilk & Bourbon

$ | **SOUTHERN** | Buttermilk & Bourbon is Chef Jason Santos's take on New Orleans fare, with dishes like beignets topped with powdered sugar, buttermilk biscuits paired with house-made sausage gravy, and fried chicken and waffles, served in a cool lower-level space. Weekend brunch offers banana-cinammon French toast, duck confit hash, and s'mores bacon. **Known for:** Southern cuisine; fun scene; buttermilk fried chicken. [$] *Average main: $25* ✉ *160 Commonwealth Ave., Back Bay* ☎ *617/266–1122* 🌐 *www.buttermilkbourbon.com* ⏲ *No lunch* [M] *Back Bay.*

The Capital Grille

$$$$ | **STEAKHOUSE** | A carnivore's utopia awaits within the clubby, dark-wood walls of this beloved steak house favored by those on expense accounts. Adjust your starched napkin and tuck into such staples as lobster and crab cakes, a massive shellfish platter, and succulent meats such as the 24-ounce dry-aged porterhouse. **Known for:** clubby feel; stellar wine list; swell crowd. [$] *Average main: $40* ✉ *900 Boylston St., Back Bay* ☎ *617/262–8900* 🌐 *www.thecapitalgrille.com* [M] *Hynes.*

★ Davio's Northern Italian Steakhouse

$$$$ | **ITALIAN** | Comfy armchairs and a grand, high-ceilinged dining room give diners a heightened sense of self-importance, beginning with lunch when the city's power elite stop in for great pastas (half portions are available), prime NY-aged steaks and oversize salads. For dinner, some patrons snag quick, pretheater bites at the bar while others opt for a more leisurely experience, lingering over sophisticated Italian dishes like tagliatelle Bolognese and succulent grilled veal chops with creamy potatoes and Port wine sauce. **Known for:** delectable Italian classics; generous portions; elegant setting and service. [$] *Average main: $39* ✉ *75 Arlington St., Back Bay* ☎ *617/357–4810* 🌐 *www.davios.com* ⏲ *No lunch weekends* [M] *Arlington.*

★ Deuxave

$$$ | **MODERN AMERICAN** | At the corner of two avenues (Commonwealth and Massachusetts), which is how this restaurant got its name (deux is French for "two"), you'll find this snazzy, dark-wood enclave serving sophisticated dishes like spice-crusted Ahi tuna and braised pork belly, pan-seared Atlantic halibut, and organic chicken with parsnip and Foie Gras agnolotti. Make sure to pair your meal with a bottle from the thoughtfully

crafted and surprisingly affordable wine list and served by an attentive staff. **Known for:** modern French food; nine-hour French onion soup; reasonably priced wine list. $ *Average main: $35* ✉ *371 Commonwealth Ave., Back Bay* ☎ *617/517–5915* ⊕ *www.deuxave.com* 🚭 *No credit cards* Ⓜ *Hynes.*

★ Grill 23 & Bar

$$$$ | STEAKHOUSE | Pinstripe suits, dark paneling, Persian rugs, and waiters in white jackets give this single-location steak house a posh tone, and the kitchen places a premium on seasonal, organic ingredients and sustainable and humanely raised meats; the divine coconut cake is worth saving room for dessert. Two bars, a big, buzzing one overlooking Berkeley Street and a quieter, smaller one on the second floor by the cozy fireplace, serve excellent drinks, specialty Scotches, and bar bites, along with the full menu. **Known for:** locally owned steak house; Brandt family beef; party-dress vibe. $ *Average main: $40* ✉ *161 Berkeley St., Back Bay* ☎ *617/542–2255* ⊕ *grill23.com* 🕒 *No lunch* Ⓜ *Back Bay/South End.*

Joe's American Bar & Grill

$$ | AMERICAN | Despite its classy New-bury Street address, Joe's (with another location on the waterfront) dishes up kitschy July 4 decor, along with myriad burgers, hearty salads, clam chowder, and affordable kid-friendly options like pasta with butter and grilled cheese sandwiches served with a complimentary hot fudge sundae (or a fruit cup for those health-conscious parents). The warm oversize chocolate chip cookie brought to the table in a small black skillet crowned with vanilla ice cream, chocolate sauce, and candied pecans, however, is reason enough to stop by. **Known for:** kid-friendly offerings; affordable prices; unfussy American classics. $ *Average main: $21* ✉ *181 Newbury St., Back Bay* ☎ *617/536–4200* ⊕ *www.joesamerican. com* Ⓜ *Copley.*

Krasi

$$ | GREEK | This comfortable Greek meze and wine bar is the real deal, with a Greek rotisserie in the open kitchen featuring rotating meat—lamb, chicken, or pork—as well as seafood and vegetable options, plus an amazingly long list of almost 200 Greek wines. Cozy banquettes are perfect for dining, but to see the action, some of the bar seats have a front row view of the kitchen. **Known for:** authentic Greek fare; impressive wine-by-the-glass menu; friendly service. $ *Average main: $30* ✉ *48 Gloucester St., Back Bay* ☎ *617/536–0230* ⊕ *krasiboston.com* 🕒 *No lunch* Ⓜ *Copley.*

Ostra

$$$$ | SEAFOOD | Boston has plenty of great seafood restaurants, but this sophisticated option near the Theater District turns out delicate and exquisitely prepared catches of the day fit for a king (and some say costing a king's ransom). Settle in with a seasonal cocktail in the sleek, pearl-white dining room before tucking into any one of the glistening raw fish tartares followed by a simply pre-pared entrée, whether it's a salt-crusted branzino for two or broiled Maine lobster. **Known for:** exquisite seafood dishes; ele-gant setting; top-notch service. $ *Aver-age main: $42* ✉ *1 Charles St., Back Bay* ☎ *617/421–1200* ⊕ *ostraboston.com.*

Porto

$$$ | MEDITERRANEAN | In a spanking white space next to the Prudential Center, chef/co-owner Jody Adams, former owner of the beloved and now shuttered Rialto restaurant, takes Mediterranean fare up a notch, with starters like a meze board brimming with hummus, saffron peppers, tzatziki, baba ganoush, and muhammara, and entrées like littleneck clams and house-made spaghetti wowing diners. Other popular dishes include grilled lamb chops and shareable paella. **Known for:** artful seafood preparations; bountiful raw bar; elegant Back Bay setting. $ *Average main: $35* ✉ *Ring Rd., next door to Saks*

5th Ave., Back Bay ☎ *617/536–1234* 🌐 *www.porto-boston.com.*

Rochambeau

$$$ | BISTRO | This two-story French-inspired bistro and café offers a stylish spot to sip a latte and enjoy a quiche in the morning, power lunch at mid-day, and dine on dishes like duck l'orange or the plate of the day, such as lemon chicken tangine or trout almandine at night. The weekend brunch menu includes classics like croque madame, with ham, gruyere and bechamel on brioche, topped with a sunny-side-up egg and a to-die-for cinnamon skillet bread. **Known for:** romantic setting; great service; buzzy scene. [$] *Average main: $35* ✉ *900 Boylston St., Back Bay* ☎ *617/247–0400* 🌐 *rochambeauboston.com* [M] *Back Bay.*

★ Saltie Girl

$$$ | SEAFOOD | Step into this snug Back Bay raw bar specializing in snappy cocktails and luscious preparations of all things seafood and you'll fall hook, line, and sinker for everything on the menu, including platters of fresh-shucked oysters on crushed ice, torched salmon belly with charred avocado, smoked fish that would make a New York deli owner proud, seafood-topped toasts, and arguably the best warm lobster roll in the city, a butter-drenched affair overflowing with fresh lobster meat. Rounding out the menu and decorating the restaurant's walls are 80-plus tins of domestic and imported gourmet fish and shellfish (including caviar!) served in all their oily goodness with bread, butter, smoked salt, lemon, and sweet pepper jam. **Known for:** creative seafood dishes; large tinned seafood selection; hip crowd. [$] *Average main: $25* ✉ *281 Dartmouth St., Back Bay* ☎ *617/267–0691* 🌐 *saltiegirl.com.*

★ Select Oyster Bar

$$$$ | SEAFOOD | Snug quarters and no desserts can't quell the stream of diners pouring into this uptown enclave eager to savor oysters and seductive seafood combinations as salmon crudo with pisatchio oil, Maine lobster cabbage-kale Thai salad, and tomato bouillabaisse with saffron aioli. With 70% of the restaurant's catch coming from New England, plus a thoughtful libations list and polished service, you have all the ingredients for a good time, whether you're sitting at the bar, the front communal table, or in the three-season alfresco area out back. **Known for:** lip-smacking seafood dishes; 20% pretax service charge automatically added to each bill; cozy, relaxed atmosphere. [$] *Average main: $36* ✉ *50 Gloucester St., Back Bay* ☎ *857/293–8064* 🌐 *www.selectboston.com* [M] *Hynes.*

Sonsie

$$$ | AMERICAN | Café society blossoms along Newbury Street, particularly at Sonsie, where a well-heeled crowd sips coffee up front or angles for places at the bar. Lunch and dinner dishes veer toward basic bistro fare with an American twist such as kale Caesar salad with grilled chicken and pan-roasted salmon with potatoes, chard, and beet "ketchup." The restaurant is a terrific place for weekend brunch, when the light pours through the long windows, and is at its most vibrant in warm weather, when the open doors make for colorful people-watching. **Known for:** American bistro favorites; sceney vibe; Sunday brunch. [$] *Average main: $25* ✉ *327 Newbury St., Back Bay* ☎ *617/351–2500* 🌐 *sonsieboston.com* [M] *Hynes.*

Sorellina

$$$$ | ITALIAN | Set in an all-white dining room, everything about this upscale Italian spot is oversized, from its space near Copley Square to its flavor-packed portions of grilled octopus with squid-ink couscous, homemade pasta with Wagyu meatballs, and bone-in veal chops over soft polenta. Just save room for dessert: it's always a highlight here. **Known for:** modern Italian cooking; bountiful portions; edgy decor. [$] *Average main: $42* ✉ *1 Huntington Ave., Back Bay* ☎ *617/412–4600* 🌐 *www.sorellinaboston.com* [M] *Copley, Back Bay.*

Stephanie's on Newbury

$$$ | AMERICAN | Here's comfort food at its best—sophisticated enough for parents (lobster pot pie), yet simple enough for kids (burgers and pasta). The attractive space has plenty of booths for spreading out in. **Known for:** favorite of locals; large portions; friendly service. $ *Average main: $30* ✉ *190 Newbury St., Back Bay* ☎ *617/236–0990* ⊕ *www. stephaniesonnewbury.com* ⊟ *No credit cards* Ⓜ *Copley.*

Summer Shack

$$ | SEAFOOD | FAMILY | Boston uberchef Jasper White's casual New England seafood restaurant is a boisterous, bright, fun eatery next to the Prudential Center (he also has one in Cambridge and at Mohegan Sun in Connecticut), where creamy clam chowder and fried Ipswich clams share menu space with golden crab cakes and cedar-planked, maple-lemon glazed salmon. In addition to a handful of chicken and meat dishes for those not into seafood, White features the most succulent lobsters in the city (he has a patented process for cooking them), all brought to you by an eager-to-please staff. **Known for:** fresh seafood; succulent lobster; fun, casual atmosphere. $ *Average main: $24* ✉ *50 Dalton St., Back Bay* ☎ *617/867–9955* ⊕ *www.summershackrestaurant.com* Ⓜ *Hynes.*

Uni

$$$$ | ASIAN FUSION | Inside the tasteful boutique Eliot Hotel lies an innovative *izakaya* (informal Japanese gastropub), owned by Boston star chefs-partners Ken Oringer and Tony Messina, who offer boldly flavored renditions of Asian street food—Chiang Mai duck carnitas; Wagyu beef dumplings; shrimp teriyaki fried rice; and dozens of tempting sashimi and nigiri choices. Although the bites can add up price-wise, the menu has a sprinkling of inexpensive dishes, like chicken steam buns and roasted celery root. **Known for:** creative raw fish options; trendy feel; small plate format. $ *Average main:*

$45 ✉ *Eliot Hotel, 370 Commonwealth Ave., Back Bay* ☎ *617/536–7200* ⊕ *www. uni-boston.com* ⊗ *No lunch* Ⓜ *Hynes.*

☕ Coffee and Quick Bites

J.P. Licks

$ | CAFÉ | Simple but sublime cones have made many addicted to the fun and funky likes of J.P. Licks, which serves a traditional stable of ice-cream flavors, like peanut butter cookies 'n' cream and mint chip, along with hard and soft frozen yogurt offerings, best smothered with the shop's superb hot fudge sauce and any of the wet (whipped cream, marshmallow sauce) and dry (M&M's, Heath Bar) toppings. **Known for:** Boston-based business; creative flavors; coffee beans roasted in-house. $ *Average main: $6* ✉ *1106 Boylston St., Back Bay* ☎ *857/233–5805* ⊕ *www.jplicks.com.*

Pavement Coffeehouse

$ | AMERICAN | Enjoy coffee, snacks, and Wi-Fi access in this hip basement spot, one of several scattered about the city. Tea lovers needn't feel left out—there are plenty of excellent options, including jade oolong and chamomile medley. **Known for:** roasting their own coffee beans; amazing hand-crafted bagels; lots of vegan options. $ *Average main: $10* ✉ *286 Newbury St., Back Bay* ☎ *617/859–9515* ⊕ *www.pavementcoffeehouse.com* Ⓜ *Hynes, Copley.*

Trident Booksellers & Café

$ | AMERICAN | Folks gather at the two-story Trident Booksellers & Café to review literary best sellers, thumb through the superb magazine selection, and chow down on items from the perpetual breakfast menu. The restaurant also serves lunch and dinner and has an excellent beer selection, as well as wine. **Known for:** beloved local bookstore; variety of events, from trivia to talks; lemon ricotta stuffed French toast. $ *Average main: $15* ✉ *338 Newbury St., Back Bay* ☎ *617/267–8688* ⊕ *www.tridentbookscafe.com* Ⓜ *Hynes.*

Hotels

The Back Bay and the South End are what locals call the "well-heeled" sections of Boston, meaning money talks here—think the likes of Mandarin Oriental or Fairmont Copley Plaza. The streets are lined with upscale, stylish hotels (old and new), boutique hotels, and inns.

Boston Marriott Copley Place

$$ | HOTEL | FAMILY | It's busy-busy, with throngs of tourists and business travelers, but you can't beat the location of this 38-story megahotel, which sports three entrances—a street-level door, a glass sky bridge from the Prudential Center, and a walk-in from the Copley mall—ensuring that you rarely have to go outside to shop or eat, which is especially nice in winter. **Pros:** good service; comfortable beds; prime Copley Square location; on-site Starbucks. **Cons:** chaotic lobby; not for those who want an intimate, boutique experience; massive in size. $ *Rooms from: $185* ⊠ *110 Huntington Ave., Back Bay* ☎ *617/236–5800, 800/228–9290* ⊕ *www.marriott.com* ⇌ *1147 rooms* ⦿ *No meals* Ⓜ *Copley, Back Bay.*

Boston Park Plaza

$ | HOTEL | FAMILY | Step into a true piece of Boston history at the esteemed Park Plaza, one of the city's most identifiable landmarks since 1927, but don't worry—while the hotel is historic, modern updates make it an upscale place to stay and is an ideal place for tourists looking for old-world charm and excellent service. **Pros:** access to a 20,000-square-foot health club; Top Golf swing suite in gym; tons of historic value; windows that open. **Cons:** bathrooms are small; guest rooms vary in size and can be small; $29 facilities fee per room, per night. $ *Rooms from: $204* ⊠ *50 Park Plaza, at Arlington St., Back Bay* ☎ *617/426–2000, 800/225–2008* ⊕ *www.bostonparkpla-za.com* ⇌ *1060 rooms* ⦿ *No meals* ⟳ *Dogs allowed for $75 cleaning fee, weight limit may apply* Ⓜ *Arlington.*

Charlesmark Hotel

$ | HOTEL | Hipsters and romantics who'd rather spend their cash on a great meal than a hotel bill have put this late 19th-century former residential row house in the heart of the Back Bay on the map. **Pros:** fantastic price for the location; free Wi-Fi; all rooms have safes and refrigerators. **Cons:** some might feel crowded by compact rooms and hallways; no valet; no turndown service. $ *Rooms from: $189* ⊠ *655 Boylston St., Back Bay* ☎ *617/247–1212* ⊕ *www.thecharlesmarkhotel.com* ⇌ *40 rooms* ⦿ *Free Breakfast* Ⓜ *Copley.*

The Colonnade Hotel

$$ | HOTEL | FAMILY | The conveniently located Colonnade Hotel offers clean, modern environs injected with hues of khaki, chocolate, and chrome. **Pros:** roof-deck pool; across from Prudential Center shopping; close to Hynes Convention Center. **Cons:** Huntington Avenue can get clogged with rush-hour traffic; on summer days the pool is packed by 11 am; parking is expensive. $ *Rooms from: $269* ⊠ *120 Huntington Ave., Back Bay* ☎ *617/424–7000, 800/962–3030* ⊕ *www.colonnadehotel.com* ⇌ *285 rooms* ⦿ *No meals* Ⓜ *Back Bay, Prudential Center.*

Copley Square Hotel

$$$ | HOTEL | The chic Copley Square Hotel offers high-tech registration pods, cushy mattresses, and in-room iPod docks—not too shabby for a place that opened in 1891 and has provided respite to a century of celebrities like Babe Ruth, Ella Fitzgerald, and Billie Holiday. **Pros:** free Wi-Fi; free nightly wine tastings; cool bar and club scene. **Cons:** small rooms; rooms facing Huntington Avenue can be noisy; not ideal for older couples seeking peace and quiet. $ *Rooms from: $350* ⊠ *47 Huntington Ave., Back Bay* ☎ *617/536–9000* ⊕ *www.copleysquare-hotel.com* ⇌ *143 rooms* ⦿ *Free Breakfast* Ⓜ *Copley, Back Bay.*

★ **Eliot Hotel**

$$ | **HOTEL** | One of the city's best small hotels, located on posh Commonwealth Avenue, expertly merges the old blue-blood Boston aesthetic with modern flair (like contemporary rugs mingling with crystal chandeliers); everyone from well-heeled Sox fans to traveling CEOs to tony college parents have noticed. **Pros:** great location near Fenway and Newbury Street; top-notch restaurant; pet-friendly; beautiful rooms. **Cons:** can be pricey; some complain of elevator noise; parking is expensive. $ *Rooms from: $285* ✉ *370 Commonwealth Ave., Back Bay* ☎ *617/267–1607, 800/443–5468* ⊕ *www.eliothotel.com* ⇌ *95 rooms* ○○ *No meals* Ⓜ *Hynes.*

★ **Fairmont Copley Plaza**

$$$ | **HOTEL** | **FAMILY** | Since 1912, this decadent, unabashedly romantic hotel has welcomed guests in style, immediately impressing as they enter under the trademark red awning, flanked by golden lion statues, into the lobby decked out in Italian marble, stunning coffered ceilings, and gorgeous crystal chandeliers. **Pros:** prime Back Bay location, centrally located in Copley Square; luxurious gym; 24-hour daily in-room dining. **Cons:** small bathrooms; valet parking is expensive; due to the historical nature, room sizes vary greatly. $ *Rooms from: $350* ✉ *138 St. James Ave., Back Bay* ☎ *617/267–5300, 866/540–4417* ⊕ *www.fairmont.com/copley-plaza-boston* ⇌ *383 rooms* ○○ *No meals* Ⓜ *Copley, Back Bay.*

Four Seasons Hotel Boston

$$$$ | **HOTEL** | **FAMILY** | This Public Garden–facing spot keeps a surprisingly low profile in Boston—and that's OK by the jeans-clad millionaires and assorted business types who cluster in the glossy lobby or use the courtesy car. **Pros:** close to Newbury Street and the Public Garden; signature Four Seasons service; pet-friendly. **Cons:** pricey during peak times; valet service can be slow; can be hard to get a table at The Bristol.

$ *Rooms from: $710* ✉ *200 Boylston St., Back Bay* ☎ *617/338–4400, 800/819–5053* ⊕ *www.fourseasons.com/boston* ⇌ *273 rooms* ○○ *No meals* Ⓜ *Arlington.*

Hilton Boston Back Bay

$$ | **HOTEL** | Rooms at the Back Bay Hilton are relatively spacious, with plush "Serenity" bedding, Suite Dreams mattresses, and cozy, down-filled comforters. **Pros:** oversize showers; good 7th-floor fitness center; indoor pool. **Cons:** room service is not 24/7; fee for Wi-Fi (except in lobby); parking is expensive. $ *Rooms from: $290* ✉ *40 Dalton St., Back Bay* ☎ *617/236–1100, 888/874–0663* ⊕ *www.bostonbackbay.hilton.com* ⇌ *395 rooms* ○○ *No meals* Ⓜ *Prudential, Hynes.*

★ **Inn@St. Botolph**

$$ | **B&B/INN** | **FAMILY** | The posh yet homey 16-room Inn@St. Botolph follows an edgy hotel model—no front desk, no restaurant, no keys, and no valet (there is, however, an office on-site that is staffed 24/7). **Pros:** guests get 25% off meals at Columbus Hospital Group restaurants; free Wi-Fi; self-service laundry on-site. **Cons:** DIY parking; no traditional front desk check-in services; may be too "off the beaten path" for some. $ *Rooms from: $279* ✉ *99 St. Botolph St., Back Bay* ☎ *617/236–8099* ⊕ *www.innatstbotolph.com* ⇌ *16 rooms* ○○ *Free breakfast* Ⓜ *Prudential.*

Lenox Hotel

$$ | **HOTEL** | **FAMILY** | A good alternative to chain-owned, big-box Back Bay hotels, the boutique family-owned Lenox offers top-notch service, three food and beverage outlets, 24-hour room service, a fitness center, and a business center in an ideal location. **Pros:** mini-refrigerator in every room; complimentary bottled water; historic/architectural charm; free Wi-Fi. **Cons:** some bathrooms are small; no minibar; costly parking. $ *Rooms from: $285* ✉ *61 Exeter St., Back Bay* ☎ *617/536–5300, 800/225–7676* ⊕ *www.lenoxhotel.com* ⇌ *214 rooms* ○○ *No meals* Ⓜ *Back Bay, Copley.*

Loews Boston Hotel

$$$ | **HOTEL** | **FAMILY** | The former headquarters of the Boston Police Department houses the sleek Loews Boston Hotel, which boasts a cool glass-and-marble lobby, a stylish restaurant, Precinct Kitchen + Bar, and manages to combine the building's history with 21st-century amenities. **Pros:** delicious restaurant with a great patio; welcoming staff; pet-friendly. **Cons:** bar-side rooms can be loud; parking is expensive; restaurant is pricey. [$] *Rooms from: $300* ✉ *154 Berkeley St., Back Bay* ☎ *617/266–7200, 855/495–6397* 🌐 *www.loewshotels.com/boston-hotel* 🛏 *225 rooms* 🍴 *No meals* [M] *Back Bay.*

Mandarin Oriental, Boston

$$$$ | **HOTEL** | The Mandarin Oriental, Boston manages to combine classic New England elegance with the luxurious touches the brand is known for around the world, including top-notch service, amenities galore, and public areas adorned with museum-quality art, while large guest rooms include contemporary Asian design and oversize bathrooms with soaking tubs and separate walk-in showers. **Pros:** amazing service; very quiet; good-size rooms. **Cons:** small fitness center; rates are exorbitant; valet parking is expensive. [$] *Rooms from: $795* ✉ *776 Boylston St., Back Bay* ☎ *617/535–8888* 🌐 *www.mandarinoriental.com/boston* 🛏 *150 rooms* 🍴 *No meals* [M] *Prudential, Copley, Back Bay.*

Newbury Guest House

$$ | **B&B/INN** | Located in the heart of Boston's most fashionable shopping street, a homey feel and personalized service are at the soul of this elegant and historic 1882 brownstone, which features natural pine flooring, blue Victorian furnishings, and prints from the Museum of Fine Arts. **Pros:** cozy and homey; free Wi-Fi; perfect base for shopping. **Cons:** rooms go quickly year-round; small bathrooms; limited parking. [$] *Rooms from: $298* ✉ *261 Newbury St., Back Bay* ☎ *617/670–6000, 800/437–7668* 🌐 *www.newburyguesthouse.com* 🛏 *35 rooms* 🍴 *Free Breakfast* [M] *Back Bay, Hynes, Copley.*

The Newbury Boston

$$$ | **HOTEL** | **FAMILY** | Standing guard at the corner of fashionable Newbury Street and the Public Garden, the old-school elegant former Taj Boston had a top-to-bottom facelift in 2020, with a fresh, contemporary look and amenities that include exclusive Byredo bath products, Frette robes and linens, in-room Nespresso Vertuo espresso-maker, and access to The Library and Fitness Center, along with preferred seating at The Street Bar. **Pros:** white-glove service; amazing views; proximity to shopping, dining, and the park. **Cons:** all this luxury will cost you; pricey to park; not all rooms face the park. [$] *Rooms from: $400* ✉ *1 Newbury St., Back Bay* ☎ *617/536–5700* 🌐 *www.thenewburyboston.com* 🛏 *315 rooms* 🍴 *No meals* [M] *Arlington.*

Westin Copley Place Boston

$$$ | **HOTEL** | If the idea of sleeping in an upscale mall appeals to you, the Westin, which has its own pod of retail shops and restaurants, is also connected by a covered skywalk to Copley Place (more high-end shopping) and the Hynes Convention Center. **Pros:** great location close to shopping and tourist spots; guided running tours in the summer and fall; Gretta Cole Spa on site. **Cons:** big and busy feeling; pool area is nothing special; some say it's overpriced. [$] *Rooms from: $279* ✉ *10 Huntington Ave., Back Bay* ☎ *617/262–9600, 888/937–8461* 🌐 *www.westincopleyplaceboston.com* 🛏 *945 rooms* 🍴 *No meals* [M] *Copley, Back Bay.*

☾ Nightlife

BARS

Bristol Bar

CAFES—NIGHTLIFE | This elegant restaurant and bar boasts floor-to-ceiling views of the Public Garden and a relaxed luxury setting that's enjoyable at nearly any time of day. Despite the fancy digs, one of the restaurant's signature dishes (available at both lunch and dinner) is the Bristol burger, though, of course, it's a premium version, made with dry-aged NY strip steak, short rib and brisket, topped with Cabot clothbound cheddar, and bacon aioli. On weekdays, power breakfasts and lunches are followed by a vibrant dinner scene, and weekends offer three meals a day plus a lively bar scene with signature cocktails. ✉ 200 Boylston St., Back Bay ☎ 617/338–4400 ⊕ www.fourseasons. com/boston/dining/the_bristol_lounge. html Ⓜ Arlington, Boylston.

Bukowski Tavern

BARS/PUBS | This narrow barroom has a literary flair and more than 100 brews for your sipping pleasure, served by a no-nonsense bar staff. You'll see many a beer nerd hanging out at the bar, but hungry folks also come to the funky joint for the creative burgers, hot dogs, and other comfort foods. Food is served until 1 am Sunday through Wednesday (1:30 am Thursday through Sunday). Make sure to bring cash; no credit cards are accepted. ✉ 50 Dalton St., Back Bay ☎ 617/437–9999 ⊕ www.bukowskitav-ern.net Ⓜ Hynes.

Champions Sports Bar

BARS/PUBS | Located inside the Boston Marriott Copley Place, this bar calls all sports fans (rabid, yet civilized) with 40 TV screens—including a 12' x 24' whopper where you surely won't miss a play. Visiting-team fans are welcome but may expect to be drowned out by cheers for home teams. Champions is not just about sports and beer (36 taps and scores of bottles): there's smooth waitstaff, a wine and cocktail list, and lengthy menu of typical bar favorites, from wings and burgers to tacos. ✉ Boston Marriott Copley Pl., Copley Pl. Mall, 2nd level, 110 Huntington Ave., Back Bay ☎ 617/927–5304 ⊕ www.championsbos-ton.com Ⓜ Prudential Center.

★ Oak Long Bar + Kitchen

BARS/PUBS | This stunning flagship bar in the 1912 Fairmont Copley Plaza Hotel is a "see and be seen" hot spot, with the original sky-high coffered ceilings, catbird views over Copley Square, and top-notch bartenders. Inside, coveted barstools are filled with an upscale crowd, while outside in warm weather, patrons can sit at outdoor tables while perusing a menu of signature martinis, single malts, shareable platters, and desserts. People-watch and enjoy a panorama that encompasses the Boston Public Library and Trinity Church in this historic spot. ✉ Fairmont Copley Plaza, 138 St. James Ave., Back Bay ☎ 617/267–5300 ⊕ www.fairmont.com/copleyplaza Ⓜ Copley.

Sonsie

BARS/PUBS | The crowd spilling through French doors onto the sidewalk café in warm weather consists of trendy cosmopolitans, fun-loving professionals, local sports celebs, and scenesters who have flocked to the contemporary spot for more than 20 years. The sophisticated jazz-rock soundtrack remains at a civilized volume as you dine, sip, and people-watch. Hungry? There's breakfast after 8, with specialty coffees from a Presse espresso coffee-bar, a weekday lunch, weekend brunches from 9:30 am to 3:30 pm, and daily dinner and late-night menus until 12:30 am. ✉ 327 Newbury St., Back Bay ☎ 617/351–2500 ⊕ sonsieboston.com Ⓜ Hynes.

MUSIC CLUBS
Red Room @ Cafe 939
CAFES—NIGHTLIFE | By day a Berklee College coffee and snack bar, the Cafe by night opens its tidy, scarlet, 200-capacity concert space. Run, booked, and played by students, it's an ideal all-ages venue for aspiring student bands and indies on the rise; everyone from Hozier to Karmin has played here. Refreshments are light (soft drinks, noodles), and so is the cover charge, which varies based on the event. There are a dozen eateries within 200 yards. ⊠ *939 Boylston St., Back Bay* ☎ *617/747–2261* ⊕ *www.berlkee.edu/ cafe939* Ⓜ *Hynes.*

# Performing Arts

MUSIC
Berklee Performance Center
CONCERTS | The main stage for the internationally renowned Berklee College of Music, the "BPC" is best known for its jazz and pop programs, but also hosts folk, world, and rock acts, and pop stars like Talking Heads, Aimee Mann, Snarky Puppy, and Melody Gardot. Bargain alert: BPC stages a wealth of excellent student and faculty shows, and showcases sets and clinics by visiting artists that cost next to nothing. ⊠ *136 Massachusetts Ave., Back Bay* ☎ *617/266–7455 box office, 617/747–2261 performance center* ⊕ *www.berklee.edu/BPC* Ⓜ *Hynes.*

Boston Philharmonic Orchestra
MUSIC | The charismatic Benjamin Zander—whose signature preconcert chats help audiences better understand the blockbuster symphonies they're about to hear—heads up Boston Philharmonic. Performances at Harvard's Sanders Theatre, New England Conservatory's Jordan Hall, Symphony Hall, and a variety of other locales often encompass symphonies by Beethoven, Mahler, Shostakovich, and Brahms, plus lots of concertos. ☎ *617/236–0999* ⊕ *www. bostonphil.org.*

Boston Pops
MUSIC | Under the agile baton of Keith Lockhart, Boston Pops (largely Boston Symphony musicians) perform a bracing blend of American standards, movie themes, and contemporary vocal numbers (with top-tier guests) during May and June at Symphony Hall, plus 40 festive holiday-season concerts. Outdoor concerts on July 3 and 4 at the Hatch Memorial Shell are followed by concerts at Boston Symphony Orchestra's summer home, Tanglewood in Lenox, Massachusetts, in July and August. The free outdoor concerts are packed; be sure to arrive early with blankets, folding chairs, and a picnic. ☎ *617/266–1200, 888/266– 1200 box office* ⊕ *www.bso.org.*

Boston Symphony Orchestra
MUSIC | Founded in 1881, the Boston Symphony is one of America's oldest and most venerable orchestras, with dynamic Latvian conductor Andris Nelsons at the helm. Its home season at Symphony Hall runs from September through April. In July and August the music migrates to Tanglewood, the orchestra's bucolic summer home in the Berkshire Mountains in Lenox, Massachusetts. Including tours to Carnegie Hall and China, and the Boston Pops concerts, the BSO performs more than 250 concerts annually. ⊠ *301 Massachusetts Ave., Back Bay* ☎ *617/266– 1200, 888/266–1200 box office* ⊕ *www. bso.org* Ⓜ *Symphony.*

New England Conservatory's Jordan Hall
CONCERTS | One of the world's acoustic treasures, New England Conservatory's Jordan Hall is ideal for solo and string quartet recitals yet spacious enough for chamber and full orchestras. The pin-drop intimacy of this all-wood, 1,000-seat hall is in demand year-round for ensembles visiting and local. Boston Philharmonic and Boston Baroque perform here regularly. Dozens of free faculty and student concerts, jazz and classical, are a best-kept secret. ■**TIP**➔ **The lobby box office is open 1½ hours before the start of**

any ticketed show, in addition to its normal daytime hours. ✉ *30 Gainsborough St., Back Bay* ☎ *617/585–1260 box office* ⊕ *necmusic.edu* Ⓜ *Symphony.*

Odyssey Opera of Boston

THEMED ENTERTAINMENT | Odyssey Opera House, under the able leadership of founder and conductor Gil Rose, presents classic and modern operas at various venues throughout the city including the Calderwood Pavilion at the Boston Center for the Arts, Jordan Hall, B.U. Theatre, and Suffolk University's Modern Theatre. ✉ *Jordan Hall, 30 Gainsborough St., Boston* ☎ *617/826–1626* ⊕ *www. odysseyopera.org* Ⓜ *Symphony.*

★ **Symphony Hall**

CONCERTS | One of the world's best acoustical concert halls—some say *the* best—has been home since 1900 to the Boston Symphony Orchestra (BSO) and the Boston Pops. Led by conductor Keith Lockhart, the Pops concerts take place in May and June and around the winter holidays. The hall is also used by visiting orchestras, chamber groups, soloists, and local ensembles. Rehearsals and daytime concerts for students are open to the public, with discounted tickets. If you can't attend a concert, you can still see the magnificent hall on a free guided tour. Visit the venue's website for dates and times. ✉ *301 Massachusetts Ave., Back Bay* ☎ *617/266–1492* ⊕ *www.bso. org* Ⓜ *Symphony.*

THEATER

Huntington Theatre Company

THEATER | Boston's largest resident theater company consistently performs a high-quality mix of 21st-century plays and classics under the artistic direction of Peter DuBois, and commissions playwrights to produce original dramas. The Huntington performs at two locations: Boston University Theatre and the Calderwood Theatre Pavilion in the South End. ✉ *Boston University*

Theatre, 264 Huntington Ave., Back Bay ☎ *617/266–7900 box office* ⊕ *www. huntingtontheatre.org* Ⓜ *Symphony.*

 Shopping

This is the neighborhood of the elegant Mandarin Oriental Hotel—so need we say more about the shops you'll find here? Just in case: elegant, chic, modern, stylish. It's also home to Newbury Street, Boston's version of LA's Rodeo Drive. It's a shoppers' paradise, from high-end names such as Anne Fontaine to tiny specialty shops such as the Fish and Bone with up-to-the-minute art galleries and dazzling jewelers thrown into the mix.

Parallel to Newbury Street is Boylston Street, where you'll find a few standout shops such as Pompanoosuc Mills (hand-crafted furnishing) scattered among the other chains and restaurants.

ANTIQUES

Brodney Antiques & Jewelry

ANTIQUES/COLLECTIBLES | In addition to plenty of porcelain and silver, Brodney claims to have the biggest selection of estate jewelry in New England. Shoppers will also find plenty of antiques, furniture, paintings, and more. ✉ *176 Newbury St., Back Bay* ☎ *617/536–0500* ⊕ *www.brodney.com* ☯ *Closed Sun.* Ⓜ *Copley.*

ART GALLERIES

Childs Gallery

ART GALLERIES | The large selection of works for sale in this gallery, established in 1937, includes paintings, prints, drawings, watercolors, and sculpture from the 1500s to the present. For a special memento with more weight than a Red Sox hat, pick out a piece from the gallery's impressive collection of Boston expressionism and Boston School impressionism art. ✉ *169 Newbury St., Back Bay* ☎ *617/266–1108* ⊕ *www.childsgallery.com* ☯ *Closed Mon.* Ⓜ *Copley.*

Copley Society of Art

ART GALLERIES | After more than a century, this nonprofit membership organization continues to present the works of well-known and aspiring New England artists, as well as out-of-town and foreign members. Styles of artists range from traditional and academic realists to contemporary and abstract painters, photographers, and sculptors. Each year, the gallery hosts between 15 and 20 exhibitions. ✉ *158 Newbury St., Back Bay* ☎ *617/536–5049* ⊕ *www.copleysociety.org* ⊙ *Closed Mon., except by appt.* Ⓜ *Copley.*

Gallery NAGA

ART GALLERIES | Specializing in contemporary paintings since 1977, primarily oil, watercolor, acrylic, and mixed media, this striking gallery in the neo-Gothic stone Church of the Covenant also displays sculpture, and furniture beyond your everyday tables and chairs. ✉ *67 Newbury St., Back Bay* ☎ *617/267–9060* ⊕ *www.gallerynaga.com* ⊙ *Closed Sun. and Mon, and mid-July–Aug.* Ⓜ *Arlington.*

Krakow Witkin Gallery

ART GALLERIES | Emerging and established regional and international artists fill the walls here. Mediums include contemporary painting, photography, drawing, and sculpture. The gallery has an exhibition program which runs three shows simultaneously, with six to seven rotations from September through July. ✉ *10 Newbury St., 5th fl., Back Bay* ☎ *617/262–4490* ⊕ *www.krakowwitkingallery.com* ⊙ *Closed Sun. and Mon.* Ⓜ *Arlington.*

Vose Galleries

ART GALLERIES | Established in 1841, Vose specializes in 19th- and 20th-century American art, including the Hudson River School, Boston School, and American impressionists. Over the five floors of galleries, visitors will find artwork displayed in living and dining rooms settings furnished with antiques, which provides a homelike scene for viewing. ✉ *238 Newbury St., Back Bay* ☎ *617/536–6176* ⊕ *www.vosegalleries.com* ⊙ *Closed Sun. and Mon.* Ⓜ *Copley, Hynes.*

BEAUTY

Bella Santé

SPA/BEAUTY | For top-notch facials, body scrubs, and massages, as well as medical-grade treatments and peels, head to this elegant, tranquil day spa. In addition to a well-trained staff, you'll find pristine facilities, including a locker room stocked with a bevy of tonics, lotions, and hair products. First-time guests receive a discount on select treatments. ✉ *38 Newbury St., Back Bay* ☎ *617/424–9930* ⊕ *www.bellasante.com* Ⓜ *Arlington.*

Exhale

SPA/BEAUTY | This Zen-like sanctuary is deceptively large. The subterranean lower level houses a first-rate spa, selection of nourishing body and skin-care products, and a yoga studio. Upstairs, you'll find a core fusion studio and boutique offering soft clothing, candles, jewelry, and more. There's another location at the Battery Wharf Hotel. ✉ *28 Arlington St., Back Bay* ☎ *617/532–7000* ⊕ *www.exhalespa.com* Ⓜ *Arlington.*

Fresh

PERFUME/COSMETICS | You won't know whether to wash with these body products or snack on them. Load up on shea butter–rich bars in such enticing scents as grapefruit, mangosteen, and sugar-lemon. The brown-sugar face polish with strawberry seeds will set your face aglow and might just leave you hungry. ✉ *121 Newbury St., Back Bay* ☎ *617/421–1212* ⊕ *www.fresh.com* Ⓜ *Copley.*

BOOKS

Trident Booksellers & Café

BOOKS/STATIONERY | This two-story shop with windows overlooking Newbury Street is known as much for its eclectic collection of books and magazines as its all-day breakfast menu. Follow the pack and order either the lemon-ricotta-stuffed French toast or homemade corned beef hash and then settle in with a favorite read. Feel free to stay through lunch, dinner, and beyond, as the store's open until midnight daily, making it a popular spot with students. A full slate of events, from game nights to author talks, is scheduled almost daily. ✉ *338 Newbury St., Back Bay* ☏ *617/267–8688* ⊕ *www.tridentbookscafe.com* Ⓜ *Hynes.*

CLOTHING
Alan Bilzerian

CLOTHING | Satisfying the Euro crowd, this store sells luxe men's and women's clothing by such fashion darlings as Yohji Yamamoto and Ann Demeulemeester. Shoppers can also pick up snazzy items for the home, such as $10,000 vintage sterling silver candlesticks or $12,000 crystal balls. ✉ *34 Newbury St., Back Bay* ☏ *617/536–1001* ⊕ *www.alanbilzerian. com* ⏰ *Closed Sun.* Ⓜ *Arlington.*

All Too Human

CLOTHING | Boston native and Tufts graduate, Jessica Knez, a former buyer for Bergdorf Goodman, stocks laser-hot labels, like Proenza Schouler and Dries Van Noten, at her fashion-forward concept store for men and women. To entice an even broader audience, the store also displays edgy, rotating art installations. ✉ *236 Clarendon St., Back Bay* ☏ *857/350–3951* ⊕ *www.alltoohumanboston.com* ⏰ *Closed Sun.*

Anne Fontaine

CLOTHING | You can never have too many white shirts—especially if they're designed by this Parisienne. The simple, sophisticated designs are mostly executed in cotton and priced at $395 and up. Complete your outfit with the store's selection of sleek skirts, slacks, and accessories; the store also carries dresses and outerwear. ✉ *280 Boylston St., Back Bay* ☏ *617/423–0366* ⊕ *www.annefontaine.com* Ⓜ *Arlington, Boylston.*

Betsy Jenney

CLOTHING | Ms. Jenney herself might easily wait on you in this small, personal store, where the well-made, comfortable lines cater to women who cannot walk into a fitted size-4 suit—in other words, most of the female population. The designers found here, such as Nicole Miller, are fashionable yet realistic. ✉ *114 Newbury St., Back Bay* ☏ *617/536–2610* ⊕ *www.betsyjenney.com* Ⓜ *Copley.*

Chanel

CLOTHING | This spacious branch of the Parisian couture house carries suits, separates, bags, shoes, cosmetics, and, of course, a divine selection of little black dresses. ✉ *6 Newbury St., Back Bay* ☏ *617/859–0055* ⊕ *www.chanel.com/ en_US/fashion.html* Ⓜ *Arlington.*

Giorgio Armani

CLOTHING | This top-of-the-line Italian couturier is known for his carefully shaped jackets, soft suits, and mostly neutral palette. Upscale options abound for men, women, and children. ✉ *22 Newbury St., Back Bay* ☏ *617/267–3200* ⊕ *www.armani.com* Ⓜ *Arlington.*

Lilly Pulitzer

CLOTHING | No tropical or trendy vacation is complete without your splashy pink, lime, yellow, and turquoise Lilly Pulitzer resort wear, available here along with shoes, home decor, and children's clothing. ✉ *133 Newbury St., Back Bay* ☏ *617/536–6423* ⊕ *www.inthepinkonline.com* Ⓜ *Copley.*

Ministry of Supply

CLOTHING | Inspired by the temperature-regulating materials used for NASA's astronaut clothes, three MIT students started this men and women's clothing store that features stretchy, moisture-wicking, wrinkle-free, machine-washable slacks, shirts, blouses, blazers, and jackets designed by a former Theory designer (think clean and elegant) in a simple palate of mainly white, black, gray, and blue. Interested in creating a bespoke blazer or top on-site? The store's 3-D print knitting machine can finish a garment in about two hours, with extra time needed to hand-finish various details. ⊠ *299 Newbury St., Back Bay* ☎ *855/667–1920* ⊕ *www.ministryofsupply.com* Ⓜ *Hynes.*

CRAFTS
★ Society of Arts & Crafts
CRAFTS | More than a century old, this is the country's oldest nonprofit crafts organization. In addition to selling a fine assortment of ceramics, jewelry, glass, woodwork, and furniture from a rotating roster of more than 400 of the country's finest artists, the soaring space sponsors free art exhibits, and a featured artist in residence, who you can see working in the studio. ⊠ *100 Pier 4, Suite 200, Back Bay* ⊹ *Above Ocean Prime restaurant on 2nd fl.* ☎ *617/266–1810* ⊕ *www.societyofcrafts.org* ◷ *Closed weekends* Ⓜ *Silver Line MBTA to Court St. station.*

GIFTS
Whitney + Winston
GIFTS/SOUVENIRS | Looking for the perfect gift for that special baby, hostess, or doggie in your life? Founded by the owners of Crush women's clothing boutique, this cheerful shop has everything from picnic blankets and picture frames to cashmere wraps and ceramic tea sets. ⊠ *113 Charles St., Back Bay* ☎ *617/720–2600* ⊕ *www.whitneyandwinston.com.*

JEWELRY
Shreve, Crump & Low
JEWELRY/ACCESSORIES | Since 1796, Shreve has specialized in high-end treasures, including gems and handcrafted platinum rings, as well as men's and women's watches and high-quality antiques. But don't get the impression that you can't afford anything here: one of the store's best-selling items is a $99 ceramic pitcher called "The Gurgling Cod," in honor of the state fish. ⊠ *39 Newbury St., Back Bay* ☎ *617/267–9100* ⊕ *www.shrevecrumpandlow.com* ◷ *Closed Sun.* Ⓜ *Arlington.*

Small Pleasures
JEWELRY/ACCESSORIES | From Victorian-era tourmaline cocktail rings to mint-condition pocket watches, vintage lovers should not miss the antique and estate jewelry that fills these cases. The staff is notably helpful and informed. The shop also offers jewelry and watch repair, restringing, and custom jewelry design. ⊠ *Copley Pl., 142 Newbury St., Back Bay* ☎ *617/267–7371* ⊕ *www.small-pleasures.com* ◷ *Closed Sun.* Ⓜ *Copley.*

MUSIC STORES
Newbury Comics
MUSIC STORES | This renowned pop-culture store carries vinyl, CDs, DVDs, quirky gifts, and an especially good lineup of independent pressings. You'll find three other locations on JFK Street in Cambridge, inside the CambridgeSide Galleria mall, and inside the Faneuil Hall Marketplace. ⊠ *348 Newbury St., Back Bay* ☎ *617/236–4930* ⊕ *www.newburycomics.com* Ⓜ *Hynes.*

SHOPPING CENTERS
Copley Place
SHOPPING NEIGHBORHOODS | An indoor shopping mall in the Back Bay, Copley Place includes such high-end shops as Christian Dior and Louis Vuitton. It is anchored by the pricey but dependable Neiman Marcus and offers a few dining options, such as Legal Sea Foods and Caffe Nero. ⊠ *100 Huntington Ave., Back Bay* ☎ *617/262–6200* ⊕ *www.simon.com/mall/copley-place* Ⓜ *Copley, Back Bay.*

Prudential Center
SHOPPING NEIGHBORHOODS | A skywalk connects Copley Place to the Prudential Center. The Pru, as it's often called, contains popular chain stores such as Ann Taylor and Sephora and is anchored by Saks 5th Avenue and Lord and Taylor. The giant food hall, Eataly, offers plenty of options for eating, from to-go sandwiches to sit-down dining, as well as shopping for items like olive oil and wine. ⊠ *800 Boylston St., Back Bay* ☎ *800/746–7778* ⊕ *www.prudentialcenter.com* Ⓜ *Prudential.*

SPECIALTY STORES
The Fish and Bone
SPECIALTY STORES | This boutique is dedicated to all things cat and dog. Choose from the enormous selection of collars, toys, and food. Of note is that none of the food the shop carries has artificial dyes, flavors or preservatives. ✉ *217 Newbury St., Back Bay* ☎ *857/753–4176* ⊕ *www.thefishandbone.com* Ⓜ *Arlington.*

THRIFT SHOPS
Castanet Designer Consignment
OUTLET/DISCOUNT STORES | Chanel purses, Rick Owens jackets, and Hermès bracelets have all graced this jam-packed couture-quality consignment shop, located on the second floor, which finds gently worn gems from fashion lovers across the country. Its picky choices are your gain. ✉ *175 Newbury St., 2nd fl., Back Bay* ☎ *617/536–1919* ⊕ *www.shopcastanet.com* ⊗ *Closed Sun. and Mon.* Ⓜ *Arlington.*

Revolve
OUTLET/DISCOUNT STORES | Come here to snag a vintage Chanel bag, some Manolo Blahnik heels, or the perfect designer dress to complete your outfit. The store receives designer booty every day, which they sell for about one-third of the retail price. Handbag hounds regularly stop in to peruse the store's generous selection. ✉ *262 Newbury St., Back Bay* ☎ *617/262–0720* ⊕ *www.revolveboutiques.com.*

Activities

BIKE RENTALS
Back Bay Bicycles
BICYCLING | Road bikes rent here for $45 per day (weekly rates are also available). City bikes rent for $35. ✉ *362 Commonwealth Ave., Back Bay* ☎ *617/247–2336* ⊕ *www.papa-wheelies.com.*

Community Bicycle Supply
BICYCLING | This South End place rents cycles from April through October. The $25 daily rate also includes a helmet and lock. ✉ *496 Tremont St., at E. Berkeley St., South End* ☎ *617/542–8623* ⊕ *www.communitybicycle.com* Ⓜ *Back Bay.*

The South End

The South End lost many residents to the Back Bay in the late 19th century, but in the late 1970s, middle-class professionals began snapping up town houses at bargain prices and restoring them. Solidly back in fashion now, the South End's redbrick row houses in various states of refurbished splendor now house a mix of ethnic groups, the city's largest gay community, and some excellent shops and restaurants.

Today a large African American community resides along Columbus Avenue and Mass Ave. (short for Massachusetts Avenue), which marks the beginning of the predominantly black neighborhood of Roxbury. Boston's gay community also has a strong presence in the South End. If you like to shop, you'll have a blast in this area, which focuses on home furnishings and accessories, with a heavy accent on the unique and handmade. At the northern tip of the South End, where Harrison Avenue and Washington Street lead to Chinatown, are several Chinese supermarkets. South of Washington Street is the "SoWa" District, home to a large number of art galleries, many of which have relocated here from pricey Newbury Street. From May through October, the excellent SoWa Open Market on Sunday is a great excursion, packed with artists, food trucks, and a farmers' market.

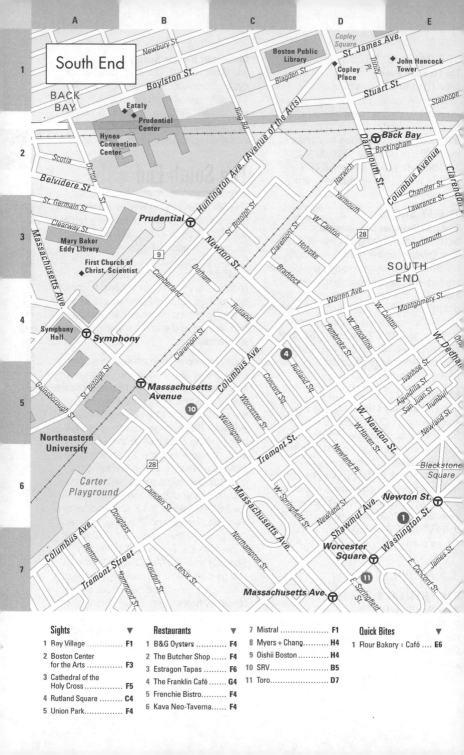

Sights

Bay Village

NEIGHBORHOOD | This pocket of early-19th-century brick row houses, near Arlington and Piedmont streets, is a fine, mellow neighborhood (Edgar Allan Poe was born here). Its window boxes and short, narrow streets make the area seem a toylike reproduction of Beacon Hill. Note that, owing to the street pattern, it's difficult to drive to Bay Village, and it's easy to miss on foot. ⊠ *Bounded (roughly) by Arlington, Stuart, Charles, and Marginal Sts., South End* ⊕ *www.bayvillage.net.*

Boston Center for the Arts

ARTS VENUE | Of Boston's multiple arts organizations, this nonprofit arts-and-culture complex is one of the most lively and diverse. Here you can see the work of budding playwrights, check out rotating exhibits from contemporary artists, or stop in for a curator's talk and other special events. The BCA houses six performance spaces, a community music center, the Mills Art Gallery, and studio space for some 40 Boston-based contemporary artists. ⊠ *539 Tremont St., South End* ☎ *617/426–5000* ⊕ *www.bcaonline.org* 🎫 *Free* Ⓜ *Back Bay/South End.*

Cathedral of the Holy Cross

RELIGIOUS SITE | This enormous 1875 Gothic cathedral dominates the corner of Washington and Union Park streets. The main church of the Archdiocese of Boston and therefore the seat of Cardinal Archbishop Seán Patrick O'Malley, Holy Cross is also New England's largest Catholic church. It's also home to an 1875 Hook and Hastings pipe organ, the largest instrument ever built by that company. ⊠ *1400 Washington St., South End* ☎ *617/542–5682* ⊕ *holycrossboston.com* Ⓜ *Back Bay.*

Rutland Square

PLAZA | Reflecting a time when the South End was the most prestigious Boston address, this slice of a park is framed by lovely Italianate bowfront houses. ⊠ *Rutland Sq. between Columbus Ave. and Tremont St., South End.*

Union Park

NEIGHBORHOOD | Cast-iron fences, Victorian-era town houses, and a grassy area all add up to one of Boston's most charming slice of a neighborhood. ⊠ *Union Park St. between Shawmut Ave. and Tremont St., South End.*

🍴 Restaurants

Home to lovely Victorian brownstones, art galleries, and the city's most diverse crowd, the South End is Boston's cultural engine. It's also ground zero for local foodies, who flood the scores of ethnic resto-bars that morph from neighborhood bistros into packed hot spots as the evening progresses. Some of the city's most popular restaurants inhabit the small square between Berkeley Street and Massachusetts Avenue to the west, and Harrison Avenue and Columbus Avenue to the north.

B&G Oysters

$$$ | SEAFOOD | B&G Oysters' Chef Barbara Lynch (of No. 9 Park, the Butcher Shop, Sportello, DRINK, and Menton fame) offers a style-conscious seafood restaurant with fresher than fresh oysters from both coasts; creative, seasonal dishes; and New England classics, including one of the best lobster rolls in the city. Designed to imitate the inside of an oyster shell, the iridescent bar glows with silvery, candlelighted tiles and a sophisticated crowd that in warm weather fills the hidden outdoor patio strung with tiny white lights. **Known for:** excellent wine list; delicate portions; stylish setting. 🄢 *Average main: $30* ⊠ *550 Tremont St., South End* ☎ *617/423–0550* ⊕ *www.bandgoysters.com* Ⓜ *Back Bay.*

The Butcher Shop

$$$ | **AMERICAN** | Chef Barbara Lynch, one of the city's most acclaimed chefs, reenvisioned the classic meat market as a polished wine bar–cum–hangout, serving those who either want to stop in for a glass of wine and a casual, quick snack of homemade prosciutto and artisanal cheeses or relax longer over dinner specials like tagliatelle Bolognese, roasted bone marrow with grilled bread, and beef tenderloin with crispy potatoes. **Known for:** excellent cooked and cure meats; rustic atmosphere; friendly service. [$] *Average main: $30* ✉ *552 Tremont St., South End* ☎ *617/423–4800* 🌐 *www.thebutchershopboston.com* [M] *Back Bay.*

Estragon Tapas

$$$ | **SPANISH** | The urbane 1930s decor makes this South End Spanish restaurant feel high-class, but the tapas plates and easy-to-share fish and meat dishes make dining here an entirely casual experience. A selection of traditional tapas, such as grilled Spanish sausage on toast and grilled leeks *romesco* (spicy red pepper–almond sauce) can easily fill up two people when coupled with entrées like paella (vegetarian or nonvegetarian) or the grilled lamb skewers. **Known for:** tapas/rice dishes; authentic flavors; comfortable setting. [$] *Average main: $30* ✉ *700 Harrison Ave., South End* ☎ *617/266–0443* 🌐 *www.estragontapas.com* ⏲ *Closed Sun. No lunch* [M] *Newton.*

The Franklin Café

$$ | **AMERICAN** | With a full menu served until 1:30 am, this place has jumped to the head of the class by keeping things simple yet effective, from the well-crafted cocktails to the homey cuisine: think skillet-smoked mussels, lasagna, and steak frites. The vibe tends to feel more like a bar than a restaurant (hence the many bartender awards), so be forewarned that it can get loud and the wait for a table (there are only seven booths and two tables) can be long. **Known for:** gastropub fare; neighborhood feel; open late. [$] *Average main: $22* ✉ *278 Shawmut Ave., South End* ☎ *617/350–0010* 🌐 *www.franklincafe.com* ⏲ *No lunch* [M] *Union Park.*

Frenchie Boston

$$$ | **FRENCH** | Step down into this charming bistro and you'll feel like you've been transported to Paris, with a menu of classic French fare dressed up a bit, such as escargot toast or foie gras on brioche, paired with one of two dozen wines by the glass, all served with a smile by an attentive staff. The intimate bar is a buzzy spot in the evenings, and the tables fill up fast with diners lingering over mussels in white wine, beef bourguignon, and steak frites. **Known for:** authentic French food; lively atmosphere; cozy solarium in back. [$] *Average main: $35* ✉ *560 Tremont St., South End* ☎ *857/233–5941* 🌐 *www.frenchieboston.com* [M] *Back Bay.*

★ Kava Neo-Taverna

$$$ | **GREEK** | This sweet little whitewashed taverna serves authentic Greek cuisine, with many ingredients imported directly from the Mediterranean, such as the feta, fish, and octopus. Order some crisp white wine off the mainly Greek wine list to sip with a parade of homestyle dishes, from tasty meze plates to entrées like grilled lamb chops. **Known for:** authentic Greek favorites; taverna feel; high-quality ingredients. [$] *Average main: $27* ✉ *315 Shawmut Ave., South End* ☎ *617/356–1100* 🌐 *www.kavaneotaverna.com* ⏲ *No lunch weekdays.*

★ Mistral

$$$$ | **FRENCH** | Boston's fashionable set flocks to this long-popular South End restaurant with polished service and upscale yet unpretentious French-Mediterranean cuisine with fail-safe favorites like tuna tartare, duck with cherries, and French Dover sole. The seasonally tweaked menu rarely changes—but no one's complaining; a luxurious à la carte brunch is served on Sunday. **Known for:** sophisticated Mediterranean cuisine; superb service; white-cloth, country French decor.

$ *Average main: $36* ⊠ *223 Columbus Ave., South End* ☎ *617/867–9300* ⊕ *mistralbistro.com* ☾ *No lunch* Ⓜ *Back Bay.*

★ Myers + Chang

$$ | **CHINESE** | Pink and orange dragon decals cover the windows of this all-day Chinese café, where Joanne Chang (of Flour bakery fame) taps her familial cooking roots to create shareable platters of creative dumplings, wok-charred udon noodles, and stir-fries brimming with fresh ingredients and plenty of hot chili peppers, garlic, fresh herbs, crushed peanuts, and lime. The staff is young and fun, and the crowd generally follows suit. **Known for:** Asian soul food; fabulous cocktails; great service. $ *Average main: $22* ⊠ *1145 Washington St., South End* ☎ *617/542–5200* ⊕ *www.myersand-chang.com* Ⓜ *Back Bay.*

Oishii Boston

$$$ | **JAPANESE** | Although the entrance to this superb sushi restaurant may elude you, simply follow the crowds of raw-fish fans streaming into the sleek, gray, industrial space, to find edible aquatic enchantment in the form of tuna tartare with caviar and crispy shallots tempura, lobster maki in a daikon radish wrapper, and seafood risotto in a sizzling hot pot. The vibe is stylish and so are the diners. **Known for:** high-end Japanese sushi; quiet atmosphere; minimalist decor. $ *Average main: $35* ⊠ *1166 Washington St., South End* ☎ *617/482–8868* ⊕ *www.oishiiboston.com* ☾ *Closed Mon.* Ⓜ *East Berkeley.*

SRV

$$$ | **ITALIAN** | SRV, short for Serene Republic of Venice, bills itself as a bacaro, or Italian wine bar, which here in the South End translates into a happening cocktail scene, where the chic set gathers to sip on Aperol Spritz and negroni *bianco* before tucking into tantalizing small plates and hand-crafted pastas made from flour the chefs mill themselves from durum wheat berries. Sharing is the way to go and once you've forked up some two-bite pork-beef meatballs and marinated olives it's time for pastas and risottos, like the ricotta gnudi or the lobster, pomodorini, and squid ink tagliatelle. **Known for:** Venetian bar bites; cocktail party buzz; casual, fun feel. $ *Average main: $35* ⊠ *569 Columbus St., South End* ☎ *617/536–9500* ⊕ *www.srvboston.com* ☾ *No lunch.*

★ Toro

$$$ | **SPANISH** | Chefs Ken Oringer and Jamie Bissonnette's tapas joint, which now has an outpost in Manhattan, is a lively, popular spot where the small plates such as grilled corn with aioli and cotija cheese are hefty enough to make a meal out of a few, or you can share the regular or vegetarian paella with a group. A predominantly Spanish wine list complements the plates. **Known for:** excellent traditional tapas; cozy, small dining room; cult following. $ *Average main: $35* ⊠ *1704 Washington St., South End* ☎ *617/536–4300* ⊕ *www.toro-restaurant.com* Ⓜ *Massachusetts Ave.*

😊 Coffee and Quick Bites

★ Flour Bakery + Café

$ | **AMERICAN** | **FAMILY** | When folks need coffee, a great sandwich, or an irresistible sweet, like a pecan sticky bun, lemon tart, or double chocolate cookie—or just a place to sit and chat—they come to one of owner Joanne Chang's eight Flour bakeries, including this one in the South End. A communal table in the middle acts as a gathering spot, around which diners enjoy morning pastries, homemade soups, hearty bean and grain salads, and specialty sandwiches, which change with the seasons. **Known for:** scrumptious sweets; delicious salads and sandwiches; laid-back setting. $ *Average main: $9* ⊠ *1595 Washington St., South End* ☎ *617/267–4300* ⊕ *www.flourbakery.com* Ⓜ *Massachusetts Ave.*

Hotels

The Back Bay and the South End are what locals call the "well-heeled" sections of Boston, meaning money talks here—think the likes of Mandarin Oriental or Fairmont Copley Plaza. The streets are lined with upscale, stylish hotels (old and new), boutique hotels, and inns.

Revolution Hotel

$ | HOTEL | This hotel is an intriguing mix of luxurious touches—like pillowtop beds and free Wi-Fi—and more downscale amenities, like shared bathrooms and tiny rooms, but for those who don't mind some odd quirks, the price is right for this South End spot. **Pros:** original artwork; inexpensive; whimsical; pet-friendly. **Cons:** inconvenient parking; small rooms; some rooms have shared bathrooms. ⓢ *Rooms from: $126* ✉ *40 Berkeley St., South End* ☎ *617/848–9200* ⊕ *therevolutionhotel.com* ⤳ *177 rooms* ⦿ *No meals* Ⓜ *Back Bay.*

Staypineapple

$ | B&B/INN | This small property, part of small brand of hotels, has a fresh, contemporary style with lots and lots of yellow accents along with complimentary Wi-Fi, plush pillow top beds, and marble bathrooms with walk-in glass showers. **Pros:** can't beat the price; friendly staff; the South End is a prime location for foodies. **Cons:** area parking is brutally hard or expensive; rooms can be noisy; might be too quirky for some. ⓢ *Rooms from: $225* ✉ *26 Chandler St., South End* ☎ *857/444–6111, 800/842–3450* ⊕ *www.staypineapple.com/south-end-boston* ⤳ *56 rooms* ⦿ *No meals* Ⓜ *Back Bay.*

Nightlife

Sedate tree-lined streets of newly repointed brick town houses cast demure impressions, but the South End is a truly lively area with cafés, restaurants, theaters, parks, and recreational enclaves. A stroll along long, narrow Southwest Corridor Park (reclaimed as the Orange Line was built) links walkers from Copley Square (Back Bay Station) to Forest Hills Station, 5 miles away. Along winding lanes of flowering crab trees and community and butterfly gardens, an array of moms with strollers, bikers, dogwalkers, and skateboarders pass tennis courts, summer lawn concerts at Titus Sparrow Park, and kids playing basketball.

BARS
Clerys

BARS/PUBS | Open-windowed, multiroomed Clerys can be your neighborhood bar, Irish pub, dance hall, sports hub, trivia game spot, or even the home for local Georgia Bulldogs sports fans. Expect long lines on weekend nights in this high-traffic club near Copley Square; its several rooms bustle with young professionals local 9-to-5ers. ✉ *113 Dartmouth St., South End* ☎ *617/262–9874* ⊕ *www.clerysboston.com* Ⓜ *Copley.*

Club Café

BARS/PUBS | This smart multiroom club and restaurant for Boston gays, lesbians, and their straight friends is livelier than ever going into its fourth decade. Behind a stylish restaurant, patrons dance in the "video lounge" or watch classic music videos, cult flicks, and TV shows. There are trivia, karaoke, and Edge Boston events weekly; Napoleon Cabaret hosts singers nightly. A weekly Sunday Tea from 5 to 10 pm is free. ✉ *209 Columbus Ave., South End* ☎ *617/536–0966* ⊕ *www.clubcafe.com* Ⓜ *Back Bay/South End.*

★ Darryl's Corner Bar & Kitchen

CAFES—NIGHTLIFE | This longtime neighborhood soul-food and jazz hangout still looks spiffy, and features real Southern cooking and live bands nearly nightly at light cover charges. Come for favorites like mac and cheese or glorified chicken and waffles, and on Sunday there is an all-you-can-eat blues brunch starting at 10 am. Theatergoers receive dining discounts. ✉ *604 Columbus Ave., South End* ☎ *617/536–1100* ⊕ *www.dcbkboston.com* Ⓜ *Massachusetts Ave.*

Delux Café

BARS/PUBS | This unpretentious, cozy bar on a quiet corner attracts old-timers and young professionals with modest drinks and affordable comfort food. The quesadillas are worth the wait for a table. Yellowing posters, dim lights, and a '60s soundtrack add to the quirky, retro vibe. Wine list? Couple of reds, whites, sparklers. Entertainment? Talk to the bartender or your friends. Cash only. ✉ *100 Chandler St., South End* ☎ *617/338–5258* ☞ *Cash only* Ⓜ *Back Bay/South End.*

Franklin Café

BARS/PUBS | A neighborhood institution for more than 20 years, The Franklin's renowned for creative cocktails, local microbrews, fine wines, and modern American food. There's no sign: just look for the white martini logo (or folks waiting for a dinner table) to know you're there. A full menu is served until 1:30 am every single night of the week, and the bar is open until 2 am. ✉ *278 Shawmut Ave., South End* ☎ *617/350–0010* ⊕ *www.franklincafe.com* Ⓜ *Back Bay.*

★ JJ Foley's Cafe

BARS/PUBS | Family-owned and-operated since 1909, JJ Foley's Cafe (or "Foley's," as regulars call it) is one of the most authentic Irish bars in Boston. There's an intimate dining room, as well as a more casual bar area where everyone from former Boston mayors to Justin Timberlake have enjoyed a pint. Better yet, it's open until 2 am. The pub food is great; order a sky-high plate of nachos if you dare. ■ **TIP→ Don't mistake this Foley's with the JJ Foley's Bar & Grill in Downtown Boston; despite similar names, the South End Foley's is the real thing.** ✉ *117 E. Berkeley St., South End* ☎ *617/728–9101* ⊕ *www. jjfoleyscafe.com* Ⓜ *Tufts Medical Center.*

The Trophy Room

BARS/PUBS | Tucked under the Staypineapple Boston inn, this gay bar is popular with the local after-work crowd who enjoy live performances from local artists and apps like nachos and chicken fingers. Casually dressed locals drop by for the large beer list and steak and eggs during the hopping weekend brunches (10 am–3 pm), which feature long, tall mimosas. ✉ *26 Chandler St., South End* ☎ *617/482–4428* ⊕ *www.trophyroomboston.com* Ⓜ *Back Bay/South End.*

MUSIC CLUBS

★ Beehive

MUSIC CLUBS | An underground bohemian bistro featuring delicious food, libations, and live music nightly, the Beehive is nestled under the historic Cyclorama building. The performers might play jazz, blues, R&B, reggae, or Latin music while patrons enjoy craft cocktails and wines. Dine on Mediterranean meze platters, daily special pastas, and comfort entrées. If jazz is your jam, don't miss the weekend live jazz brunch from 9:30 am to 3 pm (music 10 am–2:30 pm); Sunday nights feature blues. ✉ *541 Tremont St., South End* ☎ *617/423–0069* ⊕ *www. beehiveboston.com* Ⓜ *Back Bay.*

★ Wally's Café

MUSIC CLUBS | A rare gem for jazz and blues fans, Wally's Café, founded in 1947, is the oldest continuously operating family-owned jazz club in America. Patrons may see nostalgic stars like Branford Marsalis or Esperanza Spalding drop by, because the place is internationally renowned for its steady stream of heated performances by local bands and guests. Wally's diverse crowd attracts regulars from the South End and Roxbury, and music-hungry students, especially from Berklee College of Music. It's jammed every night of the year and there's never a cover. Monday it's blues and Thursday it's Latin jazz. Daily jam sessions run from 6 to 9 pm; bring your horn! Arrive early if you want a seat, because the line can be brutal. ⊠ *427 Massachusetts Ave., South End* ☎ *617/424–1408* ⊕ *www.wallyscafe.com* ⊠ *Free* Ⓜ *Massachusetts Ave., Symphony.*

 **Performing Arts**

DANCE
Boston Dance Alliance

DANCE | This group serves as a clearinghouse for an amazing array of local dance companies' classes, performances, and workshops. Visit the alliance's website for upcoming performances and venues. ⊠ *19 Clarendon St., South End* ☎ *617/456–6295* ⊕ *www.bostondancealliance.org* Ⓜ *Back Bay.*

Boston Ballet

DANCE | The city's premier dance company performs at the Boston Opera House. Shows have included *Romeo & Juliet*, classic Balanchine, and *La Sylphide*. And, of course, if you're visiting during the holidays, be sure to score seats to the *Nutcracker.* ⊠ *19 Clarendon St., South End* ☎ *617/695–6955* ⊕ *www.bostonballet.org* Ⓜ *Back Bay.*

THEATER
Huntington Theatre Company

THEATER | Boston's largest resident theater company consistently performs a high-quality mix of 21st-century plays and classics under the artistic direction of Peter DuBois, and commissions playwrights to produce original dramas. The Huntington performs at two locations: Boston University Theatre and the Calderwood Theatre Pavilion in the South End. ⊠ *Boston University Theatre, 264 Huntington Ave., Back Bay* ☎ *617/266–7900 box office* ⊕ *www.huntingtontheatre.org* Ⓜ *Symphony.*

🛍 Shopping

The South End continues to benefit from the ongoing gentrification that has brought high real-estate prices and trendy restaurants to the area. Housed in what were at one time derelict buildings, chic home-furnishings, restaurants, bakeries, and gift shops line Tremont Street, starting at Berkeley Street. If you want to bring Fido or carry home a doggie treat, this is the neighborhood: there are oodles of chichi pet boutiques here, along with plenty of water bowls and dog biscuits. ■TIP➜ **The MBTA's Silver Line bus runs through the South End.**

ART GALLERIES
Alpha Gallery

ART GALLERIES | This gallery specializes in paintings, drawings, watercolors, and mixed media works from contemporary American and foreign artists. It also has a fine selection of master prints and works from 20th-century American masters. The gallery exhibits emerging, mid-career, and established artists, as well as special shows of master artists such as Pablo Picasso, Fairfield Porter, Max Beckmann, and others. ⊠ *460 C Harrison St., South End* ☎ *617/536–4465* ⊕ *www.alphagallery.com* ⊗ *Closed Sun. and Mon.* Ⓜ *Silver Line MBTA.*

Bromfield Art Gallery

ART GALLERIES | Tucked among dozens of art studios in the artsy SOWA (South of Washington) area, this artist-run, members-only gallery mounts monthly shows featuring contemporary art in all forms, including printmaking, video, acrylic, ink drawing, and pastels. ⊠ *450 Harrison Ave., South End* ☎ *617/451–3605* ⊕ *www.bromfieldgallery.com* ⊗ *Closed Mon. and Tues.* Ⓜ *Tufts Medical Center.*

Samsøn Projects

ART GALLERIES | A truly cross-cultural blend of exhibits, this gallery shows the experimental works of young contemporary and emerging artists. It also creates and presents programs that aim to explore the diversity of cultures and voices that shape contemporary art and ideas today. ⊠ *450 Harrison Ave., #29, South End* ☎ *617/357–7177* ⊕ *www.samsonprojects.com* ⊗ *Closed Sun.–Tues.* Ⓜ *Tufts Medical Center.*

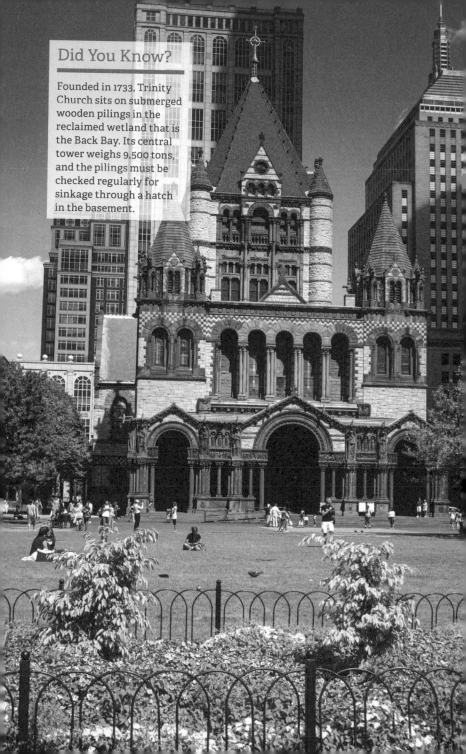

Did You Know?

Founded in 1733, Trinity Church sits on submerged wooden pilings in the reclaimed wetland that is the Back Bay. Its central tower weighs 9,500 tons, and the pilings must be checked regularly for sinkage through a hatch in the basement.

BOOKS

Ars Libri Ltd.

BOOKS/STATIONERY | It's easy to be drawn into the rare and wonderful books on display here. The airy space is filled with tomes on photography and architecture, out-of-print art books, monographs, and exhibition catalogs. Since 1976, it has been a source for scholars, collectors, and artists. All periods and all fields of art history are covered here, from antiquity to the present. ⊠ *500 Harrison Ave., South End* ☎ *617/357–5212* ⊕ *www. arslibri.com* ☺ *Closed Sun.* Ⓜ *Back Bay.*

CLOTHING

CouCou

CLOTHING | When you want your tot to standout sartorially, head to this globally sourced boutique packed with a thoughtfully curated selection of clothes; you'll also find toys and crafts, as well as a play room in the back of the store, a boon for frazzled parents with their little ones in tow. ⊠ *24 Union Park, South End* ☎ *617/936–4082* ⊕ *coucou-boston. myshopify.com* ☺ *Closed Mon.*

Flock

CLOTHING | This boho-chic boutique brims with cotton T-shirts, floral dresses, and vintage-inspired jewelry, along with whimsical gift items, like handmade keepsake boxes filled with colorful images and antique baubles. ⊠ *274 Shawmut Ave., South End* ☎ *617/391–0222* ⊕ *www.flockboston.com* Ⓜ *Back Bay.*

Viola Lovely

CLOTHING | Fashionistas flock to this sleek, white boutique to stock up on edgy tops, soft jackets, nipped waist dresses, and flattering slacks from established and emerging designers, like Bodice Studio, Lorod, and Rokh. The cute satchels, jewelry, and footwear will complete your magazine-worthy look. ⊠ *1409 Washington St., South End* ☎ *857/277–0746* ⊕ *www.violalovely.com* ☺ *Closed Mon.*

HOME FURNISHINGS

Gifted

GIFTS/SOUVENIRS | Enchanting homemade gifts from a rotating group of more than 60 artists (including the owner, Marie Corcoran) fill this dreamy boutique. Scoop up dainty charm and gemstone pendants, vegan handbags, men's ties and cufflinks, or a cute caterpillar wooden wall clock for that special little one in your life. This store has something for everyone, including you. ⊠ *2 Dartmouth St., South End* ☎ *617/716–9924* ⊕ *www. giftedboston.com* Ⓜ *Back Bay.*

Hudson Interior Designs

HOUSEHOLD ITEMS/FURNITURE | Jill Goldberg offers full-scale, in-home design services, but you can also pick up custom furniture and cool home goods, such as decorative throw pillows, marbleized pottery bowls, rugs, and luscious-smelling candles, at the store. ⊠ *12 Union Park St., South End* ☎ *617/292–0900* ⊕ *hudsonboston.com* ☺ *Closed Mon.* Ⓜ *Back Bay, Prudential.*

Lekker Home

HOUSEHOLD ITEMS/FURNITURE | Dutch design with contemporary panache pervades the neighborhood's coolest furniture and home goods store. This is a great place to pick up a sleek dining set, the perfect accent table, some funky china, or a statement pendant light. ⊠ *38 Wareham St., South End* ☎ *617/737–7307* ⊕ *www.lekkerhome. com* Ⓜ *Back Bay.*

Olives & Grace

GIFTS/SOUVENIRS | This indie boutique specializing in small-batch, handcrafted goods from artists, food makers, and gift producers across the country. From calming essential oils and craft cocktail kits to etched glasses and leather journals, the treasures in this shop are easy to browse and impossible to resist. ⊠ *623 Tremont St., South End* ☎ *617/236–4536* ⊕ *www. olivesandgrace.com* Ⓜ *Back Bay.*

SoWa Open Market

OUTDOOR/FLEA/GREEN MARKETS | From May through October, the excellent SoWa Open Market on Sunday is a great excursion, packed with artists, food trucks, and a farmers' market. ✉ *460 Harrison Ave., Back Bay* ☎ *857/362–7692* ⊕ *www. sowaboston.com* ⊗ *Closed Nov.–Apr.*

TOYS

Tadpole

TOYS | This independent shop is a treasure trove of board games, dolls, trucks, blocks, books, and every other necessity for a kid's toy chest. Stock up on baby gear and essentials as well. ✉ *58 Clarendon St., South End* ☎ *617/778–1788* ⊕ *www.shoptadpole.com* Ⓜ *Back Bay.*

Chapter 8

FENWAY AND KENMORE SQUARE

8

Updated by
Kim Foley MacKinnon

⊙ Sights	🍴 Restaurants	🛏 Hotels	⬤ Shopping	▽ Nightlife
★★★★☆	★★★★☆	★★★☆☆	★★☆☆☆	★★★★☆

FENWAY PARK

Take yourself out to a ball game at legendary Fenway Park.

For baseball fans a trip to Fenway Park is a religious pilgrimage. The Boston Red Sox have played here since 1912. The oldest Major League Baseball ballpark is one of the last of its kind, a place where the scoreboard is hand-operated and fans endure uncomfortable seats.

For much of the ballpark's history Babe Ruth's specter loomed large. The team won five titles by 1918 but endured an 86-year title drought after trading away the Sultan of Swat. The Sox "reversed the curse" in 2004, defeating the rival Yanks in the American League Championship Series after being down 3–0 in the series (an unheard of comeback in baseball) and sweeping the St. Louis Cardinals in the World Series. The Red Sox won again in 2007, against the Colorado Rockies, and again against the Cardinals in 2013, the first time since 1918 that the team cinched the series in its hometown and once more in 2018 against the Los Angeles Dodgers. The curse is no more.

FENWAY PARK TOURS

If you can't see the Sox, you can still see the Green Monster up close by going on a tour of the park. The one-hour Fenway walking tours run year-round, and if you go on the day's last tour on a home-game day, you can watch batting practice. Tours run hourly from 9 am to 5 pm (or four hours before game time) and cost $21. Check the site for info on premium tours. ☎ 617/226–6666 ⊕ boston.redsox.mlb. com/bos/ballpark/ tour.jsp.

THE NATION

The Red Sox have the most rabid fans in baseball. Knowledgeable and dedicated, they follow the team with religious-like intensity.

THE GREEN MONSTER

Fenway's most dominant feature is the 37-foot-high wall that looms over left field. It's just over 300 feet from home plate and in the field of play, so deep fly balls that would have been outs in other parks sometimes become home runs. The Monster also stops line drives that would have been over the walls of other stadiums.

THE MUSIC

Fans sing "Take Me Out to the Ballgame" during the seventh-inning stretch in every ballpark, but at Fenway they also sing Neil Diamond's "Sweet Caroline" at the bottom of the eighth. If the Sox win, the Standells' "Dirty Water" blasts over the loudspeakers.

THE CURSE

In 1920 the Red Sox traded pitcher Babe Ruth to the Yankees, where he became a home-run-hitting baseball legend. Some fans—most famously *Boston Globe* columnist Dan Shaughnessy, who wrote a book called *The Curse of the Bambino*—blamed this move for the team's 86-year title drought, but others will claim that "The Curse" was just a media-driven storyline used to explain the team's past woes. Still, fans who watched a ground ball roll between Bill Buckner's legs in the 1986 World Series or saw Aaron Boone's winning home run in the 2003 A.L.D.S. swear the curse was real.

THE WEATHER

If you plan on catching a game at Fenway in the spring, bring warm clothes or a blanket. It can get chilly, especially in the stands. April lows are in the 40s and in May it can still get down to 50.

VISIT THE NATION

Not lucky enough to nab tickets ahead of time? Try your luck at Gate E two hours before the game, when a handful of tickets are sold. There's a one-ticket limit, so everyone in your party must be in line.

If that doesn't yield results, you can still experience the Nation. Head down to the park and hang out on Jersey Street, which borders the stadium. On game days it's closed to cars and filled with vendors, creating a street-fair atmosphere. Duck into a nearby sports bar and enjoy the game with other fans who weren't fortunate enough to secure seats. A favorite is the **Cask'n Flagon**, at Brookline Avenue and Lansdowne Street, across the street from Fenway.

The closest you can get to Fenway without buying a ticket is the **Bleacher Bar** (⌂ *82A Lansdowne St.*). There's a huge window in the center field wall overlooking the field. Get here early—it starts filling up a few hours before game time.

NEIGHBORHOOD SPOTLIGHT

TOP REASONS TO GO

- **Root for the home team:** The *only* team in the eyes of Red Sox Nation at Fenway Park.

- **Immerse yourself in art:** See masterpieces at the MFA and the Isabella Stewart Gardner Museum.

- **Listen to beautiful music:** Relish the perfect acoustics of a concert at Symphony Hall.

- **Eat seafood:** Head to Island Creek Oyster Bar for super-fresh seafood.

- **Explore the outdoors:** Enjoy the outdoors in the Emerald Necklace parks.

GETTING HERE

The Green Line is the way to go when it comes to getting to Fenway; get off at the Kenmore or Fenway stop for a short walk to the ballpark. Also know that it *is* possible to drive around this part of town. With a little hunting, on-street parking can usually be found on nongame days; if not, many lots and garages are within reasonable walking distance of Fenway Park.

PLANNING YOUR TIME

Although this area can be walked through in a couple of hours, art lovers could spend a week here, thanks to the glories of the MFA and the Isabella Stewart Gardner Museum. (■**TIP→ Avoid Tuesday, when the Gardner is closed.**) If you're visiting between spring and early fall, take a tour of Fenway Park—or better yet, catch a game.

The Fenway and Kenmore Square area is generally safe, and is home to thousands of college students attending Boston University, Wheelock, Simmons, and Emmanuel, to name only a few of the nearby institutions. While the main strips—Beacon Street, Commonwealth Avenue, and Brookline Avenue—can be choked with pedestrians during game day, the marshy area of the Fens is quiet and poorly lighted: avoid walking there alone at night.

QUICK BITES

- **Blackbird Doughnuts.** It's hard to resist sampling more than one doughnut at this artisanal shop, which offers flavors like Boston Cream and Cake Batter. ⊠ *20 Kilmarnock St., Fenway* ⊕ *www.blackbird-doughnuts.com/fenway* Ⓜ *Fenway Station.*

- **Bleacher Bar.** Nothing beats a dog and a beer at Fenway when you're enjoying the game on a warm summer's night. If you don't have a ticket, you can enjoy the same vibe at this hidden bar with a view into center field, and enough historical Red Sox memorabilia to open its own museum. ⊠ *82A Lansdowne St., Fenway* ⊕ *www.bleacherbarboston.com* Ⓜ *Kenmore.*

- **Saloniki Greek.** Two-time James Beard–award winner chef Jody Adams offers classic Greek bites; think pitas, salads, and other favorites. ⊠ *4 Kilmarnock St., Fenway* ⊕ *www.salonikigreek.com* Ⓜ *Fenway.*

- **Timeout Market Boston.** Some of Boston's top chefs have outlets at this open concept food hall; there's also a couple of bars and lots of space to spread out. ⊠ *401 Park Dr., Fenway* ⊕ *www.timeoutmarket.com/boston* Ⓜ *Fenway Station.*

The Back Bay Fens marshland gave this neighborhood its name, but two iconic institutions give it its character: Fenway Park, which in 2004 saw the triumphant reversal of an 86-year drought for Boston's beloved Red Sox, and the Isabella Stewart Gardner Museum, the legacy of a high-living Brahmin who attended a concert at Symphony Hall in 1912 wearing a headband that read "Oh, You Red Sox." Not far from the Gardner is another major cultural magnet: the Museum of Fine Arts. Kenmore Square, a favorite haunt for Boston University students, adds a bit of youthful flavor to the mix.

After the outsize job of filling in the bay had been completed, it would have been small trouble to obliterate the Fens with gravel and march row houses straight through to Brookline. But the planners, deciding that enough pavement had been laid between here and the Public Garden, hired vaunted landscape architect Frederick Law Olmsted to turn the Fens into a park. Olmsted applied his genius for heightening natural effects while subtly manicuring their surroundings; today the Fens park consists of irregularly shaped reed bound pools surrounded by broad meadows, trees, and flower gardens.

The Fens marks the beginning of Boston's Emerald Necklace, a loosely connected chain of parks designed by Olmsted that extends along Fenway, Riverway, and Jamaicaway to Jamaica Pond, the Arnold Arboretum, and Franklin Park.

 Sights

Along the fens unclaimed by the Back Bay, where Olmstead's Emerald Necklace winds along museum row, you'll find ball fields, the Kelleher Rose Garden, and extensive, lovingly maintained victory gardens in the shadow of Fenway Park and lively upper Boylston Street. Along "Avenue of the Arts" (aka Huntington Avenue) are Symphony Hall, New England Conservatory, Northeastern University, the Museum of Fine Arts, the Isabella Stewart Gardner Museum, and

Museum College of Art. In the middle are Berklee College of Music, Boston Conservatory, and the Massachusetts Historical Society.

★ Boston Red Sox

The Boston Red Sox may be New England's most storied professional sports team of all time. For 86 years, the club suffered a World Series drought, a streak of bad luck that fans attributed to the "Curse of the Bambino," which was spelled in 1920 when the Sox sold Babe Ruth to the New York Yankees. All that changed in 2004, when a maverick squad broke the curse in a thrilling seven-game semifinals series against the Yankees, followed by a four-game sweep of St. Louis in the finals. Repeat World Series wins in 2007, 2013, and 2018 have cemented Bostonians' sense that the universe is back in order. Today, home games are played at Fenway Park from April to October. ⊠ *Fenway Park, 4 Jersey St., Kenmore Square* ⊕ *www.mlb. com/redsox/tickets/single-game-tickets* Ⓜ *Kenmore Square, Fenway.*

★ Emerald Necklace Conservancy

NATURE PRESERVE | FAMILY | The six large public parks known as Boston's Emerald Necklace stretch 7 miles from the Back Bay Fens to Franklin Park in Dorchester, and include Arnold Arboretum, Jamaica Pond, Olmsted Park, and the Riverway. The linear parks, designed by master landscape architect Frederick Law Olmsted more than 100 years ago, remain a well-groomed urban masterpiece. ⊠ *125 The Fenway, The Fenway* ☎ *617/522– 2700* ⊕ *www.emeraldnecklace.org.*

★ Fenway Park

SPORTS VENUE | FAMILY | Fenway Park is Major League Baseball's oldest ballpark and has seen some stuff since its 1912 opening. For one, it's the home field for the Boston Red Sox, which overcame the curse of the bambino to win World Series championships in 2004, 2007, 2013, and 2018. Ticket-holding Sox fans can browse display cases mounted inside Fenway

Did You Know?

Park before and during a ballgame; these shed light on and show off memorabilia from particular players and eras of the club team's history. Fenway offers hour-long behind-the-scenes-style guided walking tours of the park; there are also specialized tour options. ⊠ *4 Jersey St., Gate D, Kenmore Square* ☎ *617/226– 6666 tours* ⊕ *www.mlb.com/redsox/ball-park/tours* ⊠ *$21* Ⓜ *Kenmore, Fenway.*

★ Isabella Stewart Gardner Museum

MUSEUM | A spirited society woman, Isabella Stewart came in 1860 from New York to marry John Lowell Gardner, one of Boston's leading citizens. She built a Venetian palazzo to hold her collected arts in one of Boston's newest neighborhoods. Her will stipulated that the building remain exactly as she left it—paintings, furniture, and the smallest object in a hall cabinet—and that is as it has remained. The palazzo includes such masterpieces as Titian's *Europa,* Giotto's *Presentation of Christ in the Temple,* Piero della Francesca's *Hercules,* and John Singer Sargent's *El Jaleo.* Spanish leather panels, Renaissance hooded fireplaces, and Gothic tapestries accent salons; eight balconies adorn the majestic Venetian courtyard. There's a Raphael Room, Spanish Cloister, Gothic Room, Chinese Loggia, and a magnificent Tapestry Room for concerts. On March 18, 1990, thieves disguised as police officers stole 12 works, including Vermeer's *The Concert.* None of the art has been recovered, and because Mrs. Gardner's will prohibited substituting other works for any stolen art, empty expanses of wall identify spots where the paintings once hung.

■TIP➜ **A quirk of the museum's admission policy waives entrance fees to anyone named Isabella and on your birthday.** ✉ *25 Evans Way, The Fenway* ☎ *617/566–1401* ⊕ *www.gardnermuseum.org* 🎫 *$15* ⊘ *Closed Tues.* Ⓜ *Museum.*

Kenmore Square

NEIGHBORHOOD | Two blocks north of Fenway Park is Kenmore Square, where you'll find shops, restaurants, and the city's iconic sign advertising Citgo gasoline. The red, white, and blue neon sign from 1965 is so thoroughly identified with the area that historic preservationists fought, successfully, to save it. The old Kenmore Square punk clubs have given way to a block-long development of pricey stores and restaurants, as well as brick sidewalks, gaslight-style street lamps, and tree plantings. In the shadow of Fenway Park between Brookline and Ipswich is **Lansdowne Street,** a nightlife magnet for the trendy who have their pick of dance clubs and pregame bars. The urban campus of Boston University begins farther west on Commonwealth Avenue, in blocks thick with dorms, shops, and restaurants. ✉ *Convergence of Beacon St., Commonwealth Ave., and Brookline Ave., The Fenway* Ⓜ *Kenmore.*

★ Museum of Fine Arts

MUSEUM | **FAMILY** | The MFA's collection of approximately 450,000 objects was built from a core of paintings and sculpture from the Boston Athenæum, historical portraits from the city of Boston, and donations by area universities. The MFA has more than 70 works by John Singleton Copley; major paintings by Winslow Homer, John Singer Sargent, Fitz Henry Lane, and Edward Hopper; and a wealth of American works ranging from native New England folk art and Colonial portraiture to New York abstract expressionism of the 1950s and 1960s.

More than 30 galleries contain the MFA's European painting and sculpture collection, dating from the 11th century to the 20th. Contemporary art has a dynamic

home in the MFA's dramatic I. M. Pei–designed building. ✉ *465 Huntington Ave., The Fenway* ☎ *617/267–9300* ⊕ *www.mfa.org* 🎫 *$25 (good for 2 days in a 10-day period)* Ⓜ *Museum.*

Restaurants

No longer just a place to grab a slice of pizza before a Red Sox game, this area adjacent to Fenway Park and Boston University blooms with restaurants along tree-lined streets that specialize in BBQ, oysters, tacos, and faculty-friendly bistro fare.

★ Island Creek Oyster Bar

$$$ | SEAFOOD | As the name indicates, this Hotel Commonwealth restaurant specializes in seafood, beginning with oysters that come fresh from the restaurant's own oyster farm in nearby Duxbury Bay, as well as Maine, Prince Edward Island, and Puget Sound (Washington). Beyond raw options, look for panfried crab cakes, steamed little neck clams, chowders, bisques, and daily fish selections ranging from cornmeal-crusted skate wing and herb-crusted cod to grilled Maine salmon and New Bedford monkfish with Maine yellow eye beans and chorizo. **Known for:** superb oysters; delish seafood dishes; loud, lively, fun feel. Ⓢ *Average main: $34* ✉ *500 Commonwealth Ave., Kenmore Square* ☎ *617/532–5300* ⊕ *www.islandcreekoysterbar.com* Ⓜ *Kenmore.*

★ Sweet Cheeks Q

$$ | SOUTHERN | Red Sox fans, foodies, and Fenway residents flock to this meat-lover's mecca, where Texas-style barbecue is the name of the game. Hefty slabs of dry-rubbed heritage pork, great northern beef brisket, and plump chickens cook low and slow in a jumbo black smoker then come to the table heaped on a tray lined with butcher paper, along with homemade sweet pickles, shaved onion, and your choice of "hot scoops" (collard greens, mac 'n' cheese) or "cold scoops" (coleslaw, potato salad). **Known**

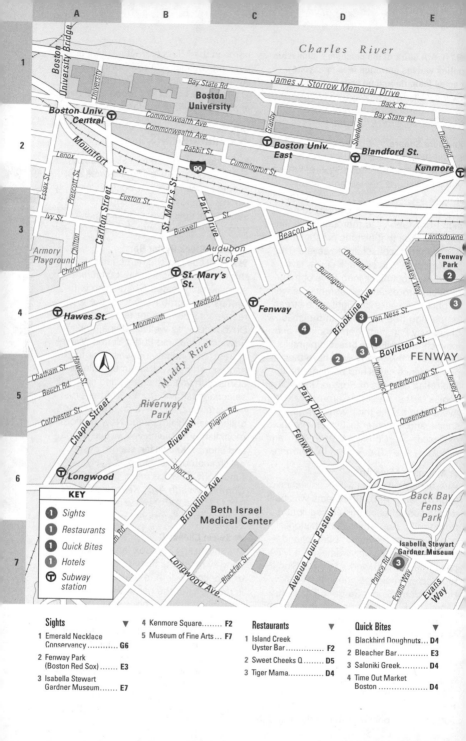

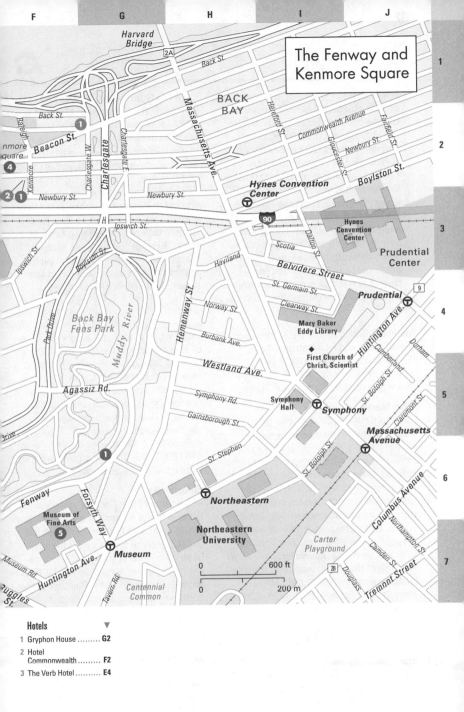

The Fenway and Kenmore Square

Hotels ▼

1 Gryphon House **G2**
2 Hotel
 Commonwealth **F2**
3 The Verb Hotel **E4**

A Good Walk

With Boston's two major art museums on this itinerary, a case of museum fatigue could set in. However, both the Museum of Fine Arts and the Isabella Stewart Gardner Museum are surrounded by the sylvan glades of Fenway—a perfect oasis and time-out location when you're suffering from gallery overload. From the intersection of Massachusetts and Huntington avenues, with the front entrance of Symphony Hall on your right, walk down Huntington Avenue. On your left is the New England Conservatory of Music and, on Gainsborough Street, its recital center, Jordan Hall.

Between Huntington Avenue and Fenway is the **Museum of Fine Arts (MFA)** and, just around the corner, the **Isabella Stewart Gardner Museum.** If you prefer to pay homage to the Red Sox: from Symphony Hall, go north on Mass Ave., turn left on Commonwealth Avenue, and continue until you reach **Kenmore Square**; from here it's a 10-minute walk down Brookline Avenue to Jersey Street and **Fenway Park.** If you get hungry, the Timeout Market Boston food hall offers plenty of tasty choices and is just down the street from Fenway Park.

for: finger-licking barbecue; scrumptious sides; jeans and T-shirt atmosphere. $ *Average main: $22* ✉ *1381 Boylston St., The Fenway* ☎ *617/266–1300* ⊕ *www.sweetcheeksq.com* Ⓜ *Fenway.*

Tiger Mama

$$ | ASIAN FUSION | Chef-owner Tiffany Faison of the beloved barbecue spot, Sweet Cheeks, has another popular Fenway eatery with her spacious, brightly colored Asian restaurant. Tiki cocktails and a bevy of umami-rich plates, like ginger-chili ribs with peanut crumble, coconut marinated chicken with tamarind sauce, and curried Singapore street noodles tangled with greens, pay homage to South East Asia. **Known for:** innovative Asian fare; tiki drinks; lively and fun vibe. $ *Average main: $18* ✉ *1363 Boylston St., The Fenway* ☎ *617/425–6262* ⊕ *www.tigermamaboston.com.*

☕ Coffee and Quick Bites

Blackbird Doughnuts

$ | AMERICAN | Creative, delicious and irresistible, these sweet treats from Blackbird Doughnuts have a cult following—even rock star Adele praised

them when in town for a concert. One of several outposts in the city, the Fenway location is tiny and it's a good idea to get there early before your fave flavor sells out. **Known for:** fan favorite Boston Cream; creative, unusual flavors; turn your doughnut into an ice-cream sandwich with soft serve. $ *Average main: 3* ✉ *20 Kilmarnock St., The Fenway* ☎ *617/482–9000* ⊕ *www.blackbirddoughnuts.com/fenway* Ⓜ *Fenway.*

Bleacher Bar

$ | AMERICAN | This Fenway restaurant is famous for its enormous garage window which looks into Fenway Park, but it's also a fun place to relax with friends, nosh on nachos or fries, and catch all sorts of sporting events on the TV. **Known for:** sneaky way to see a Red Sox game; beers and burgers; sports fans. $ *Average main: $13* ✉ *82A Lansdowne St., The Fenway* ☎ *617/262–2424* ⊕ *www. bleacherbarboston.com* Ⓜ *Kenmore.*

Saloniki Greek

$ | GREEK | Chef Jody Adams' fast-casual Greek concept offers classic flavors and everything from lamb meatballs to meze plates in a lively, fun atmosphere. Pitas stuffed with lamb, pork, chicken thighs, or Impossible meatballs fly out of the kitchen, while sides like zucchini-feta fritters and grilled Halloumi are hard to put down. **Known for:** pita bread cooked in front of you; The George, a lamb meatball rollup; Greek fries. $ *Average main: $15* ✉ *4 Kilmarnock St., The Fenway* 🕾 *617/266–0001* ⊕ *www.salonikigreek. com* Ⓜ *Fenway.*

Time Out Market Boston

$ | **INTERNATIONAL** | A food hall curated by the media company known for its magazines and books, Time Out Market Boston features 15 dining outlets run by some of Boston's most acclaimed chefs, plus two bars, a demo cooking area, and communal seating. The 25,200-square-foot space is a fun place to sample everything from sweet treats at Union Square Donuts to meatballs at Chef Michael Schlow's, one of the city's most acclaimed chefs. **Known for:** variety of eateries; fun vibe; located in historic building. $ *Average main: $15* ✉ *401 Park Dr., The Fenway* 🕾 *978/393-8088* ⊕ *www. timeoutmarket.com/boston* Ⓜ *Fenway.*

Hotels

If you have tickets for a Red Sox baseball game at Fenway Park, this is the area you want to stay in. If you're a museum hound, you'll also be able to walk to the Museum of Fine Arts and Isabella Stewart Gardner Museum as well as to Downtown. Boston University is a stone's throw from here and lots of students means lots of visiting parents. Book early.

★ Gryphon House

$$ | **B&B/INN** | The staff in this value-packed, four-story, 19th-century brownstone is helpful and friendly, and the suites are thematically decorated: one evokes rustic Italy; another is inspired by neo-Gothic art. **Pros:** elegant suites are lush and spacious; gas fireplaces in all rooms; free Wi-Fi. **Cons:**

may be too fussy for some; no elevator; no wheelchair access. $ *Rooms from: $265* ✉ *9 Bay State Rd., Kenmore Square* 🕾 *617/375–9003, 877/375–9003* ⊕ *www. innboston.com* ⇆ *8 suites* ⦿ *Free breakfast* Ⓜ *Kenmore.*

★ Hotel Commonwealth

$$$ | **HOTEL** | Luxury and service without pretense make this hip spot a solid choice. **Pros:** down bedding; perfect locale for Red Sox fans; happening bar scene at Eastern Standard; free Wi-Fi. **Cons:** area is absolutely mobbed during Sox games; small gym; pricey rates. $ *Rooms from: $399* ✉ *500 Commonwealth Ave., Kenmore Square* 🕾 *617/933–5000, 866/784–4000* ⊕ *www. hotelcommonwealth.com* ⇆ *245 rooms* ⦿ *No meals* Ⓜ *Kenmore.*

The Verb Hotel

$$$ | **HOTEL** | A rock 'n' roll reimagining of a classic midcentury hotel, the stylish Verb is filled to the brim with carefully curated historic music memorabilia. **Pros:** stylish pool scene; Bigelow bath products in the showers; free Wi-Fi. **Cons:** may be too unique for some people; one-way cooling/heating system; valet only parking option. $ *Rooms from: $314* ✉ *1271 Boylston St., The Fenway* 🕾 *855/695–6678* ⊕ *www.theverbhotel.com* ⇆ *94 rooms* ⦿ *No meals* Ⓜ *Fenway.*

Nightlife

BARS

House of Blues

MUSIC CLUBS | Around the corner from Fenway Park and girded with bars and restaurants, the city's juggernaut among nightclubs books a wide array of bands into its barnlike music hall nightly. Tickets are $25–$45, with VIP box seats usually $15–$20 more. The Foundation Room (upscale VIP lounge) opens to the public for an additional fee, and promises "high-class debauchery." ✉ *15 Lansdowne St., The Fenway* 🕾 *888/693–2583* ⊕ *www. houseofblues.com* Ⓜ *Kenmore.*

Machine

DANCE CLUBS | The granddaddy of Boston gay bars, Machine, is still cranking, and you can chalk your cue at the downstairs Pool Room. They host various theme nights like All-Star Mondays, a raucous weekly drag show. On Friday, the crowd is age 18-plus, a rare late-night option for 18- to 20-year-olds. ⊠ *1254 Boylston St., The Fenway* ☎ *617/536–1950* ⊕ *www. machineboston.club* Ⓜ *Fenway.*

BOWLING ALLEYS AND POOL HALLS

Lucky Strike Social Boston

GATHERING PLACES | Often called the city's best (and certainly biggest) playground for grown-ups, this multistory complex has something for (almost) everyone. Home to Cheeky Monkey Brewing Company on the first floor, 150 games of all kinds and a bar and restaurant on the second floor, and 25 pool tables, 12 plasma screens, 16 bowling lanes, and an 800-square-foot video wall on the third floor, it's impossible to be bored. ⊠ *145 Ipswich St., The Fenway* ☎ *617/437–0300* ⊕ *www.jilliansboston.com* Ⓜ *Kenmore.*

BROOKLINE AND JAMAICA PLAIN

Updated by
Kim Foley MacKinnon

👁 **Sights**
★★★☆☆

🍽 **Restaurants**
★★★☆☆

🛏 **Hotels**
★★☆☆☆

🛍 **Shopping**
★★★☆☆

🍸 **Nightlife**
★★☆☆☆

NEIGHBORHOOD SNAPSHOT

TOP REASONS TO GO

■ **Check out the Larz Anderson Auto Museum:** Classic car aficionados will want to see the oldest automobile collection in the United States.

■ **Visit the Frederick Law Olmsted National Historic Site:** America's preeminent landscape architect's home and office make for a fascinating tour.

■ **Sample beer at Samuel Adams Brewery:** Tour the home of Boston's own award-winning beers. Free samples at the end are the highlight of the tour.

■ **Explore the Arnold Arboretum:** The 281-acre Arboretum, a living lab open to the public, offers a breath of fresh air, with more than 4,000 plants and trees, a visitor center and walking paths.

■ **Walk around or boat on Jamaica Pond:** Part of Boston's Emerald Necklace, Jamaica Pond is an outdoor oasis for locals and visitors alike.

GETTING HERE

Although driving to these suburbs is relatively painless, they're not called the "streetcar suburbs" for nothing. To reach the Arnold Arboretum in Jamaica Plain, take the Orange Line to the end at Forest Hills. To access the restaurants and shops in Jamaica Plain, get off a few stops earlier at the Green Street stop. Brookline is accessible via the C and D lines of the Green Line.

PLANNING YOUR TIME

Timing all depends on which areas you decide to explore. Each neighborhood merits a half day, especially factoring in travel time from Boston proper and a leisurely lunch or dinner.

Generally, most of these neighborhoods are safe, particularly in the areas where these attractions reside. But use common sense: stick to well lighted areas and avoid walking alone late at night.

QUICK BITES

■ **Brassica Kitchen + Cafe.** Across from the Forest Hills T stop, this spot serves coffee, pastries, and sandwiches during the day; by night, it's a hip place to dine and drink. ⊠ *3710 Washington St., Jamaica Plain* ⊕ *www.brassicakitchen.com* Ⓜ *Forest Hills.*

■ **J. P. Licks.** Treat yourself to a few scoops of what is arguably some of the Boston area's best ice cream. ⊠ *659 Centre St., Jamaica Plain* ⊕ *www.jplicks.com* Ⓜ *Green Street.*

■ **Otto Pizza.** This outpost of the popular Portland, Maine pizzeria offers creative pies, along with slices, perfect for a quick snack. ⊠ *289 Harvard St., Brookline* ⊕ *www.ottoportland.com* Ⓜ *Coolidge Corner.*

■ **Zaftigs Delicatessen.** This modern Jewish deli serves breakfast all day and classics like chicken matzo ball soup. ⊠ *335 Harvard St., Brookline* ⊕ *www.zaftigs. com* Ⓜ *Coolidge Corner.*

The expansion of Boston in the 1800s went beyond the Back Bay and the South End. As the working population of the Downtown district swelled and public transportation grew, outlying suburbs started to become part of the city proper. Today, most of these neighborhoods are technically in the city of Boston, yet have managed to keep their own distinct personalities and charms.

Among the streetcar suburbs are Jamaica Plain (now part of Boston proper) and Brookline—rural retreats barely more than a century ago that are now popular and mostly densely settled neighborhoods. Jamaica Plain is a hip, young neighborhood with a strong lesbian and ecofriendly population; brunch and a wander through the neighborhood's quirky stores or through the Arnold Arboretum make for a relaxing weekend excursion. Jamaica Plain also borders Franklin Park, an Olmsted creation of more than 500 acres, noted for its zoo. Farther west, Brookline is composed of a mixture of the affluent and students.

Brookline

Located 4 miles from downtown Boston, Brookline is mainly a residential area, but there are significant reasons to visit, from seeing the birthplace of JFK to checking out the home and office of landscape architect Frederick Law Olmsted to dining at great local restaurants. Surrounded by Boston on three sides,

Brookline truly feels like a part of the city, though like other outlying towns, it started out as an agricultural community in the 17th century.

 Sights

Frederick Law Olmsted National Historic Site

HISTORIC SITE | Frederick Law Olmsted (1822–1903) is considered the nation's preeminent creator of parks. In 1883, at age 61, while immersed in planning Boston's Emerald Necklace of parks, Olmsted set up his first permanent office at Fairsted, an 18-room farmhouse dating from 1810, to which he added another 18 rooms for his design offices. Plans and drawings on display include such projects as the U.S. Capitol grounds, Stanford University, and Mount Royal Park in Montréal. You can also tour the design rooms (some now in use as an archive library) where Olmsted and staff drew up their plans; highlights include a 1904 "electric blueprint machine," a kind of primitive photocopier. The 1¾-acre site incorporates many trademark Olmstedian

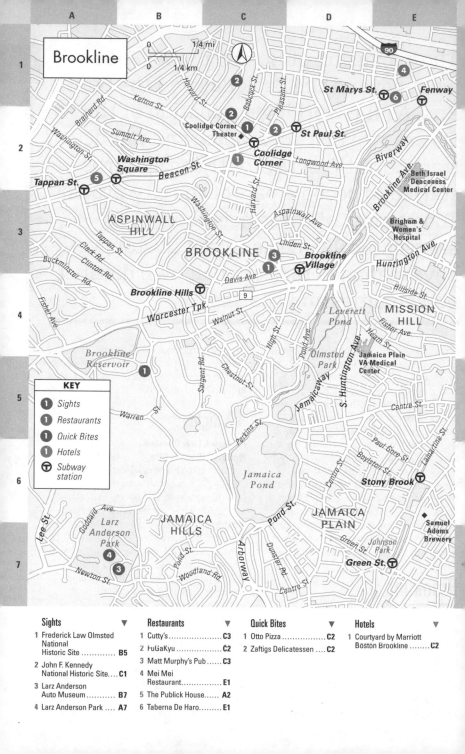

Brookline

0 — 1/4 mi
0 — 1/4 km

Sights ▼	Restaurants ▼	Quick Bites ▼	Hotels ▼
1 Frederick Law Olmsted National Historic Site **B5**	1 Cutty's **C3**	1 Otto Pizza **C2**	1 Courtyard by Marriott Boston Brookline **C2**
2 John F. Kennedy National Historic Site.... **C1**	2 FuGaKyu **C2**	2 Zaftigs Delicatessen **C2**	
3 Larz Anderson Auto Museum **B7**	3 Matt Murphy's Pub **C3**		
4 Larz Anderson Park **A7**	4 Mei Mei Restaurant................ **E1**		
	5 The Publick House...... **A2**		
	6 Taberna De Haro......... **E1**		

KEY

- ❶ Sights
- ❶ Restaurants
- ❶ Quick Bites
- ❶ Hotels
- Ⓣ Subway station

designs, including areas of meadow, wild garden, and woodland; Olmsted believed body and spirit could be healed through close association with nature. The site became part of the National Park Service in 1980; Olmsted's office played an influential role in the creation of this federal agency. Call ahead to inquire about house tour hours, which change with the seasons, though the grounds are open year-round. ⊠ *99 Warren St., Brookline* ☎ *617/566–1689* ⊕ *www.nps.gov/frla/ index.htm* ⊠ *Free* ⊙ *Closed Jan.–Mar.* Ⓜ *Brookline Hills.*

John F. Kennedy National Historic Site

HISTORIC SITE | This was the home of the 35th president from his birth on May 29, 1917, until 1921, when the family moved to nearby Naples and Abbottsford streets. Rose Kennedy provided the furnishings for the restored 2½-story, wood-frame structure. You can pick up a brochure for a walking tour of young Kennedy's school, church, and neighborhood. To get here, take the MBTA Green Line to Coolidge Corner and walk north on Harvard Street four blocks. The house is open by appointment only November through May. ⊠ *83 Beals St., Brookline* ☎ *617/566–7937* ⊕ *www.nps.gov/jofi* ⊠ *Free* Ⓜ *Coolidge Corner.*

★ Larz Anderson Auto Museum

MUSEUM | In the late 1800s and early 1900s, wealthy socialites Larz and Isabel Anderson, who lived in Brookline (among other places), started a car collection. They bought a car almost every year from 1899 to 1948 and kept the cars at their Brookline estate in a castle-like carriage house, built in 1888 and originally constructed to stable horses. Later it came to house the car collection. After Isabel's death in 1948 (Larz passed away in 1937), the building was turned into a museum. Today, visitors can see 14 of their cars in this special collection. ⊠ *15 Newton St., Brookline* ☎ *617/522–6547* ⊕ *larzanderson.org* ⊠ *$10* ⊙ *Closed Mon.* Ⓜ *Forest Hills.*

Larz Anderson Park

CITY PARK | FAMILY | This is Brookline's largest park and was once the home of wealthy socialites Larz and Isabel Anderson, who left the estate to the town in 1951. It's now home to a large lawn at the top of the hill, playing fields, a pond, a seasonal outdoor ice rink, and the Larz Anderson Auto Museum. The top of the hill offers great views of Boston. ⊠ *23 Newton St., Brookline* ⊹ *From Forest Hills T station, take 51 bus toward Cleveland Circle and get off at Clyde and Whitney Sts. The park is a 5-min walk* ☎ *617/879–5650* ⊕ *www.brooklinema. gov/Facilities/Facility/Details/Larz-Anderson-Park-87* Ⓜ *Forest Hills.*

🍴 Restaurants

Going to Brookline is a nice way to get out of the city without really leaving town. Although it's surrounded by Boston on three sides, Brookline has its own suburban flavor, seasoned with a multitude of historic—and expensive—houses and garnished with a diverse ethnic population that supports a string of sushi bars and a small list of kosher restaurants. Most Brookline eateries are clustered in the town's commercial centers: Brookline Village, Washington Square, Longwood, and bustling Coolidge Corner.

★ Cutty's

$ | AMERICAN | Don't be fooled by this self-named "sandwich shop," which belies the care, creativity, and culinary quality of the luscious offerings found in this diminutive establishment featured on the Food Network's Diners, Drive-Ins, and Dives. The owners' cooking school experience and recipe development work in a magazine test kitchen help explain why their offerings will blow your socks off—whether it's a brioche breakfast sandwich stuffed with egg, homemade chorizo, mozzarella, and cilantro or the succulent roast beef and roasted shallot sandwich with cheddar and Thousand Island dressing. **Known for:** superb sandwiches; locally sourced

Frederick Law Olmsted lived and worked at Fairsted, the circa 1810-residence while he was planning Boston's Emerald Necklace; the home is now a National Historic Site.

ingredients; no-frills setting. *$ Average main: $10* ⊠ *284 Washington St., Coolidge Corner* ☎ *617/505–1844* ⊕ *www.cuttyfoods.com* ⊘ *Closed Sun. No dinner* Ⓜ *Brookline Village.*

FuGaKyu

$$ | **JAPANESE** | The name in Japanese means "house of elegance" and the gracious and efficient service hits the mark at this flagship location, along with the interior's tatami mats, rice-paper partitions, and wooden ships circling a moat around the sushi bar. The extensive menu is both elegant and novel, with thick slabs of superfresh sashimi, inventive maki rolls, and plenty of cooked items, like panko-crusted pork cutlet and chicken teriyaki for those not into seafood or raw fish. **Known for:** excellent sushi and sashimi; attentive service; private, screened-in booths. *$ Average main: $25* ⊠ *1280 Beacon St., Brookline* ☎ *617/734–1268* ⊕ *www.fugakyu.net* Ⓜ *Coolidge Corner.*

Matt Murphy's Pub

$$ | **IRISH** | Boston has dozens of Irish pubs, but very few are notable for food—this pub being a welcome exception, making real poetry out of thick slabs of bread and butter served on wooden boards, giant servings of soup, fish-and-chips presented in a twist of newspaper, and shepherd's pie. Don't miss the house-made ketchup with your french fries or the traditional Irish breakfast (served at brunch) consisting of Irish sausage and bacon, potatoes, black and white pudding, beans, and eggs. **Known for:** cozy Irish cooking; traditional pub; lively crowd. *$ Average main: $24* ⊠ *14 Harvard St., Brookline* ☎ *617/232–0188* ⊟ *No credit cards* Ⓜ *Brookline Village.*

Mei Mei Restaurant

$ | **ASIAN FUSION** | After hitting the culinary jackpot with their wildly successful Chinese-American comfort-food truck several years ago, siblings Andrew, Margaret, and Irene Li brought the same concept to this casual exposed-brick and hardwood eatery. Now run by youngest sister Irene, the restaurant uses as many local, sustainable, and humanely raised ingredients as possible to create a tempting menu, with The Double Awesome scallion pancake sandwich a favorite mainstay. **Known for:** Asian comfort food; sustainable business practices; cheerful service. [$] *Average main: $11* ✉ *506 Park Dr., Brookline* ☎ *857/250–4959* 🌐 *www.meimeiboston.com* ⏲ *Closed Mon.*

The Publick House

$$ | AMERICAN | What started as a simple neighborhood beer bar has reached cult-like status for Brookline-ites and beyond. Serving dozens and dozens of out-of-the-ordinary and artisanal beers, the bar also offers tasty sandwiches, smaller entrées, and main dishes, of which the most beloved is the customizable mac and cheese, with additions that include tomato, mushrooms, spinach, caramelized onions, asparagus, cherry peppers, broccoli, bacon, andouille sausage, and shrimp. **Known for:** standout beer selection; great pub fare; chummy feel. [$] *Average main: $20* ✉ *1648 Beacon St., Brookline* ☎ *617/277–2880* 🌐 *publickhousebrookline.com* [M] *Washington Sq.*

Taberna de Haro

$$ | SPANISH | With a cozy, saffron yellow interior, one of Boston's original tapas bars has a nearly all-Spanish wine list (more than 320 bottles, 60 of which are Sherry and Manzanilla) and authentic hot and cold tapas and *raciones* (medium-size plates), including such classics as a tortilla Española, shrimp in garlic oil, braised eggplant, and jamón Serrano, along with favorite entrées like paella. An outdoor patio fills up in warm weather. **Known for:** authentic Spanish tapas; warm atmosphere; bountiful Sherry and Manzanilla selection. [$] *Average main: $20* ✉ *999 and 1001 Beacon St., Brookline* ☎ *617/277–8272* 🌐 *www.tabernaboston.com* ⏲ *Closed Sun.* [M] *Coolidge Corner.*

Coffee and Quick Bites

Otto Pizza

$ | PIZZA | FAMILY | Almost always packed, Otto Pizza delivers on tasty, delicious classics like cheese, pepperoni or margherita, but where it really shines is with oddball combinations, like butternut squash, ricotta, and cranberry or mashed potato, bacon, and scallion. Diners can enjoy sit-down service, paired with a beer or glass of wine, or simply get a slice to go at this bustling joint. **Known for:** creative toppings; lively vibe; friendly service. [$] *Average main: $14* ✉ *289 Harvard St., Brookline* ☎ *617/232–0014* 🌐 *www.ottoportland.com* [M] *Coolidge Corner.*

Zaftigs Delicatessen

$ | AMERICAN | FAMILY | How refreshing to have a contemporary version of a Jewish delicatessen offering genuinely lean corned beef, a modest slice of cheesecake, low-sugar homemade borscht, and a lovely whitefish-salad sandwich. If you believe breakfast is the most important meal, know it's served all day, meaning you can skip the hour-long weekend brunch waits and enjoy a plate of the area's best pancakes and stuffed French toast any weekday. Just try to leave room for one of the goodies (cupcakes, conga bars) in the bakery case. **Known for:** contemporary Jewish food; great breakfasts; friendly service. [$] *Average main: $17* ✉ *335 Harvard St., Brookline* ☎ *617/975–0075* 🌐 *www.zaftigs.com* [M] *Coolidge Corner.*

Hotels

If you don't want to pay Boston or Cambridge prices, then staying in Brookline is your best bet. Located 4 miles from Boston, Brookline is an easy T ride into the city.

Courtyard by Marriott Boston Brookline
$$$ | **HOTEL** | **FAMILY** | If you don't mind the anonymity and predictability of a chain hotel—and don't mind staying outside of Boston proper—this is a decent choice. **Pros:** kid-friendly with adjoining rooms; 1 mile from Fenway Park and Longwood Medical Center; roomy bathrooms; free Wi-Fi. **Cons:** staff can be indifferent; dull decor; might be too far of a walk to downtown Boston for some people. [$] *Rooms from: $350* ✉ *40 Webster St., Brookline* ☎ *617/734–1393, 866/296–2296* 🌐 *www.marriott.com/bosbl* 🛏 *188 rooms* 🍴 *No meals* [M] *Beacon St.*

Performing Arts

FILM

★ Coolidge Corner Theatre
FILM | This lovingly restored art deco theater presents an eclectic and exciting selection of world cinema: first-run art films, foreign films, documentaries, and classics. Two intimate screening rooms also offer occasional special programming highlighting experimental films and video. The independent nonprofit art house also holds book readings, private events, and popular midnight cult movies. One of Coolidge's signature programs is Science on Screen, a creative pairing of films with introductions by renowned science experts; the program has expanded to more than 50 independent theaters nationwide. ✉ *290 Harvard St., Brookline* ☎ *617/734–2501, 617/734–2500 recorded info* 🌐 *www.coolidge.org* [M] *Coolidge Corner.*

Shopping

Brookline, 4 miles west of Boston, lies on the Green Line of the MBTA. Centered on Coolidge Corner, the area brims with shops selling everything from Russian tchotchkes to ethnic foods. Book lovers should not miss Brookline Booksmith (✉ *279 Harvard St.*), an independent bookstore "dedicated to the fine art of browsing," with creaky wooden floors, a friendly staff, and a drool-worthy selection of hardcovers and paperbacks.

BOOKS

★ Brookline Booksmith
BOOKS/STATIONERY | Since 1961 this independent bookseller has anchored Harvard Street, and enriched the Coolidge Corner community with poetry readings, book clubs, and author talks. Browse the well-edited selection of best sellers, hardcovers, and paperbacks, as well as the area toward the back packed with cards and fun gifts that range from cutting boards and tea towels to leather notebooks and printed scarves. **■ TIP→ Head downstairs for thousands of used books.** ✉ *279 Harvard St., Brookline* ☎ *617/566–6660* 🌐 *www.brooklinebooksmith-shop.com* [M] *Coolidge Corner.*

GIFTS

Boston General Store
GIFTS/SOUVENIRS | This is the sort of shop every neighborhood should have—a warm, welcoming space filled with beautifully crafted, mainly locally sourced products. Bamboo pet brushes share space with handwoven French market baskets, fruit and flower cocktail syrups, vintage fabric neckties, and fragrances from a Boston-area perfumer, who uses only botanicals (no synthetics!) to create her scents. ✉ *305 Harvard St., Coolidge Corner* ☎ *617/232–0103* 🌐 *www.bostongeneralstore.com.*

Jamaica Plain

Before Prohibition, Jamaica Plain was home to a thriving beer industry, the remnants of which can be seen in the neighborhood's 19th-century brick breweries, long since converted to offices and lofts. That said, Sam Adams and Turtle Swamp Brewing are two great places that pay homage to that history, with lively breweries and beer gardens. Other attractions in this slightly funkier

The 281-acre Arnold Arboretum of Harvard University contains more than 4,000 plants like rhododendrons, azaleas, lilacs, magnolias, and fruit trees.

part of Boston include open spaces like the Arnold Arboretum, Jamaica Pond (part of the Emerald Necklace),and plenty of independent restaurants, bars, and shops. It's easy enough to get to J.P., as it is called by locals, via the Orange Line on the MBTA.

Sights

★ Arnold Arboretum of Harvard University
GARDEN | FAMILY | This 281-acre living laboratory, 6 miles from downtown Boston, established in 1872 in accordance with the terms of a bequest from New Bedford merchant James Arnold contains more than 4,000 kinds of woody plants, most from the hardy north temperate zone. The rhododendrons, azaleas, lilacs, magnolias, and fruit trees are eye-popping when in bloom, and something is always in season from early April through September. The Larz Anderson bonsai collection contains individual specimens imported from Japan. In the visitor center there is a 40-to-1 scale model of the arboretum (with 4,000 tiny trees).

If you visit during May, Lilac Sunday on Mother's Day is a celebration of blooming trees and picnicking (the only day it's allowed). ⊠ *125 Arborway , at Centre St., Jamaica Plain* ⊹ *Take MBTA Orange Line (Forest Hills stop) or Bus 39 from Copley Sq. to Custer St. stop in Jamaica Plain (3 blocks away)* ☎ *617/524–1718* ⊕ *www. arboretum.harvard.edu* ✉ *Donations accepted* Ⓜ *Forest Hills.*

Jamaica Pond and Boat House
CITY PARK | FAMILY | Part of Boston's Emerald Necklace, Jamaica Pond is a delightful way to escape from the city and enjoy nature. A 1.5-mile paved path runs entirely around the large pond, which is actually a glacial kettle hole, and is a big draw for walkers and joggers. The pond is stocked with trout and salmon each year and those with a permit can fish. From May to October, Courageous Sailing operates out of the Jamaica Pond Boat House and provides lessons and equipment for rowing and sailing on the pond, except when youth classes are in session; call ahead to confirm. One-hour

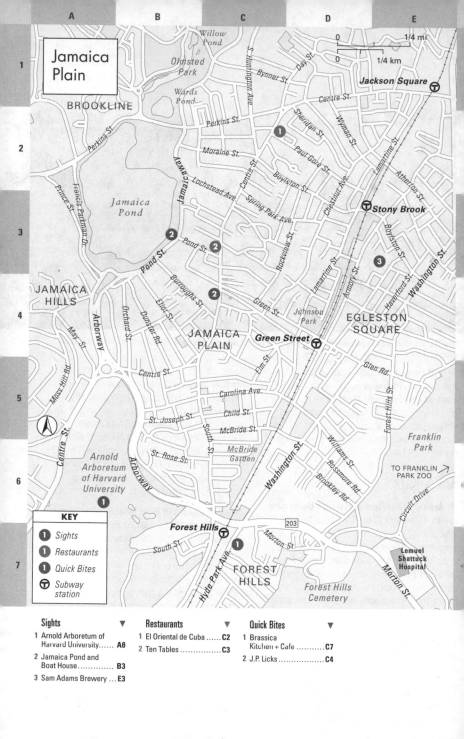

Jamaica Plain

BROOKLINE

Willow Pond

Olmsted Park

Wards Pond

Jamaica Pond

JAMAICA HILLS

Arnold Arboretum of Harvard University

JAMAICA PLAIN

Green Street

Stony Brook

Jackson Square

Johnson Park

EGLESTON SQUARE

Franklin Park

TO FRANKLIN PARK ZOO

Forest Hills

FOREST HILLS

Forest Hills Cemetery

Lemuel Shattuck Hospital

203

Day St.

Bynner St.

Centre St.

S. Huntington Ave.

Perkins St.

Perkins St.

Moraine St.

Sheridan St.

Paul Gore St.

Wyman St.

Lamartine St.

Atherton St.

Centre St.

Boylston St.

Chestnut Ave.

Jamaicaway

Lochstead Ave.

Spring Park Ave.

Rockview St.

Lamartine St.

Boylston St.

Washington St.

Haverford St.

Armory St.

Francis Parkman Dr.

Prince St.

Pond St.

Burroughs St.

Eliot St.

Dunster Rd.

Orchard St.

Arborway

May St.

Moss Hill Rd.

Centre St.

Centre St.

Green St.

Elm St.

Carolina Ave.

Child St.

McBride St.

McBride Garden

St. Joseph St.

St. Rose St.

South St.

Arborway

Washington St.

Williams St.

Rossmore Rd.

Brookley Rd.

Glen Rd.

Forest Hills St.

Circuit Drive

South St.

Hyde Park Ave.

Morton St.

Morton St.

0   1/4 mi
0   1/4 km

KEY

1 Sights
1 Restaurants
1 Quick Bites
Ⓣ Subway station

kayak and sailboat rentals are $20 (rowboats are $15; $10 with a fishing license). Cash or check only. Of course, you can walk around the pond year-round. ✉ *Jamaica Way and Pond St., Jamaica Plain* ☎ *617/522–5061* 🌐 *courageoussailing.org/jamaica-pond* [M] *Stony Brook, Green.*

Sam Adams Brewery

WINERY/DISTILLERY | Tour the Boston Beer Company's Jamaica Plain facility, where it conducts research and develops new products (the bulk of Samuel Adams production is done elsewhere). The entertaining hour-long tour is free to all, and includes a tasting for those over 21 and you get to keep your glass. Smell and taste the components of brewing: hops, malt, and barley; look at the flavoring process and hear about—perhaps even see—new beers in development. On fair-weather weekends, arrive early to avoid long waits. Tours run continuously 11 am–5 pm Monday through Saturday. Whether you take a tour, you can enjoy a beer in the Boston Tap Room, which is open daily. The brewery also offers specialty tours (for a fee); visit the website for more information. **■ TIP→ Parking is limited, so consider taking the T to Stony Brook.** ✉ *30 Germania St., Jamaica Plain* ☎ *617/368–5080* 🌐 *www.samueladams.com* 🕓 *Closed Sun. (no tours, but Tap Room open)* [M] *Stony Brook.*

🍴 Restaurants

This neighborhood is a kind of mini-Cambridge: multiethnic and filled with cutting-edge artists, graduate students, political idealists, and yuppie families. Recently the area, known for its affordable and unusual ethnic spots, has seen a swell of a more gentrified—but no less creative—sort.

El Oriental de Cuba

$ | **CUBAN** | This cozy spot with wooden tables and walls full of artwork—featuring tropical fruit, Cuban street life, and magazine covers—serves a large variety of authentic Cuban food, including a restorative chicken soup, a classic Cuban sub, superb rice and beans (opt for the red beans over the black), and sweet "tropical shakes." The menu, written in both English and Spanish, begins with breakfast, mainly various preparations of eggs with added ham, chorizo, or cheese, and Cuban espresso or Cuban iced coffee with milk. *Tostones* (twice-fried plantains) are beloved during cold New England winters by the city's many Cuban transplants, who will also find such dishes as oxtail, braised beef tongue, and *monfongo* (fried mashed green plantains with pork rinds and garlic oil). **Known for:** simple, quality Cuban cuisine; generous menu selection; homey setting. [$] *Average main: $15* ✉ *416 Centre St., Jamaica Plain* ☎ *617/524–6464* 🌐 *www.elorientaldecuba.net* [M] *Stony Brook.*

Ten Tables

$$$ | **FRENCH** | Jamaica Plain's postage stamp–size, candlelit space is an enchanting mix of Gallic elegance and chummy neighborhood revelry—both in the atmosphere and the food. Simple but high-quality dishes such as lamb meatballs with tomato jam, duck-fat dumplings with Cognac cream, and house-made pasta with garden vegetables seamlessly seal the deal. **Known for:** New England bistro fare; locally sourced ingredients; snug feel. [$] *Average main: $27* ✉ *597 Centre St., Jamaica Plain* ☎ *617/524–8810* 🌐 *www.facebook.com/TENTABLES* 🕓 *No lunch* [M] *Stony Brook.*

☕ Coffee and Quick Bites

Brassica Kitchen + Cafe

$ | **AMERICAN** | This tiny spot, tucked into a row of businesses across from the Forest Hills T station, is a café by day, serving coffee, breakfast and lunch, and a lively restaurant and bar by night. The decor is cozy and warm, with all the wood counters, tabletops and shelves made from antique woods repurposed from an old farmhouse. **Known for:**

creative and playful menu; excellent service; neighborhood favorite. [$] *Average main: $16* ✉ *3710 Washington St., Jamaica Plain* ☎ *617/477–4519* 🌐 *www.brassicakitchen.com* 🕒 *No dinner Sun. and Mon.* [M] *Forest Hills.*

JP Licks

$ | **AMERICAN** | For almost 40 years, J.P. Licks has been serving up delicious homemade ice cream and frozen yogurt, later adding its own roasted coffee and baked goods, in a fun, funky atmosphere. **Known for:** creative ice cream flavors; awesome ice cream cakes; low-key vibe. [$] *Average main: $6* ✉ *659 Centre St., Jamaica Plain* ☎ *617/524–6740* 🌐 *www.jplicks.com* [M] *Green Street.*

Hotels

Overnight options in JP are limited to a few small B&Bs.

Nightlife

Great swaths of green—the Arboretum, Jamaica Pond, and Emerald Necklace stretching miles to Fenway—set "J.P." apart from other streetcar suburbs. Centre Street runs the cultural gamut with Cuban, Mexican, Indian, Irish, and Dominican restaurants. Cafés and bars are wide open to gays and lesbians and everyone else.

BARS

Midway Café

MUSIC CLUBS | This very popular Jamaica Plain café books a lively mix of nightly rock bands, DJs, and noise artists. There's punk, soul, R&B, and Thursday a raucous lesbian (straights, too) dance party and "queeraoke." Cover varies nightly; check for show age-restrictions. ✉ *3496 Washington St., Jamaica Plain* ☎ *617/524–9038* 🌐 *www.midwaycafe.com* [M] *Green Street, Forest Hills.*

BREWPUBS AND BEER GARDENS

Turtle Swamp Brewing

BREWPUBS/BEER GARDENS | This lively and fun brewery and beer garden boasts more than a dozen types of beers which can be enjoyed on-site—indoors or outside at picnic tables. The flagship brew is the aptly named Orange Line IPA. The brewery often hosts food trucks, so patrons can enjoy a pint with different types of food, though customers are also welcome to bring their own food to enjoy as well. A second beer garden is located in nearby Roslindale. ✉ *3377 Washington St., Jamaica Plain* ☎ *617/522–0038* 🌐 *turtleswampbrewing.com* [M] *Green Street.*

Chapter 10

THE SEAPORT, SOUTH BOSTON, AND EAST BOSTON

Updated by
Leigh Harrington

⊙ **Sights**
★★★☆☆

🍴 **Restaurants**
★★★★★

🛏 **Hotels**
★★★★☆

🛍 **Shopping**
★☆☆☆☆

🍸 **Nightlife**
★★★☆☆

NEIGHBORHOOD SNAPSHOT

TOP EXPERIENCES

■ **Explore Camelot:** Visit the John F. Kennedy Presidential Library & Museum and the Edward M. Kennedy Institute for the U.S. Senate.

■ **Appreciate an architectural marvel:** The Institute of Contemporary Art/Boston leans over Boston Harbor in opposition to physics.

■ **Take in stunning views:** The unparalleled, 360-degree views from Boston Harborwalk of the water and the city's other neighborhoods can't be beat.

■ **Eat out:** The Seaport District is known for its abundant culinary offerings, from gourmet local bakeries to top national steakhouses.

■ **Swing it:** Geometrically unique swings for adults can be found at the Lawn on D. Snag a beer there, too.

GETTING HERE

Accessing the Seaport District is relatively easy, but the neighborhood is large. From South Station, you can walk anywhere along Fort Point Channel, but for farther afield take the Silver Line. If you're headed to South Boston, take a Red Line train and get off at Andrew or Broadway. By car, both the Seaport and South Boston have a moderate amount of street (free after 8 pm and all day Sunday) and lot parking.

East Boston poses more of a challenge. It's long, lean, and residential, so the best way to explore is by vehicle. Taking public transit is not impossible; ride the Blue Line to Maverick, Wood Island, Orient Heights, or Suffolk Downs and be sure to know where you want to exit. Blue Line and Silver Line trains service Logan Airport.

GOOD TO KNOW

Travelers looking for a vibrant nightlife scene should visit South Boston after dark, particularly along Broadway, with its abundance of bars and restaurants.

QUICK BITES

■ **Bon Me.** Expect chef-crafted contemporary versions of Vietnamese street food. ✉ *313 Congress St., Fort Point* ⊕ *www.bonmetruck.com* Ⓜ *South Station, Courthouse.*

■ **KO Pies.** Australian-style meat pies and craft beer served with stunning water views is hidden away on the East Boston waterfront. ✉ *256 Marginal St., Bldg. 16, East Boston* ⊕ *www. kocateringandpies.com* Ⓜ *Maverick.*

■ **Yankee Lobster Co.** This family-owned fish market and take-out seafood shack has been serving the local catch since 1950. ✉ *300 Northern Ave., Seaport District* ⊕ *www.yankeelobstercompany.com* Ⓜ *Silver Line Way.*

PLANNING YOUR TIME

■ You'll spend some time getting around the Seaport. Ambitious travelers can see two museums in a day, have a beer at Harpoon Brewery, and walk part of the Harborwalk. If you have only a few hours, plan an early dinner to enjoy topnotch dining and sunset water views.

■ Safety isn't a concern in the Seaport and South Boston. East Boston is also safe, but it's once rough reputation follows it.

While distinctly different, the Seaport, South Boston, and East Boston have one major commonality: Boston Harbor. Historically, the Seaport has supported the textile and commercial fishing industries with its working piers. South Boston and Fort Independence have safeguarded the city from attack by sea since 1643. And in East Boston, Donald McKay built record-setting clipper ships.

Today, a lot has changed. Over the last 10 years, the Seaport has transformed from an industrial no-man's-land to a vibrant, bustling extension of downtown Boston. Luxury hotels and residences, manicured micro-parks, upscale restaurants both local and national in name, and cutting-edge cultural institutions have all found homes here. Development projects remain in the works, so the face of the Seaport will continue to adjust for years to come.

Heavily populated—and Irish—South Boston has experienced its own renaissance, more so in the form of putting polish on existing multifamily homes and old-timey bars rather than making room for new construction. The neighborhood's residents, both Southie lifers and young professional transplants, walk and walk: they walk to meals, they walk to Boston's best stretch of beaches, and they walk to and around Castle Island for exercise year-round.

For the last century-plus, East Boston has been a haven for immigrants, first Italian and then Latino, and today's population reflects this heritage. Eastie features arguably the city's biggest tourist attraction—Logan Airport—but there are only a few other cultural sites to see unless you count the abundance of authentic Latin restaurants.

The Seaport

What's the appeal of the Seaport District? Bostonians have only been able to answer that question recently. As the neighborhood becomes developed and its former life as a parking lot wasteland fades from peoples' minds, locals have realized its gorgeous potential, something the Moakley Courthouse, the Institute of Contemporary Art/Boston, and restaurateur-chef Barbara Lynch recognized more than a decade back.

Start your visit to the Seaport District at South Station, which is actually just across the Fort Point Channel in the heart of downtown. From there, it's an easy walk to historical and cultural sites like the Boston Tea Party Ships & Museum, Fan Pier, and the Boston Children's

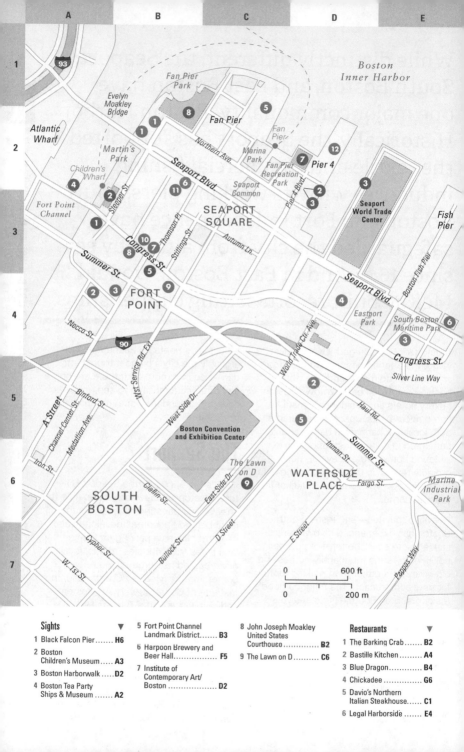

Sights ▼

1 Black Falcon Pier....... **H6**

2 Boston
 Children's Museum..... **A3**

3 Boston Harborwalk.....**D2**

4 Boston Tea Party
 Ships & Museum **A2**

5 Fort Point Channel
 Landmark District.......**B3**

6 Harpoon Brewery and
 Beer Hall.................**F5**

7 Institute of
 Contemporary Art/
 Boston **D2**

8 John Joseph Moakley
 United States
 Courthouse..............**B2**

9 The Lawn on D **C6**

Restaurants ▼

1 The Barking Crab.......**B2**

2 Bastille Kitchen **A4**

3 Blue Dragon.............**B4**

4 Chickadee **G6**

5 Davio's Northern
 Italian Steakhouse......**C1**

6 Legal Harborside **E4**

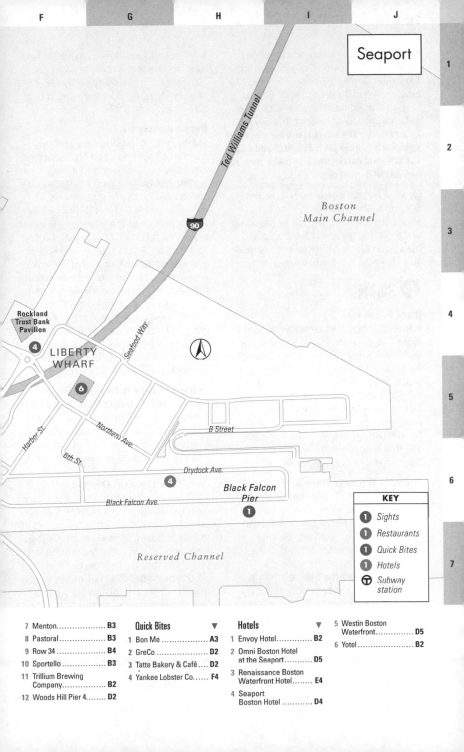

Seaport

Ted Williams Tunnel

90

Boston Main Channel

Rockland Trust Bank Pavilion

4 LIBERTY WHARF

6

Seafood Way

Harbor St.

Northern Ave.

6th St.

B Street

Drydock Ave.

4

Black Falcon Pier

1

Black Falcon Ave.

Reserved Channel

Museum. If your destination is farther afield, say the Boston Convention and Exhibition Center, Harpoon Brewery, the Seaport World Trade Center, or Boston Design Center, head to South Station's subway concourse to catch the Silver Line. ■TIP→ **The Silver Line operates three different branches (SL1, SL2, SL3) and each has different destinations, so make sure you hop on the correct one.**

Of all of Boston's neighborhoods, the Seaport is the least "Bostonian" in appearance. In fact, with all its skyscrapers and shiny glass, the Seaport could have been plucked straight out of New York. It's new, it's fresh, it's young.

Sights

Black Falcon Pier
MARINA | Surrounded by water on three sides, Black Falcon Pier is a stop on Boston's Harborwalk that seekers of amazing views won't want to miss. There's not much to do out this way at the end of the Seaport District except gaze at the fishing vessels, barges, and cruise ships navigating the inner harbor. Next door, Boston Design Center offers shopping and dining options. ⊠ *Black Falcon Pier, Seaport* Ⓜ *Dry Dock, Black Falcon.*

★ Boston Children's Museum
MUSEUM | **FAMILY** | The country's second-oldest children's museum has always been ahead of the curve with creative hands-on exhibits, cultural diversity, and problem solving. Some of the most popular stops are also the simplest, like the bubble-making machinery and the two-story climbing maze. At the Japanese House you're invited to take off your shoes and step inside a Kyoto silk merchant's home. The "Boston Black" exhibit stimulates dialogue about ethnicity and community, and children can dig, climb, and build at the Construction Zone. In the toddler PlaySpace, children under three can run free in a safe environment. There's also

a full schedule of special exhibits, festivals, and performances. ⊠ *308 Congress St., Fort Point Channel* ☎ *617/426–6500* ⊕ *www.bostonchildrensmuseum.org* ⊡ *$18* Ⓜ *South Station.*

Boston Harborwalk
TRAIL | For the last 30-plus years, a number of agencies and organizations have been collaborating to create a waterfront walking path along Boston's shoreline—currently, it stretches 43 miles. Boston's Seaport District boasts a hearty portion of the Harborwalk, which winds from Fort Point Channel, around Fan Pier, up Seaport Boulevard and out and around Black Falcon Cruise Terminal. Along the way, pedestrians can see art exhibits, stationary viewfinders, open green spaces, and incredible Boston Harbor views. Marked signs point the way, and maps can be found online. ⊠ *Seaport* ⊹ *Congress St. Bridge by Children's Museum* ⊕ *www.bostonharborwalk.org* Ⓜ *South Station.*

★ Boston Tea Party Ships & Museum
LOCAL INTEREST | **FAMILY** | Situated at the Congress Street Bridge near the site of Griffin's Wharf, this lively museum offers an interactive look at the past in a place as close as possible to the actual spot where the Boston Tea Party took place on December 16, 1773. Actors in period costumes greet patrons, assign them real-life Colonial personas, and then ask a few people to heave boxes of tea into the water from aboard historical reproductions of the ships forcibly boarded and unloaded the night Boston Harbor became a teapot. There are 3-D holograms, talking portraits, and even the Robinson Half Tea Chest, one of two original tea chests known to exist. ■TIP→ **Abigail's Tea Room (you don't need a museum ticket for entry) features a tea tasting of five tea blends that would have been aboard the ships.** ⊠ *Congress St. Bridge, Fort Point Channel* ⊕ *www.bostonteapartyship.com* ⊡ *$30* Ⓜ *South Station.*

Boston Children's Museum is the country's second-oldest children's museum.

Fort Point Channel Landmark District

HISTORIC SITE | This historic district, which was designated by the City of Boston in 2009, features the city's largest, most cohesive grouping of late 19th and early 20th-century industrial loft buildings. Boston Wharf Company owned and developed the area from 1836 to 1882. Today, the small, walkable, revitalized area sits between Fort Point Channel and the Seaport District and is home to Boston Children's Museum, Boston Tea Party Ships & Museum, working artist studios, and a variety of restaurants. ⊠ *Bounded by Seaport Blvd., Summer St., Boston Wharf Rd., and Fort Point Channel, Fort Point Channel.*

Harpoon Brewery and Beer Hall

WINERY/DISTILLERY | Harpoon Brewery holds Massachusetts' first-ever brewing permit, obtained in 1986 by three college friends who wanted to create a fresh beer culture in their hometown. Today, Harpoon features guided tours of its Seaport District facility, sharing its story, fun facts, and samples with beer lovers from around the globe. Harpoon's on-site beer hall pours a rotating lineup of limited-edition and pilot beers, nonbrand beers and ciders, and it serves handmade pretzels and dips. ⊠ *306 Northern Ave., Seaport* ☎ *617/456–2322* ⊕ *www.harpoonbrewery.com* ⊠ *$5* Ⓜ *Silver Line Way, Harbor Street.*

★ Institute of Contemporary Art/Boston

MUSEUM | The ICA mounts temporary exhibits by the contemporary art world's brightest talents, as well as curated pieces from its permanent collection, all of which are as cutting edge as the breathtaking, cantilevered edifice jutting out over Boston Harbor that houses them. The ICA's fourth floor is where most happens: incredible art and stunning water views. The Poss Family Mediatheque serves as a great resting spot for families. Live programming, from film festivals to outdoor live music concerts take place regularly. Don't miss the ICA Store on ground level, where you can pick up an inventive trinket of your own. ⊠ *25 Harbor Shore Dr., Seaport* ☎ *617/478–3100* ⊕ *www.icaboston.org* ⊠ *$15* ⊗ *Closed Mon.* Ⓜ *Courthouse.*

John Joseph Moakley United States Courthouse
BUILDING | Believe it or not, the public is welcomed in for a visit to this architectural wonder and federal house of justice. Galleries across the courthouse feature rotating exhibitions on a variety of themes, from maritime history to the judicial system. Don't miss Ellsworth Kelly's permanent installation "The Boston Panels" in the courthouse's entry rotunda. It's not uncommon to see a tall ship or a charter vessel docked outside, in season. ✉ *Fan Pier, 1 Courthouse Way, Seaport* ☎ *617/261–2440* 🌐 *www.moakleycourthouse.com.*

★ The Lawn on D
CITY PARK | **FAMILY** | Stop, rest awhile, and have some fun. That's the purpose of The Lawn on D, a free-to-all open green space that features a plethora of geometrical swings, games like bocce, cornhole, and ping-pong, and chairs for lounging. In warmer weather, you can often catch a live concert or film screening here, or a public art installation. A concession stand makes sure visitors are well-fed. The only catch? You can't bring Fido. ✉ *420 D St., Seaport* 🕒 *Closed Nov.–Apr., and during private events* [M] *World Trade Center, Silver Line Way.*

🍴 Restaurants

As the Seaport District has grown, so, too, has the quality of its dining options. A few, blue-collar "fish shacks" remain in operation as testaments to the area's lucrative industry, serving the fresh catch their fishermen bring in daily from nearby Atlantic waters. About 10 years ago, a second wave of large-scale and upscale national steak houses, Mexican restaurants, sports bars, and American seafood restaurants kicked-off, with Legal Sea Foods leading the way with its three-floor flagship Legal Harborside—it is appropriate that this Boston-born restaurant reside here, since its commercial world headquarters has anchored a corner of the Seaport long before Bostonians called it "the Seaport."

As the neighborhood continues to develop, more and more local chefs and restaurateurs open their own kitchens, featuring an array of cuisine styles, from New England farm-to-table to Italian, coastal, and Boston's only Relais & Chateaux property. As well as destination restaurants, local and national quick-eat chains have populated to serve the area's fast-growing crowd of 9–5 professionals.

The Barking Crab
$$$ | **SEAFOOD** | **FAMILY** | Decked out in cheery colors of yellow, red, and green, this is, believe it or not, a real seaside clam shack located smack dab in the middle of Boston. An outdoor patio and lobster tent in summer features stunning views of the financial district; in winter, dining retreats indoors to a warmhearted version of a waterfront dive, where you'll encounter a classic New England clambake or oysters and littlenecks from the raw bar, followed by meaty, golden crab cakes. **Known for:** traditional New England seafood platters; crowded deck in summer; kitchy confines. [$] *Average main: $35* ✉ *88 Sleeper St., Fort Point Channel* ☎ *617/426–2722* 🌐 *www.barkingcrab.com* [M] *Courthouse, South Station.*

★ Bastille Kitchen
$$$ | **BRASSERIE** | Clubby, homey, grand: all describe the look and feel of this Fort Point–located, contemporary French restaurant that will provide one of the best meals you've ever eaten in Boston. At first glance, the ambience can feel a little sceney, but that all falls away when you taste the chef's take on brasserie staples like moules frites, garlic escargot, duck à l'orange, and salmon Provençal. **Known for:** excellent service; outstanding food; tucked away, in-the-know location. [$] *Average main: $30* ✉ *49 Melcher St., Fort Point Channel* ☎ *617/556–8000* 🌐 *www.bastillekitchen.net* 🕒 *Closed Sun.* [M] *South Station.*

Blue Dragon

$$$ | ASIAN FUSION | Old Shanghai meets stylish South Boston at acclaimed chef Ming Tsai's uber-popular Asian gastropub, set in an abandoned triangular diner in the Fort Point neighborhood. Folks regularly stop in to slurp up tiki-inspired cocktails and share small-plate versions of funky Asian mash-ups. **Known for:** nut-free kitchen; signature chocolate chip cookie dessert; industrial vibe. $ *Average main: $25 ⊠ 324 A St., Fort Point Channel ☎ 617/338–8585 ⊕ www.bluedragon-bos.com* M *South Station.*

Chickadee

$$$ | MODERN AMERICAN | At the far eastern end of the city and tucked into the Innovation and Design Building, Chickadee is a restaurant you'd wish to stumble over. Make the trek on the Silver Line or by car to sample chef-owner John daSilva's curated seasonal menu, rife with unique preparations and locally sourced ingredients—think snacks like a sour cream and onion doughnut with caviar and crème fraîche. **Known for:** whole food focused; original, unique cocktails; free parking. $ *Average main: $34 ⊠ 21 Drydock Ave., Seaport ☎ 617/531–5591 ⊕ www.chickadeerestaurant.com* ⊗ *No dinner Sun.* M *Drydock Avenue.*

Davio's Northern Italian Steakhouse

$$$$ | STEAKHOUSE | This popular Boston-born restaurant splits its focus between grilled all-natural steaks and chops and hearty, Italian-inspired dishes. Diners can't get enough of Davio's signature spring rolls, stuffed with Philly cheesesteak, chicken parm, or shrimp, and pasta is made in-house. **Known for:** Italian takes on spring rolls; à la carte steaks and decadent side dishes; excellent wine list. $ *Average main: $51 ⊠ 50 Liberty Dr., Seaport ☎ 617/261–4810 ⊕ www.davios.com/seaport* M *Courthouse.*

★ Legal Harborside

$$$$ | SEAFOOD | Three huge floors, three different menus, and one spectacular view makes Legal Harborside a worthy flagship for Boston's iconic Legal Sea Foods brand. The first level pays tribute to Legal's 1950s fish market with a casual vibe and simple menu of seafood favorites; a raw bar shucks a dozen-plus varieties of fresh oysters, too. **Known for:** prime waterfront location; excellent seafood options; Legal Seafood's flagship restaurant. $ *Average main: $40 ⊠ 270 Northern Ave., Seaport ☎ 617/477–2900 ⊕ www.legalseafoods.com/restaurants/boston-legal-harborside* M *World Trade Center.*

Menton

$$$$ | FRENCH | Those for whom price is no object will want to dine here, at Barbara Lynch's luxurious, France-meets-Italy-inspired eatery that's arguably the best restaurant in town. It's Boston's only Relais & Châteaux awarded property, a prestigious honor in the hospitality industry. **Known for:** opulent dishes, like foie gras brûlée; extravagant prices; excellent wine list. $ *Average main: $165 ⊠ 354 Congress St., Fort Point Channel ☎ 617/737–0099 ⊕ www.mentonboston.com* M *South Station.*

Pastoral

$$ | ITALIAN | FAMILY | Satisfy your pizza craving with a crispy, wood-fired, thin-crust pie from this Fort Point neighborhood joint. A dozen and a half options run from the traditional margherita to the more inventive lasagna or the ham and brussel sprouts. **Known for:** wood-fired pizza; craft beer and Italian wine; casual vibe. $ *Average main: $21 ⊠ 345 Congress St., Fort Point Channel ☎ 617/345–0005 ⊕ www.pastoralfortpoint.com* M *South Station.*

★ Row 34

$$$ | SEAFOOD | This modern beer-bar-meets-oyster-bar vibes boisterous energy contained only by its soaring ceilings. A neighborhood crowd comes for the excellent menu devoted to raw oysters, fried seafood, a variety of "rolls," and fish-based entrées. **Known for:** local oysters fresh from restaurant's own oyster farm; seafood—carnivores and vegetarians should head elsewhere; excellent selection of American craft beer. $ *Average main: $27* ⊠ *383 Congress St., Seaport* ☎ *617/553–5900* ⊕ *www.row34. com* Ⓜ *World Trade Center.*

★ Sportello

$$ | ITALIAN | One of the city's most widely awarded chefs, Barbara Lynch had the foresight to create a culinary statement in the Seaport, long before it was cool to do so. Her Italian trattoria, Sportello, serves rustic, market-fresh fare in a chic, white, upscale "diner"-like setting, where diners can order à la carte, try a two- or three-course prix-fixe (at lunch), or have the kitchen cook up a three-course family style meal of their choosing for the table. **Known for:** pasta made in-house daily, by hand; casual, modern vibe; top-quality ingredients. $ *Average main: $22* ⊠ *348 Congress St., Fort Point Channel* ☎ *617/737–1234* ⊕ *www. sportelloboston.com* Ⓜ *South Station.*

Trillium Brewing Company

$$ | AMERICAN | FAMILY | When it comes to craft beer, a lot of Bostonians get excited about Trillium, even more so now that the native brewer moved to these much bigger digs and also opened a summer beer garden on the Greenway. So do as the locals do, bring the kids along to quench your thirst in the ever-crowded ground-level tap room (sorry, no flights) or sit for a quieter meal upstairs to enjoy a menu that's meant to keep you reaching for more with dips and deviled eggs, charcuterie trays, bowls, burgers, and bolognese. **Known for:** pints are comparably expensive; hazy IPAs; fantastic roof deck. $ *Average main: $20* ⊠ *50 Thomson Pl., Fort Point Channel* ☎ *857/449–0083* ⊕ *www.trilliumbrewing. com* Ⓜ *Courthouse.*

★ Woods Hill Pier 4

$$$$ | MODERN AMERICAN | Kristin Canty's brand new restaurant features floor-to-ceiling windows and sweeping, 270-degree views of the Boston Harbor waterfront. Neutral tones and vertical ceiling panels that mimic ocean waves create a cozy environment and a place where you can hang out for a while, which is ideal since the well-curated menu features mid-sized plates that are meant to be shared; plan to order two to three per person. **Known for:** incredible panoramic views of Boston Harbor; pasture-raised, sustainable and organic farm-to-table ingredients; a killer Sunday brunch. $ *Average main: $40* ⊠ *300 Pier 4 Blvd., Seaport* ☎ *617/981–4577* ⊕ *www.woodshillpier4.com* Ⓜ *Courthouse.*

☕ Coffee and Quick Bites

Bon Me

$ | VIETNAMESE | Bon Me's moniker is a whimsical take on Vietnam's signature sandwich, the bahn me, and the versions that this local fast-casual restaurant serves are authentic to its spirit, if not its traditional ingredients. Diners can create their own bowls (salad, noodle, or rice) selecting from a variety of proteins, veggies, and sauces. **Known for:** tasty proteins like char siu bbq pork, Chinese salt and pepper chicken, and roasted paprika tofu; spicy ginger lemonade that will flare your nostrils; customized bowls, so the kids will eat, too. $ *Average main: $10* ⊠ *313 Congress St., Fort Point Channel* ☎ *857/350–4035* ⊕ *www.bonmetruck. com* Ⓜ *South Station, Courthouse.*

GreCo

$ | **GREEK** | Options for fast-casual meals along Seaport Boulevard grow by the day, but a solid choice for good old-fashioned working man's Greek food comes from this Boston-born modern outpost. Ingredients in the pita sandwiches, salads, and build-your-own meals are so good, you'll be licking house-made spicy feta and lemon yogurt off your fingers. **Known for:** build-your-own salads, pitas, and plates; several types of doughy loukoumas; plenty of seating. Ⓢ *Average main: $12* ✉ *200 Pier 4 Blvd., Seaport* ☎ *617/572–3300* ⊕ *www.grecoboston. com* Ⓜ *World Trade Center.*

★ Tatte Bakery & Café

$ | **ISRAELI** | You've never had kouign-amann or Jerusalem bagels quite like Tzurit Or's, the owner and recipe mastermind behind this upscale bakery and café. Many baked goods are staples, but the majority of the café menu featuring heartier plates changes with season, all with a Middle Eastern spin. **Known for:** Or's take on traditional North African shakshuka, served with challah bread; signature nut tarts that are as pretty as they are tasty; convivial atmosphere. Ⓢ *Average main: $12* ✉ *200 Pier 4 Blvd., Seaport* ☎ *617/765–7600* ⊕ *www.tatte-bakery.com* Ⓜ *Courthouse.*

Yankee Lobster Co.

$ | **SEAFOOD** | **FAMILY** | There's nothing fresher than eating fish the same day it's caught, and that's what you get at this family-owned seafood shack in the Seaport District. Open since 1950, the local favorite serves fresh oysters, crab cakes, fried oysters and clams, steamers, and lobster. **Known for:** lobster, lobster, lobster; being simple and authentic; limited seating options. Ⓢ *Average main: $16* ✉ *300 Northern Ave., Seaport* ☎ *617/345–9799* ⊕ *www.yankeelobster-company.com* Ⓜ *Silver Line Way.*

 # Hotels

Envoy Hotel

$$$$ | **HOTEL** | Visitors and locals like to hang out at the Envoy, whose design-forward aesthetic provides a comfortable yet stylish vibe. **Pros:** 24-hour fitness center includes Peloton bikes; full restaurant menu is available for in-room dining; beautiful views overlooking the Fort Point Channel. **Cons:** bar crowds can be loud and rowdy; alarm clocks only available by request; no rollaway beds available. Ⓢ *Rooms from: $450* ✉ *70 Sleeper St., Seaport* ☎ *617/338–3030* ⊕ *www.theenvoyhotel.com* ⟿ *136 rooms* ⎟⊙⎟ *No meals* Ⓜ *Courthouse.*

★ Omni Boston Hotel at the Seaport

$$$$ | **HOTEL** | Opened in 2021, this brand new Omni hotel debuts a chic, modern counterpoint to its grand dame Downtown property, the Omni Parker House. **Pros:** year-round, outdoor, heated pool with bar area; multiple food and drink options on-site; brand new accommodations. **Cons:** far from Back Bay and Beacon Hill shopping; tight restrictions on pet policy. Ⓢ *Rooms from: $399* ✉ *450 Summer St., Seaport* ☎ *888/444–6664, 617/476–6664* ⊕ *www.omnihotels.com* ⟿ *1055 rooms* ⎟⊙⎟ *No meals* Ⓜ *World Trade Center, Silver Line Way.*

Renaissance Boston Waterfront Hotel

$$$ | **HOTEL** | Set near to Boston's working fish piers, the Renaissance plays to a watery theme—in the modern lobby, blue-and-green glass orbs complement a suspended glass lighting fixture and the spiral staircase was created to look like a nautilus shell. **Pros:** sleek lobby Capiz Bar and Lounge; close to airport transportation and convention center; on-site fitness center. **Cons:** fee for Internet usage; hordes of conventioneers; far from the Back Bay and Boston Common. Ⓢ *Rooms from: $325* ✉ *606 Congress St., Seaport* ☎ *617/338–4111,*

888/796–4664 ⊕ marriott.com/hotels/
travel/boswf-renaissance-boston-water-
front-hotel ⇆ 471 rooms ⏐⊚⏐ No meals
Ⓜ World Trade Center.

Seaport Boston Hotel

$$$ | HOTEL | FAMILY | Adjacent to the World
Trade Center and not far from Boston
Convention and Exhibition Center, the
Seaport Hotel is awash with badge-wear-
ing, convention-going suits. **Pros:**
beautiful on-site Wave Health & Fitness
Club; great location for anyone attending
a convention; multiple on-site dining
options. **Cons:** slow elevators; swamped
during conventions; far from the Back
Bay and South End. Ⓢ Rooms from:
$300 ⊠ Seaport World Trade Center, 1
Seaport La., Seaport ☎ 617/385–4000,
800/440–3318 ⊕ www.seaportboston.
com ⇆ 428 rooms ⏐⊚⏐ No meals Ⓜ World
Trade Center.

Westin Boston Waterfront

$$ | HOTEL | Located in Boston's Seaport
district, the Westin is connected to the
Boston Convention & Exhibition Center
and provides comfortable accommodations and exceptional service. **Pros:** close
to the Institute of Contemporary Art/
Boston; pet-friendly for animals up to
40 lbs.; Westin's signature "heavenly"
beds. **Cons:** clusters of meeting-goers;
lobby can get hectic; not within walking
distance of the Back Bay and South End.
Ⓢ Rooms from: $285 ⊠ 425 Summer St.,
Seaport ☎ 617/532–4600 ⊕ www.mar-
riott.com/hotels/travel/bosow-the-wes-
tin-boston-waterfront ⇆ 793 rooms
⏐⊚⏐ No meals Ⓜ World Trade Center.

Yotel

$$ | HOTEL | One of only three in the
United States, Yotel Boston fits perfectly in the city's rapidly developing and
innovative Seaport District putting smart
technology at the forefront, featuring
airline-style self-service check-in and
Technowalls in each room, which allows
guests to stream movies and music from
their own devices. **Pros:** free Wi-Fi; aller-
gen-free cabins; digital check-in. **Cons:**

not within walking distance to the Back
Bay and Newbury Street; those who
aren't fans of technology won't appreciate the high-tech style; no room service.
Ⓢ Rooms from: $170 ⊠ 65 Seaport Blvd.,
Waterfront ☎ 617/377–4747 ⊕ www.
yotel.com/en/hotels/yotel-boston ⇆ 326
rooms ⏐⊚⏐ No meals Ⓜ Courthouse.

Nightlife

BARS

⭐ **Drink**

BARS/PUBS | Barbara Lynch handles this
elegant den of iniquity as only a chef of
world-wide acclaim would—like a restaurant. Behind the bar, tenders chip ice off
a giant block and use herbs, infusions,
and elixirs to custom create a top-shelf
libation for your palate, that is, there is
no drink list. Low, beamed ceilings and
a wooden bar that snakes through the
space maximizes room for a discerning
cocktail crowd. A limited menu features
snacks and things, including a burger
made from Wagyu beef, of course. Drink
is one of the best bars in Boston, and it's
hugely popular, so you'll likely wait in line
to get in, but once you do, there's room
to breathe. ⊠ 348 Congress St., Fort
Point Channel ☎ 617/695–1806 ⊕ www.
drinkfortpoint.com Ⓜ South Station.

Kings

BARS/PUBS | Calling all gamers—at least,
the old-fashioned sort—to this massive
bar and restaurant that entertains with
upscale-style bowling, billiards, darts,
air hockey, shuffleboard, foosball, and
more. The '80s kids among us can wax
nostalgic while playing the retro arcade
games they remember from their child-
hood, including PAC-MAN, Super Mario
Bros., and Teenage Mutant Ninja Turtles.
For the hungry, the kitchen makes such
tasty fare as burgers, pub-style pizza,
wings, tacos, and more. Kings' Draft
Room serves up mega-sized 34-ounce
beers and sports. Anyone under age 18
must be accompanied by an adult, and
no one under age 21 is admitted after 10

pm (or 6 pm on Saturday). ✉ *60 Seaport Blvd., Seaport* ☎ *617/401–0025* ⊕ *www. kings-de.com* Ⓜ *Courthouse.*

Lucky's Lounge

BARS/PUBS | This low-lit, subterranean den mixes gin cocktails with a heady dash of live music for an experience locals have been loving since 2003. Think Favreau's *Swingers* meets Frank Sinatra and the Rat Pack. In fact, Lucky's is the worst-kept secret this side of the Fort Point Channel, and Bostonians wouldn't have it any other way. ✉ *355 Congress St., Fort Point Channel* ☎ *617/357–5825* ⊕ *luckys-lounge.com* Ⓜ *South Station.*

COMEDY CLUBS
Laugh Boston

COMEDY CLUBS | More than 300 people per show can share a laugh with the local comics and national headliners who take the stage at one of Boston's favorite comedy clubs. Doors are open to anyone ages 16 and older, because comedic material is typically R-rated. ✉ *425 Summer St., Seaport* ☎ *617/725–2844* ⊕ *www.laughboston.com* Ⓜ *World Trade Center.*

🛍 Shopping

For as large a neighborhood as the Seaport District is, shopping options are few and far between. Some upmarket national and international brands have set up shop along Seaport Boulevard, and a few local entrepreneurs have moved in.

CLOTHING
For Now

CLOTHING | A finely curated but always changing selection of apparel, shoes, accessories, skin care, and jewelry from emerging, small, and independent local retailers are what's in store here. Owned and operated by two Boston-based women, For Now feels like a place where you can figure it out, whether you're talking about your style or your approach to life. ✉ *68 Seaport Blvd., Seaport* ☎ *857/233–4639* ⊕ *www. itsfornow.com* Ⓜ *Courthouse.*

FOOD
Cardullo's

FOOD/CANDY | Cardullo's has been a local standout for gourmet global food items for the last 70 years, although it recently opened its Seaport location, a bit of a departure from its Harvard Square origins. Artisan and international wines and beer, chocolates and sweets, jams, crackers, teas and coffee, cured meats, cheese, and foodstuffs made in the New England region stock the shelves. A deli counter serves awesome sandwiches to-go. ✉ *99 Seaport Blvd., Seaport* ☎ *857/350–4579* ⊕ *www.cardullos.com* Ⓜ *Courthouse.*

SHOPPING MALL AND MARKETS
Boston Design Center and Market Stalls

HOUSEHOLD ITEMS/FURNITURE | Boston Design Center caters to design professionals and features more than 60 showrooms across seven floors, spotlighting luxury home decor product lines from fine art to lighting to floor coverings. For history lovers and collectors of the past, come browse all manner of high quality and fine antiques at the second floor Market Stalls, many from individual, Boston-area dealers. ✉ *1 Design Center Pl., Seaport* ⊕ *www. bostondesign.com* ⊙ *Closed weekends* Ⓜ *Boston Design Center.*

SPECIALTY SHOPS
Reebok FITHUB

SPORTING GOODS | Welcome to the global headquarters of this popular fitness lifestyle brand. Shop around the expansive space for unique, limited-edition sneaker styles as well as Reebok's Classics range, loads of running apparel, backpacks, and more. Fans can personalize exclusive, handmade shoes and other products at the in-store YourReebok Customization Shop. ✉ *25 Drydock Ave., Seaport* ☎ *617/772–0267* ⊕ *www.reebok. com* Ⓜ *Boston Design Center.*

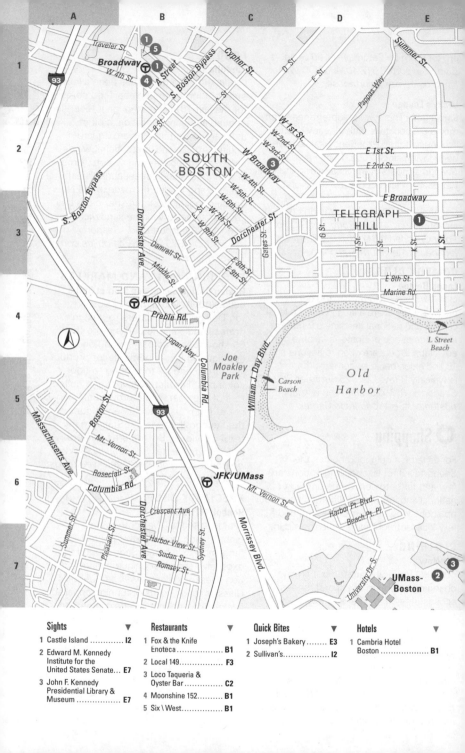

Map Legend

Sights ▼	**Restaurants** ▼	**Quick Bites** ▼	**Hotels** ▼
1 Castle Island **I2**	1 Fox & the Knife Enoteca **B1**	1 Joseph's Bakery **E3**	1 Cambria Hotel Boston **B1**
2 Edward M. Kennedy Institute for the United States Senate... **E7**	2 Local 149................. **F3**	2 Sullivan's.................. **I2**	
3 John F. Kennedy Presidential Library & Museum **E7**	3 Loco Taqueria & Oyster Bar **C2**		
	4 Moonshine 152.......... **B1**		
	5 Six \ West................. **B1**		

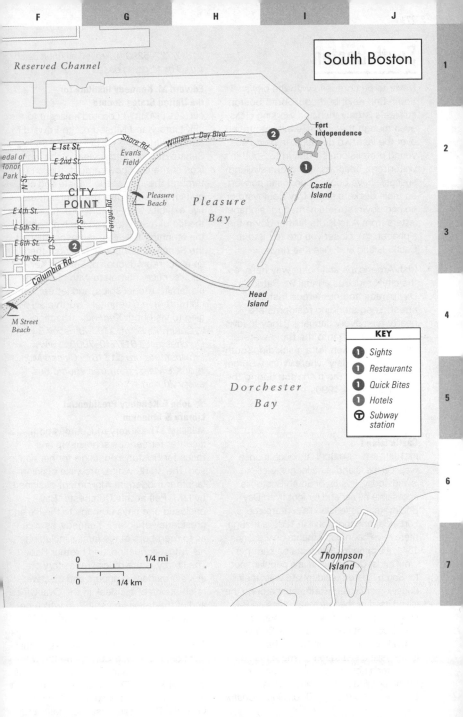

Reserved Channel

Fort
Independence

William J. Day Blvd.

Shore Rd.

Evan's
Field

E 1st St.

E 2nd St.

E 3rd St.

edal of
lonor
Park

CITY
POINT

Pleasure
Beach

Pleasure
Bay

Castle
Island

Farragut Rd.

E 4th St.

E 5th St.

E 6th St.

E 7th St.

P St.

N St.

Columbia Rd.

M Street
Beach

Head
Island

Dorchester
Bay

KEY

1 *Sights*

1 *Restaurants*

1 *Quick Bites*

1 *Hotels*

Ⓣ *Subway station*

0   1/4 mi

0   1/4 km

Thompson
Island

South Boston

Never to be confused with the city's South End neighborhood, South Boston still feels largely Irish and working class, even though the area has fully gentrified over the last two decades. In doing so, young professionals—drawn to Southie's waterfront, beaches, and green walking spaces—have bought condos in converted triple deckers along Day Boulevard or up and down streets named for alphabet letters from A to P. The farther down the alphabet, the closer you are to historic Castle Island and Pleasure Bay.

Irish-Americans still hold sway here, as the city's raucous annual St. Patrick's Day parade and numerous Irish bars attest. Long-standing residents are hearty folk; every January 1 they follow tradition and run into the frigid waters off L Street Beach for a quick dip. Southie is also famously where Whitey Bulger held court over the Irish mob during the 1980s and early 1990s.

 Sights

Castle Island

HISTORIC SITE | FAMILY | Although it once was, Castle Island is no longer, well, an island. Today, this tip of South Boston is accessible by car and by foot from Day Boulevard. Castle Island's centerpiece is Fort Independence, built in 1801, although, there have been battlements onsite since 1644; it's open for free tours on summer weekends. Castle Island is a popular spot for South Boston residents to walk their dogs, jog or cycle, whether just around the island itself or the water-set Pleasure Bay Loop. There's also a nice playground for kids. If you get peckish, stop by Sullivan's (open February through November), a Castle Island institution for more than 60 years, for a hot dog and fries. Views of the harbor and its outlaying islands are expansive. ⊠ *2010 Day Blvd., South Boston*

☎ *617/727–5290* Ⓜ *Broadway (then catch Bus 9 or 11 going east).*

Edward M. Kennedy Institute for the United States Senate

COLLEGE | FAMILY | Located adjacent to the JFK Library and Museum, the Edward M. Kennedy Institute for the United States Senate offers another view of the workings of the U.S. government, this one through the lens of the Senate and one of its most influential members. Interactive exhibits take visitors through a day in the life of a senator, and the highlight is the stunning full-scale representation of the Senate Chamber. In addition, there's an exact reproduction of Senator Kennedy's office, complete with photos of his family, model ships, and letters from his mother. It's definitely worth planning to visit both Kennedy attractions. ⊠ *Columbia Point, 210 Morrissey Blvd., Dorchester* ☎ *617/740–7000* ⊕ *www. emkinstitute.org* 🎫 *$16* ⊗ *Closed Mon.* Ⓜ *JFK/UMass, then free shuttle bus every 20 min.*

★ John F. Kennedy Presidential Library & Museum

MUSEUM | The library-museum is both a center for serious scholarship and a focus for Boston's nostalgia for her native son. The stark, white, prowlike building (another modernist monument designed by I. M. Pei) at this Dorchester Bay–enclosed site pays homage to the life and presidency of John F. Kennedy, as well as to members of his family, including his wife, Jacqueline, and brother Robert. The library is the official repository of JFK's presidential papers and displays re-creations of his desk in the Oval Office and of the television studio in which he debated Richard M. Nixon in the 1960 election. Permanent exhibits focus on his life before politics, the 1960 Presidential election, the Peace Corps, and the U.S. space program. Two theaters show films about JFK's life. There's also a permanent display on the late Jacqueline Kennedy Onassis. The facility also includes a store

Built in 1801, Fort Independence is the centerpiece of Castle Island; it's open for free tours on summer weekends.

and a small café. ✉ *Columbia Point, Dorchester* ☎ *617/514–1600* 🌐 *www.jfklibrary.org* 🎫 *$14* [M] *JFK/UMass, then free shuttle bus every 20 min.*

🍴 Restaurants

★ Fox & the Knife Enoteca

$$$ | MODERN ITALIAN | James Beard Award–winning Best Chef Karen Akunowicz steps up with hearty, traditional Italian food (not to be confused with Italian-American) inspired by her time as a chef and pasta maker in Italy. Locals love it so much that in order to score a table, especially on the weekends, you have to book a reservation about a month or so out. **Known for:** award-winning chef; handmade pastas; aperitivo program. [$] *Average main: $25* ✉ *28 W. Broadway, South Boston* ☎ *617/766–8630* 🌐 *www.foxandtheknife.com* [M] *Broadway.*

Local 149

$$ | MODERN AMERICAN | FAMILY | Pop art murals decorate the interior of this former Irish pub, and while that's been the case for the last decade or so, Local 149 features an old, well polished wooden bar and a modern, pubby vibe. It's very much a neighborhood joint, albeit an upscale one, and Southie residents in a range of ages meet up here for large portions from the cheeseburger to the chorizo-crusted cod. **Known for:** neighborhood hangout; popular weekend brunch; mule cocktails. [$] *Average main: $18* ✉ *149 P St., South Boston* ☎ *617/269–0900* 🌐 *www.local149.com.*

Loco Taqueria & Oyster Bar

$ | MEXICAN | Make a reservation in advance to secure a table at this South Boston taqueria that's popular with folks in their 20s and 30s. Tacos make up a large portion of the menu, and boy are they good; you order singly, which means you can mix and match to try a few varieties. **Known for:** tasty tacos; extensive, expert tequila list; long waits, loud atmosphere. $ *Average main: $14* ✉ *412 W. Broadway, South Boston* ☎ *617/917–5626* 🌐 *www.locosouthboston.com.*

Moonshine 152

$$ | **FUSION** | Diners who appreciate flavor and spice will adore chef-owner Asia Mei's creative kitchen endeavors, which often mix up elements of American, Chinese, Mexican, Vietnamese, Thai, and Spanish cuisines. A lively local crowd comes for dinner and late-night dining (served until 1:30 am) to get their hands on such craveable dishes as buffalo fried cheese curds and fish tacos, but the menu does change frequently. **Known for:** craveable food served 'til the wee hours; unpretentious atmosphere; friendly service. $ *Average main: $22* ✉ *152 Dorchester Ave., South Boston* ☎ *617/752–4191* 🌐 *www.moonshine152.com* [M] *Broadway.*

Six \ West

$$$ | **MODERN AMERICAN** | Within South Boston's brand new Cambria hotel, Six \ West serves drinks and food for every meal of the day in a couple different on-site locations, including a lobby-level restaurant space, an outdoor patio, and a rooftop bar and lounge (open seasonally). On the chef-driven menu, select from upscale snacks and sandwiches with a global spin, meant to share; even breakfast goes above and beyond with housemade Pop Tarts, a variety of toasts, and unique plates. **Known for:** local chef-driven menu; spectacular rooftop dining space with skyline views; interesting craft cocktails. $ *Average main: $35* ✉ *6 W. Broadway, South Boston* ☎ *857/496–0245* 🌐 *www.sixwestbroad.com* [M] *Broadway.*

Coffee and Quick Bites

Joseph's Bakery

$ | **BAKERY** | **FAMILY** | If you're in the neighborhood and jonesing for Sicilian-style pizza, a fruit pie, or anything in between, make a stop at this Italian bakery. Two worlds collide in a tiny space: bagels, scali bread, turnovers and fig squares, cookies, 20 kinds of pie, and cupcakes on one side, hot foods like plated specials, pizza, and calzones on the other. **Known for:** Sicilian pizza; brewed flavored coffee; desserts. $ *Average main: $8* ✉ *258 K St., South Boston* ☎ *617/269–2186* 🌐 *www.josephsbakerysouthboston.com.*

Sullivan's

$ | **FAST FOOD** | **FAMILY** | Family-owned and established in 1951, this beach-style dairy bar serves fried seafood, hot dogs, hamburgers, and soft-serve ice cream at Castle Island every spring, summer, and fall. Don't expect frills or indoor seating—there is no need since its surroundings provides sloping lawns, picnic tables, benches, and beachy vistas for lunching. **Known for:** long lines but quick service; fried seafood, burgers, and hot dogs; great views. $ *Average main: $10* ✉ *2080 Day Blvd., South Boston* ☎ *617/268–5685* 🌐 *www.sullivanscastleisland.com* ⏲ *Closed in winter.*

Hotels

Cambria Hotel Boston

$$ | **HOTEL** | One of very few lodgings in South Boston outside of the Seaport District, this brand new hotel attracts a younger, trendy traveler with simple, but well appointed, guest rooms, a predilection for contemporary art, and snazzy dining and drinking options on-site, including a stellar seasonal roof deck. **Pros:** large, 24-hour fitness center; seasonal rooftop bar with spectacular views; easy walk to the South End, Back Bay, and Seaport District. **Cons:** no pets; no cribs, no extra

The 300-acre Belle Isle Marsh Reservation is all that remains of the salt marsh landscape that once covered Boston when the early settlers arrived.

beds available; far from most of Boston's universities. [$] *Rooms from: $250* ✉ *6 W. Broadway, South Boston* ☎ *617/752–6681* 🌐 *www.cambriaboston.com* 🛏 *159 rooms* 🍴 *No meals* [M] *Broadway.*

East Boston

A drive through the Callahan Tunnel and into East Boston shows off street after street of multifamily homes and commercial squares laden with restaurants and markets catering to its varied ethnic communities, primarily Italian, Asian, and Latino. But, in the last few years, this waterfront neighborhood—"Eastie" as it's called by longtime locals—has begun to undergo a renaissance as modern, luxury apartments pop up on Jeffries Point. Any visitor to Boston who arrives by plane has been to Eastie—it's home to Logan International Airport. We'll let you in on a secret: East Boston features absolutely amazing views of Boston Harbor and the downtown skyline.

👁 Sights

Belle Isle Marsh Reservation

NATIONAL/STATE PARK | This 300-acre patch of remaining wetland environment is indicative of the salt marsh landscape that covered Boston when early settlers arrived and which today has been filled in. As you walk or run Belle Isle's gravel paths, listen to the sound of the marsh's diverse bird community, which includes American Kestrel, Belted Kingfisher, Great Blue Heron, Northern Harrier and the Saltmarsh Sparrow. Boardwalks venture into the marsh for great viewing and photo opps. ✉ *1399 Bennington St., East Boston* ☎ *617/727–5350* 🌐 *www.mass.gov/locations/belle-isle-marsh-reservation* [M] *Suffolk Downs.*

Downeast Cider House

WINERY/DISTILLERY | You've got to really look for the garage doors that marks the entrance to this local taproom. Once you make it inside the industrial space, you can take an hour-long tour or just simply sample Downeast's fresh,

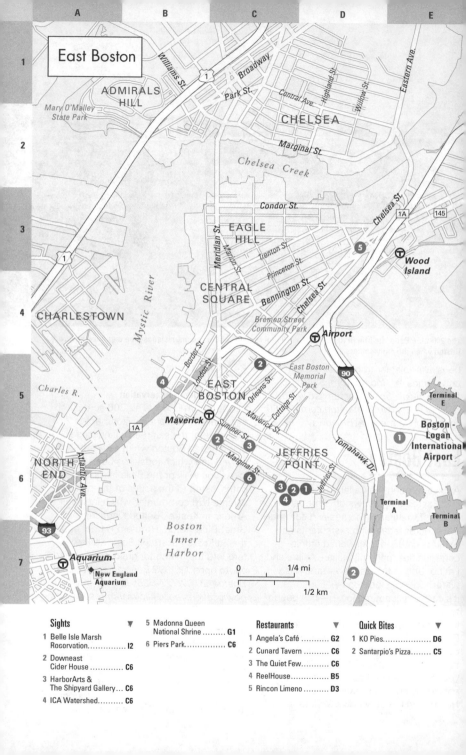

East Boston

A B C D E

1

ADMIRALS HILL

Mary O'Malley State Park

Williams St.

Broadway

Park St.

Central Ave.

Highland St.

Willow St.

Eastern Ave.

CHELSEA

2

Marginal St.

Chelsea Creek

3

Condor St.

EAGLE HILL

Meridian St.

Marion St.

Trenton St.

Princeton St.

Bennington St.

Chelsea St.

Chelsea St.

1A

145

Ⓣ **Wood Island**

Ⓢ **5**

CHARLESTOWN

4

CENTRAL SQUARE

Bremen Street Community Park

Ⓣ **Airport**

Mystic River

5

Charles R.

④

Border St.

London St.

EAST BOSTON

②

Orleans St.

Cottage St.

East Boston Memorial Park

90

Terminal E

1A

Ⓣ **Maverick**

Summer St.

Maverick St.

②

③

JEFFRIES POINT

Tomahawk Dr.

①

Boston-Logan International Airport

6

NORTH END

Atlantic Ave.

Marginal St.

⑥

③②①

④

Jeffries St.

Terminal A

Terminal B

93

7

Ⓣ **Aquarium**

▲ **New England Aquarium**

Boston Inner Harbor

②

0 ____ 1/4 mi

0 ____ 1/2 km

Sights ▼		Restaurants ▼	Quick Bites ▼
1 Belle Isle Marsh Rocervation........**I2**	5 Madonna Queen National Shrine.........**G1**	1 Angela's Café...........**G2**	1 KO Pies.................**D6**
2 Downeast Cider House.............**C6**	6 Piers Park.................**C6**	2 Cunard Tavern..........**C6**	2 Santarpio's Pizza........**C5**
3 HarborArts & The Shipyard Gallery... **C6**		3 The Quiet Few...........**C6**	
4 ICA Watershed..........**C6**		4 ReelHouse..............**B5**	
		5 Rincon Limeno..........**D3**	

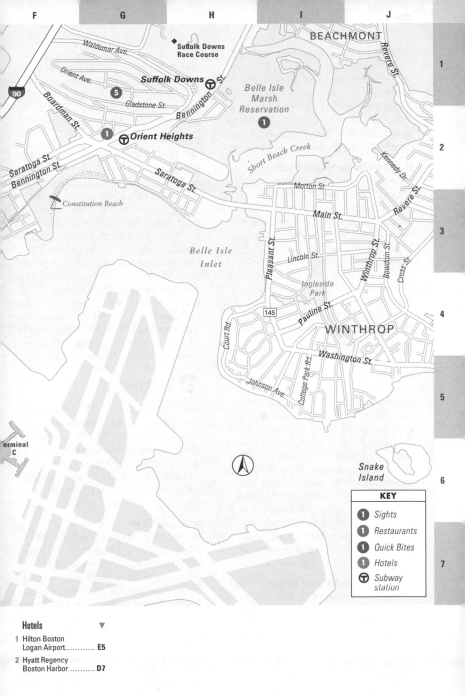

F   G   H   I   J

BEACHMONT

Waldemar Ave.

◆ Suffolk Downs
Race Course

Orient Ave.

90

Suffolk Downs Ⓣ St.

5

Gladstone St.

Boardman St.

Bennington St.

Belle Isle
Marsh
Reservation

1

Revere St.

1

1 Ⓣ **Orient Heights**

Saratoga St.
Bennington St.

Saratoga St.

Short Beach Creek

Kennedy Dr.

Constitution Beach

Morton St.

Main St.

Revere St.

*Belle Isle
Inlet*

Pleasant St.

Lincoln St.

Winthrop St.

Bowdoin St.

Cross St.

Ingleside
Park

145

Pauline St.

WINTHROP

Court Rd.

Washington St.

Johnson Ave.

College Park Rd.

**Terminal
C**

Snake
Island

KEY	
1	*Sights*
1	*Restaurants*
1	*Quick Bites*
1	*Hotels*
Ⓣ	*Subway station*

Hotels ▼

unfiltered cider varieties from its eight taps—many of which are only available at the cider house. You can bring the kiddos along to the taproom, but anyone under the age of 21 can not participate in a tour. ⊠ *256 Marginal St., East Boston* ☎ *857/301–8881* ⊕ *www.downeastcider. com* ⊗ *Closed Mon.–Wed.* Ⓜ *Maverick.*

HarborArts & the Shipyard Gallery

MARINA | Whimsical murals on cement barriers, colorful wooden chairs mounted on the outside wall of a commercial building, large-scale sculpture: together these pieces and more generate an arty feel in the industrial setting of East Boston's working shipyard. HarborArts curates a rotating collection of works by local and international artists across 14 acres, completely open to the public for perusal. ⊠ *256 Marginal St., East Boston* ☎ *617/982–3244* ⊕ *www.harborartsbos-ton.com* Ⓜ *Maverick.*

ICA Watershed

MUSEUM | FAMILY | The Institute of Contemporary Art/Boston's seasonal outpost first opened in 2018 after renovating a dilapidated former copper pipe facility in East Boston's working shipyard and marina. Every summer, a single artist makes the 15,000-square-foot space his or her own, installing large-scale, immersive artwork. A smaller gallery delves into the shipyard's history. ⊠ *256 Marginal St., East Boston* ⊕ *www.icaboston.org/ica-watershed* ⊗ *Closed Oct.–Apr.* ⌕ *Water shuttle transportation from Seaport museum to Watershed included with museum admission* Ⓜ *Maverick.*

Madonna Queen National Shrine

RELIGIOUS SITE | FAMILY | A 40-ish-foot golden and green statue of the Virgin Mary standing atop a globe dominates the Pope Paul VI Pilgrim Plaza that welcomes curious visitors and religious pilgrims to this Roman Catholic shrine that Cardinal Medeiros dedicated in 1978. From its perch in Orient Heights, the shrine also boasts some pretty spectacular views of Logan Airport and the downtown skyline.

Beneath the plaza, a sprawling sanctuary offers a quiet retreat and some holy relics are on display. Holy masses offered in English, Spanish, and Portuguese, weekly. ⊠ *150 Orient Ave., East Boston* ☎ *617/569–8792* Ⓜ *Orient Heights.*

Piers Park

CITY PARK | FAMILY | Sandwiched between Marginal Street and Boston Harbor, the gorgeous, landscaped, waterfront Piers Park features a grassy, green retreat from urban life and sweeping views of downtown Boston to the southwest. It is so named because of its many long piers that jut into the inner harbor. For a bit of historical knowledge: it's also in close proximity to the facility site where naval architect Donald McKay built his reputedly fast clipper ships. Take a stroll down the promenade and let the kiddos enjoy the large playground. ⊠ *95 Marginal St., East Boston* ☎ *617/561–6677* ⊕ *www.piersparksailing.org* Ⓜ *Maverick.*

🍴 Restaurants

Mirroring the makeup of its residents, East Boston's restaurant scene satisfies a variety of tastes, from the authentically ethnic to modern American. Foodies can dig into some of the city's best Latino and Italian fare, while closer to Eastie's coast, new, upscale restaurants serve up trendier, chef-driven options.

★ Angela's Café

$$ | MEXICAN | FAMILY | Colorful and airy, this East Boston Mexican restaurant reflects the culture of many living in the neighborhood, and its eponymous cook re-creates dishes from her native Puebla. Locals love it for its authenticity and extensive selection of small, snacky plates (mmm, queso fundido) and hearty main courses (chilaquiles, mole poblano). **Known for:** house-made guacamole; chicken and queso chilaquiles; brunch, particularly the brunch dish Central American, which features scrambled eggs, ham and avocado, cheese and sour cream, fried

plantains and corn tortillas. $ *Average main: $21* ⊠ *1012 Bennington St., East Boston* ☎ *617/874–8251* ⊕ *www.angelas-cafeboston.com* Ⓜ *Orient Heights.*

Cunard Tavern

$$ | **AMERICAN** | Luxury apartment rentals and modern condo developments are the latest thing to transform this once industrial stretch of the Boston Harbor waterfront. This gastropub, fittingly situated at the former site of Cunard S.S. **Known for:** notable brunch; seasonal roof deck with great views and a walk-up window bar; higher prices for what you get. $ *Average main: $24* ⊠ *24 Orleans St., East Boston* ☎ *617/567–7609* ⊕ *www.cunardtavern.com* Ⓜ *Maverick.*

The Quiet Few

$ | **AMERICAN** | One look at the neighborhood bar's menu will have you holding back belly laughs, even as it's grumbling with hunger, as it contains all things pickled and drenched in beer cheese, but plates are actually interesting and well thought-out and ingredients top-notch. Big spenders will appreciate two caviar (à la East Boston Oysters) and champagne combos. **Known for:** huge selection of whiskies, including flights and top-shelf, off-the-menu options; the Italian sausage meatballs, served over fried mozzarella; getting very crowded during peak hours. $ *Average main: $13* ⊠ *331 Sumner St., East Boston* ☎ *617/561–1061* ⊙ *www.thequietfew.com* Ⓜ *Maverick.*

ReelHouse

$$$ | **AMERICAN** | Modern, shiny, and bright, ReelHouse's dining room serves up waterfront views through large panel windows and fresh New England line-caught seafood prepared by award-winning chef Marc Orfaly. A number of plates are designed to be shared—and should be!—like the smoked trout toast and crispy calamari. **Known for:** awesome outdoor deck; seafood dishes; service can be iffy. $ *Average main: $26* ⊠ *The Eddy, 6 New St., Boston* ☎ *617/895–4075* ⊕ *www.reelhouseboston.com* Ⓜ *Maverick.*

Rincon Limeno

$$ | **PERUVIAN** | **FAMILY** | Authentic Peruvian food is beautifully presented in a wonderfully warm and inviting space. It is recommended to sip a much-talked-about pisco sour while perusing the menu, which includes traditionally prepared dishes, seafood and ceviche, and smaller plates called piqueo. **Known for:** lemony ceviche mixto; anticuchos, a Peruvian classic; long lines, so making a reservation is advised. $ *Average main: $23* ⊠ *409 Chelsea St., East Boston* ☎ *617/569–4942* ⊕ *www.rinconlimeno.com* Ⓜ *Wood Island.*

☕ Coffee and Quick Bites

KO Pies

$ | **AUSTRALIAN** | **FAMILY** | Picnic tables in a covered patio—or, in-season, a faux-grassy knoll overlooking the East Boston Shipyard and harbor—serve as seating for this Aussie-inspired beer garden and meat pie paradise. Order bevvies and food inside first—you'll smell the personal-sized pies baking whose flavors wrapped in shortcrust range from braised lamb shank, beef stew, and curried veggie to a monthly special. **Known for:** a real belly bomb aka the "pie floater"—a pie topped with mashed potatoes, mushy peas, and gravy; house-made lamingtons and anzac biscuits; a sweet and delicious key lime pie that is only made occasionally and isn't on the menu—you have to ask for it!. $ *Average main: $8* ⊠ *East Boston Shipyard & Marina, 256 Marginal St., East Boston* ☎ *617/418–5234* ⊕ *www.kocateringandpies.com* ⊙ *Closed Mon. and Tues.* Ⓜ *Maverick.*

Santarpio's Pizza

$ | **PIZZA** | **FAMILY** | This family-owned East Boston pizza joint started way back in 1903 and has been a local favorite ever since. The well-done and crispy, traditional style pies feature veggies, 'chovies, garlic, and meat; don't try to order a Hawaiian. **Known for:** wildly popular cheese, sausage and garlic topping combination; really long lines during peak hours; casual, no-frills atmosphere. ⓢ *Average main: $13* ✉ *111 Chelsea St., East Boston* ☎ *617/567–9871* ⊕ *www. santarpiospizza.com* ⊟ *No credit cards.*

Hotels

Hilton Boston Logan Airport

$$$ | HOTEL | FAMILY | Quiet rooms, competitive prices, and the only hotel actually connected to the airport make this newly renovated Hilton a good choice for in-and-out visitors to Boston. **Pros:** attached via skywalk to Logan terminals A and E; most rooms have great views of downtown Boston; free shuttle to subway or water taxi. **Cons:** standard check-in time is late, at 4 pm; not walking distance to attractions, restaurants, or shopping; not much to do in area. ⓢ *Rooms from: $350* ✉ *1 Hotel Dr., East Boston* ☎ *617/568–6700* ⊕ *www.bostonlogan.hilton.com* ⇗ *599 rooms* ⦿ *No meals* Ⓜ *Airport.*

Hyatt Regency Boston Harbor

$$ | HOTEL | FAMILY | Half the rooms at this hotel have sweeping views of either the city skyline or the ocean; the other half overlooks Logan Airport runways. **Pros:** close to airport; 24-hour airport shuttle; restaurant and bar on-site. **Cons:** late standard check-in, at 4 pm; fee for Wi-Fi; effort to get to downtown sights. ⓢ *Rooms from: $330* ✉ *101 Harborside Dr., East Boston* ☎ *617/568–1234, 800/233–1234* ⊕ *www.hyatt.com/en-US/ hotel/massachusetts/hyatt-regency-boston-harbor/bosha* ⇗ *270 rooms* ⦿ *No meals* Ⓜ *Airport.*

Chapter 11

CAMBRIDGE AND SOMERVILLE

Updated by
Cheryl Fenton

⊙ Sights	🍴 Restaurants	🛏 Hotels	🛍 Shopping	🍸 Nightlife
★★★★☆	★★★★★	★★☆☆☆	★★★★☆	★★★★★

NEIGHBORHOOD SNAPSHOT

TOP REASONS TO GO

■ **Take it all in:** Browse the new- and used-book stores, trawl the artsy boutiques, grab a cup of coffee, and people-watch in Harvard Square.

■ **Do the museum circuit:** The Harvard Art Museums; the Semitic Museum for ancient Near Eastern collections; the Peabody and the Natural History Museum for artifacts and culture; the MIT Museum.

■ **Be surprised with art at a tech university:** Visit MIT to wander its campus (full of hidden works of art), visit its museum, and see Pritzker Prize–winning architect Frank Gehry's Seuss-like Stata Center.

■ **Visit the country's first university:** Breathe the rarefied air of Harvard with an official tour (or an irreverent unofficial one) and a stroll around its famous "Yard."

■ **Walk the Charles River:** Follow Memorial Drive to spend some time along the famous river. The busy road is closed to traffic on Sunday from the last Sunday of April until the second Sunday of November.

GETTING HERE

Just minutes from Boston, Cambridge is easily reached by taking the Red Line train (otherwise known as the T) outbound to any stop past Charles/MGH station. There are stops at MIT (Kendall Square), Central Square, Harvard Square, Porter Square, Davis Square (actually in Somerville), and Alewife. Harvard Square is the best place to begin any visit to Cambridge, but driving (and parking) here is a small nightmare. Do yourself a favor and take the T. If you insist on driving, suck it up and park in a garage. (Street parking is usually limited to two hours, and most spots are permit only.) Driving is less of a pain in other parts of Cambridge, but you're still better off getting around via the T. Try to spend as much time as possible exploring on foot. This is a walking town, and you will want to spend more time exploring the sites than looking for a parking spot.

QUICK BITES

■ **Mr. Bartley's Burger Cottage.** Try this Harvard institution with a menu that includes dozens of riffs on the humble burger. ✉ *1246 Massachusetts Ave., Harvard Square* ⊕ *www.mrbartley.com* Ⓜ *Harvard.*

■ **Felipe's Taqueria.** A good bet for tasty Mexican food. ✉ *21 Brattle St., Brattle Street* ⊕ *www.felipestaqueria.com* Ⓜ *Harvard.*

■ **Toscanini's.** Known for their coffee and homemade ice cream. ✉ *159 1st St., Central Square* ⊕ *www.tosci.com* Ⓜ *Central.*

■ **Veggie Grill.** Popular with vegans and vegetarians for plant-based burgers, sandwiches, and bowls. ✉ *57 John F. Kennedy St., Harvard Square* ⊕ *www.veggiegrill.com* Ⓜ *Harvard.*

PLANNING YOUR TIME

■ Most visitors don't go beyond Harvard Square and Harvard Yard, but Cambridge is a one-of-a-kind city filled with funky restaurants, independent shops, unique art, historic sites, and lots of independent bookstores. If you plan to visit Harvard's natural history or art museums or explore other Cambridge neighborhoods like Kendall, Inman and Central Squares, give yourself a day or two.

Boston's Left Bank—an uber-liberal academic enclave—is a must-visit if you're spending more than a day or two in the Boston area. Cambridge is packed with world-class cultural institutions, quirky shops, restaurants galore, and tons of people-watching.

The city is punctuated at one end by the funky architecture of MIT and at the other by the grand academic fortress that is Harvard University. Civic life connects the two camps into an urban stew of 100,000 residents who represent nearly every nationality in the world, work at every kind of job from tenured professor to Uber driver, and are passionate about living on this side of the river.

The Charles River is the Cantabrigians' backyard, and there's virtually no place in Cambridge more than a 10-minute walk from its banks. Strolling, running, rollerblading, or biking is one of the great pleasures of Cambridge, and your views will include graceful bridges, the distant Boston skyline, crew teams rowing through the calm water (possibly training for October's annual Head of the Charles, the largest two-day regatta in the world), and the elegant spires of Harvard soaring into the sky.

No visit to Cambridge is complete without an afternoon (at least) in Harvard Square. It's a hub, a hot spot, and home to every variation of the human condition: Nobel laureates, homeless buskers, trust-fund babies, and working-class Joes. Farther along Massachusetts Avenue is Central Square, an ethnic melting pot of people and restaurants. Ten minutes more bring you to MIT, with

its eclectic architecture from postwar pedestrian to Frank Gehry's futuristic fantasyland. In addition to providing a stellar view, the Massachusetts Avenue Bridge, spanning the Charles from Cambridge to Boston, is also notorious in MIT lore for its Smoot measurements.

Planning

Visitor Information

CONTACTS Cambridge Visitor Information Booth. ⊠ *Harvard Sq., , near MBTA station entrance, Harvard Square* ☎ *617/497–1630* ⊕ *www.cambridgeusa. org* Ⓜ *Harvard.*

Cambridge

Harvard Square

In Cambridge all streets point toward Harvard Square. In addition to being the gateway to Harvard University and its various attractions, Harvard Square is home to the tiny yet venerable folk-music venue Club Passim (Bob Dylan played here, and Bonnie Raitt was a regular during her time at Harvard), first-run and

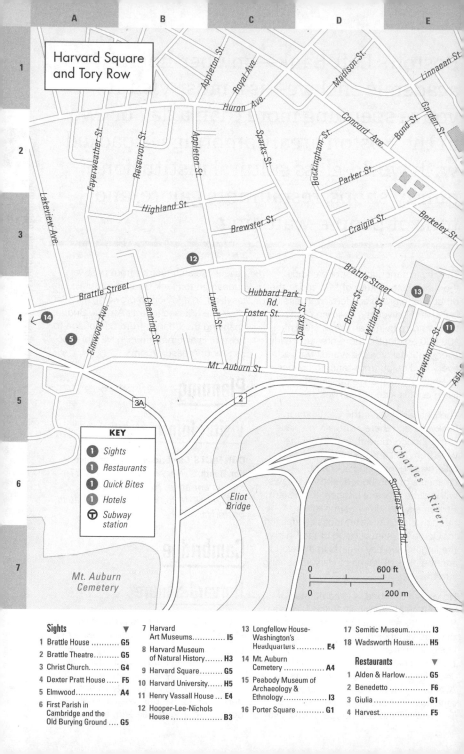

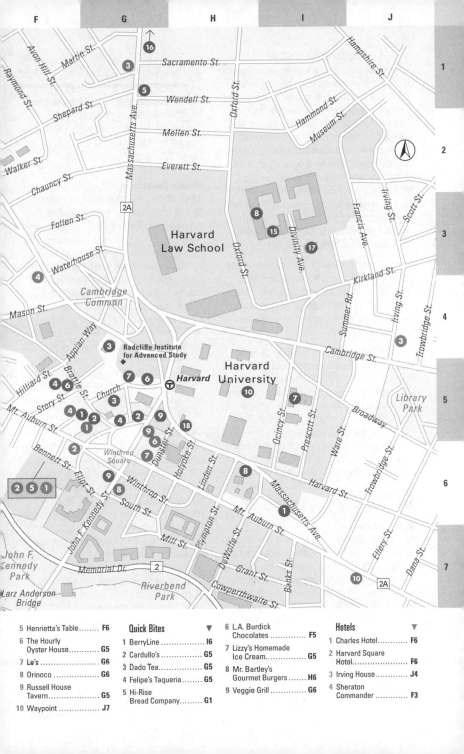

5 Henrietta's Table **F6**	**Quick Bites** ▼	6 L.A. Burdick Chocolates **F5**	**Hotels** ▼
6 The Hourly Oyster House **G5**	1 BerryLine **I6**	7 Lizzy's Homemade Ice Cream **G5**	1 Charles Hotel **F6**
7 Le's **G6**	2 Cardullo's **G5**	8 Mr. Bartley's Gourmet Burgers **H6**	2 Harvard Square Hotel **F6**
8 Orinoco **G6**	3 Dado Tea **G5**	9 Veggie Grill **G6**	3 Irving House **J4**
9 Russell House Tavern **G5**	4 Felipe's Taqueria **G5**		4 Sheraton Commander **F3**
10 Waypoint **J7**	5 Hi-Rise Bread Company **G1**		

vintage movie theaters, concert and lecture venues, and a tempting collection of eclectic, independent shops. Harvard Square is a multicultural microcosm. On a warm day street musicians coax exotic tones from their Andean pan flutes and *erhus*, Chinese stringed instruments, while cranks and local pessimists pass out pamphlets warning against all sorts of end-of-the-world scenarios. In the small plaza atop the main entrance to the Harvard T station known as "the Pit," you'll find students and activists gathering alongside artists selling their work. It's a wonderful circus of humanity.

Porter Square is about a mile northwest of Harvard Square. The area consists of several blocks along Mass Ave. that has shopping and restaurants including Cambridge's Little Japan in the Porter Exchange building.

Harvard Square's Brattle Street, a long stretch that begins in center of Harvard Square, is where you'll find several shops and eateries as you make your way down away from the Square. Follow it for the short walk to its legacy—historical Tory Row—the nickname given by purist Cantabrigians to the part of Brattle Street where many Loyalists had mansions at the time of the Revolutionary War.

Sights

Brattle House

HOUSE | This charming yellow 18th-century, gambrel-roof Colonial once belonged to the Loyalist William Brattle. He moved to Boston in 1774 to escape the patriots' anger, then left in 1776 with the British troops. From 1831 to 1833 the house was the residence of Margaret Fuller, feminist author and editor of *The Dial*. Today it's the office of the Cambridge Center for Adult Education, and is listed on the National Register of Historic Places. ✉ *42 Brattle St., Brattle Street* ☎ *617/547–6789* ⊕ *www.ccae.org* Ⓜ *Harvard*.

Mobile Tour

The Cambridge Office for Tourism offers a walking tour for your mobile device on its website ⊕ *www.cambridge-usa.org*.

Brattle Theatre

ARTS VENUE | For the last half century, the Brattle Theatre has served as the square's independent movie house, screening indie, foreign, obscure, and classic films, from nouveau to noir. Occupying a squat, barnlike building from 1890, it is set improbably between a modern shopping center and a colonial mansion. The resident repertory company gained notoriety in the 1950s when it made a practice of hiring actors blacklisted as Communists by the U.S. government. Check the website for current offerings and events. ✉ *40 Brattle St., Brattle Street* ☎ *617/876-6837* ⊕ *www.brattlefilm.org* ▨ *Tickets from $9* Ⓜ *Harvard*.

Christ Church

RELIGIOUS SITE | This modest yet beautiful gray clapboard structure was designed in 1761 by Peter Harrison, the first architect of note in the colonies (he designed King's Chapel). During the Revolution, members of its mostly Tory congregation fled for their lives. The organ was melted down for bullets and the building was used as a barracks during the Siege of Boston. (Step into the vestibule to look for the bullet hole left during the skirmish.) Today, the organ facade takes inspiration from the original 1762 gallery organ. Martha Washington requested that the church reopen for services on New Year's Eve in 1775. The church's historical significance extends to the 20th century: Teddy Roosevelt was a Sunday-school teacher here (and famously fired because he remained Dutch Reformed rather than becoming an Episcopalian), and Martin

Luther King Jr. spoke from the pulpit to announce his opposition to the Vietnam War. ✉ *0 Garden St., Harvard Square* ☎ *617/876–0200* ⊕ *www.cccambridge. org* Ⓜ *Harvard.*

First Parish in Cambridge and the Old Burying Ground

RELIGIOUS SITE | Next to the imposing church on the corner of Church Street and Mass Ave. lies the spooky-looking colonial Old Burying Ground. Known as the most historic cemetery in Cambridge, it was established around 1635 and houses 17th- and 18th-century tombstones of ministers, Continental Congressmen, authors, early Harvard presidents, and Revolutionary War soldiers. The wooden Gothic Revival church, known locally as "First Church" or "First Parish," was built in 1833 by Isaiah Rogers. The congregation dates to two centuries earlier, and has been linked to Harvard since the founding of the college. ✉ *3 Church St., Harvard Square* ☎ *617/876–7772* ⊕ *www. firstparishcambridge.org* Ⓜ *Harvard.*

★ Harvard Art Museums

MUSEUM | This is Harvard University's oldest museum and, in late 2014, it became the combined collections of the Busch-Reisinger, Fogg, and Arthur M. Sackler museums. All three were united under one glorious, mostly glass roof, under the umbrella name Harvard Art Museums. Housed in a facility designed by award-winning architect Renzo Piano, the 204,000-square-foot museum is spread over seven levels, allowing more of Harvard's 250,000-piece art collection, featuring European and American art from the Middle Ages to the present day, to be seen in one place. Highlights include American and European paintings, sculptures, and decorative arts from the Fogg Museum; Asian art, Buddhist cave-temple sculptures, and Chinese bronzes in the Arthur M. Sackler; and works by German expressionists, materials related to the Bauhaus, and postwar contemporary art from German-speaking

Europe from the Busch-Reisinger Museum. In addition to the gallery spaces, there's a 300-seat theater, Jenny's café, a museum shop, the Calderwood Courtyard, plus conservation and research labs. ✉ *32 Quincy St., Harvard Square* ☎ *617/495–9400* ⊕ *www.harvardartmuseums.org* 🎟 *$20* Ⓜ *Harvard.*

★ Harvard Museum of Natural History

MUSEUM | **FAMILY** | The Harvard Museum of Natural History (which exhibits specimens from the Museum of Comparative Zoology, Harvard University Herbaria, and the Mineralogical and Geological Museum) reminds us nature is the original masterpiece. Cases are packed with zoological specimens, from tiny hummingbirds and deer mice to rare Indian rhinoceros and one of the largest Amazon pirarucu ever caught. View fossils and skeletons alongside marvelous minerals, including a 1,600-pound amethyst geode. Harvard's world-famous Blaschka "Glass Flowers" is a creative approach to flora, with more than 4,300 hand-blown glass plant models. The museum combines historic exhibits drawn from the university's vast collections with new and changing multimedia exhibitions such as *New England Forests and Mollusks: Shelled Masters of the Marine Realm,* and the renovated Earth & Planetary Sciences gallery. ✉ *26 Oxford St., Harvard Square* ☎ *617/495–3045* ⊕ *www.hmnh.harvard.edu* 🎟 *$15; ticket includes admission to adjacent Peabody Museum* Ⓜ *Harvard.*

★ Harvard Square

PLAZA | **FAMILY** | Tides of students, tourists, and politically charged proponents are all part of the nonstop pedestrian flow at this most celebrated of Cambridge crossroads. Harvard Square is where Massachusetts Avenue, coming from Boston, turns and widens into a triangle broad enough to accommodate a brick peninsula (above the T station). The restored 1928 kiosk in the center of the square once served as the entrance

to the MBTA station, and is now home to lively street musicians and artists selling their paintings and photos on blankets. Harvard Yard, with its lecture halls, residential houses, libraries, and museums, is one long border of the square; the other three are composed of clusters of banks, retailers, and restaurants.

Time in the Square raises people-watching to a high art form. On an average afternoon you'll hear earnest conversations in dozens of foreign languages; see every kind of youthful uniform from slouchy sweats to impeccable prep; wander by street musicians playing guitars and flutes; and wonder at how students reading text books out in the sunshine can get any work done among the commotion.

The historic buildings are worth noting. It's a thrill to walk though the big brick-and-wrought-iron gates to Harvard Yard on up to Widener Library, the University's flagship library. More than 50 miles of bookshelves snake around this imposing neoclassical structure, designed by one of the nation's first major African American architects, Julian Abele. It holds more than 3.5 million volumes in 450 languages, but is unfortunately not open to the public.

Across Garden Street, through an ornamental arch, is **Cambridge Common,** decreed a public pasture in 1631. It's said that under a large tree that once stood in this meadow George Washington took command of the Continental Army on July 3, 1775. A stone memorial now marks the site of the "Washington Elm." Also on the Common is the Irish Famine Memorial by Derry artist Maurice Harron, unveiled in 1997 to coincide with the 150th anniversary of "Black '47," the deadliest year of the potato famine. At the center of the Common a large memorial commemorates the Union soldiers who lost their lives in the Civil War. On the far side of the Common is a fantastic park and newly renovated playground. ⊠ *Harvard Square* ⊕ *www. harvardsquare.com* Ⓜ *Harvard.*

Harvard University

COLLEGE | The tree-studded, shady, and redbrick expanse of **Harvard Yard**—the very center of Harvard University—has weathered the footsteps of Harvard students for hundreds of years. In 1636 the Great and General Court of the Massachusetts Bay Colony voted funds to establish the colony's first college, and a year later chose Cambridge as the site. Named in 1639 for John Harvard, a young Charlestown clergyman who died in 1638 and left the college his entire library and half his estate, Harvard remained the only college in the New World until 1693, by which time it was firmly established as a respected center of learning. Local wags refer to Harvard as WGU—World's Greatest University—and it's certainly the oldest and most famous American university.

Although the college dates from the 17th century, the oldest buildings in Harvard Yard are from the 18th century (though you'll sometimes see archaeologists digging here for evidence of older structures). Together the buildings chronicle American architecture from the Colonial era to the present. **Holden Chapel,** completed in 1744, is a Georgian gem. The graceful **University Hall** was designed in 1815 by Charles Bulfinch. An 1884 statue of John Harvard by Daniel Chester French stands outside; ironically for a school with the motto of "Veritas" ("Truth"), the model for the statue was a member of the class of 1882 and not Harvard himself. **Sever Hall,** completed in 1880 and designed by Henry Hobson Richardson, represents the Romanesque revival that was followed by the neoclassical (note the pillared facade of Widener Library) and the neo-Georgian, represented by the sumptuous brick houses along the Charles River, many of which are now undergraduate residences. **Memorial Church,** a graceful steepled edifice of modified Colonial Revival design, was dedicated in 1932. Just north of the Yard is **Memorial Hall,** completed in 1878 as a memorial to Harvard men who died in the Union cause; it's High Victorian both inside and out. It also contains the 1,166-seat Sanders Theatre, which serves as the university's largest lecture hall, site of year-round concerts by students and professionals, and the venue for the festive Christmas Revels.

Many of Harvard's cultural and scholarly facilities are important sights in themselves, but most campus buildings, other than museums and concert halls, are off-limits to the general public.

The **Harvard Information Center,** in the Smith Campus Centre, has a small exhibit space, distributes maps of the university area, and offers free student-led tours of Harvard Yard. The tour doesn't include visits to museums, and it doesn't take you into campus buildings, but it provides a fine orientation. The information center is open year-round (except during spring recess and other semester breaks). From the end of June through August, guides offer tours every half hour; however, it's best to call ahead to confirm times. You can also download a mobile tour on your smart phone. ⊠ *Bounded by Massachusetts Ave. and Mt. Auburn, Holyoke, and Dunster Sts., 1350 Massachusetts Ave., Harvard Square* ☎ *617/495–1573 Information Center* ⊕ *www.harvard.edu* Ⓜ *Harvard.*

Peabody Museum of Archaeology & Ethnology

MUSEUM | With one of the world's outstanding anthropological collections, the Peabody Museum is among the oldest anthropology museums in the world. Its collections focus on Native American and Central and South American cultures and are comprised of more than 1.2 million objects. The Hall of the North American Indian is particularly outstanding, with art, textiles, and models of traditional dwellings from across the continent. The Mesoamerican room juxtaposes ancient relief carvings and weavings with contemporary works from the Maya and other peoples. Of special note is the museum's only surviving collection of objects acquired from Native American people during the Lewis and Clark expedition. ⊠ *11 Divinity Ave., Harvard Square* ☎ *617/496–1027* ⊕ *www.peabody.harvard.edu* ⊠ *$15, includes admission to the adjacent Harvard Museum of Natural History* Ⓜ *Harvard.*

Porter Square

NEIGHBORHOOD | FAMILY | About a mile northwest of Harvard Square lies Porter Square, an area that consists of several blocks along Mass Ave. that boast shopping centers and eateries. Within the nearby Porter Exchange building, you'll discover Cambridge's Little Japan, a hidden enclave of vendors selling noodles, baked goods, bubble tea, sushi, and gift items (mostly cash only). As you walk north (away from Harvard) past the heart of Porter Square, you'll find pretty much every ethnic eatery imaginable, many of them excellent and far cheaper than Harvard Square restaurants. There are also quite a few unique shops along the way, including thrift shops and music stores. ⊠ *Porter Square* ⊹ *The Porter Square T stop is on Red Line.*

Semitic Museum

MUSEUM | An almost unknown gem, this Harvard institution serves as an exhibit space for Egyptian, Mesopotamian, and ancient Near East artifacts and as a center for archaeological exploration. The museum's extensive temporary collections rotate, while more permanent exhibits include life-sized casts of famous Mesopotamian monuments, authentic mummy coffins, and tablets containing the earliest forms of writing. Free lectures are held weekly, and the building also houses the Department of Near Eastern Languages and Civilization. ⊠ *6 Divinity Ave., Harvard Square* ☎ *617/495–4631* ⊕ *www.semiticmuseum.fas.harvard.edu/* ⊠ *Free; donations appreciated* ⊙ *Closed Sat.* Ⓜ *Harvard.*

Wadsworth House

HOUSE | On the Harvard University side of Harvard Square stands the Wadsworth House, a yellow clapboard structure built in 1726 as a home for Harvard presidents. It served as the first Massachusetts headquarters for George Washington, who arrived on July 2, 1775, just a day before he took command of the Continental Army. The building traded presidents in for students (such as Ralph Waldo Emerson) and visiting preachers as its boarders, and today, it houses Harvard's general offices. ⊠ *1341 Massachusetts Ave., Harvard Square* ⊕ *www.harvard.edu* ⊗ *Closed to the public.* Ⓜ *Harvard.*

Restaurants

Alden & Harlow

$$$ | **MODERN AMERICAN** | This boisterous subterranean restaurant with a 30-seat bar and industrial-chic design specializes in rustic, seasonal snacks and small plates layered with flavor. Whether it's brunch or dinner, start with an expertly made cocktail before you dig into a menu that includes little dishes like clams with smoked pig's tail; chicken-fried local rabbit; and pickled corn pancakes. **Known for:** flavor-packed sharing plates; terrific cocktails; boisterous feel. Ⓢ *Average main: $28* ⊠ *40 Brattle St., Harvard Square* ☎ *617/864–2100* ⊕ *www.aldenharlow.com* ⊗ *No lunch* Ⓜ *Harvard.*

★ Benedetto

$$$ | **ITALIAN** | Chef Michael Pagliarini, whose devoted fan base will wait hours for his mouthwatering pastas and Italian food at Giulia up the street, is turning out an even more ambitious menu of seasonal Italian small bites, silky pastas, and mains. Start with a cocktail and some chicken liver mousse crostini and grilled octopus while you figure out whether to get the Ossabaw Island pork tortellini or the pappardelle with foraged mushrooms before your entrée of skate wing with brown butter or the Rohan duck over lentils. **Known for:** masterful Italian cooking; elegant airy setting; incredible pastas. Ⓢ *Average main: $33* ⊠ *The Charles Hotel, 1 Bennett St., Harvard Square* ☎ *617/661–5050* ⊕ *www.benedettocambridge.com* ⊗ *No lunch.*

★ Giulia

$$$ | **ITALIAN** | With exposed brick walls and soft lighting, the heart and soul of this charming Italian restaurant is its communal pasta table at which Chef Michael Pagliarini spends hours hand-rolling superlative pastas for dishes like buckwheat pizzoccheri and pasta *alla bolognese*. Plates such as house-made lamb sausage, octopus and smoked squid, and Sardinian flatbread are original, generous, and, of course delicious. Known for its romantic nature, it's the perfect place for lovers to linger over a chocolate terrine and a cappuccino. **Known for:** excellent Italian food; silky pastas; warm, softly lit space. Ⓢ *Average main: $30* ⊠ *1682 Massachusetts Ave., Harvard Square* ☎ *617/441–2800* ⊕ *www.giuliarestaurant.com* ⊗ *Closed Sun.*

★ Harvest

$$$ | **AMERICAN** | Once a favorite of former Cambridge resident Julia Child, this sophisticated shrine to New England cuisine has been a perennial go-to spot for Harvard students when their parents are in town for more than 45 years. The seasonal menu could feature Cape scallop crudo, fresh pasta with braised veal and pesto, or fresh Cape lobster with lemon hollandaise. **Known for:** elegant New England cuisine; expansive wine list; pretty patio dining area. Ⓢ *Average main: $34* ⊠ *44 Brattle St., on walkway, Brattle Street* ☎ *617/868–2255* ⊕ *harvestcambridge.com* Ⓜ *Harvard.*

Henrietta's Table

$$$ | **AMERICAN** | Located in The Charles Hotel, this cheerful, country-style restaurant is named after chef-owner Peter Davis's pet pig, Henrietta. Davis is passionate about working with small area growers and purveyors, as well as harvesting veggies and honey from the restaurant's rooftop garden and hives, which is evident in his fresh, honest, wholesome, New England–style dishes, like juicy Yankee pot roast, cracker crusted scrod, and creamy Maine crab-corn chowder. **Known for:** farm-fresh comfort food; inviting, sunny setting; New England farm-sourced ingredients. [$] *Average main: $29* ✉ *1 Bennett St., Harvard Square* ☎ *617/661–5005* 🌐 *www.henriettastable.com* [M] *Harvard.*

The Hourly Oyster House

$$$ | SEAFOOD | This dimly lit, nautically inspired spot pays homage to the ocean in not only decor but tasty fare. Against a backdrop of sailing ships and vessels, antiqued mirrors, and chandelier bubble-like bulbs, day-time appetites fill up on beer-battered fish-and-chips, po'boys, and lobster rolls, while the dinner crowd enjoys entrées like red curried mussels, Carolina trout meunière, seared salmon, and an oyster bar that features dozens of the bivalve beauties, as well as a massive chilled grand seafood tower. **Known for:** cozy atmosphere; chilled seafood tower; quick bar dining. [$] *Average main: $28* ✉ *15 Dunster St., Harvard Square* ☎ *617/765–2342* 🌐 *www.thehourlycambridge.com* [M] *Harvard.*

Le's

$ | VIETNAMESE | FAMILY | Vietnamese noodle soup called *pho* is the name of the game in this quick and casual eatery (it's set inside the Garage, a small mall in Harvard Square); at less than $10, it's a meal unto itself with chicken, shrimp, or beef, steaming hot in a big bowl. Fresh salads, rice plates, steamed vermicelli, seafood entrees, and stir-fries are offered as well as crispy spring rolls, summer rolls, and Chinese chicken wings. **Known for:** terrific Vietnamese; low prices; fast service. [$] *Average main: $9* ✉ *35 Dunster St., Harvard Square* ☎ *617/864–4100* 🌐 *lesrestaurantcambridge.cafecityguide.website/* [M] *Harvard.*

★ Orinoco

$$ | LATIN AMERICAN | Don't miss this red clapboard, Pan-Latin American restaurant located down an alleyway in Harvard Square. Owner Andres Banger's dream to bring bountiful plates of superfresh family fare from his home country of Venezuela to Cambridge (as well as Brookline Village and the South End) rewards diners with delectable, palm-sized *arepas,* or crispy, hot, corn-flour pockets stuffed with beans, cheese, chicken, or pork; *pabellon criollo,* moist shredded beef with stewed beans, rice, and plantains; and red chili adobo–marinated, charred *pollo* (chicken). **Known for:** Venezuelan specialties; generous portions; great value. [$] *Average main: $18* ✉ *56 JFK St., Harvard Square* ☎ *617/354–6900* 🌐 *www.orinocokitchen.com* ⏲ *Closed Mon.*

Russell House Tavern

$$ | AMERICAN | The seasonally inspired menu at this New American tavern brings American classics to the table, featuring signatures like the R. House burger (with cheddar, bacon, and caramelized onions on an English muffin), a selection of tavern pizzas, and steak frites. **Known for:** New England classics; lively Saturday night scene; small brick patio. [$] *Average main: $20* ✉ *14 JFK St., Harvard Square* ☎ *617/500–3055* 🌐 *www.russellhousecambridge.com* [M] *Harvard.*

Waypoint

$$$$ | SEAFOOD | Chef-owner Michael Scelfo looked seaward to inform the menu of his second venture after Alden & Harlow. Named aptly for a plot on a map, Waypoint is his step forward on the path to coastal-inspired fare that includes an excellent raw bar with crudos, bivalves, and the celebrated caviar served with doughnut holes, along with whole-fish roasts, slow-roasted meats, indulgent seafood pasta dishes, and inventive pizzas. **Known for:** lusty seafood-rich fare; hip, happening vibe; extensive absinthe offerings. [$] *Average*

main: $36 ⊠ 1030 Massachusetts
Ave., Harvard Square ☎ 617/864–2300
⊕ www.waypointharvard.com.

☕ Coffee and Quick Bites

BerryLine
$ | CAFÉ | Two postdoctoral-fellowship
students founded this two-location tasty
oasis that serves superlative soft frozen
yogurt made from milk, cane sugar,
fresh fruit, and other natural ingredients.
The shop has featured well over 150
frozen yogurt flavors like rose, chocolate
coconut, passion fruit, and green tea,
and dedicated staff bakers create many
of the homemade toppings including
the cheesecake chunks, chewy mochi
bits, brownie bites, and honey-nut
granola. **Known for:** award-winning fro yo;
homemade bakery toppings; fresh fruit
add-ons. $ Average main: $3 ⊠ 3 Arrow
St., Harvard Square ☎ 617/868–3500
⊕ www.berryline.com.

Cardullo's
$ | DELI | This snug, nearly 70-year-old
shop (family-owned-and-operated up
until a few years ago) in Harvard Square
purveys exotic imports, including cheeses, chocolates, biscuits, jams, olive oils,
and mustards, along with sandwiches,
cheeses and charcuterie to go. You'll also
find a generous assortment of cham-
pagnes and domestic caviar, fine wines,
and assorted beers. **Known for:** New
England goods; made-to-order sandwiches and charcuterie; international gourmet
sweet shop. $ Average main: ⊠ 6 Brattle
St., Harvard Square ☎ 617/491–8888,
800/491–8288 ⊕ www.cardullos.com
⊘ No dinner Ⓜ Harvard.

Dado Tea
$ | CAFÉ | FAMILY | Named after the art of
the tea ceremony, the new-age feel to
this shop starts with organic teas and
coffee (displayed in canisters behind
the counter) and extends to hearty meal
options such as hot noodle soups, cold
noodle salads, multigrain and gluten-free

wraps, vegan dishes, baked goods, and
smoothies. Linger over free Wi-Fi. **Known
for:** loose leaf organic teas; noodle bowls;
bubble teas. $ Average main: $7 ⊠ 50
Church St., Harvard Square ☎ 617/547–
0950 ⊕ www.dadotea.com Ⓜ Harvard.

Felipe's Taqueria
$ | MEXICAN | Cafés abound on Brattle
Street, but Felipe's is a good bet for fresh
ingredients and authentic recipes that
build out a quick hit menu of Mexican
grab-and-go dishes. Start off with their
queso fundido or guac, then fill up on
heaping Super Burritos, baha-style tacos,
and chimichangas. **Known for:** tacos;
cheap eats; super burritos. $ Average
main: $8 ⊠ 21 Brattle St., Brattle Street
☎ 617/354–9944 ⊕ www.felipestaqueria.
com.

Hi-Rise Bread Company
$ | AMERICAN | Step into Hi-Rise for
sweets or a gourmet sandwich made
on freshly baked breads created from
exclusively organic whole wheat, rye,
and white flours and corn from small
and independent mills. Try the Fern's
Problem Solver with roasted turkey,
Monterey Jack, avocado, and Russian
dressing on grilled sourdough bread, or
Kate's Rough Ride with avocado, tomato,
coleslaw, cucumber, red leaf lettuce,
Russian dressing on whole grain. **Known
for:** apple pie; fresh bread; unique sandwiches. $ Average main: $13 ⊠ 1663
Massachusetts Ave., Harvard Square
☎ 617/492–3003 ⊕ www.hi-risebread.
com Ⓜ Harvard.

L.A. Burdick Chocolates
$ | AMERICAN | This charming artisanal
chocolatier is a staple for locals and
tourists alike, who come for its famously adorable signature chocolate mice,
chocolate bonbons, and chocolate bars.
The elegant, life-changing hot cocoa
may be just the thing to restore flagging
spirits or weary feet with variations on
the classic milk chocolate, including
dark, spicy, and white. **Known for:** dreamy
drinking chocolate; chocolate milk and

244

penguins; cozy atmosphere. $ *Average main: $10* ✉ *52 Brattle St., Brattle Street* ☎ *617/491–4340* ⊕ *www.burdickchocolate.com* Ⓜ *Harvard.*

Lizzy's Homemade Ice Cream

$ | **CAFÉ** | Barely bigger than a shoebox, this Harvard Square take-out parlor offers more than 50 fabulous flavor options like orange-pineapple and Charles River Crunch (a dark-chocolate ice cream with almond toffee nuggets), along with a small selection of frozen yogurts, Tofutti, "lite" ice creams, and sorbet, plus soda fountain favorites including frappes and sundaes. Adult-only flavors include Bailey's and Rum Raisin, and for those looking for just "a tiny taste," the mini-cone, topped with a golf ball–size scoop, hits the spot. **Known for:** homemade ice cream; take out service; Tofutti dairy-free treats. $ *Average main: $5* ✉ *29 Church St., Harvard Square* ☎ *617/354–2911* ⊕ *www.lizzysicecream.com.*

Mr. Bartley's Gourmet Burgers

$ | **AMERICAN** | **FAMILY** | It may be perfect cuisine for the student metabolism: a huge variety of variously garnished thick burgers with sassy names (many of them celebrities), deliciously crispy regular and sweet-potato fries, award-winning onion rings, and toppings like an egg or mac n' cheese. There's also a competent veggie burger, along with comforting dinner fare like baked meat loaf, fried chicken, and franks and beans. **Known for:** creative burgers; thick frappes; loud atmosphere. $ *Average main: $15* ✉ *1246 Massachusetts Ave., Harvard Square* ☎ *617/354–6559* ⊕ *www.mrbartley.com* ☾ *Closed Sun. and Mon.* Ⓜ *Harvard.*

Veggie Grill

$ | **VEGETARIAN** | This California-based fast chain makes living that plant-based life a little easier. The extensive meat-free menu features burgers, sandwiches, bowls, entrée salads, tacos, burritos, and desserts that are all free of meat, dairy, eggs and other animal products, so you can fill up on tasty meals without sacrificing your dietary restrictions. **Known for:** Beyond Burgers, Tacos and Burritos; vegan menu; heaping bowls. $ *Average main: $10* ✉ *57 John F. Kennedy St., Harvard Square* ☎ *617/430–4004* ⊕ *www.veggiegrill.com* Ⓜ *Harvard.*

Hotels

★ Charles Hotel

$$$ | **HOTEL** | **FAMILY** | It used to be that the Charles was *the* place to stay in Cambridge, and while other luxury hotels have since arrived to give it a little healthy competition, this Harvard Square staple is standing strong. **Pros:** two blocks from the T Red Line to Boston; on-site jazz club and hip Noir bar; on-site 4,000-square-foot Corbu Spa & Salon. **Cons:** luxury comes at a price; restricted pool hours for children; coffee pots and tea kettles are available by request only. $ *Rooms from: $399* ✉ *1 Bennett St., Harvard Square* ☎ *617/864–1200, 800/882–1818* ⊕ *www.charleshotel.com* ⇤ *295 rooms* ❀ *No meals* Ⓜ *Harvard.*

Harvard Square Hotel

$ | **HOTEL** | If you don't feel like shelling out a week's salary to stay at the venerable Charles, check in to the next-door Harvard Square Hotel, where you'll get the location and convenience for half the cost. **Pros:** awesome location; all guest room windows open; complimentary Wi-Fi, tea, and coffee in the lobby café. **Cons:** parking costs extra; no gym; no restaurant. $ *Rooms from: $189* ✉ *110 Mt. Auburn St., Harvard Square* ☎ *617/864–5200, 800/458–5886* ⊕ *www.harvardsquarehotel.com* ⇤ *73 rooms* ❀ *No meals* Ⓜ *Harvard.*

Irving House

$ | **B&B/INN** | On a residential street three blocks from Harvard Square, this four-story gray clapboard guest house is a bargain. **Pros:** free Wi-Fi; good location and price; coffee, tea, and pastries are available until 10 pm. **Cons:** small parking lot is first come, first served; some rooms with shared baths; four floors are not served by elevator; dining room is in the basement. $ *Rooms from: $85* ⊠ *24 Irving St., Harvard Square* ☎ *617/547–4600, 877/547–4600* ⊕ *www. irvinghouse.com* ⌐ *44 rooms* ¶○¶ *Free Breakfast* Ⓜ *Harvard.*

Sheraton Commander

$ | **HOTEL** | The stately 1927 Harvard Square landmark overlooking Cambridge Common park features classic furnishings (hello four-poster beds) in handsome, warm tones, but it's the hotel's signature bright-red neon sign towering overhead that really puts it on the map as a Cambridge classic. **Pros:** central Harvard Square location; pet-friendly; 24/7 gym. **Cons:** small bathrooms; some rooms have views of the parking lot; it's an older building. $ *Rooms from: $189* ⊠ *16 Garden St., Harvard Square* ☎ *617/547–4800, 800/325–3535* ⊕ *www. marriott.com* ⌐ *175 rooms* ¶○¶ *No meals* Ⓜ *Harvard.*

Nightlife

Town meets gown at Harvard Square, and glitz meets not-so-nerdy MIT at biotech-booming Kendall Square. As "Mass Ave." (Massachusetts Avenue) bends beyond the Charles, it connects both campuses and Porter Square's ethnic restaurants and jolly scenesters. Inman Square's music spots, Brattle Street's patrician serenity, and the bustle of Cambridgeside's mall and hotel pubs and dining rooms enrich the fabric.

BARS

Alden & Harlow

BARS/PUBS | This subterranean haunt adjacent to Brattle Theater provides fascinating pre- or postmovie dining with provocative locally sourced, rustic American fare like cheesy smoked grits, charred broccoli, or a burger that you once needed a secret code to order. Bartenders pour creative cocktails, local craft brews, and a fluid list of 50 edgy boutique wines. The late-night menu (to 1 am weeknights, 2 am weekends) offers favored fried smelts, broiled oysters with bacon, and crispy rabbit. ⊠ *40 Brattle St., Harvard Square* ☎ *617/864–2100* ⊕ *www. aldenharlow.com* Ⓜ *Harvard Sq.*

Grendel's Den

BARS/PUBS | This quintessential grad-student hangout is cavelike, low-lit, and brick-walled. During early evenings, tasty entrées like buffalo chicken dip, burritos, brisket nachos, and burgers are half-priced with a $4-per-person drink (inside only; not on outdoor patio). Named after Grendel, the antagonist in the Old English poem of *Beowulf*, there's nothing but neighborhood love here as you raise a pint. ⊠ *89 Winthrop St., Harvard Square* ☎ *617/491–1160* ⊕ *www.grendelsden. com* Ⓜ *Harvard.*

Temple Bar

BARS/PUBS | The chef here emphasizes house-made everything—entrées to condiments. After exploring Cambridge, saddle up to the long copper bar and kick back with a signature barrel-aged cocktail and savory gin or rum concoctions. The list is long, with inventive drinks such as the Lord of Storm's End (bourbon, Amaro Nonino, Tamsworth Blue Lion Chicoree) and Walking on Sunshine (Vodka, maraschino liqueur, GTs Gingerberry Kombucha). Be prepared to be impressed by bar menu lamb sliders and garganelli Bolognese, or choose a sit-down dinner affair. ■**TIP→ There's free parking in the rear after 6 pm.** ⊠ *1688 Massachusetts Ave., Harvard Square* ☎ *617/547–5055* ⊕ *templebarcambridge.com* Ⓜ *Porter, Harvard.*

★ Toad

BARS/PUBS | This is where local hipsters make their home. Bands, beers, and burgers sum up this snug and amiable little Porter Square hideaway attached to Christopher's. The bar is maple, the toads ceramic, and microbrews on tap are a dozen-plus. Nightly music comes in many a stripe, and usually in double bills at 7 and 10 pm. Check out Sunday spins after 5 pm: bring your own vinyl. Twelve taps, Toad T-shirts, and never a cover charge: what's not to like? ⊠ *1912 Massachusetts Ave., Porter Square* ☎ *617/497–4950 recording* ⊕ *www.toadcambridge.com* Ⓜ *Porter.*

MUSIC CLUBS
Beat Brew Hall

MUSIC CLUBS | An American brasserie and bar located in the heart of Harvard Square, Beat is inspired by the hippie and beat movements of the mid-20th century. There's daily live music by cutting-edge musicians in jazz, blues, and world music, and the bar celebrates American spirits, American artisanal wines crafted by small-batch winemakers with heart and soul, and craft beers (there are more than 40 in house). A fresh, seasonal, and wholesome menu includes dishes that draw influence and flavors from around the world. Bonus points for the DJs, pool, and parlor games in the No No Room. ⊠ *13 Brattle St., Harvard Square* ☎ *617/499–0001* ⊕ *www.beatbrasserie. com* Ⓜ *Harvard.*

Club Passim

MUSIC CLUBS | Joan Baez, Bob Dylan, Josh Ritter, Lake Street Dive—thousands of folkies have strummed and warbled their way through Club Passim, one of America's oldest (1958) and most renowned clubs for Americana and roots music. Audience participation is encouraged, so be ready to sing along. The uber-cozy brick basement has a kitchen that's open for relaxed live music Sunday brunch and dinner (which is only available to ticket holders). If you travel with your guitar, call about open-mike nights. Classes and workshops at their school around the corner carry on folk traditions. Acoustic bands perform nightly; expect to pay a $12–$20 cover. ⊠ *47 Palmer St., Harvard Square* ☎ *617/492–7679 box office* ⊕ *www.passim.org* Ⓜ *Harvard.*

Regattabar

MUSIC CLUBS | Located inside Cambridge's Charles Hotel, Regattabar is the go-to spot for jazz and world music in Cambridge, featuring regulars including leading men (Ron Carter, Joe Lovano, Lee Konitz), top guitarists (John Scofield, Mike Stern, Pat Martino), and local favorites. It was even listed in *Rolling Stone* magazine as one of the best jazz bars in the nation. Tickets for shows run about $20–$40. The dimly lit 220-seat club with subtle nautical decor offers tasty fare and drinks. ⊠ *Charles Hotel, 1 Bennett St., Harvard Square* ☎ *617/661– 5000 calendar, 617/395–7757 tickets* ⊕ *www.regattabarjazz.com* Ⓜ *Harvard.*

⭐ Performing Arts

DANCE
José Mateo's Ballet Theatre

DANCE | This troupe is building an exciting, contemporary repertory under Cuban-born José Mateo, the resident artistic director-choreographer. Performances, which include Dance Saturdays and an original *Nutcracker,* take place October through April at the **Sanctuary Theatre,** a beautifully converted Gothic revival church at Massachusetts Avenue and Harvard Street in Harvard Square. The vibe is intimate cabaret-style seating with 250 seats each with its own perfect view. ⊠ *400 Harvard St.* ☎ *617/354–7467* ⊕ *www.ballettheatre.org* Ⓜ *Harvard.*

FILM
Brattle Theatre

FILM | A classic moviegoer's iconic den with 230 seats, Brattle Theatre shows classic movies, art house, new foreign and indie films, theme series, and directors' cuts. Tickets sell out for its Valentine's Day screenings of *Casablanca;* the Bugs Bunny Film Festival in February; March's *Underground Film Festival; Trailer Treats,* an annual fundraiser featuring classic and modern movie previews; and DocYard, a stunning series of documentaries. At Christmastime, expect seasonal movies like *It's a Wonderful Life* and *Holiday Inn*. Enjoy a rotating selection of local beers and wines. ⊠ *40 Brattle St., Harvard Sq.* ☎ *617/876–6837* ⊕ *brattlefilm.org* Ⓜ *Harvard.*

Harvard Film Archive

FILM | Screening independent, foreign, classic, and experimental films rarely seen in commercial cinemas, Harvard Film Archive is open to the public Friday through Monday. The 188-seat theater, with pristine film and digital projection, is located in the basement of the stunning brick-and-glass Carpenter Visual Arts Center, Le Corbusier's only American building. A division of Harvard Library, this is one of the country's largest and most significant university-based motion picture collections—more than 36,000 audio visual global items from almost every period in film history. Tickets are $10; seniors and students, $8. ⊠ *Carpenter Center for the Visual Arts, 24 Quincy St.* ☎ *617/495–4700* ⊕ *hcl.harvard.edu/hfa* Ⓜ *Harvard.*

LECTURES
Forum

The church sponsors the popular lecture series *Forum* on Wednesday at 7 pm September through May, featuring well-known authors and academics. It's one of public radio's longest-running public affairs programs covering a wide range of topics, from the environment and policies to religion and science. There's even the occasional comedian weighing in. ⊠ *3 Church St., Harvard Square* ☎ *617/495–2727* ⊕ *www.cambridgeforum.org* Ⓜ *Harvard.*

MUSIC
★ Sanders Theatre

CONCERTS | This gilt-wood jewel box of a stage is the preferred venue for many of Boston's classical orchestras and the home of Harvard University's many ensembles. Located in the Memorial Hall, 180-degree stage design and superb acoustics afford intimacy and crystal projection. A favorite of folk, jazz, and world-music performers, the 1,000-seat Sanders hosts the holiday favorite, *Christmas Revels,* a traditional participatory Yule celebration. Winston Churchill, Martin Luther King, Wynton Marsalis, Leonard Bernstein, and Oprah Winfrey have lectured at this famed seat of oratory and music. ⊠ *Harvard University, 45 Quincy St., Harvard Sq.* ☎ *617/496–2222 box office* ⊕ *www.fas.harvard.edu/~memhall/sanders.html* Ⓜ *Harvard.*

THEATER
★ American Repertory Theater

THEATER | Founded by Robert Brustein and since 2009 under the helm of Tony Award–winning director Diane Paulus, the ART is one of America's most celebrated regional theaters, winning Tonys for Broadway originals *All the Way* and *Once* and revivals of *The Glass Menagerie, Pippin,* and *The Gershwins' Porgy and Bess.* The ART often premieres new works and seeks to expand the boundaries of theater through productions such as *Waitress, Finding Neverland,* and *Natasha, Pierre & The Great Comet of 1812* among others. The Loeb Drama Center, home of the ART, houses two theaters: the Mainstage and The Ex, a smaller black box often staging productions by the irreverent Harvard-Radcliffe Dramatic Club. OBERON, the ART's "club theater" with flexible stage design, engages young audiences in immersive theater (and has attracted national acclaim for its groundbreaking model) with gay, alternative, and cutting-edge programming. ⊠ *64 Brattle St., Harvard Sq.* ☎ *617/547–8300* ⊕ *americanrepertorytheater.org* Ⓜ *Harvard.*

Hasty Pudding Theatricals

THEATER | The oldest (1844) collegiate theatrical company in the United States still has all-male casts, though women participate in the troupe's staging and production. Its single annual madcap show plays at its theater in February and March, then tours to New York and Vegas. The troupe infamously honors

Harvard University's Radcliffe Quad is surrounded by undergrad housing; it's about a 12-minute walk, or half a mile, from Harvard Square.

actors as Man and Woman of the Year in an annual awards ceremony, complete with a celebrity roast and drag-queen and boa-laden party parade through the streets of Cambridge for the chosen woman. The 2020 honorees were Ben Platt and Elizabeth Banks. ⊠ *Harvard Sq., 12 Holyoke St.* ☎ *617/495–5205* ⊕ *www. hastypudding.org* Ⓜ *Harvard.*

🛍 Shopping

Cross over the Charles River to Cambridge, just as historic as Boston and where Harvard University's famous campus provides a beautiful backdrop for a unique and charming shopping experience. Massachusetts Avenue, Brattle Street, and Mt. Auburn Street shape the area known as Harvard Square, the place to go in Cambridge for just about anything.

A handful of chains and independent boutiques are clustered on Brattle Street.

BOOKS

Grolier Poetry Bookshop
BOOKS/STATIONERY | A beloved hangout for T. S. Eliot and E. E. Cummings when they attended Harvard, this tiny shop founded in 1927 carries classic, modern, and contemporary in-print poetry from all over the world. ⊠ *6 Plympton St., Harvard Square* ☎ *617/547–4648* ⊕ *www.grolier-poetrybookshop.org* ⊘ *Closed Sun. and Mon.* Ⓜ *Harvard.*

Harvard Book Store
BOOKS/STATIONERY | Time disappears as you browse the tables and shelves of this always-busy bookstore packed with new titles, used books, as well as remaindered books. Founded in 1932, the collection's diversity has made the store a favored destination for casual readers and academics alike, as they have plenty to discover within the floor-to-ceiling bookcases You can also stock up on Harvard University gifts, or catch an author reading. ⊠ *1256 Massachusetts Ave., Harvard Square* ☎ *617/661–1515* ⊕ *www. harvard.com* Ⓜ *Harvard.*

★ The Harvard Coop

BOOKS/STATIONERY | What began in 1882 as a nonprofit service for students and faculty is now managed by Barnes & Noble College, a separate entity that manages college campus bookstores. Housed in the same location since 1906 and affectionately called The Coop (pronounced "coop" not "co-op"), the store sells books and textbooks (many discounted), school supplies, clothes, and accessories plastered with the Harvard emblem, as well as basic housewares geared toward dorm dwellers. If you need a public restroom, you'll find it here. And if you're looking for MIT swag, they have a location on that campus as well. ⊠ *1400 Massachusetts Ave., Harvard Square* ☎ *617/499–2000* ⊕ *store. thecoop.com* Ⓜ *Harvard.*

Raven Used Books

BOOKS/STATIONERY | Looking for a stash of scholarly or literary used books? Raven's attracts local students eager to unload their university press titles. The store stocks approximately 15,000 carefully used books on topics ranging from social and political theory to art and architecture and buys more than 1,000 books weekly with discounts ranging from 50% to 80% off the cover price. It's situated next to the Christian Science Reading Room, in case you need a quiet place to settle down with your purchases. ⊠ *23 Church St., Harvard Square* ☎ *617/441–6999* ⊕ *www.ravencambridge.com* Ⓜ *Harvard.*

CRAFTS

Cambridge Artists' Cooperative

CRAFTS | Unique, handcrafted ceramics, weavings, jewelry, paper, wood, and leatherwork fill this two-level artist-owned and operated store, with more than 200 global artists represented—more than half of whom hail from New England. Spend time pursing the glass cases of artistic hand-crafted notions that greet you inside the front door, then stroll downstairs for wearable art in the forms of scarves, purses, and more. ⊠ *59A Church St., Brattle Street* ☎ *617/868–4434* ⊕ *www.cambridgeartistscoop.com* Ⓜ *Harvard.*

SHOPPING CENTERS

The Shops at the Garage

GIFTS/SOUVENIRS | Definitely one of Harvard Square's oddities, this multistory mini–shopping mall is in fact a converted parking garage with a winding walking ramp. Unique shopping opportunities include Hidden Treasures, Newbury Comics, The Hempest, and the cutesy little Japanese Anime Zakka. There's a tattoo parlor for ink enthusiasts as well as a Ben & Jerry's ice cream for frozen treats. ⊠ *36 John F. Kennedy St., Harvard Square* ☎ *617/354–5096* Ⓜ *Harvard.*

SPECIALTY SHOPS

★ Leavitt & Peirce

GIFTS/SOUVENIRS | A throwback to another era, this storied museum-like tobacco shop has been in the same location since 1883, when it served as a clubby gathering spot for young Harvard men, who puffed away while playing pool on the back billiard tables. While Harvard oars, hockey sticks, and photos still adorn the ivy-green walls, the store now caters to a broader clientele in search of quality smoking items, old-fashioned straight razors and shave brushes, chess and checker sets, and small gift items, such as beer steins. Don't miss the four chess tables on the second level, where you can rent pieces for $2 an hour (checkers and backgammon are available, too). ⊠ *1316 Massachusetts Ave., Harvard Square* ☎ *617/547–0576* ⊕ *www.leavitt-peirce.com* Ⓜ *Harvard.*

Tory Row

The stretch of Brattle Street nicknamed Tory Row remains one of New England's most elegant thoroughfares. Elaborate mansions line both sides from where it meets JFK Street to Fresh Pond Parkway. Brattle Street was once dubbed Tory Row, because during the 1770s its seven mansions, on land that stretched to the river, were owned by staunch supporters of King George. These properties were appropriated by the patriots when they took over Cambridge in the summer of 1775. Many of the historic houses are marked with blue signs, and although only two (the Hooper-Lee-Nichols House and the Longfellow National Historic Site) are fully open to the public, it's easy to imagine yourself back in the days of Ralph Waldo Emerson and Henry David Thoreau as you stroll the brick sidewalks. Mt. Auburn Cemetery, an exquisitely landscaped garden cemetery, is less than 2 miles down Brattle Street from Harvard Square.

Sights

Dexter Pratt House

COLLEGE | Also known as the "Blacksmith House," this yellow Colonial is now owned by the Cambridge Center for Adult Education. The tree itself is long gone, but this spot inspired Longfellow's lines: "Under a spreading chestnut tree, the village smithy stands." The blacksmith's shop, today commemorated by a granite marker, was next door, at the corner of Story Street. If you're lucky, you might be able to catch the celebrated Blacksmith House Poetry Series, which runs periodically throughout the year on Monday night. Tickets are $3. ⊠ *56 Brattle St., Tory Row* ⊕ *ccae.org/blacksmithpoetry* Ⓜ *Harvard.*

Elmwood

HOUSE | Shortly after its construction in 1767, this three-story Georgian house was abandoned by its owner, colonial governor Thomas Oliver. Also known as the Oliver-Gerry-Lowell House, it was home to the accomplished Lowell family for two centuries. Elmwood is now the Harvard University president's residence, ever since student riots in 1969 drove President Nathan Pusey from his house in Harvard Yard. ⊠ *33 Elmwood Ave., Tory Row* Ⓜ *Harvard.*

Henry Vassall House

HOUSE | Brattle Street's seven houses known as "Tory Row" were once occupied by wealthy families linked by friendship, if not blood. Portions of this house may have been built as early as 1636. In 1737 it was purchased by John Vassall Sr.; four years later he sold it to his younger brother Henry and his wife Penelope. It was used as a hospital during the Revolution, and the traitor Dr. Benjamin Church was held here as a prisoner. The house was remodeled during the 19th century. It's now a private residence, but from the street you can view the Colonial home with its black-shuttered windows and multiple dormers. ⊠ *94 Brattle St., Tory Row* Ⓜ *Harvard.*

Hooper-Lee-Nichols House

MUSEUM | Now headquarters of the Cambridge Historical Society, this is one of two Tory-era homes on Brattle Street fully open to the public; it's one of the older houses in Cambridge. The Emerson family gave it to the society in 1957. Built between 1685 and 1690, the house has been remodeled at least six times, but has maintained much of the original structure. The downstairs is elegantly, although sparsely, appointed with period books, portraits, and wallpaper. An upstairs bedroom has been furnished with period antiques, some belonging to the original residents. Tours are offered by appointment only. Check the website for special events and to see a virtual tour of the house. ⊠ *159 Brattle St., Tory Row* ☎ *617/547–4252* ⊕ *www.cambridgehistory.org* Ⓜ *Harvard.*

Longfellow House-Washington's Headquarters

HOUSE | Henry Wadsworth Longfellow, the poet whose stirring tales of the Village Blacksmith, Evangeline, Hiawatha, and Paul Revere's midnight ride thrilled 19th-century America, once lived in this elegant Georgian mansion. One of several original Tory Row homes on Brattle Street, the house was built in 1759 by

John Vassall Jr., and George Washington lived (and slept!) here during the Siege of Boston from July 1775 to April 1776. Longfellow first boarded here in 1837 and later received the house as a gift from his father-in-law on his marriage to Frances Appleton, who burned to death here in an accident in 1861. For 45 years Longfellow wrote his famous verses here and filled the house with the exuberant spirit of his literary circle, which included Ralph Waldo Emerson, Nathaniel Hawthorne, and Charles Sumner, an abolitionist senator. Longfellow died in 1882, but his presence in the house lives on—from the Longfellow family furniture to the wallpaper to the books on the shelves (many the poet's own). The home is preserved and run by the National Park Service; guided tours are offered Memorial Day through October. The formal garden is the perfect place to relax; the grounds are open year-round. Longfellow Park, across the street, is the place to stand to take photos of the house. The park was created to preserve the view immortalized in the poet's "To the River Charles." ⊠ *105 Brattle St., Tory Row* ☎ *617/876–4491* ⊕ *www.nps.gov/ long* ⊠ *Free* ☉ *Closed Mon. and Tues.* Ⓜ *Harvard.*

Mt. Auburn Cemetery

CEMETERY | A cemetery might not strike you as a first choice for a visit, but this one is an absolute pleasure, filled with artwork and gorgeous landscaping. Opened in 1831, it was the country's first garden cemetery, and its bucolic landscape boasts peaceful ponds, statues (including a giant Sphinx), breathtaking mausoleums, and a panorama of Boston and Cambridge from Washington Tower. More than 90,000 people have been buried here—among them Henry Wadsworth Longfellow, Mary Baker Eddy, Winslow Homer, Amy Lowell, Isabella Stewart Gardner, and architect Charles Bulfinch. The grave of engineer Buckminster Fuller bears an engraved geodesic dome. In spring local nature lovers and

bird-watchers come out of the woodwork to see the warbler migrations, the glorious blossoms, and blooming trees, while later in the year nature shows off its autumnal range of glorious color. Brochures, maps, and audio tours are at the entrance, and the cemetery is a five-minute drive from the heart of Harvard Square. ⊠ *580 Mt. Auburn St., Mt. Auburn* ☎ *617/547–7105* ⊕ *www.mountauburn.org* Ⓜ *Harvard; then Watertown (71) or Waverly (73) bus to cemetery.*

Kendall Square/ Central Square

Harvard Square may be the center of the "People's Republic of Cambridge," but the Kendall Square neighborhood is the city's hard-driving capitalist core. Gritty industrial buildings share space with sleek office blocks and the sprawling Massachusetts Institute of Technology. Although the MIT campus may lack the ivied elegance of Harvard Yard, major modern architects, including Alvar Aalto, Frank Gehry, I. M. Pei, and Eero Saarinen, created signature buildings here. To reach MIT, take the Red Line T to Kendall station; if you're headed for the MIT Museum on the western edge of the campus, the Central Square station is more convenient.

Central Square has its own draw of ethnic eateries, vintage vinyl shops, music clubs, late night dance hotspots, and consignment shops worth exploring.

◉ Sights

Massachusetts Institute of Technology

COLLEGE | Founded in 1861, MIT moved to Cambridge from Copley Square in the Back Bay in 1916. Once dissed as "the factory," particularly by its Ivy League neighbor, Harvard University, MIT mints graduates that are the sharp blades on the edge of the information

11

Cambridge and Somerville **CAMBRIDGE**

It's Hip to Be Square

In Cambridge, any commercial area where three or more streets meet in a jumble of traffic and noise has been dubbed a "square." (There are literally dozens, though most are just simple intersections.) Harvard Square draws the most visitors, but several other neighborhood squares exude their own charm. These are a few of our favorites; if you want to see where real Cantabrigians hang out.

Central Square, at Massachusetts Avenue (known by locals as "Mass Ave."), Prospect Street, and Western Avenue, has burger and beer joints, ethnic eats, music clubs, vintage record stores, and consignment shops. Cambridge's city government is here, and Ben Affleck and Matt Damon used to live here. For good eats, check out the Little Donkey (⌂ *505 Massachusetts Ave.*) or Phoenix Landing (⌂ *512 Massachusetts Ave.*), which also has dancing after 9 pm. The Central Square T stop is on the Red Line.

Somerville's **Davis Square** is just over the border from northwest Cambridge and easily accessible on the Red Line. This funky neighborhood near Tufts University is packed with great eateries, lively bars, and candlepin bowling. Harvard Square can sometimes feel a little tired after midnight, but there's still a lot of energy here late at night. At the Somerville Theater (⌂ *55 Davis Sq.*) you can enjoy cheap first-run movies ($10), excellent popcorn, and even beer and wine with your feature. Check out the hilarious Museum of Bad Art in the basement before or after your flick. The Davis Square T stop is on the Red Line.

Inman Square, at the intersection of Cambridge and Hampshire streets, has a great cluster of restaurants, cafés, bars, and shops. This place is just plain cool. One highlight includes Punjabi Dhaba (⌂ *225 Hampshire St.*), counter-service cheap and tasty late-night Indian food with Bollywood music and outstanding people-watching. Sadly, there's no T service to Inman, but you can get here from Harvard Square or Central Square on foot; it's near the intersection of Hampshire and Cambridge streets.

At **Kendall Square,** near the Massachusetts Institute of Technology (MIT) and the heart of the city's thriving biotech industry, you'll find an art-house multiplex shows first-run films and a walkable garden on top of a parking garage. The square is also a stone's throw from the Charles. The Kendall Square/MIT T stop is on the Red Line.

Porter Square, about a mile northwest of Harvard Square on Mass Ave., has several shopping centers and, within the nearby Porter Exchange, Japanese noodle and food shops. As you walk north (away from Harvard) past the heart of Porter Square, you'll pass pretty much every ethnic eatery imaginable, many of them excellent and far cheaper than Harvard Square restaurants. Standouts include one of the city's supposed first Chinese restaurants, Changsho (⌂ *1712 Massachusetts Ave.*), and popular Greek Corner (⌂ *2366 Massachusetts Ave.*), but you'll also find Indian, Thai, Bangladeshi, Vietnamese, and Himalayan. There are also quite a few unique shops along the way. The Porter Square T stop is on the Red Line.

Designed by famed architect Frank Gehry, MIT's Ray & Maria Stata Center is home to various computer science labs.

revolution. It's perennially in the top five of *U.S. News and World Report*'s college rankings. It has long since fulfilled the predictions of its founder, the geologist William Barton Rogers, that it would surpass "the universities of the land in the accuracy and the extent of its teachings in all branches of positive science." Its emphasis shifted in the 1930s from practical engineering and mechanics to the outer limits of scientific fields.

Architecture is important at MIT. Although the original buildings were obviously designed by and for scientists, many represent pioneering designs of their times. The **Kresge Auditorium,** designed by Eero Saarinen, with a curving roof and unusual thrust, rests on three, instead of four, points. The nondenominational **MIT Chapel,** a circular Saarinen design, is lighted primarily by a roof oculus that focuses natural light on the altar and by reflections from the water in a small surrounding moat; it's topped by an aluminum sculpture by Theodore Roszak. The serpentine **Baker House,** now

a dormitory, was designed in 1947 by the Finnish architect Alvar Aalto in such a way as to provide every room with a view of the Charles River. Sculptures by Henry Moore and other notable artists dot the campus. The latest addition is the Green Center, punctuated by the splash of color that is Sol LeWitt's 5,500-square-foot mosaic floor.

The East Campus, which has grown around the university's original neoclassical buildings of 1916, also has outstanding modern architecture and sculpture, including the stark high-rise **Green Building** by I. M. Pei, housing the Earth Science Center. Just outside is Alexander Calder's giant stabile (a stationary mobile) *The Big Sail*. Another Pei work on the East Campus is the **Wiesner Building,** designed in 1985, which houses the **List Visual Arts Center.** Architect Frank Gehry made his mark on the campus with the cockeyed, improbable **Ray & Maria Stata Center,** a complex of buildings on Vassar Street. The center houses computer, artificial intelligence, and information

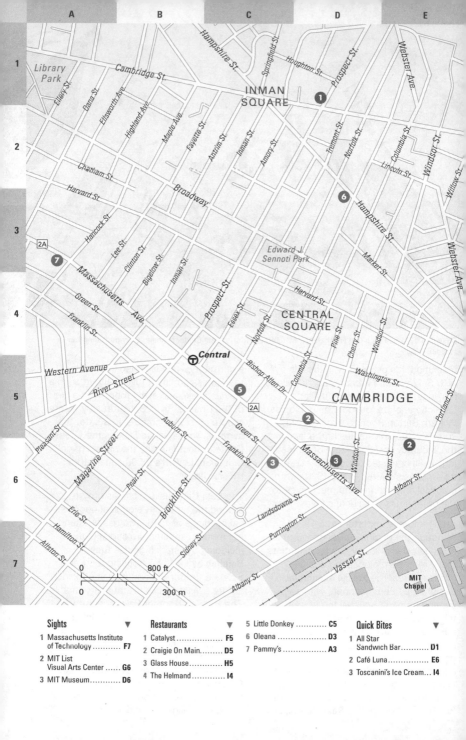

	A	B	C	D	E

Library Park

Hampshire St.

Eliot St.

Cambridge St.

Springfield St.

Houghton St.

Prospect St.

Webster Ave.

INMAN SQUARE

❶

Dana St.

Ellsworth Ave.

Highland Ave.

Maple Ave.

Fayette St.

Antrim St.

Inman St.

Amory St.

Tremont St.

Norfolk St.

Columbia St.

Windsor St.

Willow St.

Chatham St.

Broadway

Lincoln St.

Harvard St.

❻

Hampshire St.

2A

❼

Hancock St.

Lee St.

Clinton St.

Bigelow St.

Inman St.

Massachusetts Ave.

Edward J. Sennoti Park

Market St.

Webster Ave.

Green St.

Franklin St.

Prospect St.

Essex St.

Harvard St.

CENTRAL SQUARE

Ⓣ Central

Norfolk St.

Columbia St.

Pine St.

Cherry St.

Windsor St.

Washington St.

CAMBRIDGE

Western Avenue

River Street

Bishop Allen Dr.

❺

2A

❷

Portland St.

❷

Pleasant St.

Magazine Street

Auburn St.

Pearl St.

Green St.

Franklin St.

❸

Massachusetts Ave.

❸

Windsor St.

Osborn St.

Albany St.

Brookline St.

Sidney St.

Landsdowne St.

Purrington St.

Erie St.

Hamilton St.

Allston St.

0   800 ft

0   300 m

Albany St.

Vassar St.

MIT Chapel

Sights ▼
1 Massachusetts Institute
  of Technology **F7**
2 MIT List
  Visual Arts Center **G6**
3 MIT Museum............ **D6**

Restaurants ▼
1 Catalyst **F5**
2 Craigie On Main......... **D5**
3 Glass House............. **H5**
4 The Helmand **I4**

5 Little Donkey **C5**
6 Oleana **D3**
7 Pammy's **A3**

Quick Bites ▼
1 All Star
  Sandwich Bar........... **D1**
2 Café Luna................ **E6**
3 Toscanini's Ice Cream... **I4**

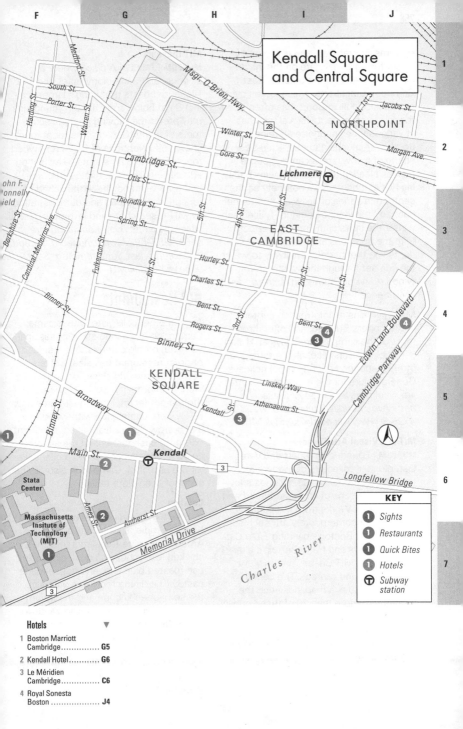

Kendall Square and Central Square

NORTHPOINT

EAST CAMBRIDGE

KENDALL SQUARE

Stata Center

Massachusetts Insitute of Technology (MIT)

Charles River

Longfellow Bridge

Lechmere

Kendall

KEY

- **1** Sights
- **1** Restaurants
- **1** Quick Bites
- **1** Hotels
- Ⓣ Subway station

Hotels ▼

1 Boston Marriott
  Cambridge............... **G5**

2 Kendall Hotel............ **G6**

3 Le Méridien
  Cambridge............... **C6**

4 Royal Sonesta
  Boston **J4**

systems laboratories, and is reputedly as confusing to navigate on the inside as it is to follow on the outside. East Campus's **Great Dome,** which looms over neoclassical Killian Court, has often been the target of student "hacks" and has at various times supported a telephone booth with a ringing phone, a life-size statue of a cow, and a campus police cruiser. Nearby, the domed **Rogers Building** has earned unusual notoriety as the center of a series of hallways and tunnels dubbed "the infinite corridor." Twice each winter the sun's path lines up perfectly with the corridor's axis, and at dusk students line the third-floor hallway to watch the sun set through the westernmost window. The phenomenon is known as "MIT-henge."

MIT maintains an information center in the Rogers Building, and offers free tours of the campus weekdays at 11 and 3. Check the schedule, as the tours are often suspended during school holidays. General hours for the information center are weekdays 9 to 5. ✉ *77 Massachusetts Ave., Kendall Square* ☎ *617/253–4795* ⊕ *www.mit.edu* Ⓜ *Kendall/MIT.*

MIT List Visual Arts Center

MUSEUM | Founded by Albert and Vera List, pioneer collectors of modern art, this MIT center has three galleries showcasing exhibitions of cutting-edge art and mixed media. Works from the center's collection of contemporary art, such as Thomas Hart Benton's painting *Fluid Catalytic Crackers* and Harry Bertoia's altarpiece for the MIT Chapel, are on view here and around campus. The center's website includes a map indicating the locations of more than 20 of these public works of art. ✉ *20 Ames St., Bldg. E 15, Kendall Square* ☎ *617/253–4680* ⊕ *listart.mit.edu* ▨ *Free* ⊘ *Closed Mon.* Ⓜ *Kendall/MIT.*

MIT Museum

MUSEUM | FAMILY | A place where art, science, and technology meet, the MIT Museum boasts the world's largest collection of holograms, though young kids may prefer the moving gestural sculptures of Arthur Ganson. The robot room shows off inventions of MIT's renowned robotics lab and an extensive exhibit on artificial intelligence. Allow an hour or two for a visit and check the schedule for special programs and demonstrations by MIT researchers and inventors. ✉ *265 Massachusetts Ave., Kendall Square* ☎ *617/253–5927* ⊕ *mitmuseum.mit.edu* ▨ *$10; free last Sun. of month, Sept.– June* Ⓜ *Kendall/MIT.*

🍴 Restaurants

Among other collegiate enthusiasms, Cambridge has a long-standing fascination with ethnic eateries. Another kind of great restaurant has also evolved here, mixing world-class cooking with a studied informality, particularly around the red-hot Technology Square area near MIT where chefs cook with wood fires and borrow flavors from every continent. For more posh tastes and the annual celebrations that come with college life (or the end of it), Cambridge also has its share of linen-cloth tables.

Catalyst

$$ | FRENCH FUSION | Chef-owner William Kovel's simple, approachable French American cuisine translates to dishes like chicken liver mousse, squid ink cavatelli, pan-roasted blue cod, and house-made pastas. The dining room has views of the semi-open kitchen and the atrium with sweeping floor-to-ceiling windows. **Known for:** modern French dishes; afterwork crowd; huge U-shape bar. ⓢ *Average main: $24* ✉ *300 Technology Sq., Kendall Square* ☎ *617/576–3000* ⊕ *www.catalystrestaurant.com* ⊘ *Closed Sun.* Ⓜ *Kendall.*

Craigie on Main

$$$ | FRENCH | This soulful, white-cloth restaurant belongs to chef-owner Tony Maws, who's passion for all things fresh and local is reflected in a daily changing menu that ranges from a slow-roasted dayboat gray sole to pork belly confit or roasted pig's head for two. Sunday is Chef's Whim Night, so after 9 pm you'll eat four to six courses of whatever Maws feels like cooking for a discounted price. **Known for:** nose-to-tail fare; locally sourced ingredients; white-cloth service. [$] *Average main: $32* ✉ *853 Main St., Central Square* ☎ *617/497–5511* 🌐 *www.craigieonmain.com* 🕓 *Closed Mon.* [M] *Central.*

Glass House

$$ | AMERICAN | A nod to East Cambridge's place as the center of the nation's glass-making industry and home to its largest glass factory, the Glass House is an eye-catching restaurant that offers tasty American cuisine that delivers a good balance between sea and land (think chimichurri-brushed Spanish octopus and grilled steak frites). While the cocktail menu is 15 creative drinks strong and the draft beer selections more than 20, the mocktail list is just as impressive with several fruity and fizzy refreshing drinks. **Known for:** poutine with lamb and ale gravy; unique patio activities; modern twists on classic dishes. [$] *Average main: $20* ✉ *450 Kendall St., Kendall Square* ☎ *617/945–9450* 🌐 *www.glasshouse-cambridge.com* 🕓 *Closed Sun.*

★ The Helmand

$$$ | AFGHAN | The area's first Afghan restaurant, named after the country's most important river, welcomes you into its cozy Kendall Square confines with Afghan rugs, a wood-burning oven, and exotic, yet extremely approachable food that reflects the motherland's location halfway between the Middle East and India. Standouts, beyond the chewy warm bread, include magical names from a far-away land like *aushak* (leek-stuffed ravioli over yogurt with beef ragu and mint), *chapendaz* (marinated grilled beef tenderloin served with cumin-spiced hot pepper–tomato puree), and a vegetarian baked pumpkin platter. **Known for:** excellent Afghan fare; enveloping atmosphere; incredible breads. [$] *Average main: $25* ✉ *143 1st St., Kendall Square* ☎ *617/492–4646* 🌐 *helmandrestaurant.com* 🕓 *No lunch* [M] *Lechmere.*

Little Donkey

$$ | FUSION | Dream team James Beard Award–winning chef-owners Jamie Bissonnnette and Ken Oringer (of Coppa, Toro fame) serve crazy-good small plates made from big, bold, unexpected combos: think Vietnamese-accented cabbage with bologna and fried squid, manti (Istanbul meat ravioli), and King Crab nachos. While burgers are indulgent—patties gilded with foie gras—you can also enjoy the Impossible Burger for plant-based protein. **Known for:** bold-flavored small plates; slushy and boozy drinks; fun atmosphere. [$] *Average main: $22* ✉ *505 Massachusetts Ave., Central Square* ☎ *617/945–1008* 🌐 *www.littledonkeybos.com.*

★ Oleana

$$$ | MEDITERRANEAN | With two restaurants (including Sofra in Cambridge) and two cookbooks to her name, chef-owner Ana Sortun continues to bewitch area diners with her intricately spiced eastern Mediterranean meze (small plates) made with fresh-picked produce from her husband's nearby Siena Farms. Oleana's menu changes often, but look for the hot, crispy-fried mussels starter and Sultan's Delight (tamarind-glazed beef with smoky eggplant puree) along with large plates of Turkish-spiced lamb and lemon chicken. **Known for:** eastern Mediterranean menu; mouthwatering small plates; deft use of spices. [$] *Average main: $27* ✉ *134 Hampshire St., Central Square* ☎ *617/661–0505* 🌐 *www.oleanarestaurant.com* 🕓 *No lunch* [M] *Central.*

Pammy's

$$$ | **MODERN ITALIAN** | Perched between Central and Harvard Squares, this New American trattoria was created by husband and wife team chef Chris and Pam Willis. The rulebook goes out the window here as the menu takes traditional Italian flavors and turns them on their tails with starters such as salmon belly with coconut risotto and fried meatballs and pasta plates of taglierini with wagyu oxtail, chocolate, and horseradish or sea scallops with charred avocado. **Known for:** unexpected flavor combos; welcoming staff; strong cocktail program. [$] *Average main: $32* ✉ *928 Massachusetts Ave., Central Square* ☎ *617/945–1761* 🌐 *www.pammyscambridge.com* 🕒 *Closed Sun.* [M] *Central Square.*

Coffee and Quick Bites

All Star Sandwich Bar

$ | **AMERICAN** | This brightly colored place with about a dozen tables turns out fresh, high-quality sandwiches and burgers, all served with coleslaw, dill pickle, and a smile. Beyond multiple beef burgers, you'll find classics like crispy, overstuffed Reubens and the famous Atomic Meatloaf Meltdown, which has been highlighted on a number of foodie networks. **Known for:** chef-quality sandwiches; creative combinations; simple setting. [$] *Average main: $12* ✉ *1245 Cambridge St., Central Square* ☎ *617/868–3065* 🌐 *www.allstarsandwichbar.com* [M] *Central.*

Café Luna

$$ | **AMERICAN** | This Cambridge hot spot is locally loved, which means there are usually long waiting times but the breakfast and lunch menus are worth it. The omelet menu is far beyond your basic egg and cheese, with combos such as fig, prosciutto, and goat cheese, and there's cinnamon swirl French toast, their 20-hour slow-cooked corned beef hash, and the signature eggs Benedict. **Known for:** epic omelets; slow-cooked corned beef; crowded college scene. [$] *Average main: $23* ✉ *612 Main St., Kendall Square* ☎ *617/576–3400* 🌐 *cafeluna-centralsq.com* [M] *Kendall/MIT.*

Toscanini's Ice Cream

$ | **CAFÉ** | If you're looking for serious ice cream, head to Toscanini's. With flavors such as gingersnap molasses, bourbon, cranberry goat cheese, burnt caramel, and green tea, this MIT establishment has few equals, especially when it comes to their microsundae—a teeny scoop of ice cream topped with excellent homemade hot fudge and real whipped cream—a perfect option for kids and adults eager for a guilt-free splurge (well, almost). **Known for:** excellent homemade ice cream; coffee drinks; unique flavors. [$] *Average main: $5* ✉ *159 1st St., Central Square* ☎ *617/491–5877* 🌐 *www.tosci.com.*

Hotels

Boston Marriott Cambridge

$$$ | **HOTEL** | Traveling businesspeople and families like the modern look and efficiency of this 26-story high-rise hotel in Kendall Square, steps from the subway and MIT. **Pros:** top-floor rooms have stunning views; on-site Starbucks coffee house; 24-hour fitness center. **Cons:** has the "chain hotel" feel; not many dining options; lots of business travelers and people with children. [$] *Rooms from: $339* ✉ *2 Cambridge Center, 50 Broadway, Kendall Square* ☎ *617/494–6600, 888/228–9290* 🌐 *www.marriotthotels.com/boscb* 🛏 *444 rooms* 🍴 *No meals* [M] *Kendall/MIT.*

Kendall Hotel

$$$ | **HOTEL** | You might think a place in such a high-tech neighborhood would be all stainless steel and chrome; think again: the Queen Anne–style Kendall Hotel is homey and ultrafriendly, bright-hued and lively—and it's convenient, with a T stop just one block away. **Pros:** quiet rooms; hot Fireman's Gourmet

buffet breakfast included; free Wi-Fi and passes to local gyms; welcome snacks and nightly reception. **Cons:** crowded with tchotchkes; no swimming pool; can feel cramped. Ⓢ *Rooms from: $390* ✉ *350 Main St., Kendall Square* ☎ *617/577–1300, 866/566–1300* ⊕ *www.kendallhotel.com* ⇆ *77 rooms* ⓘⓞⓘ *Free Breakfast* Ⓜ *Kendall/MIT.*

Le Meridien Cambridge

$$ | **HOTEL** | When the Marriott chain took over the geek-chic Le Méridien Cambridge-MIT, with its tech-savvy rooms and surroundings, some fans worried the Cambridge spot would lose its charm; but the new owners only amped up the offerings—and added some luxe touches—by displaying cool interactive lobby art from MIT and refurbishing the guest rooms with platform beds, puffy white duvets, flat-screen TVs, and ergonomically designed furniture. **Pros:** pet-friendly; close to the T (Red Line Central) and restaurants; 24-hour fitness center; free Wi-Fi. **Cons:** pricey high-season rates; tons of tech people; not really walkable to Boston sights. Ⓢ *Rooms from: $219* ✉ *20 Sidney St., Kendall Square* ☎ *617/577–0200, 800/543–4300* ⊕ *www.lemeridien.com/cambridge* ⇆ *210 rooms* ⓘⓞⓘ *No meals* Ⓜ *Central, Kendall/MIT.*

★ Royal Sonesta Boston

$$$ | **HOTEL** | **FAMILY** | Right next to the Charles River, the certified-green Sonesta has one of the best city skylines and sunset views in Boston. **Pros:** walk to Museum of Science and T to Downtown Boston; complimentary shuttle to Cambridge-area attractions; nice pool. **Cons:** pay parking; river-view guest rooms have much better view than Cambridge-view rooms; no a/c in rooms. Ⓢ *Rooms from: $379* ✉ *40 Edwin Land Blvd., off Memorial Dr., Kendall Square* ☎ *617/806–4200, 800/766–3782* ⊕ *www.sonesta.com/boston* ⇆ *400 rooms* ⓘⓞⓘ *No meals* Ⓜ *Lechmere.*

Nightlife

BARS

Cambridge Brewing Company

BARS/PUBS | This collegial, cavernous microbrewery is the oldest brew pub in the greater Boston area and has been the happy haunt for MIT techies and craft-brew geeks since its 1989 founding. They push the boundaries of beer, from bourbon barrel-aging an imperial stout to creating the first true solera aging process in the United States for beer. Order CBC's Cambridge Amber, Charles River Porter, and Tall Tale Pale Ale fresh in pints, or go for a "tower" (an 83-ounce glass "yard"). In warm weather, try to nab a coveted patio table, a catbird seat for people-watching across bricky Kendall Square. Cheerful staff serve above-average pub grub, even at weekend "beerunches." ✉ *1 Kendall Sq., Bldg. 100, at Hampshire St. and Broadway, Kendall Square* ☎ *617/494–1994* ⊕ *www.cambridgebrewingcompany.com* Ⓜ *Kendall/MIT.*

The Druid

BARS/PUBS | You can feel like you're in Dublin here, sipping well-poured pints, eyeing the dusky atmosphere, eating black-and-white pudding or rib eye roasted in Guinness. Located in vibrant Inman Square in the oldest wooden mercantile building in the city of Cambridge, Druid welcomes tourists and locals, a mix of Portuguese- and Italian-Americans, Harvard and MIT students, and young families. Irish musicians jam Saturday late day and Sunday afternoon; there's trivia Wednesday at 8 pm and a DJ Thursday at 10 pm. ✉ *1357 Cambridge St., Inman Square* ☎ *617/497–0965* ⊕ *www.druidpub.com* Ⓜ *Central, Harvard.*

★ Middlesex Lounge

BARS/PUBS | For those looking to avoid the uber-sceney clubs of Boston's Theater District, the Middlesex is a welcoming, laid-back club for all sorts of people looking to dance the night away. Rolling settees, movable in varied seating configurations for trivia, games, and nerd nights, are usually cleared by 9 pm, when a $10 cover kicks in for DJs spinning crowd-pleasing EDM and hip-hop. Feed on small plates and pressed sandwiches. The lounge is only open Thursday through Saturday, 7 pm–2 am. ⊠ *315 Massachusetts Ave., Central Square* ☎ *617/868–6739* ⊕ *www.middlesexlounge.us* Ⓜ *Central.*

The Plough & Stars

BARS/PUBS | This genuine Irish pub has doubled as a bohemian oasis for 40 steady years. Drink Guinness and Bass on tap and many Irish whiskies; hear light rock, Irish, or country music nightly, usually by 10:30. Narrow and cozy, the Plough is a comfy, noisy den for locals and students, yet a fine place to have lunch alone. The cover charge varies, but the popular $10 weekday beer and burger special remains the same. Fun fact: literary magazine *Ploughshares* was founded here. ⊠ *912 Massachusetts Ave., Central Square* ☎ *617/576–0032* ⊕ *www.ploughandstars.com* Ⓜ *Central, Harvard.*

COMEDY CLUBS

ImprovBoston

COMEDY CLUBS | This Central Square venue flips audience cues into situation comedy, complete with theme songs and commercials. Be careful when you go to the restroom—you might be pulled onstage. Performers may face off in improv competitions judged by audiences. Shows run Wednesday through Sunday, $12 to $20, with Thursday night hosting the new Best New Musical (an improved tune-driven performance). You may need that beer and wine bar. ⊠ *40 Prospect St., Central Square* ☎ *617/576–1253* ⊕ *www.improvboston.com* Ⓜ *Central.*

MUSIC CLUBS

Havana Club

DANCE CLUBS | Overlooking Central Square, this 5,400-square-foot ballroom dance floor hosts a kaleidoscope of DJs and live bands, and often free burritos or nachos. Three hundred people may show up to dance salsa, creating a lively scene for dancers at any level. Open Monday is for bachata (sultry midtempo Dominican dance), Friday and Saturday for salsa, and Tuesday blends both. With lessons at 8 or 9 pm, depending on the night, the joint really gets hopping by 9 or 10 pm. ⊠ *288 Green St., Central Square* ☎ *617/312–5550* ⊕ *www.havanaclubsalsa.com* Ⓜ *Central.*

Performing Arts

DANCE

The Dance Complex

DANCE | Performances (and classes and workshops) by local and visiting choreographers take place at Odd Fellows Hall, an intimate space that draws a multicultural crowd within its seven studios. Styles range from classical ballet to contemporary and world dance, beginner street dance moves to advanced hip-hop. Occasionally, when weather permits, performers take to the streets for fun pop-up outdoor sets. ⊠ *536 Massachusetts Ave., Central Square* ☎ *617/547–9363* ⊕ *www.dancecomplex.org* Ⓜ *Central.*

Global Arts Live

DANCE | As the metro area's premier presenter of worldwide music and dance, Global Arts Live, formerly World Music/CRASHarts, has a truly global roster featuring exciting contemporary artists in their Boston debuts (like The Bad Plus and Freshlyground), as well as world music icons such as South Africa's Ladysmith Black Mambazo and Ireland's Mary Black. Its annual blockbuster Flamenco Festival packs the Huntington Avenue Theatre. Performances unfold at many venues such as Brighton Music Hall, Berklee Performance Center,

Sinclair, Sanders Theatre, and City Winery. ☒ *720 Massachusetts Ave., Central Square* ☎ *617/876–4275* ⊕ *www. worldmusic.org* Ⓜ *Central.*

Multicultural Arts Center

DANCE | The MAC in East Cambridge supports diversity through the performing arts. They put on jazz, dance, and visiting arts programs, and have two spacious galleries showcasing international visual arts. The theater itself is a show-stopper with Victorian details and theater lighting. Galleries are open 10:30 am–6 pm and performances are usually Thursday and Saturday at 8 pm. ☒ *41 2nd St.* ☎ *617/577–1400* ⊕ *www.multiculturalartscenter.org* Ⓜ *Lechmere.*

🛍 Shopping

At the junction of Massachusetts Avenue, Prospect Street, River Street, and Western Avenue, Central Square has an eclectic mix of furniture stores, used-record shops, ethnic restaurants, and small, hip performance venues. The best word to describe the area is bohemian.

ANTIQUES
Cambridge Antique Market

ANTIQUES/COLLECTIBLES | Off the beaten track, this antiques hot spot has a selection bordering on overwhelming: five floors of goods from more than 150 dealers ranging from 19th-century furniture to vintage clothing, much of it reasonably priced. You can find everything from collectible magazines to China dolls, art work to fine silver. Head to the basement for a large selection of secondhand bikes. ☒ *201 Monsignor O'Brien Hwy.* ☎ *617/868–9655* ⊕ *www.marketantique. com* Ⓜ *Lechmere.*

CLOTHING
The Garment District

OUTLET/DISCOUNT STORES | Step into this warehouse-like building through the famous pink door and head to the second level to find a massive selection of vintage, used, and new clothing and accessories.

Boston Costume, the sister business on the first floor, draws thrift pickers to the back room to paw through an 850-pound bale of clothes that's dumped on the floor each day (twice on Saturday and Sunday); items are sold for $2 per pound ($1 on Friday). Students crowd the entire store year-round, and everyone comes at Halloween for that perfect costume. They're also known for their vintage wears, dating back to the '50s for as retro as you please. ☒ *200 Broadway, Kendall Square* ☎ *617/876–5230* ⊕ *www.garment-district. com* Ⓜ *Kendall/MIT.*

SHOPPING CENTERS
CambridgeSide Galleria

SHOPPING NEIGHBORHOODS | Macy's, T.J. Maxx, and Best Buy anchor this recently redone but basic three-story mall with a food court and sit-down restaurants; it's a big draw for local high-school kids and an easy walk from the Museum of Science. ☒ *100 CambridgeSide Pl., Kendall Square* ☎ *617/621–8666* ⊕ *www. cambridgesidegalleria.com* Ⓜ *Lechmere, Kendall/MIT via free shuttle.*

Somerville

Just north of Cambridge lies the irreverent city of Somerville, New England's most densely populated city. There is always something to see and do, as its eclectic mix of blue-collar families, young professionals, college students, and recent immigrants creates an environment that brings a ton to the table. Somerville is defined by its city squares, the most active of which are the expansive Davis and its adjacent blink-and-you'll-miss-it, Union, Ball, and Magoun. Each offers a mix of ethnic restaurants, bars and shops, and small businesses to fit every taste and occasion. In 2014, Somerville opened its latest center of art and industry: Assembly Row, a beautiful live-work-play urban environment along the Mystic River that has become a destination for even Bostonians who are always hesitant to cross The Charles River.

Sights

Assembly Row

NEIGHBORHOOD | What was once large barren fields and the former home of a Ford Assembly Plant, is now a thriving destination neighborhood along the Mystic River. Assembly Row is an open-air community of live-work-play spaces all connected by water-front walkways and parks. Retail abounds, with stores like the area's only Saks Off Fifth, Puma, Brooks Brothers, J.Crew outlet, and more. For entertainment, check out the AMC movie theater, the famed Legoland Discover Center, and the Lucky Strike Social Club, 36,000 square-feet of space with first-floor dining and bowling, games, floor shuffleboard, and an island bar on the second. There are 25 restaurants in Assembly, including the trendy River Bar (noted for its year-round fire pits), casual noodles at Totto Ramen, and award-winning BBQ at the Smoke Shop. The new 5-in-1 fitness studio FitRow has you covered for whatever workout you desire, from boxing to cycling to pilates. It also houses the Row Hotel at Assembly Row, a boutique hotel with some of the best interior design around. ⊠ *355 Artisan Way, Somerville* ⊕ *assemblyrow. com* Ⓜ *Assembly.*

Bow Market

COMMERCIAL CENTER | **FAMILY** | Once a storage building, today's Bow Market provides small-scale storefronts to established and aspiring chefs, retailers, and artists from Somerville and Greater Boston. An afternoon is well spent among the more than 30 independent food, art, and retail shops set around a public courtyard in the heart of Union Square. Maca Macaronerie, Jaju Periogis, and Hooked Fish Shop are just a few of the eateries, while shopping goes global with one-of-a-kind gifts at retailers including 9000 Things and artisinal Japanese arts and crafts at Crane & Turtle. On any given day, there could be a pop-up event like a book fair, jewelry shops, Etsy spotlights, and oysterfests. Grab a pint (or a freshly roasted Barrington coffee) at the market's Remnant Brewery, which boasts a garage door that opens whenever the weather permits. ⊠ *1 Bow Market Way, Somerville* ⊕ *bowmarketsomerville.com.*

LEGOLAND Discovery Center Boston

AMUSEMENT PARK/WATER PARK | **FAMILY** | Look for the giant Lego giraffe and you've found this mecca for building block enthusiasts. There are more than 10 Build & Play Zones, including The LEGO City Indoor Play Zone, which is full of energy-expending climbing walls, slides, a jungle gym, and the Duplo Farm, which is perfect for tiny tots to spend some quiet discovery and building time. The 4D Cinema brings LEGO movies to life with additional wind, rain, and snow effects, while the indoor rides and virtual reality experiences add in a little more interactive fun. Discover iconic Boston attractions and local buildings all made entirely out of LEGO in the infamous MINILAND attraction that used more than 1.5 million bricks. ⊠ *598 Assembly Row, Somerville* ☏ *866/228–6439* ⊕ *boston.legoland-discoverycenter.com.*

🍴 Restaurants

Just 2 miles north of Boston, Somerville is known for its eclectic mix of students, blue-collar families, indie musicians, and immigrants, all of whom help inform the hip restaurant scene here, which centers on Davis and Union squares. In addition to Spanish, Haitian, and Brazilian eateries, you'll find burger joints, BBQ, and tacos, along with a new sort of place—second restaurants from Boston star chefs, eager to share their home cooking with a democratic mix of diners.

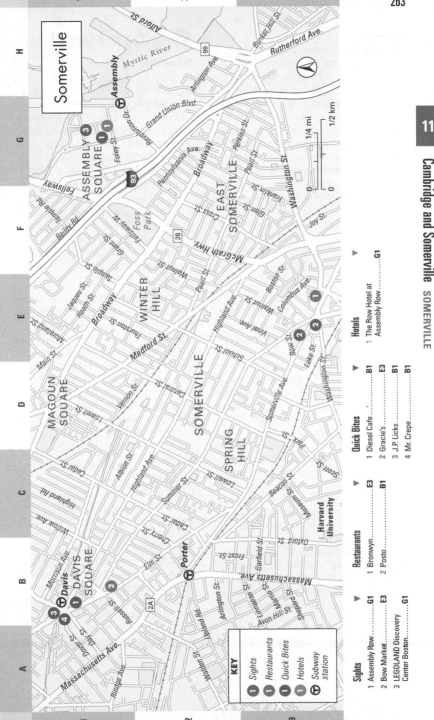

11

Cambridge and Somerville SOMERVILLE

Somerville

Mystic River

Assembly

ASSEMBLY SQUARE

99

93

28

MAGOUN SQUARE

WINTER HILL

Foss Park

EAST SOMERVILLE

SOMERVILLE

SPRING HILL

DAVIS SQUARE

Davis

Porter

Harvard University

1/4 mi
1/2 km
0
0

KEY

🔴	Sights
🔴	Restaurants
🔴	Quick Bites
🔴	Hotels
Ⓣ	Subway station

Sights ▶

1 Assembly Row G1
2 Bow Market E3
3 LEGOLAND Discovery Center Boston G1

Restaurants ▶

1 Bronwyn E3
2 Posto B1

Quick Bites ▶

1 Diesel Cafe B1
2 Gracie's E3
3 J.P. Licks B1
4 Mr. Crepe B1

Hotels ▶

1 The Row Hotel at Assembly Row G1

Bronwyn

$$ | **GERMAN** | Harkening back to his German heritage, chef-owner Tim Wiechmann and his wife, Bronwyn, the restaurant's namesake, have brought a rib-sticking yet sophisticated taste of Central and Eastern Europe to Union Square. The menu here includes juicy hand-stuffed pork sausages served with powerfully seasoned sauces, hearty dumplings, noodle dishes (try the *spaetzle* with cheddar), and sauerbraten made with Wagyu beef. **Known for:** hearty German specialties; excellent beer list; medieval manorlike setting. [$] *Average main: $23* ✉ *255 Washington St., Somerville* ☎ *617/776–9900* 🌐 *www.bronwynrestaurant.com* 💳 *No credit cards* 🕒 *Closed Mon. No lunch Sun.–Fri.*

★ Posto

$$ | **ITALIAN** | A central wood-burning oven at this Davis Square spot churns out more than a dozen varieties of excellent tomato or "white" bubble-crusted pies (try the "white" three-mushroom, fontina, and lemony spinach pizza), while the kitchen crafts scrumptious starters and mains, like "nonna'" meatballs, gnocchi with beef short ribs, and succulent swordfish with potatoes and broccoli rabe. The central brick and glass-walled dining room (with sidewalk seating during fair weather) fills nightly, as this eatery succeeds at blending classic Italian pizzeria, enoteca, and trattoria all together in a "farm chic" open air concept. **Known for:** wood-fired Italian cuisine; excellent Neopolitan pies; cheerful environment. [$] *Average main: $23* ✉ *187 Elm St., Somerville* ☎ *617/625–0600* 🌐 *www.postoboston.com* 💳 *No credit cards* 🕒 *No lunch.*

Coffee and Quick Bites

Diesel Cafe

$ | **CAFÉ** | Known as Somerville's "refueling station," this bright, window-y spot with bold local artwork and spacious tables draws in Davis Square hipsters, Tufts students, and the LGBTQ sets. Be part of the rebel crowd over veggie-friendly fare, crafted salads, soups, wraps, house-made pastries, and gourmet coffee with tasty house-made syrups in flavors like turmeric, caramel, and vanilla. **Known for:** industrial no-nonsense vibe; coffee drinks; local hangout. [$] *Average main: $5* ✉ *257 Elm St., Somerville* ☎ *617/629–8717* 🌐 *www.diesel-cafe.com* [M] *Davis.*

Gracie's

$ | **CAFÉ** | This snow-white shop makes micro batches of ice cream daily and serves it, if you wish, in a torched marshmallow-cream-lined cone. There are six All The Time Flavors (chocolate, sweet cream, black raspberry chip, mint chip, cookies n' cream, salty whiskey) and six Sometimes Flavors. **Known for:** daily-made creative ice creams; tiny location; dairy-free option available. [$] *Average main: $5* ✉ *22 Union Sq., Somerville* ☎ *617/764–5294* 🌐 *www.icecreamgracies.com.*

J.P. Lick's

$ | **CAFÉ** | Vince Petryk started this Boston ice-cream institution 40 years ago, and today, there are 16 current locations in and around Boston including Assembly Row. With all their ice cream made in-house, J.P. **Known for:** creative ice-cream flavors; their own roasted coffee; lixwiches ice-cream cookie sandwiches. [$] *Average main: $5* ✉ *4A College Ave., Somerville* ☎ *617/666–5079* 🌐 *www.jplicks.com* [M] *Davis Square.*

Mr. Crepe

$ | **CAFÉ** | For more than 20 years, this unpretentious, quick-serve creperie and café in the heart of Davis Square has been a local favorite. For the savory set, ingredients are layered together (think grilled veggies, fresh cheeses, and crispy greens), wrapped in very thin pancakes and heated until warm and toasty. **Known for:** tasty crepes; relaxed counter service; homemade soups. $ *Average main: $10* ⊠ *51 Davis Sq., Somerville* ☎ *617/623–0661* ⊕ *www.mrcrepe.com* Ⓜ *Davis Square.*

Hotels

The Row Hotel at Assembly Row

$$$$ | **HOTEL** | Part of Marriott's Autograph Collection, The Row's elegant calm pays homage to its past life as a Ford Motor Assembly Plant. **Pros:** 15 minutes by T from Boston and right next to Assembly Row; a communal pantry with coffee, tea, water, and snacks; wellness center with pool and on-demand fitness. **Cons:** limited storage in standard rooms; busy scene; rooms can be loud. $ *Rooms from: $399* ⊠ *360 Foley St., Somerville* ☎ *617/628–1300* ⊕ *www.therowhotelatassemblyrow.com* ⊂ *158 rooms* ❖ *No meals.*

▼ Nightlife

Once marginal and blue-collar, crowded Somerville is now very cool. Look at Davis Square: a hub for the T and bike paths, the square's alive with cafés, clubs, a large theater, and ethnic eateries serving BBQ, sushi, wood-fired pizza, curry, bangers and mash, pad thai, and soba. It's a prime gathering spot for Tufts University students, vintage hippies, and young thinkers, and even hosts local festivals, like Davis ArtBeat and Honk! You can catch bands in storefront bars and cafés along Somerville Avenue and Washington Street.

BARS

★ The Burren

BARS/PUBS | Your true-emerald Irish music pub pulls in devoted locals and all fans of *craic* (enjoyable environment). Enthusiastic staff and professional bartenders expertly pour Guinness on tap and serve comfort food (some of the best fish-and-chips in the area, bangers and mash, Irish stew, shepherd's pie). Dark decor, a tiny sunny west-facing patio, an old-wood library bar, and slate specials add to the allure of live Irish music—acoustic groups—most nights in both the Front and Back Rooms. On weekends, check out the Beatles brunch. ⊠ *247 Elm St., Somerville* ☎ *617/776–6896* ⊕ *www.burren.com* Ⓜ *Davis.*

The Independent

BARS/PUBS | In Somerville's Union Square, this comfortable neighborhood bar is a good spot to hit for a pint, a whiskey-based cocktail with a quaint name, quality brews (36 drafts, 60 bottles), and a fine listing of spirits. Patrons can be independent or join in the fun during Thursday's People's Karaoke, and their Sip 'n' Spin Wednesdays are popular with the vinyl crowd. Late night munchies translate to pickled veggies, popcorn, Noe's nachos, and maple buffalo wings. ⊠ *75 Union Sq., Somerville* ☎ *617/440–6022* ⊕ *www.theindo.com* Ⓜ *Bus 86, 87, 91, CT2.*

Orleans

BARS/PUBS | This American bar and restaurant opens floor-to-ceiling windows onto busy Holland Street and 14 all-sports HD screens onto diners and drinkers, except those dining on the patio. Nightly themes include Taco Fiesta Tuesday and Team Trivia Wednesday. There are weekend brunches, a $10 Burger of the Week Special, and a fully stocked bar including an extensive Scotch whiskey selection and 20 rotating taps of seasonal craft beers. ⊠ *65 Holland St., Somerville* ☎ *617/591–2100* ⊕ *www.orleansrestaurant.com* Ⓜ *Davis.*

Sacco's Bowl Haven

BOWLING | The '50s decor here "makes bowling the way it was, the way it is." Run by the Sacco family until 2010, the building and alleys in the heart of Davis Square were bought and are maintained by Flatbread Company pizzeria. Its 10 lanes are open daily until midnight (10:30 pm Sunday), and cost $30 per hour; there's a $3 fee to rent shoes. You can bowl away and enjoy organic pizza. ⊠ *45 Day St., Somerville* ☎ *617/776–0552* ⊕ *www.flatbreadcompany.com/sacco.*

Trina's Starlite Lounge

BARS/PUBS | Crazy cocktails wash down Southern comfort grub at this hip, retro joint packed with a younger crowd. The original drinks are just that—original—with concoctions like De Peach Mode (mezcal, amaro montenegro, and peach), Rockin' Chair (black tea–infused bourbon and Canton ginger cognac), and the Fallen Angel (a spicy mango margarita with a BBQ-dusted rim). Come for the cocktails and stay for the food. Their fried chicken and waffles is loved by locals, and the mac 'n cheese with hot dogs is your new guilty pleasure. ⊠ *3 Beacon St., Somerville* ☎ *617/576–0006.*

# Performing Arts

THEATER

★ Somerville Theatre

CONCERTS | This keystone of Davis Square's growing culture presents films (five screens) and easily 40 concerts a year (The Boss, Adele, U2, and Louis CK have all played here). The 900-seat theater recently celebrated its centennial with special performances, and continues to delight with special evening events like silent movies set to live music. In the coffered-ceiling, stone-tiled foyer you may buy beer, wine, popcorn, and ice cream to enjoy during the show. ⊠ *55 Davis Sq., Somerville* ☎ *617/625–5700* ⊕ *www. somervilletheatreonline.com* Ⓜ *Davis.*

Chapter 12

SIDE TRIPS FROM BOSTON

12

Updated by
Kim MacKinnon

Sights	Restaurants	Hotels	Shopping	Nightlife
★★★★★	★★★★★	★★★★★	★★★★★	★★★★★

WELCOME TO
SIDE TRIPS FROM BOSTON

TOP REASONS TO GO

★ **Early American history:** From Plimoth Plantation to Salem, Concord, and Lexington, you can visit colonial-reenactment museums, Revolutionary War battle sites, historic homes, and inns.

★ **Seafaring communities:** Set off on a whale-watch from Gloucester, warm yourself after a windy coastal walk in Rockport with clam chowder, and admire the dedicated routine of local fishermen.

★ **Revisit your reading:** Nathaniel Hawthorne's House of Seven Gables still stands in Salem. Liberate yourself with a swim in Thoreau's Walden Pond. In Concord, see where both Louisa May Alcott and Ralph Waldo Emerson penned their works.

★ **Cranberry bogs:** The bogs' red, green, gold, and blue colors dot Cape Cod and the Plymouth area.

★ **The Mayflower II:** The story of the Pilgrims' Atlantic crossing comes alive in Plymouth.

Visit Concord and Lexington and that history class from high school may suddenly come rushing back to you. The state's coast from Boston to Cape Ann is called the North Shore, visited for its beaches, quintessential New England seaside communities, and bewitching Salem. South of Boston lies more history in Plymouth and seaside scenery at Cape Cod.

1 Lexington. Where the British and the upstart Colonists first fought.

2 Concord. A literary hot spot, Emerson, the Alcotts, and Thoreau all lived in Concord.

3 Gloucester. America's oldest seaport still has vibrant harbor.

4 Salem. Famous for witches, writers, and the seafaring trade.

5 Rockport. Calling to artists for centuries, this scenic town is stunning.

6 Plymouth. Learn all about the Pilgrims' journey at several museums and memorials.

7 Provincetown. This town at the tip of the Cape Cod is a colorful spot for a day trip.

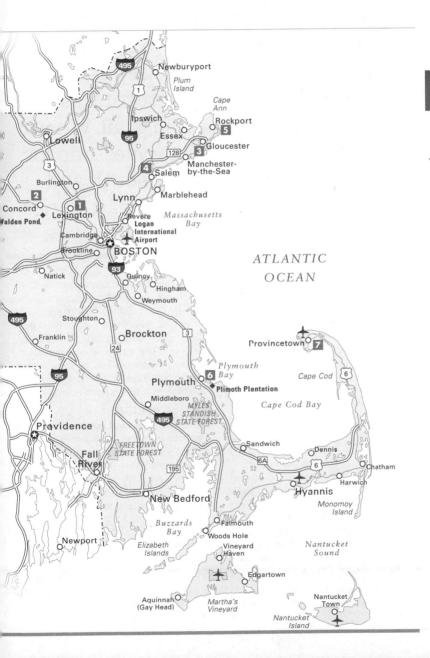

12

Side Trips from Boston   WELCOME TO SIDE TRIPS FROM BOSTON

History lies thick on the ground in the towns surrounding Boston—from Pilgrims to pirates, witches to whalers, the American Revolution to the Industrial Revolution. The sights outside the city are at least as interesting as those on Boston's Freedom Trail. When you're ready to trade history lessons for beach fun, Cape Cod to the south and the North Shore to the northeast entice sand-and-sun seekers.

Rich in more than history, the areas surrounding Boston also allow visitors to retrace the steps of famous writers, bask in the outdoors, and browse shops in funky artist communities. The haunts of literary luminaries of every generation lurk throughout Massachusetts. Head to Concord to visit the place where Henry David Thoreau wrote his prophetic *Walden* and where Louisa May Alcott's *Little Women* brightened a grim time during the Civil War. Relive Nathaniel Hawthorne's vision of Puritan-era Salem.

The seaside towns of Massachusetts were built before the Revolution, during the heyday of American shipping. On the North Shore, Gloucester is the country's oldest seaport and Rockport has artists' studios and seafood spots. South of Boston, you'll find Plymouth and the Mayflower as the town of Provincetown on the tip of Cape Cod.

In a more contemporary vein, Boston and its suburbs have become a major

destination for food and wine lovers. Internationally acclaimed chefs, including Barbara Lynch, Tiffany Faison, and Ming Tsai, draw thousands of devoted, discerning foodies to their restaurants each year. The state's extensive system of parks, protected forests, beaches, and nature preserves satisfies everyone from the avid hiker to the beach bum.

MAJOR REGIONS

Northwest of Boston, Lexington and **Concord** embody the spirit of the American Revolution. Sites of the first skirmishes of the Revolutionary War, these two quintessential New England towns were also cradles of American literature; several historic homes and small museums here are dedicated to some of the country's first substantial writers—Ralph Waldo Emerson, Nathaniel Hawthorne, Louisa May Alcott, and Henry David Thoreau.

The slice of Massachusetts' Atlantic Coast known as the **North Shore** extends past Boston to the picturesque Cape Ann

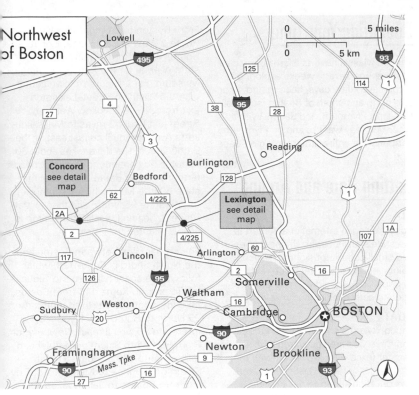

region just shy of the New Hampshire border. In addition to miles of woods and beaches, the North Shore's highlights include **Salem,** which thrives on a history of witches, writers, and maritime trades; **Gloucester,** the oldest seaport in America; and **Rockport,** rich with crafts shops and artists' studios. Bustling during the short summer season and breathtaking during the autumn foliage, the North Shore is calmer (and colder) between November and June. Since many restaurants, inns, and attractions operate on reduced hours, it's worth calling ahead off-season.

South of Boston will help you gain insight into what the earliest American settlers experienced. In **Plymouth,** learn how the Pilgrims raised food, built their homes, and survived under harsh conditions at Plimoth Plantation. As you may guess,

November in Plymouth brings special events focused on Thanksgiving. And don't forget vacation-central Cape Cod! **Provincetown,** on the tip of the Cape, is only 90 minutes by ferry from Boston.

Planning

When to Go

The dazzling foliage and cool temperatures make fall one of the best times to visit Massachusetts. Summer, especially late in the season when the water is a bit warmer, is ideal for beach vacations. Many towns save their best for winter—inns open their doors to carolers, shops serve eggnog, and lobster boats parade around Gloucester Harbor.

Budgeting Your Time

Though Massachusetts is small, you can easily spend several weeks exploring it. If you have a few days, head to a town or two north and south of Boston, such as Concord, Plymouth, and Salem. With a week you may want to add on Plymouth or spend the entire time relaxing on Cape Cod.

Getting Here and Around

AIR

Boston's Logan International Airport is the state's major airport. Trains, ferries, and small commuter flights take you to points around the state. If you're driving to Cape Cod, avoid the Friday late-afternoon-to-early-evening summer rush.

BOAT

Though Martha's Vineyard, Nantucket, and Cape Cod aren't covered in this chapter (except for Provincetown), they are popular getaway destinations from Boston. High-speed ferries provide transportation to Martha's Vineyard and Nantucket. The Bay State Cruise Co. and Boston Harbor Cruises run 90-minute ferry rides between Boston and Cape Cod's Provincetown from May through October; reservations are strongly recommended. For details on what to see and do in these destinations, see *Fodor's New England*.

CONTACT Bay State Cruise Co..
☎ *877/783–3779* ⊕ *www.baystate-cruisecompany.com.* **Boston Harbor Cruises.** ✉ *Long Wharf, 1 Seaport La., Boston* ☎ *877/733–9425, 617/227–4321, 877/733–9425* ⊕ *www.bostonharbor-cruises.com.*

CAR

Outside Boston you need a car to explore the state. Expect heavy traffic heading in and out of the city at rush hour, generally from 6 am to 9 am and 4 pm to 7 pm.

From Boston to Lexington, pick up Route 2 West in Cambridge. Exit at Routes 4/225. Turn left on Massachusetts Avenue for the National Heritage Museum. For Lexington's town center, take the Waltham Street–Lexington exit from Route 2. Follow Waltham Street just under 2 miles to Massachusetts Avenue; you'll be just east of the Battle Green. The drive takes about 30 minutes. To continue to Concord, head farther west on Route 2. Or take Interstate 90 (the Massachusetts Turnpike) to Interstate 95 North, and then exit at Route 2, heading west. Driving time is 40–45 minutes from Boston.

The primary link between Boston and the North Shore is Route 128, which follows the coast northeast to Gloucester. To pick up Route 128 from Boston, take Interstate 93 North to Interstate 95 North to Route 128. If you stay on Interstate 95, you'll reach Newburyport. From Boston to Salem or Marblehead, follow Route 128 to Route 114 into Salem or continue to Marblehead. Driving from Boston to Salem takes about 35–40 minutes; to Gloucester, about 50–60 minutes.

To get to Plymouth, take the Southeast Expressway Interstate 93 South to Route 3 (toward Cape Cod); Exits 6 and 4 lead to downtown Plymouth and Plimoth Plantation, respectively. Allow about one hour.

TRAIN

The MBTA's commuter rail offers service to Ipswich, Rockport, Salem, and Gloucester. Travel times are usually 70 minutes or less.

Massachusetts Bay Transportation Authority
☎ *800/392–6100, 617/222–3200* ⊕ *www.mbta.com.*

Hotels

Although Boston has everything from luxury hotels to charming bed-and-breakfasts, the signature accommodation outside Boston is the country inn; less extravagant and less expensive are B&B establishments, many of them in private homes. Make reservations well in advance if traveling in the summer. Smoking has been banned in all Massachusetts hotels.

Restaurants

Massachusetts invented the fried clam, and it's served in many North Shore restaurants. Creamy clam chowder is another specialty. Eating seafood in the rough—from paper plates in seaside shacks—is a revered local custom. At country inns you'll find traditional New England dinners: double-cut pork chops, rack of lamb, game, Boston baked beans, Indian pudding, and the dubiously glorified New England boiled dinner (corned beef and cabbage with potatoes, carrots, turnips, and other vegetables).

HOTEL AND RESTAURANT PRICES

Hotel prices in the reviews are the lowest cost of a standard double room in high season. Restaurant prices in the reviews are the average cost of a main course at dinner, or if dinner is not served, at lunch.

WHAT IT COSTS in U.S. Dollars			
$	$$	$$$	$$$$
RESTAURANTS			
under $15	$15–$24	$25–$32	over $32
HOTELS			
under $150	$150–$225	$226–$325	over $325

Tours

Gray Line of Boston & Cape Cod
Daily June through October and on weekends in May, Gray Line Boston & Cape Cod offers motor-coach tours from Boston to Lexington's Battle Green and Concord's Old North Bridge area. Seasonal trips to Salem, Marblehead, Newport, Cape Cod, and Plymouth, and city tours of Boston are also available. ☎ *781/986–6100, 617/720–6342, 781/986–6100* ⊕ *www.graylineboston.com.*

Lexington

16 miles northwest of Boston.

Incensed against the British, American colonials burst into action in Lexington in April 1775. On April 18, patriot leader Paul Revere alerted the town that British soldiers were approaching. The next day, as the British advance troops arrived in Lexington on their march toward Concord, the Minutemen were waiting to confront the redcoats in what became the first skirmish of the Revolutionary War.

These first military encounters of the American Revolution are very much a part of present-day Lexington, a modern suburban town that sprawls out from the historic sites near its center. Although the downtown area is generally lively, with ice-cream and coffee shops, boutiques, and a great little movie theater, the town becomes especially animated each Patriots' Day (April 19 but celebrated on the third Monday in April), when costume-clad groups re-create the Minutemen's battle maneuvers and Paul Revere rides again.

To learn more about the city and the 1775 clash, stop by the **Lexington Visitors Center.**

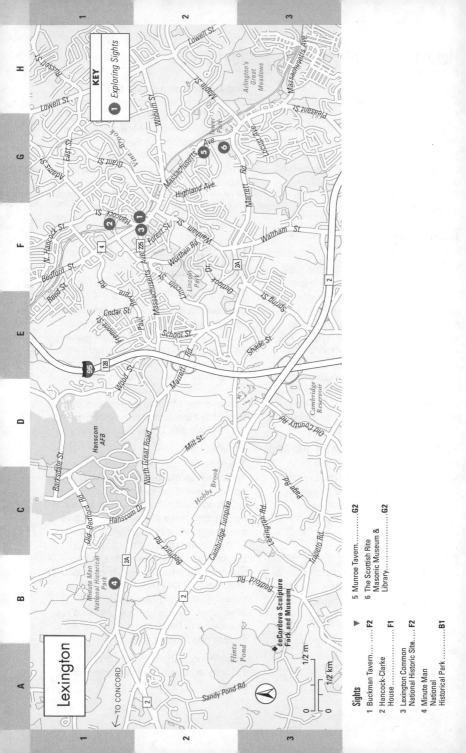

Lexington

KEY

1 *Exploring Sights*

Sights

1 Buckman Tavern............**F2**

2 Hancock-Clarke
House **F1**

3 Lexington Common
National Historic Site.....**F2**

4 Minute Man
National
Historical Park...........**B1**

5 Munroe Tavern............**G2**

6 The Scottish Rite
Masonic Museum &
Library....................**G2**

deCordova Sculpture
Park and Museum

TO CONCORD

0   1/2 km
0   1/2 m

GETTING HERE AND AROUND

Massachusetts Bay Transportation Authority (MBTA) operates bus service in the greater Boston area and serves Lexington.

ESSENTIALS

VISITOR INFORMATION Lexington Visitors Center. ⊠ *1605 Massachusetts Ave.* ☎ *781/862–1450* ⊕ *www.lexingtonchamber.org.*

Sights

Buckman Tavern

HISTORIC SITE | While waiting for the arrival of the British on the morning of April 19, 1775, the Minutemen gathered at this 1690 tavern. A half-hour tour takes in the tavern's seven rooms, which have been restored to the way they looked in the 1770s. Among the items on display is an old front door with a hole made by a British musket ball. ⊠ *1 Bedford St.* ☎ *781/862–3763* ⊕ *www.lexingtonhistory.org* ⟳ *$10* ⊙ *Closed Oct. 31–Apr.*

Hancock-Clarke House

HISTORIC SITE | On April 18, 1775, Paul Revere came here to warn patriots John Hancock and Sam Adams (who were staying at the house while attending the Provincial Congress in nearby Concord) of the advance of British troops. Hancock and Adams, on whose heads the British king had put a price, fled to avoid capture. The house, a parsonage built in 1698, is a 10-minute walk from Lexington Common. Inside is the Treasures of the Revolution exhibit, and outside, a Colonial herb garden. ⊠ *36 Hancock St.* ☎ *781/862–3763* ⊕ *www.lexingtonhistory.org* ⟳ *$10* ⊙ *Closed Oct. 31–Apr.*

Lexington Common National Historic Site

MILITARY SITE | It was on this 2-acre triangle of land, commonly referred to as simply the "Battle Green," on April 19, 1775, that the first confrontation between British soldiers, who were marching from Boston toward Concord, and the Colonial militia known as the

Take a Tour

Liberty Ride Trolley Tour. Ride along the historic Battle Road while your costumed guide recounts the exciting events of April 19, 1775, and the literary legacy that defined American identity and culture. This 90-minute trolley tour begins and ends at the Lexington Visitors Center. Purchase tickets online in advance. ⊠ *1605 Massachusetts Ave.* ☎ ⊕ *www.tourlexington.us/liberty-ride-trolley-tours* ⟳ *$28.*

Minutemen took place. The Minutemen—so called because they were able to prepare themselves at a moment's notice—were led by Captain John Parker, whose role in the American Revolution is commemorated in Henry Hudson Kitson's renowned 1900 *Minuteman* statue. Facing downtown Lexington at the tip of Battle Green, the statue's in a traffic island, and therefore makes for a difficult photo op. ⊠ *Junction of Massachusetts Ave. and Bedford St.* ⊕ *www.lexingtonma.gov/battle-green* ⟳ *Free.*

Minute Man National Historical Park

NATIONAL/STATE PARK | **FAMILY** | West of Lexington's center stretches this 1,000-acre park that also extends into nearby Lincoln and Concord. Begin your park visit at the **Minute Man Visitor Center** in Lexington to see the free multimedia presentation, "The Road to Revolution," a captivating introduction to the events of April 1775. Staffed by costumed park volunteers, the Whittemore House has a hands-on "Try on 1775!" exhibit where kids can wear Colonial clothing and gather ingredients for a meal. Continuing along Highway 2A toward Concord, you pass the point where Revere's midnight ride ended with his capture by the British; it's marked with a boulder and plaque, as well as an enclosure with wayside exhibits. You can also visit the

1732 **Hartwell Tavern,** a restored drover's (driver's) tavern staffed by park employees in period costume; they frequently demonstrate musket firing, militia drills, and talk about life in Colonial Massachusetts. ⊠ *Rte. 2A, ¼ mile west of Rte. 128* ☎ *978/369–6993* ⊕ *www.nps.gov/mima.*

Munroe Tavern

HISTORIC SITE | As April 19, 1775, dragged on, British forces met fierce resistance in Concord. Dazed and demoralized after the battle at Concord's Old North Bridge, the British backtracked and regrouped at this 1695 tavern 1 mile east of Lexington Common, while the Munroe family hid in nearby woods. The troops then retreated through what is now the town of Arlington. After a bloody battle there, they returned to Boston. ⊠ *1332 Massachusetts Ave.* ☎ *781/862–3763* ⊕ *www. lexingtonhistory.org* 🎫 *$10* ⊗ *Closed weekdays Apr. and May.*

The Scottish Rite Masonic Museum & Library

MUSEUM | View artifacts from all facets of American life, put in social and political context. Specializing in the history of American Freemasonry and Fraternalism, the changing exhibits and lectures also focus on local events leading up to April 1775 and illustrate Revolutionary-era life through everyday objects such as blacksmithing tools, bloodletting paraphernalia, and dental instruments, including a "tooth key" used to extract teeth. ⊠ *33 Marrett Rd., Rte. 2A at Massachusetts Ave.* ☎ *781/861–6559* ⊕ *www.srmml.org* 🎫 *Donations accepted.*

Concord

About 10 miles west of Lexington, 21 miles northwest of Boston.

The Concord of today is a modern suburb with a busy center filled with arty shops, places to eat, and (recalling the literary history made here) old bookstores. Autumn lovers, take note: Concord is

Tour by Phone

Cell-phone audio tours of various parts of Minute Man National Historical Park are available. They start at the visitor center, Hartwell Tavern, and Concord's North Bridge entrance—just look for the audio-tour signs and call ☎ 978/224–4905 for instructions.

a great place to start a fall foliage tour. From Boston, head west along Route 2 to Concord, and then continue on to find harvest stands and apple picking around Harvard and Stow.

GETTING HERE AND AROUND

The MBTA runs buses to Concord. On the MBTA Commuter Rail, Concord is a 40-minute ride on the Fitchburg Line, which departs from Boston's North Station.

BUS AND TRAIN CONTACT MBTA.
☎ *617/222–3200, 800/392–6100* ⊕ *www. mbta.com.*

ESSENTIALS

VISITOR INFORMATION Concord Visitor Center. ⊠ *58 Main St.* ☎ *978/369–3120* ⊕ *concordma.gov/1920/Visitor-Center.*

Sights

Concord Museum

MUSEUM | FAMILY | The original contents of Emerson's private study, as well as the world's largest collection of Thoreau artifacts, reside in this 1930 Colonial Revival building just east of the town center. The museum provides a good overview of the town's history, from its original Native American settlement to the present. Highlights include Native American artifacts, furnishings from Thoreau's Walden Pond cabin (there's a replica of the cabin itself on the museum's lawn), and one of the two lanterns hung at Boston's Old North Church to signal that the British

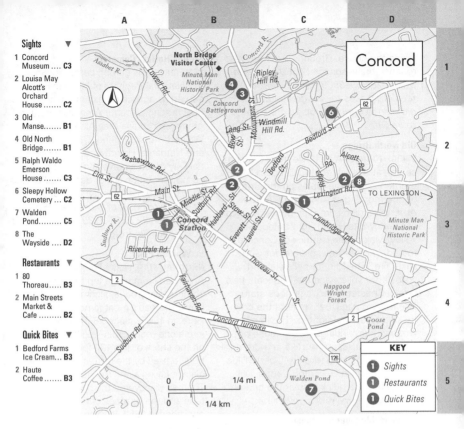

were coming by sea. If you've brought children, ask for a free family activity pack. ⊠ *200 Lexington Rd., GPS address is 53 Cambridge Tpke.* ☎ *978/369–9763* ⊕ *www.concordmuseum.org* ✉ *$12.*

Louisa May Alcott's Orchard House

HOUSE | The dark brown exterior of Louisa May Alcott's family home sharply contrasts with the light, wit, and energy so much in evidence within. Named for the apple orchard that once surrounded it, Orchard House was the Alcott family home from 1857 to 1877. Here Louisa wrote *Little Women,* based in part on her life with her three sisters; and her father, Bronson, founded the Concord School of Philosophy—the building remains behind the house. Because Orchard House had just one owner after the Alcotts left, and because it became a museum in 1911, more than 80% of the original furnishings

remain, including the semicircular shelt-desk where Louisa wrote *Little Women.* ⊠ *399 Lexington Rd.* ☎ *978/369–4118* ⊕ *www.louisamayalcott.org* ✉ *$10.*

Old Manse

HOUSE | The Reverend William Emerson, grandfather of Ralph Waldo Emerson, watched rebels and Redcoats battle from behind his home, which was within sight of the Old North Bridge. The house, built in 1770, was occupied continuously by the Emerson family for almost two centuries, except for a 3½-year period during which Nathaniel Hawthorne rented it. Furnishings date from the late 18th century. The house is open different days, depending upon the time of year. When open, tours run throughout the day and last 45 minutes, but call ahead to check. Don't whip out your camera, however: photography is prohibited inside the house. Grounds are open year-round sunrise–sunset. ✉ *269 Monument St.* ☎ *978/369–3909* ⊕ *www.thetrustees.org/places-to-visit/greater-boston/old-manse.html* ☒ *Grounds free; house tours $10.*

Old North Bridge

BRIDGE/TUNNEL | A half mile from Concord center, at this bridge, the Concord Minutemen turned the tables on the British on the morning of April 19, 1775. The Americans didn't fire first, but when two of their own fell dead from a Redcoat volley, Major John Buttrick of Concord roared, "Fire, fellow soldiers, for God's sake, fire." The Minutemen released volley after volley, and the Redcoats fled. Daniel Chester French's famous statue *The Minuteman* (1875) honors the country's first freedom fighters. The lovely wooded surroundings give a sense of what the landscape was like in more rural times. Guests who take the Liberty Ride trolley tour from Lexington Center will be treated to a quick stop at the bridge. ✉ *Concord* ⊕ *www.nps.gov/mima.*

Ralph Waldo Emerson House

HOUSE | The 19th-century essayist and poet Ralph Waldo Emerson lived briefly in the Old Manse in 1834–35, then moved to this home, where he lived until his death in 1882. Here he wrote the *Essays.* Except for artifacts from Emerson's study, now at the nearby Concord Museum, the Emerson House furnishings have been preserved as the writer left them, down to his hat resting on the newel post. You must join one of the half-hour-long tours to see the interior. ✉ *28 Cambridge Tpke., at Lexington Rd.* ☎ *978/369–2236* ⊕ *www.nps.gov/places/ralph-waldo-emerson-house.htm* ☒ *$9* ⊗ *Closed Nov.–mid-Apr., and Mon.–Wed. mid-Apr.–Oct.* ☞ *Call ahead for tour-scheduling information.*

Sleepy Hollow Cemetery

CEMETERY | This garden cemetery on the National Registry of Historic Places served as a place of inspiration and a final resting place for American literary greats like Louisa May Alcott, Ralph Waldo Emerson, Henry David Thoreau, and Nathaniel Hawthorne. Each Memorial Day Alcott's grave is decorated in commemoration of her death. ✉ *Bedford St. (Rte. 62), 24 Court La. and Bedford St.* ✛ *1 block east of Monument Sq. in Concord* ☎ *978/318–3233* ⊕ *www.friendsofsleepyhollow.org.*

★ Walden Pond

NATIONAL/STATE PARK | For lovers of Early American literature, a trip to Concord isn't complete without a pilgrimage to Henry David Thoreau's most famous residence. Here, in 1845, at age 28, Thoreau moved into a one-room cabin—built for $28.12—on the shore of this 100-foot-deep kettle hole formed by the retreat of an ancient glacier. Living alone for the next two years, Thoreau discovered the benefits of solitude and the beauties of nature. *Walden,* published in 1854, is a mixture of philosophy, nature writing, and proto-ecology. The site of the original house is staked out in stone. A full-size, authentically furnished replica of the cabin stands about ½ mile from the original site, near the Walden Pond State Reservation parking lot. During the summer, don't be shocked if you aren't allowed entrance: Walden Pond has a visitor capacity. ✉ *915 Walden St. (Rte. 126)* ✛ *To get to Walden Pond State Reservation from center of Concord—a trip of only 1½ miles—take Concord's Main St. a block west from Monument Sq., turn left onto Walden St., and head for intersection of Rtes. 2 and 126. Cross over Rte. 2 onto Hwy. 126, heading south for ½ mile* ☎ *978/369–3254* ⊕ *www.mass.gov/locations/walden-pond-state-reservation* ☒ *Free, but parking is $8 for vehicles with Massachusetts plates, $15 for vehicles with non-Massachusetts plates* ☞ *No dogs allowed.*

Literary Concord

The first wholly American literary movement was born in Concord, the tiny town west of Boston that, quite coincidentally, also witnessed the beginning of the American Revolution.

Under the influence of essayist and poet Ralph Waldo Emerson, a group eventually known as the Transcendental Club (but called the Hedges Club at the time) assembled regularly in Emerson's Concord home. Henry David Thoreau, a fellow townsman and famous proponent of self-reliance, was an integral club member, along with such others as pioneering feminist Margaret Fuller and poet Ellery Channing, both drawn to Concord simply because of Emerson's presence.

These are the names that have become indelible bylines in high-school anthologies and college syllabi, but Concord also produced beloved authors outside the Transcendentalist movement. These writers include Louisa May Alcott of *Little Women* fame and children's book author Harriet Lothrop, pseudonymously

known as Margaret Sydney. Even Nathaniel Hawthorne, whose various temporary homes around Massachusetts constitute a literary trail all their own, resided in Concord during the early and later portions of his career.

The cumulative inkwells of these authors have bestowed upon Concord a literary legacy unique in the United States, both for its influence on literature in general and for the quantity of related sights packed within such a small radius. From Alcott's Orchard House to Hawthorne's Old Manse, nearly all their houses remain standing, well preserved and open for tours.

The Thoreau Institute, within walking distance of a reconstruction of Thoreau's famous cabin in the woods at Walden Pond, is a repository of his papers and original editions. Emerson's study sits in the Concord Museum, across the street from his house. Even their final resting places are here, on Authors Ridge in Sleepy Hollow Cemetery, a few short blocks from the town common.

The Wayside

HOUSE | Nathaniel Hawthorne lived at the Old Manse in 1842–45, working on stories and sketches; he then moved to Salem (where he wrote *The Scarlet Letter*) and later to Lenox (*The House of the Seven Gables*). In 1852 he returned to Concord, bought this rambling structure called The Wayside, and lived here until his death in 1864. The home certainly appealed to literary types: the subsequent owner of The Wayside, Margaret Sidney, wrote the children's book *Five*

Little Peppers and How They Grew (1881), and before Hawthorne moved in, the Alcotts lived here, from 1845 to 1848. An exhibit center, in the former barn, provides information about the Wayside authors and links them to major events in American history. Hawthorne's tower-study, with his stand-up writing desk, is substantially as he left it. ⊠ *455 Lexington Rd.* ☎ *978/318–7863* ⊕ *www. nps.gov/mima/learn/historyculture/the-wayside.htm* ☜ *$7* ☺ *Closed in winter.*

🍴 Restaurants

80 Thoreau

$$ | **AMERICAN** | This fine-dining restaurant, located in the Concord Depot, offers new American cuisine, with much of the food on the plate coming from nearby local farms. Friendly and knowledgeable servers can help you navigate the menu, which changes with the seasons, along with what's available at the time. **Known for:** New England ingredients; creative cocktails; excellent service. [$] *Average main: $23* ✉ *80 Thoreau St.* ☎ *978/318–0008* 🌐 *www.80thoreau.com* 🕒 *Closed Sun. No lunch.*

Main Streets Market & Cafe

$$ | **AMERICAN** | Cyclists, families, and sightseers pack into this brick building, which was used to store munitions during the Revolutionary War. Wood floors and blackboard menus add a touch of nostalgia, but the extensive menu includes many modern hits, including ale mac and cheese, meat loaf, and a Yankee pot roast dinner. **Known for:** live music five nights a week; summertime ice-cream counter; open early for breakfast. [$] *Average main: $18* ✉ *42 Main St.* ☎ *978/369–9948* 🌐 *www.mainstreetsmarketandcafe.com.*

☕ Coffee and Quick Bites

Bedford Farms Ice Cream

$ | **AMERICAN** | **FAMILY** | The Concord outpost of the long-running Bedford Farms Ice Cream shop offers just as many tasty, locally made ice creams. Always making flavors include chunky chocolate pudding, green monster, and black raspberry, but there is also a list of sometimes making flavors, sorbets, sherbets, and yogurts. **Known for:** more than 60 flavors; large portions; friendly staff. [$] *Average main: $6* ✉ *68 Thoreau St.* ☎ *978/341–0000* 🌐 *www.bedfordfarmsicecream.com.*

Haute Coffee

$ | **AMERICAN** | Stop in for freshly brewed coffee and homemade baked goods, like lemon olive oil cake, Valrhona chocolate cupcakes, and a variety of scones at this cozy spot. At lunch, enjoy the soup du jour and a selection of sandwiches. **Known for:** creative pastries; coffee ground and brewed to order; gluten-free and vegan options. [$] *Average main: $8* ✉ *12 Walden St.* ☎ *978/369–9900* 🌐 *myhautecoffee.com* 🕒 *Closed Tues.*

🏃 Activities

South Bridge Boat House

BOATING | You can reach the North Bridge section of the Minute Man National Historical Park by water if you rent a canoe or kayak at the South Bridge Boat House and paddle along the Sudbury and Concord rivers. You can even paddle all the way to Sudbury or up to Billerica. ✉ *496 Main St.* ☎ *978/369–9438* 🌐 *www.southbridgeboathouse.com* 🎟 *Canoes from $16/hr; kayaks from $16/hr* 🕒 *Closed Nov. 1–Apr. 1.*

Gloucester

37 miles northeast of Boston, 8 miles northeast of Manchester-by-the-Sea.

On Gloucester's fine seaside promenade is a famous statue of a man steering a ship's wheel, his eyes searching the horizon. The statue, which honors those who go down to the sea in ships, was commissioned by the town citizens in celebration of Gloucester's 300th anniversary in 1923. The oldest seaport in the nation (with some of the North Shore's best beaches) is still a major fishing port. Sebastian Junger's 1997 book *A Perfect Storm* was an account of the fate of the *Andrea Gail,* a Gloucester fishing boat caught in the storm of the century in October 1991. In 2000 the book was made into a movie, filmed on location in Gloucester.

ESSENTIALS
VISITOR INFORMATION Cape Ann Chamber of Commerce. ⌧ *33 Commercial St.* ☎ *978/283–1601* ⊕ *www.capeannchamber.com.* **Cape Ann Chamber of Commerce, Rockport Visitor Center.** ⌧ *170 Main St., (Rte. 127), Rockport* ☎ *978/546–9372* ⊕ *www.rockportusa.com.*

 Sights

Cape Ann Museum
MUSEUM | The Cape Ann Museum celebrates the art, history, and culture of Cape Ann. The museum's collections include fine art from the 19th century to the present, artifacts from the fishing, maritime, and granite-quarrying industries, as well as textiles, furniture, a library-archives, and two historic houses. ⌧ *27 Pleasant St.* ☎ *978/283–0455* ⊕ *www.capeannmuseum.org* ⌧ *$12* ⊗ *Closed Mon.*

Hammond Castle Museum
MUSEUM | Inventor John Hays Hammond Jr., credited with more than 500 patents, including remote control via radio waves, built this structure in 1926 to resemble a "medieval" stone castle. The museum contains medieval-style furnishings and paintings, and the Great Hall houses an impressive 8,200-pipe organ. From the castle you can see Norman's Woe Rock, made famous by Longfellow in his poem "The Wreck of the Hesperus." In July and August, unique "Spiritualism Tours" are an additional option on Thursday nights (for an extra fee), with discussion of topics like the Ouija board, spirit photography, séances, and the science behind Spiritualism. ⌧ *80 Hesperus Ave., south side of Gloucester off Rte. 127* ☎ *978/283–2080* ⊕ *www.hammondcastle.org* ⌧ *$15* ⊗ *Closed Mon. and Jan.–early Apr.*

Rocky Neck
NEIGHBORHOOD | On a peninsula within Gloucester's working harbor, the town's creative side thrives in this neighborhood, one of the oldest continuously working artists' colonies in the United States. Its alumni include Winslow Homer, Maurice Prendergast, Jane Peter, and Cecilia Beaux. Call for winter hours. ⌧ *6 Wonson St.* ☎ *978/515–7004* ⊕ *www.rockyneckartcolony.org.*

Thomas E. Lannon
Consider a sail along the harbor and coast aboard the meticulously maintained 65-foot schooner *Thomas E. Lannon,* crafted in Essex in 1997 and modeled after the great vessels built a century before. From mid-May through mid-October the Ellis family offers two-hour sails, including trips that let you enjoy the sunset or music. ⌧ *63 Rogers St., next to Gloucester House restaurant* ☎ *978/281–6634* ⊕ *www.schooner.org* ⌧ *$45.*

 Beaches

Gloucester has the best beaches on the North Shore. From Memorial Day through mid-September parking costs $20 on weekdays and $25 on weekends, when the lots often fill by 10 am.

Good Harbor Beach
BEACH—SIGHT | This beach has calm, waveless waters and soft sand, and is surrounded by grassy dunes, making it perfect any time of year. In summer (June, July, and August), it is lifeguard patrolled, handicap accessible, and there is a snack bar if you don't feel like packing in food. The restrooms and showers are wheelchair accessible, and you can pick up beach toys at the concessions. On weekdays parking is plentiful, but the lot fills by 10 am on weekends. In June, green flies can be bothersome. **Amenities:** food and drink; lifeguards; parking (fee); showers; toilets. **Best for:** swimming; walking. ⌧ *Gloucester* ⌖ *Clearly signposted from Rte. 127A* ⊕ *gloucester-ma.gov* ⌧ *Parking from $30 per car.*

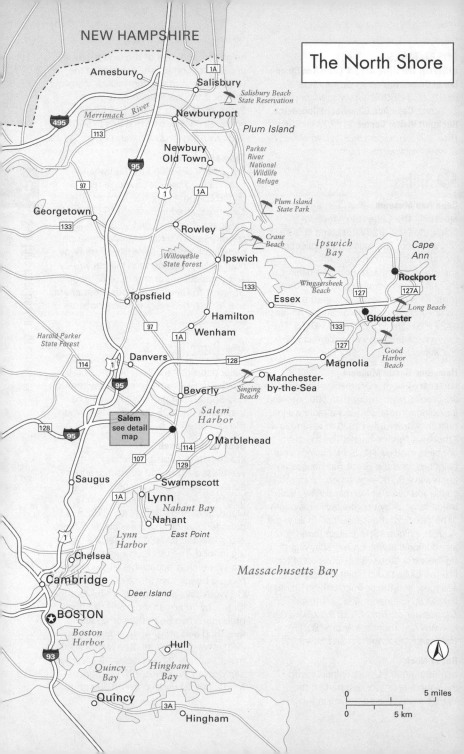

Long Beach

BEACH—SIGHT | Just as its name implies, this soft-sand beach that is half in Rockport, half in Gloucester is long, and it's also broad. It draws crowds from the houses that border it, particularly on weekends. Pay attention to the tide schedule, or you may find there's no beach to sit on. Cape Ann Motor Inn is nearby. Parking is very limited. Don't even think of parking on neighborhood streets if you don't have a town parking sticker—you will be towed. However, there is a lot on the Gloucester side. **Amenities:** none. **Best for:** swimming; walking. ✉ *Off Rte. 127A on Gloucester-Rockport town line, Off Rockport Rd.*

★ Wingaersheek Beach

BEACH—SIGHT | With white sand and dunes, Wingaersheek Beach is a well-protected cove with both a beach side and a boat side. The white Annisquam lighthouse is in the bay. The beach is known for its miles of white sand and calm waters. On weekends arrive early. The parking lot generally fills up by midmorning. It's handicap accessible and beach wheelchairs are available on request. **Amenities:** food and drink; parking (fee); toilets. **Best for:** swimming; walking. ✉ *232 Atlantic St.* ✥ *Take Rte. 128 N to Exit 13* 🌐 *gloucester-ma.gov* 🎫 *Limited parking, from $30 per car.*

🍴 Restaurants

The Franklin Cafe

$$ | **AMERICAN** | This contemporary night-spot offers bistro-style chicken, roast cod, and steak frites, perfect for the late-night crowd (it's open until midnight during the summer). Live music is on tap every Thursday evening. **Known for:** sushi available Tuesday through Saturday; friendly vibe; good service. [$] *Average main: $25* ✉ *118 Main St.* ☎ *978/283–7888* 🌐 *www.franklincapeann.com* 🕓 *No lunch.*

Passports

$ | **ECLECTIC** | **FAMILY** | In the heart of Downtown Gloucester, Passports serves a modern take on classic New England seafood. The fried oysters and house haddock are favorites here, and there's always local art hanging on the walls for patrons to buy. **Known for:** lively atmosphere; warm, fresh popovers; great, central location. [$] *Average main: $22* ✉ *110 Main St.* ☎ *978/281–3680* 🌐 *www.facebook.com/PassportsRestaurant/.*

★ Woodman's of Essex

$$ | **SEAFOOD** | **FAMILY** | According to local legend, this is where Lawrence "Chubby" Woodman invented the first fried clam back in 1916. Today this sprawling wooden shack with indoor booths and outdoor picnic tables is *the* place for seafood in the rough. **Known for:** fried clams; gluten-free options; open year-round; the popular "down-river" lobster combo plate. [$] *Average main: $20* ✉ *121 Main St. (Rte. 133), Essex* ☎ *978/768–2559, 800/649–1773* 🌐 *www.woodmans.com.*

☕ Coffee and Quick Bites

Virgilio's Italian Bakery

$ | **ITALIAN** | Since 1961, this bustling Italian bakery and deli has been making fresh breads and rolls, serving some of the tastiest sandwiches around. One of the shop's claims to fame is the now-famous Saint Joseph Sandwich, made with their Italian rolls stuffed with Italian deli meats, olive oil, and oregano. **Known for:** family-owned; tasty prepared foods; busy in summer. [$] *Average main: $7* ✉ *29 Main St.* ☎ *978/283–5295* 🌐 *www.virgiliosbakery.com* 🕓 *Closed Sun.*

Sights

1 House of the Seven Gables....... **D3**
2 Peabody Essex Museum **B4**
3 Salem Maritime National Historic Site **C4**
4 Salem Witch Museum **B3**
5 Salem Witch Trials Memorial ... **B4**

Restaurants

1 Finz Seafood & Grill **C4**
2 Ledger Restaurant and Bar **A4**

Hotels

1 Amelia Payson House........**B2**
2 The Hawthorne Hotel......... **B3**
3 The Merchant... **A4**

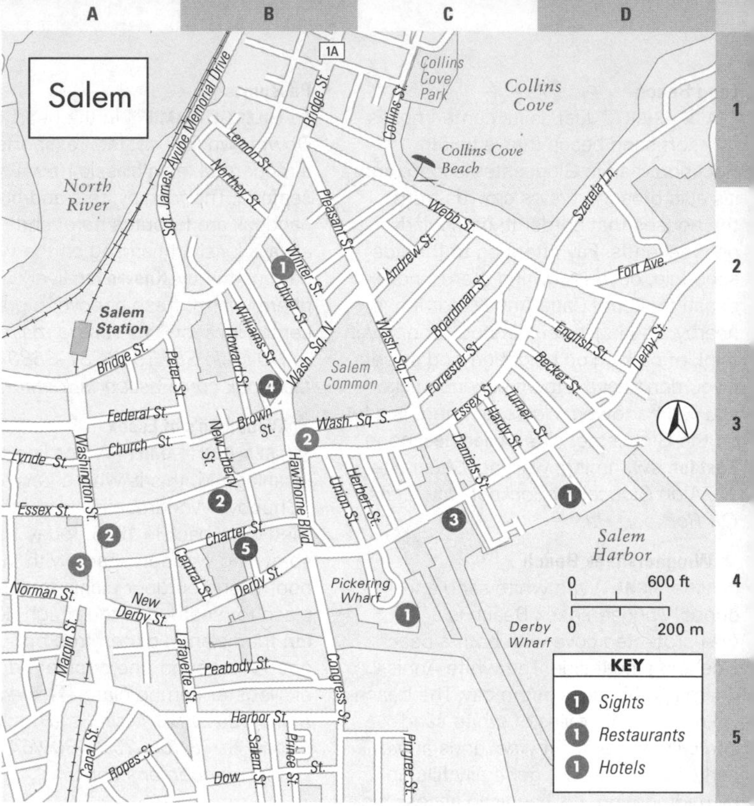

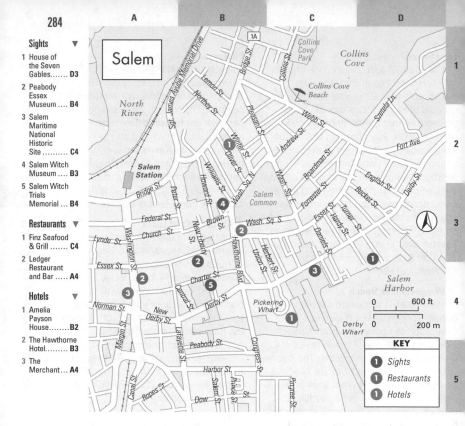

Hotels

Cape Ann's Marina Resort & Spa

$$ | RESORT | FAMILY | This year-round hotel less than a mile from downtown Gloucester comes alive in summer with an on-site restaurant and deep-sea fishing excursions. **Pros:** free Wi-Fi; full marina; indoor pool and Jacuzzi with poolside bar. **Cons:** hotel surrounded by parking lots; price hike during summer; bar area can be loud in summer. *Rooms from: $226* *75 Essex Ave.* *978/283–2116, 800/626–7660* *www.capeannmarina.com* *31 rooms* *No meals.*

Cape Ann Motor Inn

$ | HOTEL | On the sands of Long Beach, this three-story, shingled motel, open year-round, has no-frills rooms except for the balconies and ocean views. **Pros:** exceptional view from every room; kids under age 12 stay free; free Wi-Fi. **Cons:** thin walls; motel quality; no A/C. *Rooms from: $195* *33 Rockport Rd.* *978/281–2900, 800/464–8439* *www.capeannmotorinn.com* *31 rooms* *Free Breakfast.*

★ Castle Manor Inn

$ | B&B/INN | With original woodwork and cozy fireplaces, this restored 1900 Victorian inn perfectly captures the Cape Ann aesthetic. **Pros:** discount parking passes to the local beaches; historic; close to Gloucester's beaches. **Cons:** closes for the winter; roads in the area can be windy and confusing; may be too intimate for some travelers. *Rooms from: $150* *141 Essex Ave.* *978/515–7386* *www.castlemanorinn.com* *10 rooms* *No meals.*

Salem

16 miles northeast of Boston, 4 miles west of Marblehead.

Known for years as the Witch City, Salem is redefining itself. Though numerous witch-related attractions and shops still draw tourists, there's much more to the city. But first, a bit on its bewitched past...

The witchcraft hysteria emerged from the trials of 1692, when several Salem-area girls fell ill and accused some of the townspeople of casting spells on them. More than 150 men and women were charged with practicing witchcraft, a crime punishable by death. After the trials later that year, 19 people were hanged and one man was crushed to death.

Though the witch trials might have built Salem's infamy, it'd be a mistake to ignore the town's rich maritime and creative traditions, which played integral roles in the country's evolution. Frigates out of Salem opened the Far East trade routes and generated the wealth that created America's first millionaires. Among its native talents are writer Nathaniel Hawthorne, the intellectual Peabody sisters, navigator Nathaniel Bowditch, and architect Samuel McIntire. This creative spirit is today celebrated in Salem's internationally recognized museums, waterfront shops and restaurants, galleries, and wide common.

To learn more on the area, stop by the **Regional Visitor's Center.** Innovatively designed in the Old Salem Armory, the center has exhibits, a 27-minute film, maps, and a gift shop.

ESSENTIALS

VISITOR INFORMATION Destination Salem. ⊠ *81 Washington St., Suite 204* ☎ *978/741-3252, 877/725-3662* ⊕ *www. salem.org.* **Salem Armory Visitor Center.** ⊠ *2 New Liberty St.* ☎ *978/740-1650* ⊕ *www.nps.gov/ner/sama.*

Sights

House of the Seven Gables

HOUSE | Immortalized in Nathaniel Hawthorne's classic novel, this site is itself a historic treasure. Built in 1668 and also known as the Turner-Ingersoll Mansion, the house includes the famous secret staircase, a re-creation of Hepzibah's cent shop from *The House of Seven Gables*, and some of the finest Georgian interiors in the country. Also on the property is the small house where Hawthorne was born in 1804; built in 1750, it was moved from its original location a few blocks away. ⊠ *115 Derby St.* ☎ *978/744-0991* ⊕ *www.7gables.org* ⊡ *$17.*

★ Peabody Essex Museum

MUSEUM | Salem's world-class museum celebrates superlative works from around the globe and across time, including American art and architecture, Asian export art, photography, maritime art and history, as well as Native American, Oceanic, and African art. With a collection of 1.8 million works, housed in a contemplative blend of modern design, the museum represents a diverse range of styles; exhibits include pieces ranging from American decorative and seamen's art to an interactive Art & Nature Center and photography. While there be sure to tour the Yin Yu Tang house. This fabulous 200-year-old house dates to the Qing Dynasty (1644–1911) of China. The museum brought it over from China in sections and reassembled it here. ⊠ *East India Sq.* ☎ *978/745-9500, 866/745-1876* ⊕ *www. pem.org* ⊡ *$20* ☉ *Closed Mon.*

Salem Maritime National Historic Site

LIGHTHOUSE | Near Derby Wharf, this 9¼-acre site focuses on Salem's heritage as a major seaport with a thriving overseas trade. It includes the 1762 home of Elias Derby, America's first millionaire; the 1819 Custom House, made famous in Nathaniel Hawthorne's *The Scarlet Letter;* and a replica of the *Friendship,* a 171-foot, three-masted 1797

Landlubbers can go to sea at Salem's Peabody Essex Museum.

merchant vessel. There's also an active lighthouse dating from 1871, as well as the nation's last surviving 18th-century wharves. Newer to the site is the 1770 Pedrick Store House, moved from nearby Marblehead and reassembled right on Derby Wharf; the two-story structure once played a vital role in the lucrative merchant seaside trade. The grounds are open 24/7, but buildings open on a seasonal schedule. ⊠ *193 Derby St.* ☎ *978/740–1650 visitor center* ⊕ *www. nps.gov/sama/index.htm* ✉ *Free with exception of film "Witch Hunt: Exam the Evidence.".*

Salem Witch Museum

MUSEUM | An informative and fascinating introduction to the 1692 witchcraft hysteria, this museum offers a look at 1692 with 13 life-size stage sets featuring narration of what life was like at that time, plus a 15-minute guided tour through the exhibit, "Witches: Evolving Perceptions," which describes witch hunts through the years. ⊠ *19½ Washington Sq. N* ☎ *978/744–1692* ⊕ *www.salemwitchmuseum.com* ✉ *$13.*

Salem Witch Trials Memorial

MEMORIAL | Dedicated by Nobel Laureate Elie Wiesel in 1992, this quiet, contemplative space—an antidote to the relentless marketing of the merry-witches motif—honors those who died because they refused to confess that they were witches. A stone wall is studded with 20 stone benches, each inscribed with a victim's name, and sits next to Salem's oldest burying ground. ⊠ *Liberty St.* ✛ *Between Charter and Derby Sts.* ⊕ *salem.org/listing/witch-trials-memorial.*

🍴 Restaurants

Finz Seafood & Grill

$$ | SEAFOOD | This contemporary seafood restaurant on Salem Harbor treats patrons to prime canal views. Seafood potpie and lobster rolls highlight the lunch menu, while sesame-crusted tuna or steamed lobster are dinner favorites, but burgers and steaks are available for meat eaters. **Known for:** outdoor seating; classic New England seafood; large sushi

The First Witch Trial

It was in Danvers, not Salem, that the first witch trial was held, originating with the family of Samuel Parris, a minister who moved to the area in 1680 from Barbados, bringing with him two slaves, including one named Tituba. In 1691 Samuel's daughter, Betty, and niece, Abigail, began having fits. Tituba, who had told Betty and Abigail stories of magic and witchcraft from her homeland, baked a witch cake to identify the witches who were harming the girls. The girls in turn accused Tituba of witchcraft. After three days of questioning, which included beatings from Samuel and a promise from him to free her if she cooperated, Tituba confessed to meeting the devil (in the form of a black hog or dog). She also claimed there were other witches in the village, confirming the girls' accusations against Sarah Good and Sarah Osborne, but she refused to name any others. Tituba's trial prompted the frenzy that led to the deaths of 20 accused witches.

menu. $ *Average main: $24* ✉ *76 Wharf St.* ☎ *978/744–8485* ⊕ *www.hipfinz.com.*

Ledger Restaurant and Bar

$$$ | **AMERICAN** | Housed in a 200-year-old building that was once a bank—Ledger takes its name from the massive amount of banking ledgers found in the building—today diners enjoy a modern-day spin on traditional 19th-century dishes, especially live-fire cooking. Grab a cocktail while checking out the multitude of original features incorporated into the restaurant, including deposit boxes and a huge safe that serves as the restaurant's walk-in refrigerator. **Known for:** historic digs; New England cuisine; live music once a month. $ *Average main: $26* ✉ *125 Washington St.* ☎ *978/594–1908* ⊕ *www.ledgersalem.com* ⊘ *Closed Mon.*

🛏 Hotels

★ Amelia Payson House

$$ | **B&B/INN** | Built in 1845, this Greek Revival house is a comfortable bed-and-breakfast near all the historic attractions. **Pros:** fireplaces in each room; outdoor lounge with a fire pit; on-site parking. **Cons:** no children under 12; hard to get reservations; might be too quaint for some. $ *Rooms from: $225* ✉ *16 Winter St.* ☎ *978/744–8304* ⊕ *www.amelia-paysonhouse.com* ⇱ *3 rooms* ¶⊘ *Free breakfast.*

The Hawthorne Hotel

$ | **HOTEL** | Elegantly restored, this full-service historic hotel celebrates the town's most famous writer and is within walking distance from the town common, museums, and waterfront. **Pros:** lovely, historic lobby; free parking available behind hotel; free Wi-Fi. **Cons:** many rooms are small; two-night minimum June through October; pricey pet policy. $ *Rooms from: $189* ✉ *18 Washington Sq. W* ☎ *978/744–4080, 800/729–7829* ⊕ *www. hawthornehotel.com* ⇱ *93 rooms* ¶⊘ *No meals* ⌕ *$50 charge per room per night for pets.*

The Merchant

$$ | **HOTEL** | The 11-room Merchant is an intimate, design-forward Lark Hotel property in the heart of Salem's historic district. **Pros:** off-site parking at Riley Plaza is $5; free Wi-Fi; downstairs lounge with fully stocked "BYOB Mixer Bar". **Cons:** no elevator; no in-room fridge; books up quickly. $ *Rooms from: $272*

✉ *148 Washington St.* ☎ *978/745–8100* 🌐 *www.themerchantsalem.com* 🛏 *11 rooms* 🍴 *Free Breakfast.*

Performing Arts

THEATER

Cry Innocent: The People versus Bridget Bishop

THEATER | This show, the longest continuously running play north of Boston, transports audience members to Bridget Bishop's witchcraft hearing of 1692. After hearing historical testimonies, the audience cross-examines the witnesses and decides whether to send Bridget to trial or not. Actors respond in character revealing much about the Puritan frame of mind. Each show is different and allows audience members to play their "part" in history. ✉ *Old Town Hall, 32 Derby Sq.* ☎ *978/810–2588* 🌐 *www.historyalivesalem.com* 🎟 *$25.*

Rockport

41 miles northeast of Boston, 4 miles northeast of Gloucester on Rte. 127.

Rockport, at the very tip of Cape Ann, derives its name from the local granite formations. Many Boston-area structures are made of stone cut from its long-gone quarries. Today the town is a tourist center with a well-marked, centralized downtown that is easy to navigate and access on foot. Unlike typical tourist-trap landmarks, Rockport's shops sell quality arts, clothing, and gifts, and its restaurants serve seafood or home-baked cookies rather than fast food. Walk past shops and colorful clapboard houses to the end of Bearskin Neck for an impressive view of the Atlantic Ocean and the old, weather-beaten lobster shack known as Motif No. 1, a popular subject for amateur painters and photographers.

ESSENTIALS

VISITOR INFORMATION Rockport Visitor Center. ✉ *Upper Main St. (Rte. 127)* ☎ *978/546–9372* 🌐 *www.rockportusa.com.*

Restaurants

Brackett's Ocean View

$$ | **SEAFOOD** | Enormous windows in this quiet, homey restaurant offer excellent views across Sandy Bay, along with plenty of chowder, fish cakes, lobster, and other seafood dishes. While the restaurant is only open seasonally, next door is their cafe, Brothers' Brew Coffee Shop, open year-round. **Known for:** local seafood; every table has a waterfront view; great downtown location. [$] *Average main: $18* ✉ *25 Main St.* ☎ *978/546–2797* 🌐 *www.bracketts.com* 🕒 *Closed Columbus Day–mid-Apr.*

Hotels

Addison Choate

$$$ | **B&B/INN** | Just a minute's walk from both the center of Rockport and the train station, this 1851 inn sits in a prime location. **Pros:** free parking; comfortable, spacious porch for relaxing; free Wi-Fi. **Cons:** only one bedroom on the first floor; most rooms require taking the stairs; may be too intimate a setting for some. [$] *Rooms from: $299* ✉ *49 Broadway* ☎ *978/546–7543, 800/245–7543* 🌐 *addisonchoate.com* 🛏 *7 rooms* 🍴 *Free Breakfast.*

Bearskin Neck Motor Lodge

$$ | **HOTEL** | **FAMILY** | Near the end of Bearskin Neck, this small brick-and-shingle motel offers guests the best of both worlds: beautiful, oceanfront rooms, as well as easy access to shopping and restaurants. **Pros:** all rooms have balconies and unobstructed ocean views; central location; mini-refrigerators in rooms. **Cons:** lots of summertime tourists; heavy "classic motel" vibe; no pets allowed. [$] *Rooms from: $220* ✉ *64 Bearskin Neck*

☎ 978/546–6677, 877/507–6272 ⊕ www.
bearskinneckmotorlodge.com ⊗ Closed
early Dec.–Mar. ⊅ 8 rooms ❍❘ No meals.

★ **Sally Webster Inn**

$ | B&B/INN | This historic inn, which is
within walking range of shops, restaurants, and beaches, was named for a
member of Hannah Jumper's "Hatchet
Gang," teetotalers who smashed up the
town's liquor stores in 1856 and turned
Rockport into the dry town it remained
until as recently as 2008. **Pros:** full buffet
breakfast; free Wi-Fi; free parking. **Cons:**
some rooms accessed via second-floor
stairs; small bathrooms; might be too
quaint for some. Ⓢ *Rooms from: $150*
⊠ *34 Mt. Pleasant St.* ☎ *978/546–9251*
⊕ *www.sallywebster.com* ➡ *No credit
cards* ⊅ *6 rooms* ❍❘ *Free Breakfast.*

Plymouth

40 miles south of Boston.

On December 26, 1620, 102 weary
men, women, and children disembarked
from the *Mayflower* to found the first
permanent European settlement north of
Virginia (they had found their earlier landing in Provincetown to be unsuitable).
Today Plymouth is characterized by narrow streets, clapboard mansions, shops,
antiques stores, and a scenic waterfront.
To mark Thanksgiving, the town holds
activities including historic-house tours
and a parade. Historic statues dot the
town, including depictions of William
Bradford, Pilgrim leader and governor
of Plymouth Colony for more than 30
years, on Water Street; a Pilgrim maiden
in Brewster Gardens; and Massasoit,
the Wampanoag chief who helped the
Pilgrims survive, on Carver Street.

ESSENTIALS

**VISITOR INFORMATION Plymouth Visitor
Information Center.** ⊠ *130 Water St., at
Rte. 44* ☎ *508/747–7525* ⊕ *www.seeplymouth.com.*

Sights

Mayflower II

LIGHTHOUSE | FAMILY | This seaworthy
replica of the 1620 *Mayflower* was built
in England through research and a bit of
guesswork, then sailed across the Atlantic in 1957. As you explore the interior and
exterior of the ship, which was extensively refurbished in time for Plymouth's
400th anniversary in 2020, sailors in modern dress answer your questions about
both the reproduction and the original
ship, while costumed guides provide a
17th-century perspective. Plymouth Rock
is nearby. ⊠ *State Pier* ☎ *508/746–1622*
⊕ *www.plimoth.org* 🎟 *From $9; heritage
passes and combination tickets include
Plimoth Plantation and Plimoth Grist Mill*
⊗ *Closed mid-Nov.–mid-Mar.*

National Monument to the Forefathers

MEMORIAL | Said to be the largest
freestanding granite statue in the
United States, this allegorical monument stands high on an 11-acre hilltop
site. Designed by Hammet Billings of
Boston in 1854 and dedicated in 1889,
it depicts Faith, surrounded by Liberty,
Morality, Justice, Law, and Education,
and includes scenes from the Pilgrims'
early days in Plymouth. ⊠ *72 Allerton St.*
⊕ *www.seeplymouth.com/things-to-do/
national-monument-forefathers.*

Pilgrim Hall Museum

MUSEUM | FAMILY | From the waterfront
sights, it's a short walk to one of the
country's oldest public museums. Established in 1824, Pilgrim Hall Museum
transports you back to the time of the
Pilgrims' landing with objects carried
by those weary travelers to the New
World. Historic items on display include
a carved chest, a remarkably well-preserved wicker cradle, Myles Standish's
sword, and John Alden's Bible. In
addition, the museum presents the story
of the Wampanoag, the native people
who lived here 10,000 years before the
arrival of the Pilgrims, and who are still

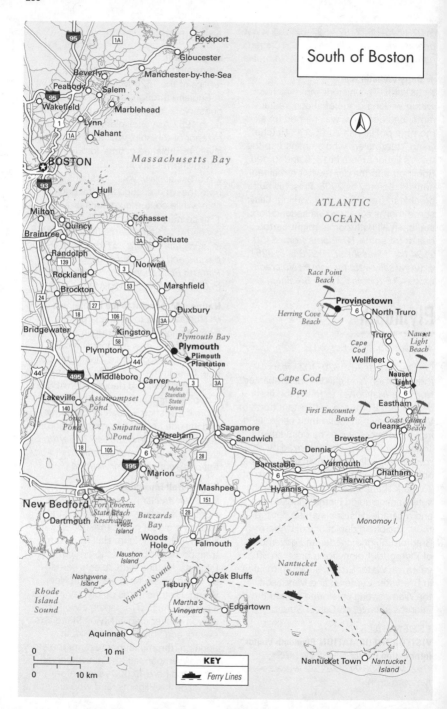

South of Boston

live here today. ⊠ *75 Court St. (Rte. 3A)* ☎ *508/746–1620* ⊕ *www.pilgrimhall.org* 🎫 *$12* ⊙ *Closed Jan.*

★ **Plimoth Plantation**

MUSEUM VILLAGE | FAMILY | Against the backdrop of the Atlantic Ocean, and 3 miles south of downtown Plymouth, this living museum shares the rich, interwoven story of the Plymouth Colony and the Wampanoag homeland through engaging daily programs and special events. A 1620s Pilgrim village has been carefully re-created, from the thatch roofs, cramped quarters, and open fireplaces to the long-horned livestock. Throw away your preconception of white collars and funny hats; through ongoing research, the Plimoth staff has developed a portrait of the Pilgrims that's more complex than the dour folk in school textbooks. Listen to the accents of the "residents," who never break out of character. Feel free to engage them in conversation about their life. Don't worry, 21st-century museum educators are on hand to help answer any questions you have as well. On the Wampanoag homesite meet native people speaking from a modern perspective of the traditions, lifeways, and culture of Eastern Woodlands Indigenous people. Note that there's not a lot of shade here in summer. ⊠ *137 Warren Ave. (Rte. 3A)* ☎ *508/746–1622* ⊕ *www.plimoth.org* 🎫 *$32* ⊙ *Closed late-Nov.–mid-Mar.*

Plymouth Rock

MEMORIAL | FAMILY | This landmark rock, just a few dozen yards from the *Mayflower II*, is popularly believed to have been the Pilgrims' stepping-stone when they left the ship. Given the stone's unimpressive appearance—it's little more than a boulder—and dubious authenticity (as explained on a nearby plaque), the grand canopy overhead seems a trifle ostentatious. Still, more than a million people a year come to visit this world-famous symbol of courage and faith. ■**TIP→ The views of Plymouth Harbor alone are worth the visit.** ⊠ *Water St.* ☎ *508/747–5360* ⊕ *www.mass.gov/ locations/pilgrim-memorial-state-park.*

🍴 Restaurants

Blue-Eyed Crab Grille & Raw Bar

$$ | CARIBBEAN | FAMILY | Grab a seat on the outside deck overlooking the water at this friendly, somewhat funky (plastic fish dangling from the ceiling), Caribbean-inspired eatery. Enjoy fruity cocktails on the patio, or hang out in the colorful dining room. **Known for:** views of the water; funky decor; tropical cocktails. 🖺 *Average main: $25* ⊠ *170 Water St.* ☎ *508/747–6776* ⊕ *www.blue-eyedcrab.com.*

Provincetown

115 miles southeast of Boston (2½ hours by car), 90 minutes by ferry.

This outermost Cape resort town known for its beautiful beaches and vibrant summer culture has long been home to tourists, artists and a dynamic LGBT community. In summer, a fast ferry whisks you from Boston to Provincetown in about 90 minutes, allowing you to skip all the notorious Cape traffic on the roads and enjoy an enjoyable boat ride. It's possible to even make a day trip, though it's more fun to spend a weekend there.

GETTING HERE AND AROUND

Cape Air has year-round service from Boston's Logan Airport to Provincetown, and Bay Stay Cruise Company offers daily, summer-season high-speed ferry service from the World Trade Center pier in Boston directly to Provincetown Terminal in 90 minutes.

CONTACTS Bay State Cruise Company. ⊠ *Commonwealth Pier, 200 Seaport Blvd., Boston* ☎ *617/748–1428, 877/783–3779* ⊕ *baystatecruisecompany.com.* **Cape Air.** ⊠ *660 Barnstable Rd., Hyannis* ☎ *800/227–3247, 508/771–6944 outside U.S.* ⊕ *www.capeair.com.* **JetBlue.** ☎ *800/538–2583* ⊕ *www.jetblue.com.*

VISITOR INFORMATION
Provincetown Chamber of Commerce.
✉ *307 Commerce St., Provincetown*
☎ *508/487–3424* ⊕ *ptownchamber.com.*

 Sights

★ Commercial Street

NEIGHBORHOOD | Take a casual stroll by the many architectural styles—Greek Revival, Victorian, Second Empire, and Gothic, to name a few—used in the design of the impressive houses for wealthy sea captains and merchants. The center of town is where you'll find the crowds and the best people-watching, especially if you try to find an empty spot on the benches in front of the exquisitely renovated Town Hall. The East End has a number of nationally renowned galleries; the West End has a number of small inns with neat lawns and elaborate gardens. There is one-way vehicle traffic on this street, though pedestrians dominate the pavement, particularly in July and August. Commercial Street runs parallel to the water, so there is always a patch of sand close at hand, should you need a break. ✉ *Provincetown* ⊕ *ptowntourism.com.*

Pilgrim Monument

MEMORIAL | The first thing you'll see in Provincetown is this grandiose edifice, somewhat out of proportion to the rest of the low-rise town. The monument commemorates the Pilgrims' first landing in the New World and their signing of the Mayflower Compact (the first Colonial American rules of self-governance) before they set off to explore the mainland. Climb the 116 steps and 60 short ramps of the 252-foot-high tower for a panoramic view—dunes on one side, harbor on the other, and the entire bay side of Cape Cod beyond. At the tower's base is a museum of Lower Cape and Provincetown history, with exhibits on whaling, shipwrecks, and scrimshaw. ✉ *1 High Pole Hill Rd., Downtown Center* ☎ *508/487–1310* ⊕ *www.pilgrim-monument.org* 🖼 *$17.*

★ Province Lands Visitor Center

NATIONAL/STATE PARK | Part of the Cape Cod National Seashore, the Province Lands stretch from High Head in Truro to the tip of Provincetown and are scattered with ponds, cranberry bogs, and scrub. More than 7 miles of bike and walking trails lace through forests of stunted pines, beech, and oak and across desert-like expanses of rolling dunes. At the visitor center you'll find short films on local geology and exhibits on the life of the dunes and the shore. You can also pick up information on guided walks, birding trips, lectures, and other programs, as well as on the Province Lands' pristine beaches, Race Point and Herring Cove, and walking, biking, and horse trails. Don't miss the awe-inspiring panoramic view of the dunes and the surrounding ocean from the observation deck. This terrain provides optimal conditions for the deer tick, which can cause Lyme disease, so use extra caution. ✉ *Race Point Rd., east of U.S. 6, Greater Provincetown* ☎ *508/487–1256* ⊕ *www.nps.gov/caco* 🖼 *Free* ⊗ *Visitor center closed Nov.–Apr.*

★ Provincetown Art Association and Museum

LOCAL INTEREST | Founded in 1914 to collect and exhibit the works of artists with Provincetown connections, this facility has a 1,650-piece permanent collection, displayed in changing exhibitions that mix up-and-comers with established 20th-century figures like Milton Avery, Philip Evergood, William Gropper, Charles Hawthorne, Robert Motherwell, Claes Oldenburg, Man Ray, John Singer Sargent, Andy Warhol, and Agnes Weinrich. A stunning contemporary wing has greatly expanded the exhibit space. The museum store carries books of local interest, including works by or about area artists and authors, as well as posters, crafts, cards, and gift items. Art classes (single day and longer) offer the opportunity to study under such talents as Hilda Neily, Selina Trieff, and Doug Ritter. ✉ *460 Commercial St., East*

Cape Cod National Seashore

The Cape Cod National Seashore, established in 1961 by President John F. Kennedy, is an expansive 27,000-acre park, extending from Chatham to Provincetown, with 30 miles of superb beaches; great rolling dunes; swamps, marshes, and wetlands; and pitch-pine and scrub-oak forest. Self-guided nature trails, as well as excellent biking and horse trails, lace through these landscapes. The Cape was a refuge and haven for JFK and we can thank him for saving this part of the region for us for the foreseeable future. A good place to get an overview of the area is at the Salt Pond Visitor Center, at the southern end of the Cape, which offers guided walks, boat tours, demonstrations, and lectures from mid-April through Thanksgiving, as well as evening beach walks, campfire talks, and other programs (many are free) in summer.

Highlights of the National Seashore include **Coast Guard Beach,** a long beach backed by low grass and heathland. A handsome former Coast Guard station is also here, though it's not open to the public. The beach has a very small parking lot that fills up early, but in season visitors can park at the Salt Pond Visitor Center or at the lot up Doane Road from the center and take a free shuttle to the beach. **Nauset Light Beach,** located adjacent to Coast Guard Beach, is a long, sandy beach backed by tall dunes, frilly grasses, and heathland. You'll find **Nauset Light** here, too, a much-photographed red-and-white lighthouse. Another popular beach is **First Encounter Beach,** ideal for watching sunsets over Cape Cod Bay. Pick up maps and more information at the Salt Pond Visitor Center (⊠ *50 Doane Rd.* ☎ *508-255–3421* ⊕ *www.nps.gov/caco.*

End ☎ *508/487–1750* ⊕ *www.paam.org* ✉ *$13* ۞ *Closed Mon.–Wed. Oct.–May.*

Beaches

Herring Cove Beach
BEACH—SIGHT | FAMILY | Herring Cove Beach is relatively calm and warm for a National Seashore beach, but it's not as pretty as some because its parking lot isn't hidden behind dunes. It's close to town, so in warm weather it's always crowded. The lot to the right of the bathhouse is a great place to watch the sunset. ■**TIP→ Daily parking is $25; the annual seashore pass grants access to all six national park beaches and costs $60. Amenities:** food and drink; lifeguards; parking (fee); toilets; showers. **Best for:** sunset; swimming; walking. ⊠ *Provincetown* ⊕ *www.nps.gov/caco/index.htm*

✑ *From late June–early Sept. $25 per vehicle, $10 per person.*

★ Race Point Beach
BEACH—SIGHT | FAMILY | Race Point Beach, one of the Cape Cod National Seashore beaches in Provincetown, has a wide swath of sand stretching far off into the distance around the point and Coast Guard station. Because of its position facing north, the beach gets sun all day long. Keep an eye out for whales offshore; it's also a popular fishing spot. ■**TIP→ Daily parking is $25; the annual seashore pass grants access to all six national park beaches is $60. Amenities:** lifeguards; parking (fee); showers; toilets. **Best for:** sunrise; sunset; surfing; swimming; walking. ⊠ *Race Point Rd., east of U.S. 6, Provincetown* ☎ *508/487–1256* ⊕ *www.nps.gov/caco/index.htm* ✑ *From late June–early Sept. $25 per vehicle, $10 per person.*

🍴 Restaurants

★ The Canteen

$ | **AMERICAN** | Bustling from breakfast until 11 pm, this casual spot specializes in classics like grilled cheese sandwiches, hand-cut fries, and local seafood in a lively spot. Order at the counter, then grab a seat at one of the picnic tables street-side or in a little shady grove out back; there's also a large beer menu with New England offerings, a good selection of wines, and delicious house-made lemonade and iced tea. **Known for:** hot or cold lobster rolls; raw bar; great atmosphere out back. [$] *Average main: $13* ✉ *225 Commercial St., Downtown Center* ☎ *508/487–3800* 🌐 *www.thecanteenptown.com.*

Lobster Pot

$$$ | **SEAFOOD** | Provincetown's Lobster Pot, a mainstay for 40 years, is fit to do battle with all the lobster shanties anywhere (and everywhere) else on the Cape; although it's often jammed with tourists, the crowds reflect the generally high quality and the water views can't be beat. The hardworking kitchen turns out classic New England cooking: lobsters, generous and filling seafood platters, and some of the best chowder around. **Known for:** locally award-winning clam chowder; local icon; extensive menu. [$] *Average main: $27* ✉ *321 Commercial St., Downtown Center* ☎ *508/487–0842* 🌐 *www.ptownlobsterpot.com* ⏲ *Closed in winter.*

★ The Mews Restaurant & Cafe

$$$ | **AMERICAN** | This perennial favorite with magnificent harbor views focuses on seafood and grilled meats with a cross-cultural flair (there's also a lighter bistro menu for smaller appetites). The view of the bay from the bar is nearly perfect, and the gentle lighting makes this a romantic spot to have a drink. **Known for:** waterfront setting; ambience; two levels of dining. [$] *Average main: $27* ✉ *429 Commercial St., East End* ☎ *508/487–1500* 🌐 *mewsptown.com.*

★ The Pointe

$$$ | **AMERICAN** | Inside the snazzy Crowne Pointe Inn, this intimate, casually handsome restaurant occupies the parlor and sunroom of a grand sea captain's mansion and serves finely crafted, healthful, modern American food with daily specials focused on local ingredients. There's a substantial wine list, with more than a hundred selections to choose from, as well as a large martini menu. **Known for:** superb service; cocktails in the lounge; truffle popcorn. [$] *Average main: $27* ✉ *Crowne Pointe Inn, 82 Bradford St., Downtown Center* ☎ *508/487–2365* 🌐 *www.provincetown-restaurant.com* ⏲ *Closed Mon.–Tues. No lunch.*

🛏 Hotels

★ Brass Key

$$$$ | **B&B/INN** | One of the Cape's most luxurious small resorts, this meticulously kept year-round getaway comprises a beautifully restored main house—originally a sea captain's home built in 1828—and several other carefully groomed buildings and cottages all centered around a beautifully landscaped pool area. **Pros:** ultraposh rooms; beautiful and secluded grounds; pool on-site. **Cons:** among the highest rates in town; not for those with children; significant minimum-stay requirements in summer. [$] *Rooms from: $375* ✉ *67 Bradford St., Downtown Center* ☎ *508/487–9005, 800/842–9858* 🌐 *www.brasskey.com* 🔑 *43 rooms* 🍴 *Free breakfast* ☞ *Pets are only allowed in certain rooms.*

★ Crowne Pointe Historic Inn and Spa

$$$$ | **B&B/INN** | Created meticulously from six different buildings, this inn hasn't a single detail left unattended—period furniture and antiques fill common areas and guest rooms; a queen-size bed is the smallest you'll find, dressed in 300-thread-count linens; treats are left on the pillow for nightly turndown service; and there's complimentary wine and cheese in the afternoon. **Pros:** great

on-site amenities like the full-service Shui Spa; posh and luxurious room decor; professional and well-trained staff. **Cons:** among the highest rates in town; significant minimum-stay requirements in summer; no children allowed. Ⓢ *Rooms from: $340* ⊠ *82 Bradford St., Downtown Center* ☎ *508/413–2213, 877/276–9631* ⊕ *www.crownepointe.com* ↝ *40 rooms* ⦿ *Free breakfast.*

★ White Porch Inn

$$$ | B&B/INN | This sterling, light-filled B&B offers a soothing respite from the bustle of town; opt for one of the carriage-house rooms for even more seclusion. **Pros:** a selection of wines and small bites are set out each afternoon for guests; steps from East End shopping and dining; enthusiastic and friendly staff. **Cons:** somewhat long walk to West End shopping and businesses; not for those with children; limited parking. Ⓢ *Rooms from: $299* ⊠ *7 Johnson St., Downtown Center* ☎ *508/364–2549, 508/487–0592* ⊕ *www.whiteporchinn.com* ↝ *10 rooms* ⦿ *Free breakfast.*

🏃 Activities

★ Art's Dune Tours

TOUR—SPORTS | Art's Dune Tours has been taking eager passengers into the dunes of Province Lands since 1946. A bumpy but controlled ride (about one hour) transports you through sometimes surreal sandy vistas peppered with beach grass, along a shoreline patrolled by seagulls and sandpipers. Head out at sunset for a stunning ride, available with or without a clambake feast; on Sunday there is a special Race Point Lighthouse Tour. ⊠ *4 Standish St., Downtown Center* ☎ *508/487–1950, 800/894–1951* ⊕ *www.artsdunetours.com* ☒ *From $32* ⊗ *Closed mid-Nov.–mid-Apr.*

★ Dolphin Fleet

WHALE-WATCHING | FAMILY | Tours are led by scientists from the Center for Coastal Studies in Provincetown, who provide commentary while collecting data on the whales they've been monitoring for years. They know many of them by name and will tell you about their habits and histories. These trips are most often exciting and incredibly thrilling with close-up encounters. ■**TIP**➜ **Look for discount coupons in local free brochures and publications, as well as online.** ⊠ *Chamber of Commerce Bldg., MacMillan Wharf, Downtown Center* ☎ *508/240–3636, 800/826–9300* ⊕ *www.whalewatch.com* ☒ *From $53.*

Index

Photo Credits

Front Cover: Eric Hill [Description: A flowery morning along Beacon Street in Boston's Back Bay]. **Back cover, from left to right:** SeanPavonePhoto/iStockphoto, Coleong/Dreamstime, Sepavo/Dreamstime. Spine: Lunamarina/Dreamstime. Interior, from left to right: Chrisc2000/Dreamstime (1). Chee-Onn Leong/Shutterstock (2). Kindra Clineff (5). **Chapter 1: Experience Boston:** Sepavo/Dreamstime (6-7). Luckydoor/Dreamstime (8). Mbastos/Dreamstime (9). Cpenler/Dreamstime (9). Photopro123/Dreamstime (10). Susch/Dreamstime.com (10). Kwanbenz/Shutterstock (10). Nic Lehoux/ Isabella Stewart Gardner Museum (10). Babar760/Dreamstime (11). Mbastos/Dreamstime (11). F11photo/Dreamstime (12). Appalachianviews/Dreamstime.com (12). Jiawangkun/Dreamstime.com (12). Kimberly Vardeman/Flickr, [CC BY 2.0] (12). Indigochyld/Dreamstime (13). Martin Thomas Photography / Alamy (14). Mikey Colon/Shutterstock (14). Smart Destinations/Flickr, [CC BY 2.0] (14). DMS Foto/Shutterstock (14). DenisTangneyJr/iStockphoto (15). Jiawangkun/Dreamstime(15).Jay Yuan/Shutterstock (22). Marcio Jose Bastos Silva/Shutterstock (22). Museum of African American History/Flickr, [CC BY 2.0] (22). LnP images/Shutterstock (22). LnP images/Shutterstock (23). alberto cervantes/Shutterstock (24). Martin Nolan/Shutterstock (24). Brent Hofacker/Shutterstock (24). Brent Hofacker/Shutterstock (24). Lauriyckas/Dreamstime (25). Alessio Orru/Shutterstock (25). Max Moraga/Shutterstock (25). rj lerich/Shutterstock (25). Dbvirago/Dreamstime (26). Elovkoff/Dreamstime (26). Spencerprice/Dreamstime (26). Michael Blanchard Photography/Boston Tea Party Ships & Museum (27). Jon Bilous/Shutterstock (27). Kindra Clineff (32). Public Domain (33). A. H. C. / age fotostock (33). Classic Vision / age fotostock (33). Classic Vision / age fotostock (33). Kindra Clineff (33). Public Domain (33). Kindra Clineff (34). Kindra Clineff (35). Kindra Clineff (35). Freedom Trail Foundation (35). Kindra Clineff (35). Tony the Misfit/Flickr, [CC BY 2.0] (35). Scott Orr/iStockphoto (35). Tim Grafft/MOTT (35). Kindra Clineff (36). Jim Reynolds/Flckr (36). Kindra Clineff (37). Public Domain (37). Kindra Clineff (38). **Chapter 3: Beacon Hill, Boston Common, and the West End:** Kindra Clineff (63). m_sovinskii/Shutterstock (72). Roman Babakin/Shutterstock (79). **Chapter 4: Government Center and the North End:** Marcio Jose Bastos Silva/Shutterstock (85). Jorge Salcedo/iStockphoto (90). m_sovinskii/Shutterstock (92). Jorge Salcedo/Shutterstock (98). **Chapter 5: Charlestown:** Maxim Gorishniak/Shutterstock (109). Page Light Studios (114). **Chapter 6: Downtown and the Waterfront:** Jon Bilous/Shutterstock (119). F11photo/Dreamstime (126). shananies/iStockphoto (138). **Chapter 7: The Back Bay and South End:** Heeb Christian / age fotostock (143). Mbastos/Dreamstime (146). Chee-Onn Leong/Shutterstock (152). Coleong/Dreamstime (180). **Chapter 8: Fenway and Kenmore Square:** Israel Pabon/Shutterstock (183). ChrisDag (184). Kindra Clineff (185, Top and Bottom). **Chapter 9: Brookline and Jamaica Plain:** Alyssa Tortora/iStockphoto (195). Wangkun Jia/shutterstock (200). Micha Weber/Shutterstock (203). **Chapter 10: The Seaport, South Boston, and East Boston:** Marcio Jose Bastos Silva/Shutterstock (207). Danita Delimont / Alamy (213). Darryl Brooks/Shutterstock (223). Miguel Rincon/Shutterstock (225). **Chapter 11: Cambridge and Somerville:** Jorge Salcedo/Shutterstock (231). Harvard Crimson (238). janniswerner/iStockphoto (248). Jorge Salcedo/Shutterstock (253). **Chapter 12: Side Trips from Boston:** DenisTangneyJr/iStockphoto (267). Peabody Essex Museum. Photography by Ken Sawyer (286). **About Our Writers:** All photos are courtesy of the writers.

*Every effort has been made to trace the copyright holders, and we apologize in advance for any accidental errors. We would be happy to apply the corrections in the following edition of this publication.

Fodor's BOSTON

Publisher: Stephen Horowitz, *General Manager*

Editorial: Douglas Stallings, *Editorial Director*; Jill Fergus, Jacinta O'Halloran, Amanda Sadlowski, *Senior Editors*; Kayla Becker, Alexis Kelly, Rachael Roth, *Editors*

Design: Tina Malaney, *Director of Design and Production*; Jessica Gonzalez, *Graphic Designer*; Mariana Tabares, *Design & Production Intern*

Production: Jennifer DePrima, *Editorial Production Manager*; Elyse Rozelle, *Senior Production Editor*; Monica White, *Production Editor*

Maps: Rebecca Baer, *Senior Map Editor*; Mark Stroud and Harry Colomb (Moon Street Cartography), David Lindroth, *Cartographers*

Photography: Viviane Teles, *Senior Photo Editor*; Namrata Aggarwal, Ashok Kumar, Carl Yu, *Photo Editors*; Rebecca Rimmer, *Photo Intern*

Business and Operations: Chuck Hoover, *Chief Marketing Officer*; Robert Ames, *Group General Manager*; Devin Duckworth, *Director of Print Publishing*; Victor Bernal, *Business Analyst*

Public Relations and Marketing: Joe Ewaskiw, *Senior Director Communications & Public Relations*

Fodors.com Jeremy Tarr, *Editorial Director*; Rachael Levitt, *Managing Editor*

Technology: Jon Atkinson, *Director of Technology*; Rudresh Teotia, *Lead Developer*; Jacob Ashpis, *Content Operations Manager*

Writers: Kim Foley MacKinnon, Cheryl Fenton, Leigh Harrington

Editor: Alexis Kelly

Production Editor: Monica White

31st Edition

ISBN 978-1-64097-302-2

ISSN 0882–0074

All details in this book are based on information supplied to us at press time. Always confirm information when it matters, especially if you're making a detour to visit a specific place. Fodor's expressly disclaims any liability, loss, or risk, personal or otherwise, that is incurred as a consequence of the use of any of the contents of this book.

SPECIAL SALES
This book is available at special discounts for bulk purchases for sales promotions or premiums. For more information, e-mail SpecialMarkets@fodors.com.

PRINTED IN CANADA

10 9 8 7 6 5 4 3 2 1

About Our Writers

Cheryl Fenton is a Boston-based freelance writer who specializes in all things lifestyle, with bylines in such publications and outline outlets as the *Boston Globe, Cooking Light,* USAToday.com, Boston.com, *Women's Health and Fitness,* and USAirways. Her career has spanned decades of reporting on the next best thing in dining, travel, interior design, fashion, beauty, and more. To see her work, visit ⊕ *www.cherylfenton.com* and follow her @cherylfenton. For this guide, Cheryl updated the Travel Smart; Government Center and the North End; Charlestown; and Cambridge and Somerville chapters.

Kim Foley MacKinnon, a Boston-based, award-winning journalist and author, contributes to *Forbes Travel,* Food Network, *U.S. News & World Report,* and the *Boston Globe,* among others. Her latest book, *Secret Boston: A Guide to the Weird, Wonderful, and Obscure,* came out in April 2020. She is a member of SATW. Visit her website, ⊕ *www.escapewithkim.com,* or follow her on Instagram and Twitter at @escapewithkim. Kim updated the Back Bay and South End, Fenway and Kenmore Square, Brookline and Jamaica Plains, and Side Trips from Boston chapters for this guide.

Leigh Harrington has been a writer and editor for 20 years, curating content for a variety of different titles, travel-oriented and otherwise. She squeezes in freelance projects around her two full-time jobs: as Senior Editor at Reviewed.com and as wife-mom to her husband and one very curious kid. When there's free time, she likes to hike and work on DIY projects. Follow her adventures at ⊕ *lahlah-land.com.* For this edition of Boston, she updated the Experience Boston; Beacon Hill, Boston Common, and the West End; Downtown and the Waterfront; and the Seaport, South Boston, and East Boston chapters.